Religion Matters

Religion Matters: How Sociology Helps Us Understand Religion in Our World focuses on religion's interplay with broader society, introducing students to the basic questions, ideas, and methods with which sociologists have analyzed the relationship between religion and society.

Since the first edition, religion as a social force has changed dramatically in its content and consequences for the world. In this new edition, the authors update the foundational lenses used to understand religion's multiple roles in society, assess the impact of technology and social media on religion and faith, draw further reflection from contemporary studies of religion and gender, and add a new chapter examining the increasing amount of religious polarization in the United States and throughout the world.

With new illustrations and connections that make this readable textbook more accessible and relevant for today's student, the second edition of *Religion Matters* remains a perfect counterpart for introductory courses concerned with the sociological study of religion.

William A. Mirola is former Dean of the College of Arts and Sciences and Professor of Sociology at Marian University in Indianapolis, IN. His publications include *Redeeming Time: Protestantism and the Eight-Hour Movement in Chicago; Religion and Class in America;* and *Sociology of Religion: A Reader.*

Michael O. Emerson is Professor and Department Head of Sociology at the University of Illinois-Chicago. He studies religion, race, and the many intersections of these. He is the author of 15 books and over 100 other publications.

Susanne C. Monahan is Associate Provost and Professor of Sociology at Western Oregon University. She is co-editor of *Sociology of Religion: A Reader* and has published articles and reviews in Journal for the Scientific Study of Religion, Review of Religious Research, Sociology of Religion, and Contemporary Sociology.

From presentation of classic approaches to understanding religion, such as those by such members of the canon as Karl Marx and Emile Durkheim, to the most timely of current events (how is the COVID pandemic affecting church life?), *Religion Matters* provides a thorough coverage of sociological approaches to religion. An excellent balance of breadth and depth, *Religion Matters* explores both how society and social change affects religion and the various ways in which religion influences society. There is something for every syllabus: religion and climate change - check; religion and controversy over sexuality - check; religion and political conflict - check; religion and immigration - check, and on and on. The authors bring an accessible writing style along with a mastery of the current research to present a balanced, informative, and stimulating approach to contemporary religion.

Rhys H. Williams, *Professor of Sociology and Director of the McNamara Center for the Social Study of Religion, Loyola University, Chicago, USA*

If recent events are any indication, religion has and continues to change individuals, communities and societies. Students of all ages must pay attention to this institution to understand how this social institution can motivate calls for liberation and equality as well as dominance and prejudice. *Religion Matters* is a vital resource for understanding our present circumstances and historical origins as they pertain to religion. It pays particular attention to the ways in which religion intersects with race, gender, and class in a unique way that sets this textbook apart from the others. A must-read.

Jerry Z. Park, *Associate Professor of Sociology, Baylor University*

Religion Matters is the perfect text to introduce students to the myriad ways that religion shapes our culture, politics, and daily lives. Written in a highly accessible style, the book covers traditional sociological theories of religion as well recent empirical research findings. It sheds light on the intersection of religion and a variety of contemporary social issues, ranging from gender equality, racism and black liberation, immigration, LGBTQI concerns, and climate change. Academically rigorous and thought-provoking, *Religion Matters* offers all that one needs to teach a compelling sociology of religion course.

Sharon Erickson Nepstad, *Distinguished Professor of Sociology, University of New Mexico*

Religion Matters

How Sociology Helps Us Understand Religion in Our World

Second Edition

William A. Mirola, Michael O. Emerson and Susanne C. Monahan

Routledge
Taylor & Francis Group

NEW YORK AND LONDON

Second edition published 2023
by Routledge
605 Third Avenue, New York, NY 10158

and by Routledge
4 Park Square, Milton Park, Abingdon, Oxon, OX14 4RN

Routledge is an imprint of the Taylor & Francis Group, an informa business

© 2023 Taylor & Francis

The right of William A. Mirola, Michael O. Emerson and Susanne C. Monahan to
be identified as authors of this work has been asserted in accordance with sections 77
and 78 of the Copyright, Designs and Patents Act 1988.

All rights reserved. No part of this book may be reprinted or reproduced or utilised
in any form or by any electronic, mechanical, or other means, now known or
hereafter invented, including photocopying and recording, or in any information
storage or retrieval system, without permission in writing from the publishers.

Trademark notice: Product or corporate names may be trademarks or registered
trademarks and are used only for identification and explanation without intent to
infringe.

First edition published by Routledge 2010

ISBN: 978-1-032-02148-5 (hbk)
ISBN: 978-1-032-02145-4 (pbk)
ISBN: 978-1-003-18210-8 (ebk)

DOI: 10.4324/9781003182108

Typeset in Bembo
by Apex CoVantage, LLC

Contents

Acknowledgments

Religion has always played important but complicated roles in our own lives, as well as in society more broadly. We wrote the first version of this book more than 10 years ago because we believed (and still do) that sociology is an insightful, but underutilized, perspective for understanding religion and its powerful effects. If that was true then, it is even more so now in light of the many changes in our world that continue to intersect with religion and religious institutions, including the explosion of social media, religious polarization in politics, religious support and opposition to LGBTQ+ rights, and many more that we will discuss here. We hope you find this second edition of our book both useful and thought provoking. Indeed, if we have answered all your questions about religion and society rather than leaving you wondering about more, we will be a bit disappointed!

We are grateful to many researchers—those who came before us as well as those who are working in this field today—for their contributions to our knowledge. We thank our editors at Taylor and Francis/Routledge, especially Tyler Bay, who took on the revision of this text and continually encouraged us, despite the challenges we faced, to see this to completion. The entire staff at Taylor & Francis/Routledge have been so supportive of our vision of a text that focused on religion's interplay with broader society presented in a conversational, undergraduate-friendly way. Charlotte Taylor was our editorial assistant who, along with others on her staff, did amazing (and efficient) work to make this volume publishable.

We are also grateful to our departments and our institutions, Marian University, the University of Illinois-Chicago, and Western Oregon University, for their support of this work. A number of individuals also deserve recognition for their assistance and feedback at various stages of this project. In particular, we would like to thank Isaiah Jeong, Tryce Prince (UIC), Bill MacDonald, Adele Pittendrigh, Kevin O'Neill, Renee Sallese, and Meredith Gardner for reading and commenting on various chapters in both this revised edition and in the first edition. We also are grateful to the reviewers who provided us with helpful feedback on how the first edition worked for their students and insightful ways to improve what we did in this volume. We could not manage to make all the changes we wished to, but we did do our best and we hope it shows.

Finally, we would like to thank you, the reader. We welcome your feedback and wish you the best on your learning adventure.

William A. Mirola
Marian University

Michael O. Emerson
University of Illinois-Chicago

Susanne C. Monahan
Western Oregon University

Figures, Tables, and Boxes

Preface

This Just in: Religion Still Matters!

- The January 6th riot was far from just a politically-driven event, it was also driven by faith! "Before self-proclaimed members of the far-right group the Proud Boys marched toward the U.S. Capitol . . . they stopped to kneel in the street and prayed in the name of Jesus . . . the group . . . prayed for God to bring 'reformation and revival.' They gave thanks for 'the wonderful nation we've all been blessed in.' They asked God for the restoration of their 'value systems,' and for the 'courage and strength to both represent you and present our culture well.' And they invoked the divine protection for what was to come . . . then they rose. Their leader declared into a bullhorn that the media must 'get the hell out of my way.' And then they moved toward the Capitol" (Dias and Graham 2021, A1).
- Who could guess that a cheeseburger could cause such a ruckus? In 2006, McDonald's agreed to alter its signature logo—the golden arches—at a dozen or so kosher Mickey Ds in Israel. According to *The Guardian International*, "The restaurant chain agreed to the change under pressure from the chief rabbi of Tel Aviv, Yisrael Meir Lau, who refused to sign kosher certificates for McDonald's branches in the city and at its university. 'When I assumed my position 10 months ago and I had to sign kashrut certificates for two [McDonald's] restaurants in Tel Aviv, I refused because my conscience wouldn't let me,' he told the Israeli newspaper, *Yedioth Ahronoth*. 'I was mainly concerned that tourists or adolescents who visit one kosher branch may jump to the conclusion that all McDonald's branches in Israel are kosher.'" At these sites, the McDonald's name will appear in blue and White, the colors of the Israeli flag, with 'kosher' alongside (McGreal 2006).
- Religion drives conflict in U.S. schools. Here's a case in point: In 2019, the *New York Times* reported that Cathedral High School, a Catholic high school in Indianapolis, fired one of its gay teachers who was legally married to their partner, following the directive of Archbishop Charles Thompson. That same year, Roncalli High School, another Indianapolis Catholic school, fired Shelly Fitzgerald and Lynn Starkey, two lesbian women who were counselors at the school, each of whom had been legally married to their same-sex partners. Interestingly, Roncalli subsequently fired Kelly Fisher, a third school counselor who was heterosexual, because she vocally supported these two women after they were fired (Herron 2019). Matthew LaBanca, a gay music teacher at St. Joseph Catholic Academy in Brooklyn faced a similar fate following his marriage to his partner in 2021 (Stack 2021). In each of these cases, the Archdiocese involved argued that the schoolteachers were "ministers" and as such could be fired for violating church teachings, even if they were not Catholic or were not teaching in fields related to religion or theology.
- France claims to be a neutral state through its secularist model known as laïcité, a complete division between a secular public life and relegation of religion to the private lives of people. This strong tradition among many French can lead its leaders to say things like every citizen must respect the French Republic because people are citizens before being religious believers.

That belief came to a head in a new bill and eventual law passed in 2021, originally dubbed the "Anti-Separatist" Law. In what opponents argue is a thinly-veiled attack on Muslim believers in France, who often do not share the secularist model, the law requires community groups to sign a charter supporting the French model, limits the possibilities of homeschooling, allows the government to shut down religious gatherings it deems "extremist," extends strict religious neutrality beyond civil servants to even private contractors of public services such as bus drivers, creates new offenses of "separatism," caps funding community groups can receive from abroad, requires full respect of the equality of males and females, and can even ban those seen as supporting terrorism from running for elected office. While many celebrated the passing of the new law, others, not surprisingly, saw the law as religious and ethnic discrimination, using the force of law to impinge on the freedom of worship and assembly (Salam 2021; Cohen 2021; Breeden 2021).

- Many Americans faced economic, social, and medical challenges during the COVID pandemic. But faith communities did too as they struggled to find ways to hold religious communities together. Thankfully, Facebook came to the rescue! Megachurch Hillsong, with its congregation of many thousands, wanted to open a site in Atlanta, Georgia. Facebook was there as a pandemic partner. More than just offering a streaming platform for its services, Facebook helped the megachurch pilot apps for financial giving, prayer sharing, and hosting worship. Other religious groups, including the South Bay Islamic Association, the Presbyterian Church (U.S.A.), and the African American Pentecostal Church of God in Christ have also worked with Facebook. For these congregations, Facebook is a tool for connection and evangelism. But others aren't so sure. Sarah Lane Richter, a theology and science lecturer at the University of Edinburgh, reminds us that "corporations are not worried about moral codes," and Bob Prichett, who founded Faithline as an online Christian ministry platform, points out that "it is dangerous to have your community anchored on a tech platform that is susceptible to all the whims of politics and culture and congressional hearings." Hillsong's pastor, however, sees it differently. He sees the partnership as a way " 'to help churches navigate and reach the consumer better . . . consumer isn't the right word,' he said, correcting himself. 'Reach the parishioner better' " (Dias 2021).

Religion Implicated

In his 2008 book *God Is Not Great*, Christopher Hitchens wrote, "Religion is poison." (13) He is not alone in his disdain for religion. Others, including Sam Harris and Richard Dawkins, have made impassioned pleas for the death of religion—an end to the madness, as some say.

Nonetheless, we note that religion remains a strong force in the United States and worldwide. Political power is—to varying degrees, in different places—distributed along religious lines, and religious groups struggle to influence and control states. Religion provides comfort, meaning, and a sense of transcendent order to people around the world, as it has for the better part of human history. Religious practice and doctrine are embedded in the daily lives of people around the world, including in the United States, and much of our social world is built on practices and beliefs that are rooted in religious traditions. This, according to religion's detractors, is the problem.

As authors, we take a different stand, viewing these realities instead as a challenge to understand religion better. Because religion is embedded to varying degrees in a wide range of social, political, and economic phenomena, it is worthwhile for us to seek a better understanding of religion's social implications.

Sociologist Max Weber called on social scientists to engage in what he called "value-free inquiry," or the dispassionate examination of phenomena guided as much as possible by empirical observation and separated as much as possible from the researcher's personal feelings about what is being observed. It is, of course, impossible for social inquiry to be entirely value-free since all observers have biases and opinions. Nonetheless, Weber urged those who observed and explained the social world to do their best to set aside their assumptions, preconceptions, biases, and values, and to focus instead on explaining—not judging—social phenomena. We do our best to follow Weber's lead in this book.

Thus, we do not argue for or against the existence of "god," either as an empirical reality or as a perception on the part of believers. Many people believe in a transcendent order, and whether or not we see the same order, religious belief and consequences are worth understanding. We also do not dispute the "reality" of religion. Religion is, as sociologist Emile Durkheim termed it, a *social fact* that has real and observable effects: it shapes human and collective behavior. That religion is intangible—beliefs, practices, experiences, and community that we cannot touch in a physical way—does not reduce its power in human society. Nor do we try to prove or debunk particular religious systems. Plenty of other books do that. The debunkers, in particular, give the impression that if only we could show fervently religious people the logical error of their thinking, they would abandon their long-held beliefs and get with the modern, rational, scientific program.

Our primary motivation in writing this book was the observation that religion is a powerful force in our social world and does not appear to be going away. Even Berger (1999, 9), who once convincingly argued the theoretical case for the inevitable decline of religion in the modern world, has conceded: "The world today is massively religious, is *anything but* the secularized world that had been predicted (whether joyfully or despondently) by so many analysts of modernity." Religion thrives. And no matter how we evaluate the content and effects of religious beliefs, practices, and communities, it behooves us to *understand* a social force like religion that has so much power in our world today. The discipline of sociology offers valuable tools for doing this.

We hope this will not be an ordinary textbook. Knowledge is a collective process that develops over time. We want you to realize that you can be part of that process. To be a learned person is to move beyond simply absorbing what others say about a topic and to critically evaluate it for its usefulness and for its holes. Perhaps in so doing, you will move our knowledge further forward, becoming part of the collective process.

Let's get started.

References

Berger, Peter. 1999. "The Desecularization of the World: A Global Overview." In *The Desecularization of the World: Resurgent Religion and World Politics*, edited by Peter Berger, 1–18. Washington, DC: Ethics and Policy Center.

Breeden, Aurelian. 2021. "France Adopts Laws to Combat Terrorism, but Critics Call Them Overreaching." *New York Times*, July 23. www.nytimes.com/2021/07/23/world/europe/france-terrorism-islamist-extremism-laws-passed.html

Cohen, Roger. 2021. "French National Assembly Backs Law to Combat Islamist Extremism." *New York Times*, February 17: A11. www.nytimes.com/2021/02/16/world/europe/france-law-islamist-extremism.html

Dias, Elizabeth. 2021. "Facebook's Next Target: The Religious Experience." *New York Times*, July 26: A12. www.nytimes.com/2021/07/25/us/facebook-church.html

Dias, Elizabeth, and Ruth Graham. 2021. "A Movement Buttressed by Grievance and God." *New York Times*, January 11. www.nytimes.com/2021/01/11/us/how-white-evangelical-christians-fused-with-trump-extremism.html

Herron, Arika. 2019. "Woman says Roncalli Fired Her for Supporting 2 Employees Fired Over Same-Sex Marriages." *Indy Star*, October 24. www.indystar.com/story/news/education/2019/10/24/woman-says-roncalli-fired-her-supporting-employees-fired-over-same-sex-marriages/2387527001/

Hitchens, Christopher. 2008. *God is Not Great: How Religion Poisons Everything*. New York: Twelve.

McGreal, Chris. 2006. "McDonald's Changes its Brand to Suit Kosher Appetites." *Guardian International Pages*, March 13: 25.

Salam, Yasmin. 2021. "Bill Aims to Tackle Rising Extremism in France. Some Say It's an Infringement of Rights." *NBC News Online*, March 29. www.nbcnews.com/news/world/bill-aims-tackle-rising-extremism-france-some-say-it-s-n1262247

Stack, Liam. 2021. "Brooklyn Diocese Fires Gay Teacher Who Wed." *New York Times*, October 28: A21. www.nytimes.com/2021/10/27/nyregion/catholic-school-teacher-fired-same-sex-marriage.html

Section I
Getting Acquainted

Why Religion?

Religion is a pervasive force around the world. As the newsflashes in the introduction suggest, religion shapes how people behave and how they think about the world and their place in it.

Before we can understand the effects of religion in our world, however, we need to understand what exactly religion is. For many Americans, the word evokes familiar images of church, worship, prayer, traditions, and pilgrimage. Religion is harder to recognize, however, when it takes less-familiar forms:

- Following strict rules that govern the killing of an animal
- Carefully washing hands before a meal
- Performing a dance or a song
- Frequently repeating a particular greeting or kind words
- Following restrictions on food or drink that have nothing to do with dieting or being a picky eater

Each of these acts is infused with religious meaning, at least to some groups of people. It is easy to overlook the significance of these acts, however, if you do not know much about religious beliefs and practices outside your own faith.

Baylor University sociologists Jerry Park and Joseph Baker reported the results of their survey exploring how often people "consume" (buy or view) religious goods (Park and Baker 2007). The survey asked about art and jewelry with religious themes, sacred books, religious music and educational materials, and bumper stickers and cards with religious content (e.g., "What would Jesus do?"). Park and Baker also collected data on specific books and visual media. For example, they asked people whether they had watched *The Passion of the Christ* or *Veggie Tales*. Had they read *God's Politics* by the liberal Christian Evangelical Jim Wallis, Rick Warren's *The Purpose-Driven Life*, or Dan Brown's *The Da Vinci Code*? Had they seen TV programs like *7th Heaven*; *This Is Your Day*, featuring Benny Hinn; or *Touched by an Angel*? Had they read any of the *Left Behind* series, a book on Dianetics, or anything by James Dobson?

Many people recognize the religious connotations of these items. But that is probably because the exemplars—the objects the researchers chose to represent religious products—represent a fairly narrow range of religions. All but two of the exemplars are associated with variants of Christianity.

DOI: 10.4324/9781003182108-2

The exceptions include Dianetics, which comes from L. Ron Hubbard's Scientology religion, and the TV show *Touched by an Angel*, which presents a world populated by spirits in human form ("angels") who are sent by an otherwise unnamed "holy father." The religion in *Touched by an Angel* is monotheistic, but it does not mention Christianity, Jesus, or a savior. This study's findings mostly tell us about buying or viewing products that are associated with the major religious traditions of Christianity.

What about less well-known religious traditions? A vast array of religious traditions exists beyond Christianity and Scientology in the United States and worldwide. Each of these traditions has its own beliefs and practices, along with associated objects that people might buy or books or other media that people might view. Wouldn't it be interesting to know about those, too?

Perhaps you do not care about the unfamiliar. As long as you follow your own beliefs and practices, you may think you do not need to understand those of others. When it comes to religion, you may just want to mind your own business. (We doubt that this describes you! If it did, why would you read this book?) But there are consequences of not seeing the religious in the unfamiliar. We offer one well-known and tragic example.

In her nonfiction book *The Spirit Catches You and You Fall Down*, author Anne Fadiman chronicles a clash of cultures between American doctors and immigrant Hmong refugees from Laos (Fadiman 1997). Doctors in Merced, California, concluded that Lia, the young daughter of a Hmong couple, had epilepsy. Over the next couple of years, the toddler had a series of traumatic grand mal seizures that caused her parents to repeatedly bring her to the local emergency room. To the doctors, Lia's treatment was obvious: a complex regimen of medications to manage epilepsy. Nonetheless, Lia's case confounded the doctors and other hospital staff. They were perplexed by crescent-shaped indentations on her skin, not knowing that the marks resulted from a healing ceremony. They were taken aback when her parents brought traditional healers to visit her. And they were grossed out by the strange foods that her parents brought to her hospital room. (Imagine what the doctors would have thought of the pig sacrifice that the family conducted in the parking lot of their apartment building!) Most of all, Lia's physicians were frustrated when her parents often seemed to ignore their medical directions.

During the years that they treated her, Lia's doctors never wondered what her parents thought was happening to her. A language barrier complicated the situation: The parents spoke no English and the doctors spoke no Hmong. But working through translators, Fadiman uncovered the parents' understanding. They explained to her that right before Lia's first grand mal seizure, her older sister slammed the door and frightened Lia's spirit away. Where Lia's doctors saw an organic condition typified by misplaced electrical impulses in the brain, Lia's family saw a spirit lost in a world where bodies and spirits live side by side, in constant interaction with each other. Even if the parents spoke English, or the doctors understood the Hmong language, how would members of an ethnic group driven from their isolated home in the mountains of Laos communicate about the presence of spirits to scientifically trained Western doctors? Animistic religion was so central and powerful to the lives of Lia and her family that Fadiman wrote of the Hmong people: "Medicine was religion. Religion was society. Society was medicine." But this sort of religion, so integrally tied to every sphere of life and populated by spirits both benign and malevolent, is invisible to doctors who are trained to see the world from a Western, scientific perspective. Their understanding of disease allows no room for the existence of spirits or the influence of the spirit world on a little girl.

Add to that the chasm in understanding the difference in the way that Lia's parents and her doctors *evaluated* the meaning of her seizures. To the doctors, the seizures were a serious medical disorder that needed to be controlled lest Lia suffer permanent brain damage. Her parents, though frightened by the severity of her seizures, believed that their daughter had a special connection to the spiritual world, a connection that could give her an elevated status in the Hmong community. As a result, they were not always sure that they wanted to "cure" her condition.

But her doctors knew none of this. When they were informed, years later, about how Lia's parents understood her condition, the doctors were incredulous. Animism, the injection of the spiritual into objects we encounter in day-to-day life, was alien to these doctors. More importantly, it never even occurred to them to *ask* the parents what they believed about their daughter's condition, not just because of a language barrier, but because the doctors took for granted their scientific explanation of events. The gap between the scientific and religious explanations became an invisible impediment to her care: It impaired trust between the doctors and the family and led to profound misunderstandings about Lia's condition, its treatment, and her prognosis. Lia's care was compromised because of a lack of cross-cultural understanding, and everyone who encountered Lia—her family, medical staff, and social workers—experienced a lot of fear, stress, and uncertainty, partly because of the severity of her illness and partly because of their lack of understanding.

Whether the Hmong beliefs reflected scientific reality or not, they exerted a real force in this situation: Religious beliefs drove how her parents responded to and understood events, despite being *unseen* by Lia's doctors. Had the doctors recognized the distinctive Hmong religion and culture, they might have approached her treatment differently and more effectively. For example, they might have worked with her family, Hmong shamans and elders, and the family's religious beliefs and traditions to develop a treatment plan. The experience of the care process for Lia, her family, and her doctors might have been transformed by better understanding.

In this instance, and in others like it, at levels of analysis from the interpersonal to the cross-national, there are practical implications of being bound by the familiar and not recognizing the pivotal role of religion in our world today. This is why we need tools to understand religion—what it is, what it does—that allow us to see beyond that which is familiar to us to appreciate a wide range of religious beliefs and their effects on ourselves and those around us.

What is Religion, Anyway?

Stop for a moment. Write or type an answer to this question: What is religion? Go ahead. Take a stab at this. We'll gladly wait.

Did you find it easy to define religion? Creating a definition that stands up under scrutiny is harder than you might expect. One approach used by sociologists (scientists who study people and human social behavior) is to create criteria that they then apply to decide whether a practice or belief indeed represents a religion. For example, Melford Spiro, an American cultural anthropologist, defined religion as "an institution consisting of culturally patterned interaction with culturally postulated superhuman beings" (Spiro 1966, 98). You may be thinking, "What in the world does that mean?" It will help if we walk through an example. Let's apply Spiro's definition to the branch of Christianity known as Catholicism. First, we'll consider whether Catholicism is an institution that consists of culturally patterned interactions. In other words, are patterns of relationships, behaviors, and beliefs embodied in it? Well, Catholicism has an organizational structure that extends from Rome into local communities worldwide. It has a hierarchy of authorities (e.g., the Pope, cardinals, archbishops, priests). It has a clearly articulated theology that covers a wide range of subjects, ritual practices, and expectations for the behavior of followers. So Catholicism meets our first criterion. As for our second criterion, do those interactions involve culturally postulated superhuman beings? "God" certainly qualifies as such a being. When we can answer "yes" to both questions, then we are dealing with a religion according to Spiro's definition.

If we consider the case of consumerism, we may answer those questions differently. Consumerism is certainly an "institution that consists of culturally patterned interactions." It is embodied in social and cultural practices including mass production, marketing, shopping, and waste disposal, and driven by beliefs about shopping being good for the economy and an enjoyable pursuit. But consumerism has no "culturally postulated superhuman beings": The "dollar as the almighty god" really is just a metaphor. Although consumerism is a powerful social force, it falls short of being a religion by Spiro's definition.

So it wasn't so difficult to define religion. But the minute you settle on criteria, someone is bound to come up with a compelling counterexample, forcing you to adjust your thinking. In part, this happens because we tend to generate definitions on the basis of what is familiar to us. If you build your definition of religion around what is most familiar to you, and you are a typical modern Westerner, you may form a definition of religion that includes a single supernatural being: a "god" such as the one found in Christianity, Judaism, and Islam. But this definition focuses too narrowly on monotheistic traditions. Our definition should include polytheistic faiths (ones with multiple gods). As you may remember from high school mythology, Greek and Roman religious belief systems were populated with a lot of gods. Some scholars have argued that the Catholic faith posits more than one "spiritual being" because it embraces a Trinitarian conception of God in which three components—the Father, the Son, and the Holy Spirit—make up the entity of God, and because Catholicism features a multitude of saints and angels.

Even if your definition of religion includes belief in god *or* gods (plural), it may unwittingly exclude other belief systems. For example, animists believe in the existence of an unseen reality (the supernatural), but not in "gods" *per se*. The Hmong people, who believe that spirits inhabit the world alongside us, are animists. And if you extend your definition of religion to encompass beliefs and practices related to the supernatural, you will still miss other belief systems commonly understood to be religious. For example, Buddhism is oriented around *practices* that are thought to lead to a richer and fuller life, but it does not involve gods, spirits, or even a supernatural realm.

Spiro provided us with a *substantive definition* of religion. A substantive definition tells us what religion is and provides criteria for elements that should be included in the category of "religion." But substantive definitions are dead ends because they are rooted in particular times, places, and cultural contexts. They blind us to what may serve as religion in other times, places, and contexts.

To avoid this trap, we may take a different approach to defining religion: thinking through what religion *does* as opposed to explaining what religion *is*. Although the content of religious systems varies widely across time and place, sociologists have identified some key *functions* that religion serves. These functions are common across widely disparate systems of belief, practice, and community:

1   Religion provides comfort and quells dissatisfaction.
2   Religion strengthens human community.
3   Religion assures its followers that there is a larger cosmic order.

Religion Provides Comfort and Quells Dissatisfaction

Perhaps the most infamous *functional definition* of religion was provided by Karl Marx when he claimed that

> Religion is the general theory of that world, its encyclopedic compendium, its logic in popular form, its spiritualistic *point d'honneur* [trans.: principle], its enthusiasm, its moral sanction, its solemn complement, its universal source of consolation and justification. . . . Religion is the sigh of the

oppressed creature, the heart of a heartless world, just as it is the spirit of a spiritless condition. It is the opium of the people.

(Marx 1843, 53–54)

Marx believed that religion arose out of oppressive conditions and supported the status quo by justifying inequality, consoling the downtrodden, and dulling the pains of daily life. To Marx, religion was fundamentally conservative in that it confirms and reinforces existing social arrangements. It justifies laws that limit people's freedoms, it validates the rule of the powerful and oppression of the weak, and it makes sense of economic inequality and other forms of social disparity. In so doing, religion also suppresses people's resistance to oppressive systems.

To serve these purposes, religion need not take any specific form, posit a god or supernatural beings, or embody particular practices. It need only justify existing conditions and soothe those who suffer. Marx's understanding of the functions of religion does not apply to all cases, of course. As we will discuss in Chapter 7, there are numerous examples in history when religious groups stood up to *challenge* existing social arrangements—unfair laws, discriminatory practices, or economic inequality—and when religion served more to drive social change than to inhibit it. Marx did not acknowledge this fairly common use of religion. Thus, his functional definition of religion—"it is the opium of the people"—is oversimplified. It nonetheless provides a useful starting point for thinking about the functions of religion: Religion provides comfort to individuals and justifications for existing social arrangements.

Religion Strengthens Human Community

The 19th-century French sociologist Emile Durkheim offers a more comprehensive explanation of the function of religion when he writes that religion is "a unified system of beliefs and practices relative to sacred things, that is to say, things set apart and forbidden—beliefs and practices which unite into one single moral community called a Church, all who adhere to them" (Durkheim 1912, 44). It is a densely worded definition, but unpacked, it contains a number of important elements of religion: belief, ritual, sacred elements, and community. It is also a strong statement that the main function of religion in society is to strengthen human communities.

On Belief and Ritual Durkheim (1912) identifies two key elements of religion: belief and ritual. According to him, beliefs are "states of opinion and consist in representations." Essentially, beliefs are what we *think*. Rituals are "determined modes of action." They are what we *do*. Recall that substantive definitions of religion typically try to define the content of religious beliefs; specifically, belief in a god or the supernatural characterizes religion.

After studying a wide variety of world religions past and present, Durkheim concluded that religions share one significant common belief. He argued that

All known religious beliefs, whether simple or complex, present one common characteristic: they presuppose a classification of all the things, real and ideal, of which men think into two classes or opposed groups, generally designated by two distinct terms which are translated well enough by the words profane and sacred.

(Durkheim 1912, 34)

But what is the *difference* between the sacred and the profane? The definition of sacred varies across religious systems, so we will not find the answer in particular objects, beliefs, persons, or practices. There are hierarchical rankings even within the categories of sacred and profane. Some sacred objects are *more* sacred than others, for example. So saying that sacred elements are superior in dignity and power to profane elements does not help us distinguish them. To solve this problem,

Durkheim settles on the "absolute" heterogeneity of these categories. That is, the sacred and pro-fane are completely and totally different from each other. Any interaction between the two must be undertaken with the greatest of care:

> The sacred thing is *par excellence* that which the profane should not touch, and cannot touch with impu-nity . . . this establishment of relations [between the sacred and the profane] is always a delicate operation in itself, demanding great precautions and a more or less complicated initiation.
>
> (Durkheim 1912, 38)

To distinguish the sacred from the profane, Durkheim does not focus on the specific content of the categories of sacred and profane, because these vary so widely across religious systems. Instead, he focuses on the way that the sacred and profane are *treated* in human societies, particularly with respect to each other:

> Sacred things are those which the interdictions protect and isolate; profane things, those to which these interdictions are applied and which must remain at a distance from the first.
>
> (Durkheim 1912, 38)

Rituals are "the rules of conduct which prescribe how a man should comport himself in the presence of these sacred objects" (Durkheim 1912, 38). Because the sacred and profane are mutu-ally exclusive and completely dissimilar categories, problems arise when the sacred and profane meet. We have trouble imagining how the two can safely mingle: What if the profane contaminates the sacred? What if the profane is transformed into the sacred? These scenarios are understood to be socially dangerous possibilities. Nonetheless, the sacred and profane do sometimes interact—for example, when humans, whose bodies may be considered profane, touch or consume sacred objects. When this happens, people generally take great care to structure their contact with ritu-als, specifying a set of steps that makes interaction between the sacred and the profane safe. Thus, humans may reach out to the sacred through prayer, liturgy, dance, or song.

We see rituals, undertaken as precautions, across numerous religious traditions. Once, after attending an Episcopal worship service in an outdoor chapel, one of the authors (Monahan) pro-posed feeding the leftover consecrated bread to the birds. She was trying to avoid having to eat it herself. The priest who had led the service was unwavering: The bread must be consumed or saved for a later worship service. It was absolutely forbidden to throw the bread on the ground or leave it for the birds. A sacred element—the consecrated bread—cannot be treated in profane ways, even for the benefit of the birds. "Ah," your author thought, "that explains why, at the end of a communion service in a Christian church, the celebrant guzzles the leftover wine up at the altar at 11 A.M. on a Sunday morning. You can't just pour it down the drain!"

Because of concerns about the profane contaminating the sacred, Judaism understands the name of God ("YHWH") to be unpronounceable by humans, preserving its mystery and majesty; Ortho-dox Judaism bans menstruating women from attending temple; and Hindus abstain from eating the meat of cows, which are sacred to them.

Thus, Durkheim argues that religion is a system with two interrelated parts: (1) beliefs about how the world is divided into distinct, mutually exclusive, and wholly encompassing spheres of the sacred and the profane; and (2) practices through which sacred objects, people, ideas, and actions can safely come into contact with the profane. But that raises the question, What is the *point* of all of this?

On Community As a class exercise early in a Sociology of Religion class, we sometimes ask students to come up with a list of questions for a survey that would measure the "religiosity" of individuals, that is, how strongly people hold their religious beliefs. We remind students that they should expect to survey a culturally and ethnically diverse group of people. (Think beyond Christianity!) What questions would you ask?

To get students started, we provide a list of questions that researchers have used in the past to measure aspects of religion. We tell students that they may use, adapt, or eliminate any of these questions. Very quickly, the class eliminates questions about specific religious beliefs. Being able to recite the Ten Commandments serves as evidence of religiosity only in people who are Christian or Jewish, and being able to recognize prominent quotes from the Qu'ran does not speak to religiosity in other traditions. Praying, attending worship services, and donating money to a church are also aspects of some religions but not others.

Common ground emerges in an intriguing place, in questions that on the surface seem not to be about religious belief and practice at all: How much time do you spend with friends who share your religious beliefs, and how likely are you to marry within your faith? In fact, most students eliminate almost all other questions before arriving at these two as ways to measure religiosity. What is intriguing is that the first question does not capture how much time a person spends participating in *religious* activities with friends who share the same beliefs, just how much time in general the person spends around such friends. Yet students conclude that it is likely to be a good measure of general religiosity. Similarly, the second question does not measure a person's engagement in religious activities with his or her spouse. Instead, it captures how likely the person is to partner for life with someone else who shares the same faith.

These questions highlight the fundamentally *social* nature of religion. That is, while religion includes beliefs and practices, these elements exist to build religious community and integrate people into that community. When students lean toward measuring the strength of religious faith through questions that focus on affiliation with other members of a religious group, they implicitly understand this.

In fact, Durkheim claims that religion happens only within a community or collective setting. Those who adhere to the notion of individual spirituality might object to that limitation, claiming that their solitary practices also constitute "religion." But Durkheim is clear that a central function of religion is to create and strengthen common bonds among members of social groups and to tie members to the group as a whole. Note that he makes no claim that individual spirituality does not exist, only that it is tangential to the cohesive function of religion for the group as a whole. The "unified system of belief and practice" matters because it emerges from the social group and belongs to the group as a whole: Beliefs and rituals are communally recounted and practiced, and together they provide vital glue that holds the social group together.

Thus, the type of people with whom you regularly interact, especially voluntary interaction on nonwork time, is generally a strong indicator of your degree of religiosity. People who hold strong religious beliefs and engage in regular religious practice often associate with others who share their beliefs and practices, irrespective of the content of the religion. Likewise, marriage within the group is a robust measure of degree of religiosity because marriage typically has both civil and religious meaning and creates a presumably permanent social tie with another person. Of course, some people marry outside their religious group. Almost everyone knows someone who has done so. But the tendency toward marrying within the group is stronger among those who profess higher levels of religiosity. In sum, religious beliefs and practices unite the community and provide a powerful foundation for the rest of social life. In Chapter 5, we will explore in more detail the ways in which religion builds community and strengthens community cohesiveness.

Religion Assures Us of Cosmic Order

Peter Berger, a sociologist and Lutheran theologian, takes a broader approach to understanding the function of religion when he argues that religion is "the audacious attempt to conceive of the entire universe as humanly significant" (Berger 1967, 28). (See Box 1.1) He argues that humans are fundamentally meaning-seeking creatures: It is our very nature to impose order on our experiences and seek meaning in day-to-day events. In so doing, we reject chaos and the possibility that events are random in nature. We see much anecdotal evidence that Berger is right about this. A child dies, and through their grief, parents vow that the child's death will "mean something": They may start a foundation, lobby for passage of a law, or speak publicly about a larger issue related to their child's death. The child's death is transformed from an isolated, random, tragic event that happens with some degree of regularity—diseases strike, drunk drivers kill, accidents happen—to an event with meaning and larger purpose, an event connected to the greater social order. Similarly, an elderly woman wins the lottery and believes that she is being repaid for a lifetime of financial struggles and generous acts. It is entirely unsatisfying to think that picking the right lottery numbers might be just dumb luck and unrelated to the moral fiber of the lucky winner to conceive that a selfish and callous person could be fortunate enough to beat the odds.

Box 1.1 Some Definitions of Religion

- *Melford Spiro (1966):* Religion is "an institution consisting of culturally patterned interaction with culturally postulated superhuman beings."
- *Karl Marx (1843):* Religion is "the opium of the people."
- *Emile Durkheim (1912):* Religion is "a unified system of beliefs and practices relative to sacred things, that is to say, things set apart and forbidden—beliefs and practices which unite into one single moral community called a Church, all who adhere to them."
- *Peter Berger (1967):* Religion is "the audacious attempt to conceive of the entire universe as humanly significant."

According to Berger, humans constantly seek order and meaning in daily events as a way to fight off the alternative—the admission that our lives are full of random unpredictability, which leaves us enmeshed in the terrifying and dark morass of chaos. Chaos, or the absence of order, is terrifying to humans because it suggests a potentially risky situation over which we have no control.

One common type of order is what Berger refers to as *nomos*, the imposition of order by humans on everyday events so that events seem more predictable and stable. Schedules and appointments, laws of science, social norms such as driving on the right side of the road, and stereotypes about other people all take masses of information, actions, and events and place them in a system of humanly constructed and understood order.

But the most robust order is *cosmos*, a conception of order that links human experience to a transcendental order, providing a sense that our lives are not mere aggregations of random events but instead that our experiences are connected to some larger sacred order. As people often say in both good and bad times, "It's all part of God's plan." Events that otherwise make no sense are explained through their connection to a cosmic order. When terrorists crashed a plane into a building, Jerry Falwell, a prominent religious leader, claimed that

> the pagans, and the abortionists, and the feminists, and the gays and the lesbians . . . the ACLU, People For the American Way . . . created an environment which possibly has caused God to lift the veil of protection.

(CNN 2001)

Falwell is convinced that such a tragic event *must* be connected to some larger and sacred order. It cannot be an accident, a fluke, or a mundane failure of airport security. The universe cannot be so cruel. It must *mean* something.

In the aftermath of Hurricane Katrina in 2005, people expressed a variety of attitudes toward those who stayed in New Orleans as the storm approached. Some of the harshest evaluations came from those whose criticisms suggested that *they* would have done things differently: "I would have hoofed it out of there" said one student who was not the least bit compassionate toward—and indeed seemed disgusted by—the people who remained behind. She even said, "They got what they deserved." This student was certain that those who stayed behind were basically flawed human beings, and she insisted that their suffering was not random but deserved. Berger's lens suggests that she had a different underlying thought, something along the following lines:

> I cannot believe that this was just a random event that happened to random people, because that would mean that someday something like this could happen to me. There is order in this world and nothing so awful could ever happen to a deserving person like me.

To admit that a terrifying and tragic event could befall anyone at any time is to acknowledge the significant degree of randomness in our day-to-day existence. It is this sense of inherent chaos that, with the help of religion, we fight so hard to fend off. Humans resist the notion that events are random by conceiving that the events are meaningful in some larger cosmic order.

A Sociological Consensus: Religion is a Human Product

Sociologists and anthropologists agree on one essential point: Religion is a product of human beings. Across time and place, human beings create religion: They originate belief systems, they develop rituals, and they form communities of faith. Sometimes this happened so far in the past that we forget religion's origins. But religion originates in human societies.

So what is the relationship between religion and its subject (e.g., God, gods, the supernatural and so on)? Think of it this way: Religion is the human system that reflects our understandings of reality, order, and appropriate ways to engage the sacred, whereas supernatural formulations such as a god or gods are posited as existing and are understood through the lens provided by religion. Religion is not the same thing as "god." Instead, religion creates the perception of a bridge between humans and what is variously called "god," the supernatural, or the cosmic order. It is a way for human beings to understand and to reach out and connect to something larger and unknowable that they believe is out there.

Many people find this understanding of religion to be contentious because it suggests that "god" does not really exist but is instead a product of human imagination. Peter Berger responds to this concern in an endnote to his book *The Sacred Canopy*, in which he points out that the claim that religion is a human creation does not speak to the question of whether "god" or some other larger cosmic order really exists (Berger 1967). The existence of "god" or that larger cosmic order is simply not empirically verifiable. Despite copious efforts by believers and nonbelievers, it is not possible to either confirm or disprove the existence of "god." Understanding religion as a human product, Berger argues, implies nothing about the existence of some ultimate reality.

What is most important to sociologists is that the *claim* of this reality drives the creation of religious beliefs, rituals, structures, and communities. Those phenomena *are* consequential and empirically observable. While there is no empirical evidence that religious structures, beliefs, and practices are inspired by some ultimate being, force, or order, there is plenty about religion that is worth exploring and understanding. Religion is real in its consequences and effects. And, of course, it feels real—in its substance—to believers.

It is worth examining the nature of religion that makes people take it for granted, the sense that it is simply *is* and always has been. Much of any institution's power lies in its ability to make its human roots invisible. In other words, when an institution—such as religion—is understood to be timeless, enduring, or emerging from other than human sources, that institution is more likely to be taken for granted (in the sense that people will believe and trust in it), and its stability is enhanced. On the other hand, when the human origins of an institution become apparent, the institution is often weakened in the eyes of observers.

Consider, for example, Jon Krakauer's account of the origins of *The Book of Mormon*, the text that lies at the heart of the Mormon faith, which in 2008 claimed over 13 million adherents. Krakauer recounts how Joseph Smith, a farmer in upstate New York, found buried treasure using "divining." On four attempts, Smith failed to find the treasure, but on the fifth attempt he supposedly was greeted by an angel named Moroni who had been sent from God, who allowed Smith to dig up a box that contained a sacred text written on golden plates. The text was written in "reformed Egyptian," a dead language, but Moroni gave Smith magic glasses that allowed Smith to read, translate, and transcribe the plates. When Smith completed the 116-page translation, Moroni reclaimed the golden plates and the magic glasses. As the story goes, the original translation was lost, and Moroni returned to Smith with the golden plates but not the magic glasses, so Smith relied on another technique for "translating" the text:

> Day after day, utilizing a technique he had learned from [a local girl], Joseph Smith would place the magic rock in an upturned hat, bury his face in it with the stack of gold plates sitting nearby, and dictate the lines of scripture that appeared to him out of the blackness. He worked at a feverish pace . . . averaging some thirty-five hundred words a day, and by the end of June 1829 the job was finished.
>
> (Krakauer 2003, 63)

The result was *The Book of Mormon*.

Krakauer's striking account lays clear the human roots of religion—how religion is originated by human beings. Whether you believe that Joseph Smith was divinely inspired or not, the account is unsettling because it suggests that a rapidly growing worldwide religion began with the mundane, if somewhat odd, act of a man who lived less than 200 years ago. In this case, the human roots of this religion are so obvious that it is hard to see how a faith—one that is obviously compelling on the basis of recent growth in its adherents—could have been founded on it.

But is the narrative of the founding of Mormonism really any more outlandish than the founding stories of other religions—stone tablets inscribed with text handed down on a mountain, or an individual who dies and comes back to life again? Or is the founding story more transparently a human product because not enough time has yet passed to render the belief system part of the taken-for-granted cultural landscape?

In his *New York Times Magazine* article, "What Is It about Mormonism?", Noah Feldman confronts the common response to this tale of the religion's origins:

> [E]ven among those who respect Mormons personally, it is still common to hear Mormonism's tenets dismissed as ridiculous. This attitude is logically indefensible insofar as Mormonism is being compared with other world religions. There is nothing inherently less plausible about God's revealing himself to an upstate New York farmer in the early years of the Republic than to the pharaoh's changeling grandson in ancient Egypt. But what is driving the tendency to discount Joseph Smith's revelations is not that they seem less reasonable than those of Moses; it is that the book containing them is so new. When it comes to prophecy, antiquity breeds authenticity. Events in the distant past, we tend to think, occurred in sacred, mythic time. Not so revelations received during the presidencies of James Monroe or Andrew Jackson.
>
> (Feldman 2008)

Over time, the human roots of a given religion become less visible, and the religion itself becomes more taken-for-granted as timelessly and universally real, rather than being the ideas and practices of a person or group at one particular point in time. None of this changes the fact that religion is a human product. It only explains how, over time, we come to overlook that uncomfortable reality.

People have also sought to uncover the human roots of older and more established religions, a practice that often causes discomfort and dissent within religious communities. In her memoir *The Spiral Staircase*, religious historian and former Catholic nun Karen Armstrong describes her surprise upon encountering "New Testament criticism," a scholarly body of work that examines in detail how the New Testament of the Bible was constructed. New Testament critics have concluded that the Bible was written years after the death of Jesus and that there were fierce political debates among the contributors about what to include and exclude. In addition, the text underwent numerous transformations at the hands of humans: It was translated from one language to another, people made copies that were slightly different versions, and people used gradual to abrupt adaptations of certain words. New Testament critics claim that, in all, decisions made by humans over time shaped the Christianity we know today, and the Bible is only the current record of a document that has been evolving for a long time, despite the fact that some people hold it to be fixed, sacred, and constant (or even literal). Bart Ehrman, a religious historian at the University of North Carolina, popularized New Testament criticism research in his books *Misquoting Jesus* (2007) and *Lost Christianities* (2005). His work and that of fellow New Testament critics have elicited strong negative responses, especially from fundamentalist Christians. For example, Darrell Bock and Daniel Wallace, theology professors at the Dallas Theological Seminary, wrote *Dethroning Jesus* to counter the claims of the New Testament critics: The book's promotional materials claim that it will "help readers understand that the orthodox understanding of Christ and his divinity is as trustworthy and sure as it ever was." For Karen Armstrong, however, this scholarship was eye-opening. After she spent a lifetime in the Catholic Church, "New Testament Criticism" challenged the previously unquestioned reality of her religious beliefs by highlighting their very human roots.

The Promise of Sociology

Students often say that they are drawn to sociology because they are "interested in people" and they have heard that "sociologists study people." Probe more deeply, and you will hear that people do "stuff" that the students want to better understand: They think, act, and feel. But the typical student has yet to grasp the full meaning of the word *people*, and with it, the inherent power of sociology.

Students of sociology often start out as closet psychologists. In order to understand people better, they take the methodological approach of focusing on individuals. They naïvely assume that if they study enough individuals—their beliefs, behaviors, and feelings—they will reach a full understanding of "people" as a group, as well. The belief has an intuitive and compelling logic on the surface, one that fits well with the way that Western culture socializes us to see the world around us as made up of individual actors with free will.

But the approach demonstrates a fundamental misunderstanding of sociology's object of study and, more important, sociology's power as a tool for explanation. To many students, the term *people* is merely the plural of *person;* it is the aggregation of two or more individuals. But to social scientists, the term *people* connotes something different: Though indeed a "people" is made up of individuals, it is noteworthy because it is larger than the mere sum of its constituent parts. Sociologists do not study individuals or "people" in the adding-up-individuals sense. "People" are not merely "persons," and sociology is not, as students often assume, the study of the experiences of individual persons, viewed in isolation from their social relationships or ties. Instead, sociology focuses on the collective itself: the nation, the community, the family, the group, the organization, and so on. It ponders all the ways that people organize themselves and examines human *arrangements*.

Those arrangements include what sociologists call "structure," or stable patterns of social relationships. Groups, communities, bureaucracies, and families are examples of institutions that demonstrate social structure. The arrangements also include "culture"—the values, norms, and knowledge of a group or society. Social practices, including recurrent patterns of behavior, are also a type of human arrangement. So the practices of going to church on Sunday, attending synagogue on the Sabbath, praying five times a day, or dipping infants in holy water all have social content and meaning. At the heart of sociology is the study of "people" in this sense, as social collectives that have ties among members, connections to other groups, shared understandings, and patterned behaviors.

How, then, can we study those human arrangements? Emile Durkheim, whose ideas about the sociology of religion we have already mentioned, was one of sociology's founders. He wrote that *social facts*—patterns of thinking, feeling, and acting—exist outside of any individual but exert force over individuals in systematic—though not wholly deterministic—ways. So when we see someone express a thought or feeling, or act in a certain way, we are often observing something larger and more significant than the individual's expression. That is, we are often observing an instance of a *pattern* that exists in society.

Our day-to-day lives are structured by an infinite number of such patterns, everything from handshaking, to "flipping the bird" (in response, of course, to different stimuli!), to valuing the newest technology, to feeling grief at a funeral. Certainly, thoughts, feelings, and actions related to religion are instances of broader patterns. A Muslim woman who wears a veil is not making a personal fashion decision but instead is engaging in the religious practice of hijab. A man who professes belief in "God's plan" did not invent that belief; instead, he is drawing on an existing pattern of belief that is widespread in his social community. Similarly, an observant Jewish person who washes his hands carefully before each meal did not invent the practice, nor does he engage in it in isolation from its larger social context. People's thoughts, feelings, and actions often have their origins in patterns of thinking, feeling, and acting that exist outside them. Those *external patterns* are what interest sociologists: We note them in the thoughts, feelings, and actions of individuals, but never forget that they have an existence *outside* the individual.

These patterns of thinking, feeling, and acting also exercise "an external constraint" over the individual: The patterns have coercive power to push us to think, feel, and act in particular ways. People often initially reject or resist the idea that there are coercive social facts, because we like to think of ourselves as individualists, actors with free will. But a closer examination of our daily lives reveals endless instances where we are following well-established patterns of thinking, feeling, and acting. To name but a few: driving on the right side of the road (in the United States), saying "excuse me" when you bump into someone, avoiding eye contact in an elevator, waiting in line, applying for college or jobs, tipping service providers, kneeling during prayer, feeling teary during a wedding (although that pattern is probably related to gender!), and so on.

You might respond that people *do* violate these patterns on occasion and so there are not really any constraints. Durkheim does not dispute that sometimes the patterns are violated, but he locates evidence of their coercive nature in the broader social *response* to violation, a response from those around us and, perhaps more interestingly, from within ourselves. When people violate existing patterns of thinking, feeling, or acting, those around them often respond in a negative way: a funny look, a sharp word, a rolling of the eyes, a denial of assistance or service, or a formal punishment. Those responses remind the transgressors of the existing patterns and of the benefits of conforming to them. In that sense, the patterns and the responses to violations exert a coercive influence over us: We become more likely to follow the patterns than to violate them because we wish to avoid negative sanctions. Violations also elicit responses from within the violator, such as heightened self-consciousness, a queasy or nervous feeling in the pit of the stomach, a feeling of guilt, or an overwhelming desire to simply *conform*. The patterns exist outside of us, but we have also internalized them.

Consider again the Islamic practice of women wearing the veil or the orthodox Judaic practice of women covering their hair (e.g., by wearing a wig or a scarf). As we stated earlier, this behavior is not merely a personal fashion choice; it is a religious imperative. In his book *The Culture of Disbelief*, legal scholar Stephen Carter considers cases in which nonbelievers reduce religious patterns or imperatives—to perform animal sacrifice, to consume an illegal substance, to rest on a specified day—to "individual choices," suggesting that a religious person has a choice about whether or not to adhere to his or her faith (Carter 1993). Carter argues that understanding religion as a "personal choice" trivializes faith because, in the lives of believers, religion is not a choice but a powerful social fact. It comprises ways of thinking, feeling, and acting that are external to and coercive over us. It is a particularly powerful social influence because it is made up of an interconnected set of beliefs, practices, structures, and communities and is central to the way that we think about and experience our lives.

To say that religion is a social fact does not, in any way, imply that what religion purports to represent and connect us to—the supernatural or a deity—is itself an empirically observable fact. But religion, the human-created system that connects communities to the unseen, is very much a "fact" in the social sense. It is observable, it exists outside any one person, and, as we will see, it exerts a tremendous influence in our world.

Suggested Reading

Berger, Peter. 1967. *The Sacred Canopy: Elements of a Sociological Theory of Religion*. Garden City, NY: Doubleday.

Bock, Darrell, and Daniel B. Wallace. 2008. *Dethroning Jesus: Exposing Popular Culture's Quest to Unseat the Biblical Christ*. Nashville, TN: Thomas Nelson.

Durkheim, Emile. 1895 (1982 trans). *The Rules of Sociological Method*. New York: Free Press.

Durkheim, Emile. 1912 (1995 trans). *The Elementary Forms of Religious Life*. New York: Free Press.

Ehrman, Bart. 2007. *Misquoting Jesus*. New York: HarperOne.

Fadiman, Anne. 1997. *The Spirit Catches You and You Fall Down*. New York: Noonday.

Geertz, Clifford. 1966. "Religion as a Cultural System." In *Anthropological Approaches to the Study of Religion*, edited by M. Banton, 1–45. London: Tavistock.

Marx, Karl. 1843 (1970 trans). "From Contribution to the Critique of Hegel's Philosophy of the Law: Introduction." In *The Marx-Engels Reader*, 2nd Edition, edited by Robert C. Tucker, 53–65. New York: W.W. Norton.

Spiro, Melford. 1966. "Religion: Problems of Definition and Explanation." In *Anthropological Approaches to the Study of Religion*, edited by M. Banton, 85–126. London: Tavistock.

2 "You Believe What?"

A Tour of Religious Belief
and Ritual Practice

1 How do beliefs, rituals, and experiences vary across religious traditions?
2 Why are religious beliefs, ritual practices, and religious experiences *all* important in the study of religion?
3 What are "worship wars" and "Sheilaism" . . . and who are the "Nones?" Are they all uniquely American religious phenomena?
4 What do sociologists think about religious beliefs, practices, and experiences?

It's one of those special or unusual years, depending on how you look at it. The day is December 21, four days before Christmas. Many American Christians are getting ready to celebrate the birth of Christ with lights, greenery, and manger scenes that include small figures of Jesus as a baby, his parents Mary and Joseph, a few shepherds, a donkey, sheep, and sometimes three kings.

In this particular year, this day is also the first day of the Jewish holiday Hanukah. Hanukah is the eight-day festival of lights that commemorates the rededication of the Jewish temple in Jerusalem in the second century B.C.E. Hanukah commemorates the miracle in which, when only enough oil remained to light the temple lamp for one day, the oil lasted eight full days, just enough time to harvest olives and make more oil.

But wait, we're not done yet. December 21 is also the festival of Yule, which is a celebration of the winter solstice, the shortest day of the year. Yule is a pre-Christian festival that continues to be celebrated by members of Wicca and other pagan groups as the time when the sun is reborn, and the Goddess gives birth to the God.

So . . . raise your hand if you've ever wondered why people still celebrate things that happened a couple of thousand years ago. Or why some ancient winter festival still matters to anyone today. Or why these very different celebrations all fall at the same time of the year, although not always all on the same day. Religious beliefs, rituals, and experiences can thrill us or revolt us. They can bring us together as a community or make people from one group want to burn outsiders at the stake. As you may already be thinking, religion is complex and not necessarily easy to understand.

If asked, a vast majority of people in North America and Europe would probably tell you that religion is what individuals believe about the sacred. They might also say that religion is about being a member of some religious group, attending religious services, or believing in God . . . but beliefs are often at the core of what makes religion, religion. But did you ever hear the old saying about two topics never to bring up in conversation? Religion and politics! Those of us living in North America and Europe, what is really the Global North, tend to see beliefs and values as highly personalized and tend to think that they should rarely, if ever, be discussed outside one's own religious group. Religion is a private matter, and we risk conflicts when we start talking to other people about what we really believe, especially to people who might believe something else! But keep in mind that this viewpoint is certainly not shared by people who live in other parts of the world, a point we will come back to later.

DOI: 10.4324/9781003182108-3

Depending on where you live, you may feel barraged by other people's religious beliefs. Or you may know that different religious groups exist in your community but may not often hear about what they believe or do. Yet even when we are in situations where religion seems to surround us, most of us know little about the diverse range of religious beliefs, practices, and experiences out there. That is sometimes true even within our own faith traditions. Roman Catholics know little about the big differences among Protestant Christian groups. Some Christians have never had a "born again" experience or the experience of being filled with the Holy Spirit in some physical way. Likewise, Christians don't know much about the different branches of Judaism or Hinduism and vice-versa. Think about it for a moment: How much do you know about the religious beliefs, practices, and experiences of your friends, classmates, or co-workers?

To understand religion in our world, you have to realize that religious beliefs, practices, and experiences are social constructs. As noted in Chapter 1, they are rooted in communities of believers and are shaped by these believers over time. So our first order of business is to examine the broad organizational families in which believers believe, act, and experience the sacred. As you will see, some religious groups are closely related to others. Figure 2.1 illustrates the interrelationships among Christians as one example of these linkages. While it is not possible for us to exhaustively cover every religion, this chapter will give you a sense of some of the differences that you might encounter within different traditions, along with some recent data on religious beliefs, practices, and experiences among Americans. As the chapter title suggests, often we are surprised at what religious people actually believe, what they do, and what they experience. We should remember, however, that beliefs and practices differ widely even within the same religion. The sociological lens will help us understand religious diversity and the consequences of beliefs, rituals, and experiences for people, communities, and entire societies.

Comparing Religious Beliefs and Practices

Of the almost 8 billion people in the world today, about 78% belong to one of the world's major religions (Pew Research Center 2015a). Although specific estimates vary, a third of the world's population (approximately 31.4%) claim to belong to some form of Christianity, making it the largest of the world's religions. Of course, we will see that Christianity encompasses a vast range of different denominations and groups. Islam is the second largest religion, with roughly 1.9 billion adherents, or approximately 25% of the population. Hindus represent another 15%, or 1.16 billion people. Buddhism makes up 6.6% of the world's population, and traditional Chinese religion and the world's indigenous and animist religious traditions together make up 5.6% of the population, or 500 million people more or less in each case. Judaism claims 14 million people, or 0.22% of the world's population.

While these statistics may make you think that the world's biggest religions (and therefore the unique beliefs, practices, and experiences of their adherents) are concise and easily understood, these broad categories barely touch the over 10,000 distinct religions in the world or the 150 religions that have a million or more followers. Even Christianity can be subdivided into well over 200 denominations in the United States alone, with many more distinct Christian groups existing worldwide (Olson et al. 2018; Jacobson 2011; Barrett 2001)! With that diversity in mind, let's explore some key beliefs, practices, and experiences that are related to these groups. Since it is the single biggest religion in the world today, we'll start with Christianity, then move on to Islam, Hinduism, and others. Hang on for the ride!

Christianity

The core beliefs and practices of Christianity focus on the life and teachings of Jesus, who is understood to be the Son of the one God and who came to earth to save humans from their sins by dying

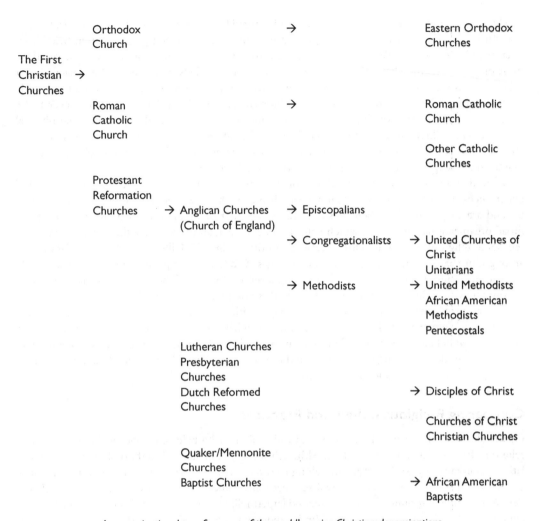

An organizational tree for some of the world's major Christian denominations.

Figure 2.1   A Denominational Tree for Some of the World's Major Christian Denominations

and returning to life again. Christians believe that the Bible, which includes the Hebrew Scriptures or "Old Testament" as well as the New Testament, is the word of God, forming the basis for their religious life and social morality, though what this means practically varies by congregation and denomination. Some Christians believe that the Bible is the literal word of God; in other words, every word is understood to be true and relevant for living today. Other Christians believe the Bible to be the "inspired" word of God, meaning that moral teachings are central to understanding one's faith and living a "good" life, though not every story or commandment is literally true or relevant for life today. There are also many Christians for whom the Bible is an important sacred text but who understand its stories and moral precepts as products of a much different historic era. As a result, the Bible may provide guidance today but no more so than other sacred texts. Most Christians believe that moral conduct in this life determines what happens to them after death. Here, too, there is much variety among denominations, but most Christians believe in an afterlife with an eventual judgment at which one must account for one's life.

Different denominations embrace and amplify different basic tenets of Christianity. We will review some differences among the main Christian denominations: the Roman Catholics, Establishment Protestants, Black Protestants, Evangelicals, and other notable Christian groups.

Catholicism

If asked, Catholics would probably say that their Church goes all the way back to the days when the first Christian communities were founded by disciples of Jesus. They include congregations around the world, including Eastern European churches under the historic jurisdiction of the Bishop of Constantinople, often called Orthodox Churches, and Western European Churches under the jurisdiction of the Bishop of Rome, called Roman Catholic.

Orthodox Churches represent one of three major branches of Christianity, along with Roman Catholicism and Protestantism. There is, however, no single hierarchy that encompasses all of these churches. Instead, Orthodox denominations reflect national heritages (e.g., the Serbian Orthodox Church or the Bulgarian Orthodox Church) and the ethnic customs of their members. Most of the Orthodox Churches have formal relationships with one another, and they hold similar doctrines that are based on ancient Christian creeds. Orthodox services tend to be beautifully elaborate and ritualistic, including the movement of priests and laity. Church architecture is also often elaborate and filled with symbolic significance.

Since the 13th century, Christians in Western Europe have used "catholic" to describe churches, communities, and individuals that are loyal to the Bishop of Rome (the Pope). During most of the Middle Ages, the Roman Church dominated European society. That domination ended with the Protestant Reformation of the 16th century, which divided European Christianity into Catholic and Protestant branches. Roman Catholicism, as a distinctive branch of Christianity, can be dated to the Council of Trent in 1545, which officially defined Roman Catholic doctrine for the first time and established the current structure of the Roman Catholic Church worldwide, which continues to be headed by the Pope.

The Roman Catholic Church is the single largest religious body in the United States and has approximately 51 million members. This number under-represents things, however. In 2015, the Pew Research Center (2015b, 18) found 45% of Americans had some close connection to Catholicism, either as members (20%), as former members (9%), as "cultural" Catholics by birth (9%), or through some less formal connection (8%). On one hand this is an amazingly large percentage but on the other, it is sobering that it includes so many who are no longer practicing Catholics or those who may occasionally attend Mass but aren't formally members of the Church. In fact, overall the number of Americans who consider themselves to be Catholic when asked about their present religion has been steadily in decline, from 24% in 2007 to the 20% noted in 2015. From a global perspective, Catholics from North America represent the smallest proportion of Catholics worldwide. Latin America is home to 39% of the world's Catholics, with another 28% living in Africa or Asia.

Catholic beliefs are formalized. Three creeds form the core of all Roman Catholic belief and doctrine: the Apostles' Creed, the Nicene Creed, and the Athanasian Creed. Creeds are formal statements of belief that people say out loud. Here is the Apostles' Creed:

> I believe in one God, the Father almighty, creator of heaven and earth.
> I believe in Jesus Christ, his only Son, our Lord.
> He was conceived by the power of the Holy Spirit and born of the Virgin Mary.
> He suffered under Pontius Pilate, was crucified, died, and was buried.
> He descended to the dead. On the third day he rose again.
> He ascended into heaven, and is seated at the right hand of the Father.
> He will come again to judge the living and the dead.

> I believe in the Holy Spirit, the holy Catholic Church, the communion of saints, the forgiveness of sins, the resurrection of the body, and the life everlasting.

As you can see in this example, creeds are statements about what Christian churches understand to be the "correct" beliefs about God, Jesus, and important doctrines. The Nicene and the Athanasian Creeds are similar to the Apostles' Creed but go into more theological detail about the nature of God, the divinity of Jesus Christ, and the relationships among God the Father, Jesus, and the Holy Spirit (the Trinity).

In addition to making these statements of belief, Roman Catholics also emphasize seven rituals or sacraments: baptism (in which babies are sprinkled with water as a sign that they are members of the community); confirmation (in which teens make a formal statement that they intend to belong to the Church); Eucharist (or Communion), which is a re-enactment of the Last Supper; reconciliation (in which individuals confess sins or bad things that they have done to a priest and receive forgiveness); matrimony (we'll assume you know that one); holy orders (in which men become priests); and anointing of the sick (with oil for healing).

Over time, seven denominations have broken away from the Roman Catholic Church while retaining many of its beliefs, liturgical styles, and basic theology. These denominations are still classified as Catholic (though the Pope may disagree!). For example, the American Catholic Church is a federation of independent churches founded in 1988 whose members are committed to basic Catholic beliefs and sacraments. They are, however, more liberal in their social and political beliefs than the Roman Catholic Church. There are also Old Catholic Churches founded by a combination of mostly Swiss, German, and Austrian Roman Catholic priests who refused to accept the dogma of papal infallibility when it was formally defined in 1870. In the United States, Old Catholics are more conservative than Roman Catholics and have attracted conservative Roman Catholic priests who opposed some of the changes brought about in the 1960s by the Second Vatican Council (such as the elimination of services in Latin). The Liberal Catholic Church was founded in 1916 as a reorganization of the Old Catholic Churches in Great Britain. It combines traditional Catholic forms of worship with freedom of individual conscience and thought. Okay, you get the idea. This diversity of traditions shows that just because someone says that he or she is Catholic doesn't mean that the person believes or worships in the same way as other Catholics. There's often more to it.

Establishment Protestantism

As we noted earlier, the Protestant Reformation broke the Roman Church's monopoly on Western Europe. A huge diversity of Protestant denominations grew out of this historical event but seven represent the core of this branch of Christianity. The label itself may sound strange to you and is not one that is commonly used in academic circles today. More often, these groups are called "mainline Protestants." Yet what makes these denominations mainline, which suggests something about their size or organizational strength? Ironically, none of these seven denominations are among the largest religious groups in the United States, nor are they growing. Since the 1970s, as a group their collective membership has been steadily declining. In fact, Roman Catholics and Southern Baptists, neither of which are ever included in this category, both outnumber them. This label reinforces that these specific Protestant groups were the powerful religious groups in American history that ran the show religiously, politically, and socially until the later decades of the 20th century. They were "mainline" as distinct from everyone else, reinforcing their cultural privilege in the American religious landscape. Today it makes sense to move away from this label that hides the power relationships between religious groups in the U.S., much less around the world.

"Establishment" Protestant denominations, a label we've adapted from Baltzell's (1964) classic study of the elite in American society, *The Protestant Establishment*, include the United Methodist

Church, the Disciples of Christ, the United Church of Christ, the Anglican or Episcopal Church, the Evangelical Lutheran Church of America, the American Baptist Church, and the Presbyterian Church, U.S.A. Each of these denominations developed out of unique historical and regional circumstances. But despite their differences, they share much in common. Each is affiliated with the National Council of Churches in the United States, supports a moderate to liberal social agenda, and generally accommodates changes in the broader culture. However, because each of these groups is linked to its counterparts in countries around the world in global denominational networks, in recent years conflicts have emerged between U.S. churches and their international counterparts, especially over issues of gender and sexuality. Once again, just because religious believers claim the same denominational identity doesn't mean they do or believe the same things. Here, we will highlight three of these denominations from the U.S. to give you a sense of their differences: United Methodists, Churches of Christ, and Anglicans.

One of the largest mainline Protestant denominations, United Methodists started as a movement within the Church of England between 1738 and 1790 under the leadership of John and Charles Wesley. Methodist churches focus on simplicity of worship (unlike the more elaborate rituals of Anglicans), love of one's neighbor (especially the poor and disadvantaged), personal piety, and evangelism. Methodists believe in the Trinity and the sinfulness of humanity. They also believe that the Bible is the inerrant (without error) word of God and that humans need to be converted and to repent, need justification by faith, sanctification, and holiness, and can expect future rewards or punishments in heaven or hell. There are two formal rituals in United Methodist churches: baptism and the Lord's Supper (communion).

In America, United Methodists represent the core of what formerly was called the Methodist Episcopal Church. Historically, this denomination drew members from among small business owners, the middle class, and the skilled working class. Although they are more liberal in their social attitudes than other types of Methodists, United Methodists share most of the same doctrines and worship styles that other Methodists follow. UMC is also a global denomination with annual conferences in different nations (www.umc.org). The UMC also belongs to the World Methodist Council (https://worldmethodistcouncil.org). It is the federation of all Methodist/Wesleyan denominations worldwide, though it has no legislative power over the member denominations.

Sometimes referred to as Churches of Christ, Christian churches trace their roots to the early 1800s when a small group of Presbyterians and Methodists set out to restore what they saw as the structure and doctrine of first-century Christians, a common theme in the founding of many Christian denominations. Followers believed that the Word of God was sufficient to form the basis for worship without the addition of any creeds or other human interpretations. This represents a significant break with Anglicans and United Methodists, since worship in both traditions includes reciting creeds and formal rituals like the Eucharist (the Lord's Supper or communion). Establishment Protestant denominations in the United States include two Christian churches, or Churches of Christ: The Disciples of Christ and the United Church of Christ (UCC). Like other Establishment Protestant groups in the U.S., Disciples and UCC churches hold liberal theological and social attitudes. Disciples of Christ churches are marked by informality, openness, individualism, and diversity. Membership is granted to anyone who professes to believe in Jesus Christ and who has been baptized by being dunked completely in water, in small pools or tanks of water often built right in the church itself. Some of the core beliefs are that Christ is the only head of the church, that the Bible is the basis for faith and practice, that Christian character is the measure of church membership, that individual members are free to interpret the Bible as they see fit, that "Christian" is an appropriate name for all followers of Christ, and that Christian unity is the goal of all believers. These churches are organized as democracies in which local congregations determine their own policies regarding programs and budgets, as well as the extent of their engagement with social issues such as war, racism, and gay rights. U.S. churches are linked to others around the world through the World Convention of Churches of Christ which, as an organization, focuses on Christian unity and evangelism.

Anglicans grew out of the Church of England, which severed its alliance with the Pope during the reign of Henry VIII in the 1500s. Britain was an empire that dominated the globe until the first half of the 20th century and exported its religious tradition to every one of its colonies. These branches were reconstituted into national churches after each colony gained independence. The Anglican Communion links these national bodies around the world. The largest Anglican Churches are in Uganda and Nigeria. In the United States, the Church of England became the Protestant Episcopal Church, now more commonly just referred to as the Episcopal Church. An American version of the *Book of Common Prayer* is the foundation of Anglican worship and belief. Anglicans, like Roman Catholics, use the Apostles' Creed and the Nicene Creed as the basis for their beliefs. For them, as for other Establishment Protestants, baptism and Holy Eucharist are central to the ritual life of the church. Worship styles vary from "high church" traditions, which have more elaborate ritual and ceremony, to "low church" traditions, which have less ceremony. American Anglicans vary considerably in their social and theological attitudes, from very conservative to very liberal, though as a group American and Canadian Anglicans are more liberal than those elsewhere in the world.

Although the preceding short discussion doesn't do justice to these groups, we hope that you're beginning to see that within Christian denominations there are points of strong unity (like belief in Jesus Christ) and points of hot disagreement (such as the elaborateness of rituals or how much the Bible and tradition should determine the way that churches operate today).

Black Protestants

The Reverend Martin Luther King, Jr., observed that Sunday mornings were the most segregated hours of the week. We will explore this idea further in Chapter 11. For now, we will focus on Black Protestantism as an independent category of denominations linked by theology and race. The core of Black Protestantism is a set of historic African American religious bodies founded in the days of slavery: the African Methodist Episcopal Church (AME), the African Methodist Episcopal Church of Zion (AMEZ), and the Christian Methodist Episcopal Church (CME). Also central, but more internally diverse, are Black Baptist churches, including those associated with the National Baptist Convention, U.S.A., and the National Baptist Convention of America. Numerous Churches of God in Christ and Pentecostal churches also fall into this category. At first glance, you might think that these denominations represent too much theological diversity to be grouped together. Yet the common experience of racial inequities that has shaped African American people makes these denominations more similar to one another in their social and religious attitudes than they are to White mainline or evangelical denominations.

Several Black Protestant denominations broke away from largely White denominations, often in protest against segregation and discrimination. Black Methodists broke away from their White Methodist counterparts in the 18th century. Although they share doctrine and liturgical traditions with United Methodists, almost all members of this church today are African Americans. For example, the AME Church, one of the largest Methodist denominations, was founded in 1787 as a protest against racial discrimination and segregation. The AMEZ Church was founded as an independent Methodist denomination in 1769 by members of New York City's John Street Church in protest against racial segregation in the Methodist Episcopal Church. The Colored Methodist Episcopal Church was created in 1870 out of the General Conference of the Methodist Episcopal Church, South. The name was changed to the Christian Methodist Episcopal Church in 1956. Its doctrines remain parallel to its parent church.

Beliefs vary widely among African American Christians. For example, members of the Church of God and Saints in Christ focus on the Old Testament doctrines. In the late 19th century,

Williams Saunders Crowdy, a son of former slaves, had a vision calling him to form a church whose aim was to live according to a literal understanding of the Old Testament law. Sometimes called Christian Israelites, members of this church have no connection to historic Judaism but celebrate Jewish holy and feast days as prescribed by the Bible. They also believe in the Seven Keys of doctrine: repentance, baptism, consumption of unleavened bread and water in the Lord's Supper, foot washing (the ritual washing of members' feet as Jesus did at the Last Supper, commanding them to do the same to each other as the symbol of being a servant to all), obedience to the Bible (especially the Ten Commandments), the holy kiss (following Saint Paul's encouragement to "greet one another with a holy kiss"—Romans 16:16), and the Lord's Prayer. Today this denomination has 40,000 members in 200 congregations.

Evangelical Protestants

Evangelical denominations include denominations such as the Assemblies of God, Holiness Churches, Missouri Synod Lutheran Churches, Churches of the Nazarene, Southern Baptists, Jehovah's Witnesses, Full Gospel, Apostolic Churches, Churches of God, and many more. Many of these churches have their roots in religious revivals of the late 19th and early 20th centuries. Historically, these denominations have resisted what they perceive to be the more liberal theology and social agendas of mainline Protestant churches. Most Evangelical groups see their standards of moral behavior as absolute, applicable to all people, and unchanging. A belief in an imminent end of the world and the return of Christ also are common among Evangelicals. Additionally, these churches emphasize the importance of having a "born-again" conversion experience. Not all churches in this category share all of these beliefs or emphasize them equally. For analytical purposes, sociologists divide the broad category of Evangelical Christians into three subgroups: Fundamentalists, Pentecostals, and Evangelicals. It is important to understand that while these groups share a common theological approach in that they hold literal views of the Bible, they vary in what this view implies for their religious practices or experiences.

Christian fundamentalism, for example, emerged as a counterforce to secularizing trends, including modernity, science, and academic scholarship. It was founded by Dwight L. Moody in the 19th century. Fundamentalist Christians establish firm boundaries between themselves and the broader culture. In some traditions, women do not cut their hair, based on St. Paul's New Testament recommendation. Others forbid members from going to the movies, wearing make-up, or listening to rock music. One example of a Christian fundamentalist church, the Apostolic Faith Church, was founded in Portland, Oregon, in 1907 by Reverend Florence L. Crawford to restore the doctrines and style of life taught by Christ and early church apostles. Christian fundamentalist churches teach the doctrines of biblical inerrancy and stress justification by faith, entire sanctification, and the baptism of the Holy Spirit as on the Day of Pentecost. Membership requires being born again and believing in the doctrines of the group. Dancing, movies, smoking, drinking, using cosmetics, gambling, and participating in other forms of popular entertainment often are banned, as is marriage to people who are not members of these churches. Christian fundamentalism is one type of relationship between religion and broader culture, a relationship we will explore in more depth in Chapter 6.

Pentecostal groups emerged in the early 20th century out of the larger Holiness movement in American Christianity. *Pentecostal* refers to the first Pentecost, the 50 days after Christ's resurrection, when the Holy Spirit was said to have come upon the early Christians, allowing them to speak unfamiliar languages. Pentecostalism's founders preached that the Gifts of the Spirits (e.g., speaking in tongues, healing the sick, and prophecy) were available to modern Christians. Exhibiting these gifts experientially is evidence of being "filled with the Spirit," an important aspect, even a requirement, of salvation and inclusion in the church community. Most Pentecostal denominations are theologically and socially conservative. They emphasize belief in the Trinity (with special emphasis on the role of the Holy Spirit), the literal and infallible interpretation of the Bible, belief in Jesus Christ as a necessary condition for salvation, the personal return of Jesus to earth, and the responsibility of believers to spread the teachings of Christ around the world. Two sacraments are commonly practiced: adult baptism (by full immersion in water) and the Lord's Supper (communion). In some Pentecostal Churches, faith healing (in which prayers and other rituals are believed to heal illnesses) is also practiced and is considered a sacrament. The Church of God in Cleveland, Tennessee, founded in 1886, is one of America's oldest Pentecostal churches. Many Pentecostal congregations separate themselves from the broader culture, though that is changing.

As a group, Evangelicals increasingly engage the outside culture in everything from their use of media to their musical styles to their dress. They include Southern Baptists and the Christian Church, also called Churches of God. The name Southern Baptist reflects the divide among Baptists that resulted from slavery and the Civil War. Although they are Biblical literalists, Southern Baptists have historically believed in the autonomy of the individual believer when it comes to reading and interpreting the Bible. Sermons are central features of their services, as is time for individuals to repent for their sins, "receive Jesus," or rededicate themselves to God. While some Southern Baptists use traditional hymns, others are increasingly adopting contemporary musical styles performed by "praise bands," groups of musicians that include drums, guitars, keyboards, and percussion. A relatively new Evangelical denomination, the Vineyard Churches International, grew out of the Vineyard movement in California in the 1970s. It adopted charismatic traditions in the 1980s, organized as a body in 1983, and is now headquartered in Texas. Like the Southern Baptists and other evangelicals, Vineyard Churches embrace evangelical and charismatic or Pentecostal theology, including belief in the infallibility of the Bible, human sin, salvation, and the open expressions of spiritual gifts such as speaking in tongues and divine healing. In contrast with old-school evangelicals, however, they make effective use of Christian rock music and informal worship styles.

Other Christian Denominations

Though they are clearly branches of Christianity, many denominations do not fit neatly into these broad categories. Consider Christian Scientists, Jehovah's Witnesses, the Latter-Day Saints (Mormons), Unitarian Universalists, and Pietist denominations such as the Society of Friends (Quakers). You may wonder: "What do any of these groups have in common with each other?" The answer is, "Not much, except that they are all Christians!" These denominations do not share any of the core characteristics associated with Evangelical churches and, unlike other Protestants, they do not belong to the National Council of Churches. Some Christians would not even consider it appropriate to label groups like Jehovah's Witnesses or Latter-Day Saints as Christians at all, making categorizing them more difficult. Nevertheless, let's take a look at some of these groups.

Mary Baker Eddy founded the Christian Science Church in 1879 with the goal of recovering the primitive Christianity of the early church and its lost practice of healing. Members seek spiritual truth through participation in Christian healing and by reading church publications and Eddy's own writings. Christian Science relies on both belief in healing and the experience of it.

Founded in the 1870s, Jehovah's Witnesses believe in one almighty God, Jehovah, and believe that Jesus Christ was the first of God's creations. They believe that Christ's sacrificial death opened the chance for humans to have eternal life and that following the destruction of wickedness, Christ and the righteous will rule the earth in a global paradise. During the 1930s and 1940s, Jehovah's Witnesses fought many court battles over freedoms of speech, press, assembly, and worship. There are now almost 6 million Jehovah's Witnesses worldwide. For many in the U.S, Jehovah's Witnesses are known for their door-to-door canvassing to distribute religious literature and attempt to gain converts to the faith.

Joseph Smith organized the Church of Jesus Christ of Latter-Day Saints, also known as the Mormon Church, in 1830. Members believe that Smith was divinely directed to restore the gospel to the earth. They recognize both the Bible and the Book of Mormon as scripture. Although Mormons resemble some conservative Protestant denominations, they differ by holding the key beliefs that both God the Father and Jesus have bodies of flesh and bone; that people will be punished for their own sins and not for original sin; and that all humans, dead or alive, can be saved. Mormons practice baptism by immersion, lay hands on people to help them receive the Holy Ghost, and participate in the Lord's Supper. They believe in the gift of speaking in tongues and in visions, prophecy, and healing. Although there are other types of Mormons that have broken away over the years, the Latter-Day Saints headquarters in Salt Lake City represents the majority of Mormons worldwide.

Pietist denominations have their roots in a 17th-century German revival movement to continue Martin Luther's reformation. They focus on the moral and spiritual life of believers. Pietism's lead theologian, Jakob Philip Spencer, encouraged pastors to build a "religion of the heart" by having small groups of Christians meet for study, prayer, and mutual encouragement. Pietism influenced the development of the early Methodist movement in England and spurred the First Great Awakening in 1740s America. Three main branches of Pietism continue today in the Brethren, Friends, and Mennonite Churches.

Brethren view the church as a community of brothers and sisters who come together to build their own inner spiritual life, to pray, and to study Scripture. They rely on the Holy Spirit to work inside each believer to bind that person to the community. They strive to live simple lives and initially tried to put even the most minute details of early Christian life into practice, including dressing in very plain clothes and refusing to take oaths or engage in lawsuits. The Society of Friends, founded in England by George Fox in the 1650s, affirms that every person possesses an Inner Light of spiritual endowment placed there by God. As a result, they reject the authority of clergy, liturgy, and sacraments; they are exceptionally service-minded; and they are outspoken in support of universal equality. Though they value the Bible, they believe that truth is unfolding and continuing. Founded in Central Europe in the 1520s, Mennonites were radical Protestants who rejected both Luther's and Calvin's reformation movements in favor of modeling their lives on Christ's Sermon on the Mount. They emphasize spiritual community and separation from secular society. You may know Mennonites, as well as Friends and Brethren, for their role in anti-war protests and their refusal to join the armed forces.

In 1961, Unitarian and Universalist churches in the United States and Canada merged to create Unitarian Universalism. This group believes in one God but is distinguished from almost all other Christian traditions by not believing that Jesus was divine or that he was the unique son of God in human form. The group values flexibility, freedom of conscience, and local autonomy. They believe that all people will be saved regardless of whether they believe in God.

As you can see, Christians hold very diverse beliefs and practices and experience their faith in unique ways. Our overview only begins to tell the story. Like all religions, Christianity reflects the broader culture, so it looks very different in Africa than it does in South Asia or Central America, and it demonstrates differences that go beyond language (Jacobson 2011). In many places, Christianity has evolved to include older local beliefs and rituals in ways that would be unrecognizable to Christians from other parts of the world. For example, as described by Philip Jenkins in *The Next Christendom*, many new Christian groups in Africa have retained traditional African religious practices such as animal sacrifice and ancestor worship. The incorporation of traditional practices is not limited to African Christianity. Jenkins (2002, 121) also quotes Taiwanese Catholic Bishop Chen Shih-Kwang: "We do mass, then we venerate the ancestors." This isn't what most North American Christians would think of as "typical" Christianity! As we will see later, understanding how new religious beliefs, practices, and experiences are shaped is key to understanding the role of religion in the contemporary world. But are these same forces shaping other religions around the world? You bet! Let's turn our attention to the other largest religious groups in our world.

Islam

Islam is the world's second-largest religion whose numbers continue to increase. Prior to the events of September 11, 2001, and the ongoing conflicts in the Middle East—especially in Iraq and Iran—most non-Muslims in North American and Europe knew little about Islam. There are five key beliefs and five pillars of ritual behavior in Islam. Muslims believe that there is one God; that there are angels; that there have been many prophets in addition to Mohammed but only one message; that there will be a final judgment; and, finally, that it is possible to know God and God's will in this life (Olson et al. 2018). Required rituals include the *Shahada*, stating that there is no God but Allah and that Mohammed is his prophet; *Salat*, praying five times a day while facing Mecca; *Zakat*, giving alms; *Siyam*, observing the one-month Feast of Ramadan, which includes daily fasting; and *Hajj*, making a pilgrimage to Mecca at least once in one's lifetime. The Qu'ran is the Muslim scripture and, like the Christian Bible, contains the direct revelation of God (Allah), providing Muslims with moral direction for their beliefs and daily life. In addition, religious laws and observances, codified in *Sharia*, shape daily life. *Imams*, who are heads of local mosques, interpret *Sharia* law and the teachings of the Qu'ran to the faithful.

As in the case of other religions, the form of Islam dictates specific beliefs and practices. There are four major forms: Shi'ism, Sunnism, Sufism, and the Nation of Islam.

The divide between Shi'a and Sunni Muslims goes back to the death of the Prophet Mohammed. One group of his followers (Sunni Muslims) believed that Mohammed wanted a close friend and companion, Abu Bakar, to be his successor because the Prophet appointed him to lead prayers at his bedside just before he died. Another group (Shi'a Muslims) thought that the Prophet wanted his son-in-law Ali to be his successor because on his way back from Hajj, he took Ali's hand and told those around him that if they wished to follow the Prophet, they should also follow Ali. Over the centuries, these two branches of Islam have sometimes conflicted.

Sufism, which is more experiential, is less a separate branch of Islam than a theological and worship tradition within Islam. Sufism teaches that God is everywhere and in everything. Sufism generally puts less emphasis on living according to strict laws and more on the subjective feeling of God's love. Sufis aim to experience divine joy all the time and use dancing as a means to help induce religious experience in worship.

The Nation of Islam is a uniquely North American expression of Muslim religion, rooted in African American communities, that was founded by Marcus Garvey and other leaders of the African Pride Movement in the early 20th century. For African Americans, the Nation of Islam provides a religious tradition that is closer to their African roots and less laden with the ideological baggage that ties Christianity to the history of slavery and segregation. While some within the Nation of Islam, including Louis Farrakan's followers, believe in Black nationalism, Warith Deen Mohammed took over the organization in 1975 and has brought it closer to traditional Islamic belief and practice. American domestic and foreign policies since 9/11 have made it vital that we understand Muslim beliefs and practices. More than ever before, the United States is now directly engaged with a variety of Islamic nations and groups. Some have developed intense hatred of the United States and its military. Others try to overcome stereotypes that equate all Muslim believers with suicide bombers in Iraq and Afghanistan. Once again, we see how religious beliefs can differ radically across traditions and groups, even within the same religion.

Hinduism

Hindu belief and practice originated in India around 1500 B.C.E. There is no single hierarchy or leader to define legitimate or appropriate beliefs and rituals. As a result, Hinduism adapts to local contexts and is a diverse faith tradition that closely reflects the region and traditions of the communities that practice it. Although Christians often assume that Hindus worship many gods and goddesses, they are actually all forms of one God, called Brahman, the original spirit and creative force of the universe. God is reflected in as many as 33 million forms and incarnations, each of which is best understood as reflecting a particular attribute of God (Kurtz 1995, 30). Behind them all is a divine unity.

Hindus see the One reflected in a trinity of Gods: Brahma, the creator of the universe; Vishnu, its maintainer; and Shiva, the destroyer who brings new life. Most Hindus worship Vishnu or Shiva, though in recent years other deities like Devi, the Mother Goddess, who is sometimes linked with Parvati, the wife of Shiva, have become popular. The worship of Krishna, either as a personification of Vishnu or as the supreme being in his own right, is also widespread among Hindus worldwide. Each manifestation of God has highly specialized functions and powers. Faithful Hindus venerate the gods and goddesses who can meet their present needs. So for example, Ganesha, an elephant-headed god, helps believers to overcome obstacles and aids people in times of trouble. Lakshmi, the consort of Vishnu, brings wealth and purity.

Hindu sacred texts include the Vedas, but their role is different from that of the Bible for Christians or the Qur'an for Muslims. Although the Vedas provide a guide for worship and rituals and include both hymns to sing and the philosophical teaching of Hinduism, most ordinary Hindus do not follow the Vedas in their worship. Instead, the narrative poem *Bhagavad Gita* is increasingly viewed as scripture by contemporary Hindus. The *Bhagavad Gita* teaches that there are three means to salvation for all: pursuing knowledge, doing work appropriate to your caste, and showing devotion to God (BBC 2014b).

Dharma is a core Hindu belief that captures the idea of duty and moral righteousness in behavior. It covers "the pursuit of all legitimate worldly ends," whether they are financial, political, social, or even sexual (Madan 2006, 18). Dharma is the goal of moral living. For Hindus, responsibilities in life depend on who one is, most importantly the social caste or varna into which one is born. The *Bhagavad Gita* reduces karma to each caste's assigned duties. Brahmans have a duty to study and teach, Kshatriyas to rule and protect, and Vaishyas to pursue trades, earn and lend money, and engage in farming and agriculture. The lowest varna, Shudras, have a duty to serve the other castes. Duties are strictly divided: Appropriate or required actions for one caste are forbidden to others, and those who deviate from their duties are believed to suffer.

Karma are the actions that one takes to achieve dharma. Karma includes the idea that all of our actions have consequences for our future reincarnations in the cycles of birth, death, and rebirth (samsara). That cycle eventually ends when one's soul is freed from this cycle (moksha) to join with the spirit of the universe. Right actions result in rewards and wrong actions in punishments, if not in this life then in the next.

Hinduism is less a collective practice than an individual one and is based more in domestic than public life. Madan (2006) notes that the head of the family conveys Hindu religious values through life cycle rituals, ritual feeding of ancestors, domestic worship of related gods and goddesses, and pilgrimages. Hindu individuals chant the names of their favorite gods and goddesses; offer them food, incense, and flowers; and perform other acts of devotion, such as pilgrimages to a deity's shrine.

Buddhism

Buddhism originated after the sixth century B.C.E. It emerged from followers of Siddhartha Gautama, the Buddha or Enlightened One, and his teachings. After many years of living a life of wealth and privilege, protected from pain and suffering, Siddhartha set out to discover the realities of material existence. He began by rejecting his past life of wealth to follow a monastic path of self-denial. Eventually, he also rejected this lifestyle and adopted the Middle Path, living a life of neither wealth nor poverty. He devoted himself to meditation and one day achieved a state of enlightenment while sitting under the Bodhi tree (i.e., the "tree of awakening"). Over time, two main traditions arose within Buddhism: Theravada and Mahayana. Other forms emerged as Buddhism spread to different Asian countries including Tibet, China, Japan, and Korea.

Theravada Buddhism is an elite form of Buddhism that is linked to the specialized life and religious devotions of monks who live together in communities called *sanghas*. In this tradition, there is no worship of a deity. Spiritual beings exist, but they are of limited significance. What matters most is meditation on the Buddha's teaching and making one's own way toward enlightenment without the help of gods or goddesses. Like other forms of Buddhism, Theravada Buddhism emphasizes the illusory character of the material world. Detachment through meditation is required to achieve enlightenment. So strong is the mandate to be detached from the material world that monks may not even touch money. They rely entirely on outside support and patronage for their food, drink, clothing, and for the upkeep of their monasteries.

Mahayana Buddhism embodies a more complex understanding of the relationship between the spiritual and material worlds. As it spread, Mahayana Buddhism was more open to local traditions and customs, and it has developed into more of a lay-oriented tradition than a monastic one. Anyone, not just monks, can achieve enlightenment and liberation from suffering (BBC 2014a). Worship of local gods and goddesses characterizes this tradition, and ritual practices include burning incense, offering food and flowers, and chanting.

Both branches of Buddhism embrace four Noble Truths and an eightfold path to enlightenment. These tenets make up the Dharma, or teaching, that all Buddhists must follow. Ideas that are central to the four Truths include the beliefs that life is suffering (Dukkha), that desire or craving is the source of all suffering (Trsna), that detachment from desire is possible (Nirvana), and that the Eightfold Path is the way to achieve enlightenment. The Eightfold Path requires those seeking enlightenment to live with Right Knowledge, Right Aspirations, Right Speech, Right Behavior, Right Livelihood, Right Effort, Right Mindfulness, and Right Absorption. Adherents will escape the endless cycle of birth, death, and rebirth if they faithfully try to live according to these principles. Like Hindus, Buddhists believe that all of our actions have consequences (karma) that shape, positively or negatively, the conditions we will experience in our future lives.

Buddhist ritual is as varied as the locales to which it has spread. Venerating the Buddha, not as God but as the example of one who has achieved enlightenment, is central to worship practices. Buddhists can worship at home, as it is not essential to go to a temple to worship with others. At home, Buddhists often set aside a room or a part of a room as a shrine that includes a statue of Buddha, candles, and an incense burner. Worship in Mahayana tradition takes the form of devotion to Buddha and to Bodhisattvas, enlightened beings who have delayed entering paradise so that they may help others attain enlightenment. It is common in this tradition to see worshippers seated on the floor facing an image of Buddha and chanting. As in the case of all religions, there are also special festivals during which members practice unique forms of worship and devotion. One such Buddhist festival is Wesak, celebrated on the full moon in May. It celebrates the Buddha's birthday and, for some Buddhists, marks both his birth and death. As a part of this festival, statues of the Buddha are ceremonially washed as a symbolic reminder for worshippers to purify their minds from greed, hatred, and ignorance (BBC 2014a).

Judaism

Although Jews represent less than one percent of the world's religious adherents, Judaism is among the world's oldest religions. Judaism gave birth to Christianity, but it takes a very different approach in its beliefs and practices. Apart from a belief in the oneness of God, there is no unifying creed among Jews. Instead, Judaism emphasizes the observance of rituals and ethical practices.

Contemporary Judaism is based on the Torah, but generally does not follow all the ritual practices, including animal sacrifice, that it mandates. Over time, as it became more difficult to observe the Torah's commandments for daily living, Jews placed more emphasis on the unfolding interpretations of these commandments, taking into account how the times and circumstances had changed from the situations that early Jews faced. Around 600 C.E., the Talmud was codified, providing a basis for how to interpret the Torah. The Talmud includes a list of 613 commandments that Jews must follow in daily life and a process for making sense of faithful religious practice in a constantly changing contemporary world.

There are two general types of Jewish rituals: seasonal liturgies that follow a lunar calendar and individual liturgies that correspond to key moments in the lives of individuals. The Jewish liturgical year begins in September with the High Holy Days of *Rosh Hashanah* and *Yom Kippur*. *Rosh Hashanah*, the Jewish New Year, is celebrated with great joy. For the 10 days that follow it, however, Jews reflect on their lives, repent of their sins and shortcomings, and try to make restitution for wrongs that they have done in preparation for *Yom Kippur*, the Day of Atonement. Other feasts follow, commemorating key moments in Jewish history. *Succoth* reminds Jews of the 40 years that the Israelites wandered in the desert following their release from slavery in Egypt. *Hanukkah* celebrates the restoration and purification of the Temple in Jerusalem during the revolt of the Jews against the Greeks. *Passover* recalls the period of slavery itself and the manner by which God freed the Jews from Egyptian bondage. *Shabuoth* commemorates the occasion when Moses received the Torah. Rituals related to the lives of individuals and families are observed weekly in Sabbath observances and more occasionally in rites of passage, such as the circumcision of male babies on the eighth day after birth and Bar Mitzvah and Bat Mitzvah ceremonies to initiate young men and women into adulthood.

The beliefs, rituals, and experiences of Jews vary depending on the branch of Judaism. Hasidic and Orthodox Jews are the most conservative: Both groups take a literal reading of the Torah and Talmud, believing that their teachings are absolute and not open to reinterpretation. Conservative Judaism follows the rules of the Torah and Talmud but allows for reinterpretation of ancient Jewish teaching in light of contemporary experience. Reform Judaism holds that the rules in the Torah related to social justice and peace are more important than the observance of rituals and dietary laws. Reconstructionist Judaism is the newest branch of Judaism. Reconstructionists hold to the importance of Jewish heritage while seeking new ways to experience the sacred in the modern world. Like the denominational differences within Christianity, different organizational branches of Judaism follow different beliefs about what is authentic or true.

We have just taken an abbreviated tour of the world's religions. We have neglected important traditions, including Baha'i, traditional Chinese religions rooted in Confucianism, Shintoism, Sihkism, Jainism, Contemporary Paganism, Wicca, and thousands of indigenous religious traditions including those of Native Americans, African tribes, and many others. Nonetheless, an important lesson emerges: Religious beliefs are reflected in practices and experiences; all three often motivate our actions both within and outside our faith communities.

Understanding Contemporary Religious Ritual Practices

Religious beliefs are never the whole story of any faith tradition. For most of the world's religious people, religion is less a matter of what you *believe* intellectually and more what you *do*—your everyday behaviors and ritual practices—and also what you *experience*—the subjective feelings, emotions, and states of being that result from these behaviors. So for example, if we try to determine what makes a "good" or "faithful" Jew, we would observe that a person's commitment is understood through his or her faithful participation in Sabbath services, celebration of Seder meals during Passover, observation of other holy days like Rosh Hashanah and Yom Kippur, hospitable and charitable behavior toward neighbors, and study of the Torah. What a Jew *believes* about the theology underlying any or all of these ritual acts is secondary to doing them.

As we have observed again and again, religious beliefs are tied to and embodied in what believers actually *do*, the rituals that they perform as part of their devotion. We have already discussed some rituals and observances across the world's religions. Rituals have fascinated sociologists because they are the visible manifestations of a religious tradition. It is not always possible to clearly observe changes in beliefs. However, since rituals always involve individual or collective action, we can observe how they evolve and adapt to new circumstances or contexts. Rituals also shape how people feel. They have a subjective component whereby individuals feel in contact with the sacred and with others in their community. Sharing experiences builds social bonds even more than sharing intellectual beliefs. By analyzing what people do and how they do it, we come to see how religious rituals strengthen and reaffirm group beliefs and unite the group that participates in them. Even when rituals are performed by an individual or family in the privacy of their own home, as happened for many religious people during the COVID pandemic in 2020, the rituals tie the believer to the Sacred and by extension to all those others who share in the same beliefs. We can also observe how the changing needs of members can alter where and how (in content or styles) religious rituals are performed.

Rituals vary by tradition. Ritual processions, sacraments, lighting candles, burning incense, praying in specific ways, and eating certain kinds of food in particular ways are common elements in many religious traditions. Sometimes rituals focus more on *how* things are done than on *what* is done. Spontaneous expressions can be a ritual act, as can shouting or dancing. Raising one's hands to the sky is a ritual act. Even prayers can be ritually formulaic. Growing up in an evangelical church, one of the authors (Mirola) learned to disparage the idea of reciting pre-written prayers out of a book as many congregations do. Church members were taught to pray spontaneously, using whatever words they wished, so he would pray: "Lord, I just want to thank you . . . I just praise you . . . I just want to ask . . ." Notice anything? The words "I just . . ." are commonly used. It may sound funny, but listen closely to prayers offered in many of today's nondenominational and evangelical churches where prayer is unscripted, be they large megachurches or small congregations of born-again Christians. You will hear this prayer structure or something similar to it coming from those who are most committed to spontaneity. Looking back, it is clear how ritualized such prayers were, no matter what the motivation was behind them. In examining the variety of religious rituals, it is imperative to look past the grand ceremonies that take place in congregations to see all the small and new forms that ritual behavior might take. Furthermore, we must keep in mind that it is never the content of an action that makes a ritual religious; rather, it is the meaning that people attach to doing something in a particular way and what they experience in a spiritual sense as a result.

Worship Styles to Meet Every Need

Religious groups around the world take diverse approaches to worship. As we have discussed, Roman Catholic and Orthodox Christians have maintained their commitment to historic liturgies that emphasize formal rituals and sacred mysteries. Many Protestant Christians embrace relative simplicity in worship and focus on preaching rather than on formal rituals like Holy Communion. One might recognize an Establishment Protestant congregation in North America by its staid formality and intellectualism and an evangelical one by its unabashed emotional joy and congregational participation. Even in Jewish traditions, different forms of worship characterize Hasidic, Orthodox, Conservative, Reform, and Reconstructionist congregations. Orthodox Jews use only Hebrew in rituals, while Reform Jews use both English and Hebrew. Also, Orthodox men worship separately from women and children, separated by a screen. Among Reform Jews and Reconstructionists, men, women, and children all sit together. Over time, the defining features of worship are transformed in response to changing culture in some groups, while other groups maintain older forms of ritual practices.

To transform or maintain tradition can be a source of intense conflict for some religious groups. In some cases, primarily in industrial countries, religious groups have entered into what we might euphemistically call *worship wars* (or in Roman Catholic contexts, "liturgy wars"). These disputes over the forms and content of rituals and religious services typically pit traditionalists against modernists. Traditionalists prefer the music, styles, and structure of their historic religious traditions, whereas modernists argue that worship styles ought to keep up with the times and follow trends and styles in the larger society. When you think about it, there have always been disagreements over worship styles. During the English Reformation in the mid-1500s, many Christians wanted to hold on to Christian traditions that were common at this time, such as elaborate processions and rituals, beautiful images of saints, the use of candles, and the use of Latin as the main language for services. Extreme Protestant reformers didn't want anything to do with such theatrical nonsense. They wanted services to be simple and to be based only on elements found in the Bible, which was now printed in English. They destroyed images, melted candles, and ripped up the ritual robes. In between these extremes were people who wanted to keep some traditions but also were happy to embrace some change. Needless to say, those worship wars resulted in people on all sides being imprisoned or burned at the stake. But note that the fights weren't really over the big belief questions, like those dealing with God or salvation. People fought over keeping or getting rid of candles. Now all this may seem silly to you. But the forms that worship takes dictate the ways that people encounter or experience the sacred. To suggest changing these forms is to challenge the sacred itself.

As we'll see in the next chapter, change in worship styles continues to occur, but so do the worship wars. Let's look at some ways in which contemporary groups have tried to redefine what authentic and relevant worship looks like.

Christian churches are maintaining and even rediscovering traditions in a wide variety of ways. Among Roman Catholic young people, it is not uncommon to see devout women wearing lace veils as head-coverings during Mass or individuals lying face-down on the ground in front of the consecrated Host (the wafer blessed during communion) during a ritual known as Eucharistic Adoration. These are traditions more common in the past that now have been readopted as expressions of authentic Catholic devotion among younger people. Many Establishment Protestant congregations have revived historic rituals and liturgies. In doing so, these churches look and sound increasingly similar to one another, whether they are Presbyterians, Methodists, or Lutherans. For instance, these denominations have adopted a common *lectionary*, or set of Biblical readings used during services. Believers practice the ritual of Holy Communion or Eucharist during Sunday morning services more frequently than in the past. And, most interesting of all, these churches have added other ritual activities throughout the church year that once were used only in Roman Catholic or Orthodox religious practices. The return of rituals such as saying prayers at the Stations of the Cross and consciously observing Ash Wednesday, Lent (the 40 days of abstinence before Easter), and Advent (the four weeks before Christmas) point to a renewed interest in historic Christian ritual and liturgy among many Establishment congregations.

Monastic traditions also are being rediscovered. During the 1990s, religious chant became popular. The Benedictine monks of Santo Domingo de Silos reached the top of the pop music charts with their CD *Chant*, and a nonreligious music group, Enigma, used chant and synthesized music to create a popular sound that was heard in dance clubs from New York to L.A. Musical ensembles specializing in medieval church music, like Chanticleer, Harry Christophers and the Sixteen, and Anonymous 4 remain popular recording artists among Establishment Protestant and Roman Catholic audiences alike.

Taizé services drawn from a French monastic community remain popular after two decades as well. Taizé is an ecumenical community of around a hundred brothers from different Christian traditions located in a small village in eastern France. Tens of thousands of people, mainly between the ages of 17 and 30, come each year to spend time at the community, reflecting on their faith. Using prayer and music from the Taizé community, Catholic and Protestant congregations around the country have added Taizé services of singing and silent meditation to their traditional worship services.

Labyrinth walking is another medieval tradition that has garnered interest among Christians. In 1991, Dr. Lauren Artress, canon for special ministries at Grace Cathedral (Episcopal) in San Francisco, created a model of the 13th-century labyrinth in Chartres Cathedral in France. Within the Christian mystical tradition, walking the labyrinth is a form of meditation. As you walk a labyrinth, you empty your mind while you meditate and pray. Labyrinth walking empowers people to find and do the things to which they feel called or drawn. Once again, through this ritual practice, one feels connected to the sacred and can find meaning and direction for other areas of one's life.

In other churches, modern elements predominate. Contemporary worship styles have proliferated in many Christian congregations and local congregations have developed a variety of alternative services. In the next chapter, we will explore some of these in depth. Some congregations offer services at times other than Sunday mornings to better fit the flow of life and work of would-be participants. Music is a prime target for stylistic makeovers. Some congregations have moved away from traditional hymns and adopted songs with more upbeat sounds that invite worshipers to sing, clap, and even dance. Words to songs are projected on a wall or screen and many congregations have a "Praise Band," complete with drums, guitars, and keyboards to play along. Preaching has also gotten a makeover. Ministers walk around more and use a more conversational style when they talk to their congregations. Many of these trends have been around since the 1960s. What is new is their adoption for the express purpose of attracting new members, especially young ones or people who identify with particular subcultures, from heavy-metal enthusiasts to marijuana smokers.

Prominent Protestant congregations in Indianapolis, Indiana—one Establishment Protestant and one Evangelical—illustrate these trends. First-Meridian Heights Presbyterian Church appeals to neighborhood residents by emphasizing

> "a community focus that is warm and inviting to everyone. Within a relaxed atmosphere, our worship service continues to offer contemporary spiritual music combined with traditional hymns and elements of a 'classic' church service. Casual clothing is welcome. Powerful, relevant messages from the perspective of the everyday world give you the energy and guidance you need to start your week filled with joy, peace, and love."
>
> (www.fmhpc.org/worship)

They also offer "Messy Church" for busy parents who don't have time for traditional Sunday morning church or older adults and empty-nesters looking for ways to connect with their faith and the local community. Messy church, they say, is "where 'kids grow up and adults don't have to' . . . a place for all ages and life stages . . . a free event where we learn about God's love through crafts, activities, story and a shared meal" (www.fmhpc.org/messy-church).

In the mid-1990s, Trader's Point Christian Church, another non-denominational church in Indianapolis, began a separate ministry for young adults called Common Ground. This new group met in a former Baptist Church building far from the main church. The services held for Common Ground participants regularly drew more than 300 college-aged and twenty-something people with little overlap with those who attended the regular Trader's Point Sunday services. At Common Ground services, the lights were dim, the music loud, and the preaching was minimal. In this congregation, the minister was more like a storyteller than a traditional preacher. Today, Common

Ground is now its own independent church with three congregations in the city. The college students got married and had children, so now the church resembles others in having children's ministries and community outreach. On their website, they say this of themselves:

> As our name indicates, Common Ground is a church that invites people of all faith and cultural backgrounds to come together to worship our creator God and his son Jesus Christ. [Our] belief statements help to motivate our life with God (Devotion), our life with each other (Community) and our life serving others (Mission). Even if your beliefs differ from those stated here, please know that you are welcome to join us on this journey toward fullness in Christ. Many of these statements are matters of scriptural interpretation and should not be used as a "test of faith." For now we know in part, but one day, we shall know fully.

> (1 Cor. 13:12)

What is interesting about this statement is they while they maintain a set of clear beliefs, they also embrace an openness to interpretation and difference, making them a church that clearly has adapted to the religious and cultural diversity of the contemporary world.

"And then there were Nones . . ."

Just as congregations vary in their rituals, so do individuals. One of the most striking trends of the last decade has been the rise of the "religious Nones," individuals who claim no religious identity whatsoever (Pew Research Center 2014, 2017b; Pew Forum 2012). Nones are a broad category too that encompasses people who are atheists (those who do not believe in any kind of god or supreme being) and agnostics (those who say a supreme being may or may not exist but there's no way for humans to know either way) make up about 31% of the unaffiliated. People who say religion is unimportant in their life make up another 39% of the Nones. The remaining 30% of Nones are those who, while not having a distinct religious identity, may still think of themselves as religious or spiritual, attend church, pray, and sometimes participate in religious rituals. Nones don't claim a specific label or identify as a member of a particular denomination or even of a religion. Now, the idea that there are people out there who reject labels or claim no formal religious identity and create their own approach to religion is hardly new. Take, for example, the now-famous phenomenon of Sheilaism that was uncovered by Bellah et al. (1985, 221) and his colleagues in their classic study *Habits of the Heart*. Sheila Larson was a nurse whom Bellah interviewed as a part of his study of community life in America. Here are her words:

> I believe in God. I'm not a religious fanatic. I can't remember the last time I went to church. My faith has carried me a long way. It's Sheilaism. Just my own little voice. . . . It's just try to love yourself and be gentle with yourself. You know, I guess, take care of each other. I think He would want us to take care of each other.

Bellah and his colleagues noted that Sheila had summed up the totality of her religious belief and practice in a few simple sentences. Sheila's example is often used to illustrate how individualized religion had become more than three decades ago, to the point that each believer practices private rituals that make sense to him or her, with no need for a religious community.

In more recent studies of American youth, Sheilaism has given way to what has been more complexly described as "monotheistic therapeutic deism" (Smith and Denton 2005). In their exploration of religion in the lives of teenagers, Smith and Denton found that teens professed a very conventional belief in God who watches things and "wants people to be good, nice, and fair to each other but who does not need to be involved in one's life except to resolve a problem" (Pearce and Denton 2011, 6). Like Sheila, what these sociologists have found was that young people in the United States claim religious faith and state they do hold specific religious beliefs, but their faith and beliefs do not, in their own estimation, directly shape their lives and actions.

The tremendous growth of religious Nones takes this trend further still. Sheila was one individual. Nones have been a steadily growing portion of the population, increasing from 36 million Americans in 2007 to 56 million by 2014 (Pew Research Center 2014, 16)! To put this in perspective, religious Nones are second only to Evangelical Protestants in terms of their proportion of the U.S. population. Many believers would likely express concern over the trend among young people to take such an informal approach to their faith. Others would not see Sheilaism or the religious Nones as a legitimate expression of religion identity, regardless of the religion involved. Yet all of these developments point to social forces that give rise to new ways for individuals to experience religion.

Are the religious trends embodied in worship wars, Sheilaism, monotheistic therapeutic deism, and Nones meaningful outside of contemporary North American Christianity? In recent years, some people have worried that traditional ritual is in permanent decline. Some think that formal ritual is dying not only in North America and Europe but also in the developing world as globalization moves other societies forward. But ritual is an essential part of religion, a way to express belief and build community. Its forms may change over time, but rituals changing is not the same as rituals dying. For example, many new Christian groups in the developing world practice unique mixes of indigenous religious rituals and mainstream Christian rituals, with 21st-century styles and even content. Let's look at examples from Africa and China.

> In 2000, the Roman Catholic archbishop of Bloemfontein, South Africa, not only suggested that Christians might be permitted to honor their ancestors through blood libations, but that ritual sacrifice of sheep or cows might be incorporated into the Mass. . . . Critics reacted with horror, as much because the suggestion violated animal rights as on grounds of heresy. . . . In keeping with the concept of consecration, the Congolese church uses a profession rite in which a drop of the candidate's blood is placed on the altar cloth. Such practices make great sense in African terms, and it would be easy to justify the practice with an arsenal of biblical texts.
>
> (Jenkins 2002, 131)

In China, every year on or around April 4th, Chinese families gather to celebrate the festival of Quingming, a traditional festival for families to honor and pray to their ancestors. (Look at YouTube for any number of videos covering this annual festival across Asia.) In addition to cleaning their graves, family members make offerings of their ancestors' favorite food and drink. They leave gifts of "money," which is burned so the dead can spend it in the next world. They even offer material gifts like cell phones to their ancestors. In participating in this ritual, families pray, make offerings to the dead, and express their familial piety in honoring those who came before them. In return, their ancestors are asked to help increase their wealth, keep them healthy, and protect them from danger. Like Christian prayers to saints, ancestor veneration in indigenous religions in Africa, or Hindu or Buddhist rituals to honor the dead, the ritual of grave sweeping sure sounds like a religious ritual. But if you ask most Chinese people, very few would claim to be religious in any sense! So like the religious Nones, just because you don't claim to be religious doesn't mean you can't believe or practice unique constellations of ideas and actions that clearly seem to come from religion. As you think about these examples, do you see them as backward-looking, superstitious religious practices? Or do you see them as innovative ways for contemporary religious believers to be in touch with the sacred in ways that link their pasts to the present and, sometimes, to the future?

And what about ritual innovation in non-Christian contexts? Most of the world's religious people practice rituals that have been handed down for centuries or even millennia. Even these religions, however, have adapted their rituals to the new contexts in which they found themselves.

For example, when Buddhism reached Japan, a 13th-century monk named Nichiren Daishonin sought to reform Buddhist practice by focusing on the Lotus Sutra as the supreme, authoritative Scripture. Nichiren encouraged followers to read this Sutra daily, but he emphasized that they should interpret it in light of the present-day situation. He believed that classical Buddhist teaching no longer led to enlightenment, but was responsible for all that was wrong in the world. While Nichiren Buddhists chant and study like other Buddhists, they also keep a small scroll, or Gohonzon, a replica of the original scroll of Nichiren, on a home altar that they face during their daily chanting.

Hinduism too has adapted its forms of worship and devotion to the local regions where it spread and now is adapting itself to the experiences of younger generations. Among Hindu immigrants to the United States, young people go to temples and participate in collective rituals much less often than their parents or grandparents. They report that they don't understand the complex rituals of the temples, usually conducted in Sanskrit, and increasingly they also feel that these rituals "superstitious" from their more secular worldview (Min 2010, 155–156). While this isn't to say these young people never participate in temple rituals, they often report doing so as a way to stay connected to their cultural heritage as Hindus and also to express a more generalized spirituality.

As religious beliefs and ritual practices move across the world and encounter different cultural contexts and the constraints of living in new times and places, we can expect them to evolve just as they have done since the first humans expressed their reliance on the natural world through religious rituals for hunting, planting, childbirth, death, and sickness.

The Role of Beliefs and Ritual Practices

Part of our job as sociologists is to describe the broad roles that religious beliefs, practices, and experiences play in shaping the dynamics of the groups that claim them and the dynamics of the communities and societies in which they are embedded. The concept of group is key; as students of religion, you can't fully understand the diversity of religious beliefs, practices, and experiences through the study of individuals alone. As Durkheim argued a century ago, religion is a social product created by the group that has consequences for the world, good as well as bad. Religion is an important means for maintaining social stability in societies around the world, but it can also be the basis for conflict and change. Because beliefs and practices are dynamic, we can't predict how they will continue to be transformed in the face of the forces of globalization, another discussion that we will return to later in the book.

Remember too that the meaning of beliefs and ritual practices is flexible and can be fought over by different groups of believers. What makes sense to one group is dismissed as superstition by another. As we will see in the next chapter, authentic beliefs and ritual practices are changing all the time. We need to expect these changes and be ready to investigate the effects of change on religious groups themselves and their communities. There's always something new to discover.

Suggested Reading

Jacobsen, Douglas. 2011. *The World's Christians: Who They Are, Where They Are, and How They Got There.* Malden, MA: Wiley-Blackwell.

Jenkins, Philip. 2002. *The Next Christendom: The Coming of Global Christianity.* New York: Oxford University Press.

Jenkins, Philip. 2006. *The New Faces of Christianity: Believing the Bible in the Global South.* New York: Oxford University Press.

Juergensmeyer, Mark (ed.). 2006. *The Oxford Handbook of Global Religions.* New York: Oxford University Press.

Olson, Roger E., Frank S. Mead, Samuel S. Hill, and Craig D. Atwood. 2018. *Handbook of Denominations in the United States*, 14th Edition. Nashville, TN: Abingdon Press.

Pearce, Lisa D., and Melinda Lundquist Denton. 2011. *A Faith of Their Own: Stability and Change in the Religiosity of America's Adolescents*. New York: Oxford University Press.

Pew Forum on Religion and Public Life. 2012. *Nones on the Rise: One-in-Five Adults Have No Religious Affiliation*. Washington, DC: Pew Research Center.

Pew Research Center. 2014. *America's Changing Religious Landscape: Findings from the 2014 U.S. Religious Landscape Survey*. Washington, DC: Pew Research Center.

Roof, Wade Clark Roof. 1999. *Spiritual Marketplace: Baby Boomers and the Remaking of American Religion*. Princeton, NJ: Princeton University Press.

Smith, Christian, and Melinda Lundquist Denton. 2005. *Soul-Searching: The Religious and Spiritual Lives of American Teenagers*. New York: Oxford University Press.

3 Downloading God, "Big-Box" Churches, and the Crystal Shop around the Corner

Religious Adaptation in the Digital Age

1 How have the Internet, social media, and other forms of digital communication shaped religious beliefs, practices, and organizations (and vice-versa) in the COVID and post-COVID world?
2 Is it possible to build an authentic virtual spiritual community that serves all the social functions of religion?
3 How do megachurches balance their size and scale while simultaneously building intimacy and community among their members?
4 Are Christian bookstores, New Age shops, organic food stores, and wellness centers only places of business, or are they new forms and contexts for religious identities and communities?

In November 2020, eight months into the COVID pandemic, the *New York Times* included a full-page expose on the impact of the pandemic and social distancing mandates on religious communities in New York City. The City's Roman Catholics, Jews, Hindus, Muslims, and Black Protestants all had a parish, synagogue, temple, mosque, or church featured in the article.

The article is clear that the City's religious communities adapted to the demands of social distancing and other public health safety measures in place to curb further spread of the virus. At the Ganesh Temple, only 30 Hindu worshippers were allowed entrance at a time, and these were limited to 15 minutes each. According to the report, although Hindu priests carried on performing ceremonies that were livestreamed, they did so in surgical masks and face guards in addition to their White robes. At the Jewish Center, an Orthodox synagogue, only 60 people, compared to the usual 500, were allowed in, and they had to register in advance online, complete a virus exposure survey, and have their temperatures taken when they entered. The Christian Cultural Center, a Black Protestant congregation, streamed its services on YouTube and Facebook and held daily prayer conference calls which attracted over 1300 members each day. And this represents only a tiny cross section of religious groups in one American city. The global pandemic, perhaps like nothing else in recent memory, highlights the adaptability of religious groups and people when facing extreme circumstances. But this adaptability also raises important sociological questions about how religious community, identity, and authority work when beliefs, practices, and experiences are taken out of the context of face-to-face communities and shifted to Zoom or are left to individuals to sort out on their own. And for religious leaders of many traditions, fear remains significant that the longer people are removed from their face-to-face worship communities, the less likely they will return once health and safety permit it. Once religion adapts social pressures for change, even temporary ones, can it ever return to how it functioned before?

The digital age of the 21st century has initiated fundamental changes to the world in which we live. Like the printing press, the telephone, and television before them, and before the pandemic, computers, cell phones, the Internet, iPods, and social media have all transformed the ways in

DOI: 10.4324/9781003182108-4

which we communicate, meet prospective love interests, read books and newspapers, and yes, even experience the sacred. A person of faith from almost any faith tradition, past or present, can search the Internet and find not only websites that house extensive information on beliefs and practices, but also entire sites for experiencing religious rituals and community with the click of a mouse. Social media outlets like Facebook have groups and forums dedicated to those interested in specific religious traditions (Brubaker and Haigh 2017). More advanced sites allow a worshipper to actually participate in a ritual via webcams and interactive technology. New religions also appear regularly online, attracting seekers and the curious public to explore and experience the sacred in new ways, from the sublime and traditional to the novel, odd, and even dangerous.

Religion in our world is changing in other ways as well. The phenomenon of suburban mega-churches across the United States put small community churches on the defensive. Megachurches offer vast auditorium seating, state-of-the-art light and sound equipment, and contemporary music, dance, and theatrical performances that seem at times more like Broadway than church. Saddleback Church, for example, founded by celebrity preacher and author Rev. Rick Warren, now with multiple campuses that span the globe, attracts over 20,000 people to its weekly services. The style of the services and the themes addressed in the preaching are contemporary. Addressing the needs and the tastes of today's churchgoers while simultaneously maintaining a classically evangelical message of faith in Jesus Christ are at the top of these churches' priority lists. They are very unlike the "little country church" on the edge of town of nostalgic memory. In many ways, these "big-box" churches represent both a break with tradition and also a conscious attempt on the part of religion to adapt to new generations of churchgoers.

New Age shops, organic food stores, Christian and non-Christian bookstores, and spas and wellness centers in big and small towns across the country provide yet another way for individuals to touch the sacred, or at least to buy things that will help them do so. Even in a Midwestern city like Indianapolis, there are more than 10 shops that cater to those interested in a wide variety of spiritual beliefs and practice. In addition to selling merchandise, they also advertise and sometimes host drumming circles, yoga classes, psychic fairs, and in-store seminars on health and wellness and eating right. In the checkout lines of stores like Whole Foods, a national grocery store chain that offers a variety of organic as well as conventional foods, one finds not *News of the World* or the *National Enquirer*, but magazines like *The Mindfulness Manual*, *Spirituality and Health*, *Yoga*, and *The Essential Guide to Happiness*, focused on Eastern religious traditions, back-to-nature lifestyles, and food and healthy living. Somehow, new forms of spirituality and even old forms of religious practice are being bought and sold along with a gallon of milk and a loaf of whole-grain bread. Of course, there are even more Christian bookstores with merchandise to match these. Some stores cater specifically to Roman Catholics, others to Evangelical Protestants, and some to Orthodox Christians. The same is true for other religious traditions. For instance, in many Indian grocery stores, one is likely to find statues of various Hindu deities along with incense and other offerings for home altars alongside traditional Indian foods. And let's not forget that Amazon.com is now a virtual purveyor of all things religious and spiritual. With your Amazon Prime account, you can order (and in some cases receive overnight) a "Mary is my Home Girl" or a "Jesus is my Home Boy" t-shirt, with a picture of either the Virgin Mary or Jesus on it, a Muslim prayer rug, a Shofar or Ram's Horn from Israel, or a Wiccan Altar supply kit.

What is fascinating to us as students of religion is how at various points in recent history all of these new expressions and contexts for religious beliefs, practices, and experiences have been both hailed as the inevitable future of all religion and condemned as threats to the traditional practice of religion. We will take a middle approach in our examination of these new contexts for religion and the sacred here. The widespread embrace of digital religion, megachurches, and alternative forms of spirituality are adaptations by religious groups and individuals to our changing world, and each has an impact on what religion looks like and how it operates. As we will explore in this chapter, the ability to download God, to get convenience and low prices at a big-box church, or even to stop by the local Christian bookstore for a new book on keeping a Christian family strong all demonstrate that religion in our world is changing into forms that are far removed from the traditional forms that we might expect to find.

These new forms also raise some complicated questions that haven't yet received clear answers, either from those within religious communities or from those of us who study them. For instance, new Zoom rituals are devoid of a "real-time" community context, thanks to the pandemic. They do not require the full participation of a believer in the same way that a church service might. Provided they have their computer video turned off, the online worshipper can multitask while worshipping. She or he might play solitaire, balance a checkbook, and, of course, take care of laundry, prepare meals, and even take phone calls without ever interrupting the ritual itself. Is this, then, the same ritual experience as the original form? Think about megachurches: What does community mean when there are 10,000 people attending a particular church service? Can big-box churches fulfill the traditional functions of religion as well as smaller congregational settings can? Whether they can or cannot, the new forms of Christianity do add to the religious vitality of communities and pressure other congregations to become more intentional about who they are and what the sacred means to them.

And what about the Christian and pagan shops, the grocery stores, and the spa treatments? Are they local means for individuals to pursue their spiritual journeys, or are they businesses pure and simple, turning spirituality into a commodity and selling it to those who can afford to buy it? Of course, we will only just begin to explore these questions in this chapter. Yet, in our examination of these new contexts for religious beliefs, practices, and experiences, we must keep in mind that religion has always adapted itself to changing conditions. Let us turn our attention first to digital religion and see how this adaptation has affected the global religious landscape.

Changing Technology, Changing Religion

Technology has had a hand in shaping Christianity since the Protestant Reformation, which was fueled by the invention of moveable type and the printing press. These developments allowed people to print Bibles, religious tracts, and other religious materials cheaply and in enough quantities that they became accessible to ordinary people. Prior to this time, of course, religious texts were painstakingly reproduced by hand and beautifully illuminated by skilled monks and nuns. Such works were accessible only to the clergy and the literate upper classes, who had both the time and the financial resources to use them.

For an ordinary person in medieval Europe, religion was visual and physical: something to be witnessed and experienced through the ceremonies of the Mass, by taking part in processions, by noticing the smell of incense that wafted through church buildings, and by participating in countless other rituals that were part of pre-Reformation Christianity. Religious leaders were the only people who had access and authority to read and interpret the Latin texts of the Bible for their congregations.

Enter the printing press: soon, religious texts that were printed in the common language of the people, instead of Latin, were widely available. Not only did access to these texts change as a result of technological innovations, but so did the form and structure of Christianity (O'Leary 1996). The most obvious shift came because nonclergy could read religious texts for themselves, since the texts were available and written in the common language. More significantly, however, was the fact that ordinary people could now *interpret* for themselves the meaning of the words of the Bible. The old forms of religious authority were undermined by this technology, and new forms of Protestant Christianity emerged that were focused not on the visual and physical aspects of rituals and beliefs, but on the printed words. Christianity was irreversibly transformed as a consequence.

It is necessary to engage in this brief look back in time in order to clarify the point that the impact of technological change on religion is not new. Furthermore, looking at the role of technology among Protestant reformers also makes it clear that technology sets in motion forces that are not always foreseen by those who use the technology to achieve religious ends. Initially, Protestant reformers probably saw the printing of religious texts as a way to replace the outdated system of church control over theology and Biblical teaching with a more appropriate system that allowed all people to have access to these texts, but the result was something akin to pandemonium. Groups battled over the true meaning of texts and split apart over different interpretations, then split again on yet other sets of issues. Much to the dismay of religious leaders, control of religion by official leaders gave way to a more democratic and individualistic approach, all thanks to technology making the texts available to everyone.

We hope that you can already begin to see the parallels between this period in history and our own time, in which technological changes whip around us daily. When television made possible the new reality of an "electronic church," Establishment Protestant Christian leaders expressed concern that religious broadcasting would reduce the numbers of people going to church and the amount of money that people gave to local congregations (Stacey and Shupe 1982, 291). Their fears were never fully realized, however, because most religious television broadcasting was dominated by evangelical pastors such as Jerry Falwell and talk show hosts like Pat Robertson, whose at-home audiences were already members of evangelical and fundamentalist congregations that were sympathetic to the messages they heard on TV. In Stacey and Shupe's (1982) early study of those who watched religious programming on TV, church attendance was highly correlated with viewing of that programming. This evidence suggests that those who watch religious television are still participating in local congregations. In short, the "electronic church" initially was a supplement to traditional church, not a replacement for it. Today, however, it is possible that those fears of religious leaders may have some foundation in reality.

Around the world today, digital religion is causing controversies, not only among Christian groups but among other world religions as well. If you Google any of the world's contemporary religions, you will be amazed not only at the number of informational sites that you will discover—what Hadden and Cowan (2000) called "religion online"—but also at the number of sites that are designed for the practitioners of these traditions, which Hadden and Cowan distinguished as "online religion." There are extensive sites that explain the religious beliefs and practices of the world's religions, discuss sacred texts, muse on the implications of religious beliefs for social and political issues, and serve as soapboxes for religious individuals and groups that seek to challenge the validity of other religions. Online religion is a way for an ever-greater number of religious groups around the world to be socially visible, and most religious groups and congregations increasingly feel pressure to maintain their own websites to communicate with their own members, to advertise services and events, and attract new members. More recently, the divides between online religion and religion online have blurred, as have the divides between online and offline religious belief, practice, and experience (Campbell 2013; Anderson and Drescher 2018).

In the last decade, a great deal of research on digital religion has documented the many ways that contemporary religious groups use digital media (see Table 3.1).

Table 3.1 Typical Religious Organizations' Purposes in Using Digital Media

1 **Proselytizing and Proclamation**
2 **Global Networking**
3 **Agenda Setting and Publishing Beliefs/Policies/Teachings**
4 **Digitalize Religious Rituals**
5 **Lifestyle Branding**

Source: (Campbell 2010; Grant et al. 2019).

However, not every religious group goes virtual in exactly the same way, and they also do not make use of all of the different social media platforms to the same extent. Some groups, for instance, use their online presence as a way to attract others to their faith. Sometimes called "e-vangelism" among Christians, social media and other digital platforms provide ways to share religious traditions and values intentionally to convert the curious or seeking into believers. The Internet provides a far more efficient way of sharing the good news with potentially thousands of people around the world than going door-to-door or standing on street corners passing out literature. Many American congregations feel that the Internet is the key way that new members can be recruited, if by no other means than providing dates and times for services and events that will bring these individuals to the congregation itself. Evangelical Christian groups use social media platforms for evangelism more than other types of Christians (Wirtz et al. 2013; Miller et al. 2013). Elsewhere in the world, especially in the Global South in parts of Africa and Southeast Asia, Facebook and YouTube are significant tools for both attracting new believers to the many new evangelical and Pentecostal churches that are springing up there as well as creating an online community among existing members through streaming services and sharing testimonials (Kgatle 2018). Traditional indigenous religious movements in these parts of the world also find these platforms useful as a means to challenge the social and religious power of Evangelical and Pentecostal Christian groups and their leaders in their communities (Kallinen 2019).

More and more, digital media is a means for religious or curious individuals around the world to actually participate in rituals, attend services, and interact with other believers virtually, both under the oversight of the religious organizations themselves as well as independently of those organizations and their leaders. As noted at the start of this chapter, the global pandemic of 2020 changed everything and forced religious groups of all traditions to deal with digital media formats. Before COVID, digital religious participation remained fairly limited in scope with limited numbers of congregations offering live broadcasts of services that viewers could watch much like they would watch a service on television. Other churches, however, were already becoming more creative. Some Catholic websites offer users the opportunity to light candles on behalf of special needs and to pray the rosary. BustedHalo.com (the name emphasizing the belief that no one is perfect but that God loves us anyhow) is a website the provides podcasts and videos aimed at young Catholics to answer questions they might have some in two minutes or less (Dearie 2018). Check out their video "Advent in 2 minutes" as an interesting example. On Anglican websites, the daily offices of morning and evening prayer are available, sometimes broadcast from a grand cathedral in England. One site, simply listed as the Mission of St. Clare (www.missionstclare.com), actually provides music so that the viewer can sing the service music in "karaoke" style. The Greek Orthodox Archdiocese of America also offers live broadcasts of divine services in New York, New Jersey, Connecticut, Michigan, and California. The requirements to shelter in place due to the pandemic made this kind of social media presence more universal in the U.S. and Europe, where clergy often broadcast services from their own homes instead of in their churches.

Islam has also had an online presence for some time. The faithful are called to prayer five times a day thanks to an iPhone app (Athan, Muslim Pro, and Pray Watch are just three among many). It is also possible to take a virtual Hajj to Mecca thanks to Instagram. WhatsApp is used as a way to say morning prayers by Muslims in Indonesia and where 30 groups of 30 individual Muslims each read one of the 30 sections of the Qur'an every day. This allows the entire Qur'an to be read collectively once a day and by each individual, once a month (Slama 2018)! In Eastern Europe, Muslims commonly share audio files on their iPhones to practice reading the Qur'an and also use Facebook as a place to discuss dimensions of Muslim belief and practice (Olson 2017).

Judaism, too, has its virtual identity on sites such as www.ritualwell.org, which provides information on a full range of Jewish rituals, with resources to assist the viewer in creating his or her own rituals. Other sites include different resources. Net.religion.jewish is a general website for Jewish internet users with news, recipes, and other relevant information, Jdate.com is an online Jewish dating service, and Aish.com is a site which, in addition to news, information on various aspects of Judaism, and Torah readings, also includes a "Place a Note in the Wall" link where an individual can submit a note or prayer virtually that will then be placed in real time in the Wailing Wall in Jerusalem (Campbell 2011). Because the COVID pandemic kept many devout Jews from being able to participate in the High Holy Days of Rosh Hashana (the Jewish New Year) and Yom Kippur (the Day of Atonement) in person, congregations sent High Holy Day boxes to families with items that would allow them to create their own at-home sanctuary for worship, including a miniature "ark" which traditionally contains the Torah in a synagogue and a bandana which could be used either as an altar cloth or as a COVID face mask (Stack 2020).

Many other religious groups, some representing seemingly long-vanished religious traditions, have joined the virtual revolution and can now be found online. Ancient Egyptian worship is one such religious tradition. It was revived in Chicago in 1988 by Tamara Siuda, recognized by the state of Illinois in 1993, and recognized by the federal government in 1999 (Krogh and Pillifant 2004). This group maintains two websites, one that presents information about beliefs and practices in ancient Egyptian religion with a virtual shrine and another that includes classes for would-be members and a password-protected portion for full members that grants access to online biweekly worship services.

More technologically savvy religious groups can take a further step toward virtual religious services. Second Life (www.secondlife.com) allows users to create avatars for themselves—alternative, animated, online selves. Users can then join virtual services and be present virtually in the online worship space. The avatar can participate physically in the service, standing, kneeling, clapping, or sitting as required. Other users who are also there can see one another's avatars and can communicate with one another before and after the services. But what happens if you don't have a specific religious identity or are a religious "none," how do you know where you belong in religious cyberspace? The answer is easy! Take the "Belief-O-Matic®" quiz on beliefnet.com. All you need to do is answer twenty questions about your beliefs and ideas about God, the afterlife, human nature, and a range of social issues and Belief-O-Matic® will tell you what religion or spiritual path (if any) best suits your beliefs. Regardless of your religious preferences, digital media technology and social media platforms of all kinds make it possible for anyone with access to the Internet, anywhere in the world, to be a part of an online religious community instantly.

Digital Spiritual Community, Identity, and Authority

For sociologists, online religion raises many important questions. Is a virtual community the same thing, in terms of its dynamics and influences on people, as a real community that is based on face-to-face interaction? What does it mean for individuals to have authentic religious identities in a technological context where having multiple personalities is commonplace? And most importantly for religious leaders, how does a religious group ensure that religious belief and practice remain orthodox when anyone can go online and circulate his or her own spin on what constitutes true beliefs and practices? Sociologists and scholars from a wide range of other disciplines have been exploring the impact of this new technological format for religion (Campbell 2013; Cheong et al. 2012; Drescher 2011; Grant et al. 2019). Let's briefly explore the issues that are emerging as we consider the impact of cyberspace on religious community, identity, and authority.

Online Faith Community

As we have already mentioned, the introduction of televised church services caused many in the religious community to fear, among other things, that this new technology would pull people out of church communities and contribute to growing social isolation. Decades later, such fears have proven to be incorrect. Those who watched religious television were also members of congregations, supplementing their religious experience with new media but not replacing it. The same fears have re-emerged about digital religion and social media. As in the past, people of many faiths supplement their offline religious practice with online additions. However, unlike television, social media makes it possible for digital religion to become an exclusive outlet for faith though the development of online relationships that bring a significant sense of community. But rather than simply being a supplement or substitute, digital media has allowed religion to evolve into something new. From what we know of those who participate in digital religion, the Internet fosters entirely new forms of relationships as well as reinvents what "community" looks like for religious believers (Campbell 2005). If these forms of interaction are not identical to older ones, proponents of digital religion ask "so what?" and point to the many positive ways that digital religion encourages community building that weaves together the face-to-face and offline experiences with those encountered online (Hoover 2012).

What online religious communities provide most clearly is access to an inexhaustible supply of active, dormant, and extinct religions. Whether one is in search of community in a Jewish synagogue or pagan coven, digital media allows one to join with others who share a set of beliefs and practices to worship, build relationships, offer spiritual and practice care, and interact by being online at the same time (Anderson and Drescher 2018). For those who follow ancient or marginalized faith traditions, joining together online is a way to build social bonds among otherwise isolated individuals. What is truly remarkable about the community-building potential of digital religion is that it can be truly global in scope, because, regardless of where you are in the world, you can join in the practice of your religion or spiritual tradition with others. Physical spaces and place no longer matter as much (Musa and Ahmadu 2012). Finally, digital religion allows a person to be a part of more than one community at a time, something that is not always possible in real time. Spiritual "seekers" can join in chat room relationships and participate in online rituals with others from the safety of their own homes. Chats can continue at all times of the day or night; there are no limits on how much interaction takes place, unlike the situation in real-time religious communities, where relationships and interactions are structured around particular times and days of the week. In the virtual practice of religion, a person can more easily explore diverse spiritual communities and experiences simultaneously.

But sociologists and religious practitioners alike (and hopefully now you, too) continue to consider whether there are limitations that balance these potentially positive aspects of online religious relationships and community. Like in the early days of religious television, the assumption has been that one significant challenge to community posed by digital religion is that, regardless of how many people we chat with online, we remain alone while we do it (Turkle 1995). Yet the evolution of this technology has been such that we can be connected to most of our offline friends and families around the clock in ways that mirror face-to-face interaction (Lundby 2012). Texting on our phones, Skype, FaceTime, Facebook, Instagram, and Twitter all allow us to connect to each other constantly, as do the thousands of social media sites. Few of us can be said to be truly alone anymore, so the question that remains is about the social impact of digital religious community membership. Do the known social benefits of relationships, such as group integration, social support during times of crisis, and the many mental and physical health benefits, emerge from digital relationships? How would you answer this question based on your own digital experience, religious or not?

Whether on- or offline, building relationships and community is an inherently messy business. All kinds of strain and conflicts are possible as individuals from different backgrounds confront one another. When a person is online, there are usually no visible indicators of that person's race, gender, class, or sexual orientation. These aspects of our selves and the obstacles that they can pose to building communities are inescapable in our real-time relationships (Schroeder et al. 1998). Digital media can free our social interactions from these identity constraints, yet are the community interactions we have as authentic as in real time? Also, if we get bored with or feel uncomfortable in an online community setting, we can simply leave the site, delete our profiles, and move on. This is less easy in offline religious communities, where one's absence may be more readily noticed and followed up on. As was evident during the pandemic, digital communities—despite the many ways that they can facilitate interaction—cannot fully replicate some central religious practices around which community is built. As many religious practitioners found, while some religious rituals can be performed at home or online, many others cannot. Digital religion makes us reflect on what a faith community looks like, how it operates, and what its social impact is on the life of its members. Clearly, we need to continue to learn a lot before we can fully appreciate how religious communities are evolving in the digital age.

Digital Religious Identity

One of the powerful implications of digital identity formation is the way in which the technology allows us to create personal "profiles" that reflect as much or as little of ourselves as we wish to reveal online. Social media allows us to be quite narrow as an online self if we so desire. We can present ourselves as devout Buddhists or Evangelical Christians or as a faithful "prayer warrior" online and that is all anyone else in our online social networks will know about us. But we also can create as many different identities as we wish, each with its own unique aspects. June, an 11-year-old who used her mom's Internet account to play online, sums up this idea when she says to an interviewer: "I don't play so many different people online—only three" (Turkle 1995, 256). Once again, the Internet frees users to present themselves as religious believers and practitioners in many different ways. Avatar religion, where we create a personal avatar and deploy it in virtual worlds like Second Life, can allow us to pick and choose a religious identity using many different markers that come from a wide array of religious traditions, or we can create a more unified identity for our avatars and send them into more clearly defined virtual religious worlds (Straarup 2012, 108). Downloaded apps on our phones or iPads related to prayer and meditation, rituals, sacred texts, and religiously based social media all allow believers to create religious multidimensional identities (Wagner 2013). As noted in the preceding mention of religious seekers—those who explore what it means to belong to many different religious and spiritual communities—digital media allows people to express their multiple spiritual interests and desires in ways that could be difficult in real time. By crafting several online personalities, one can fully participate in Ancient Egyptian religious rituals, be a "technopagan," and join an evangelical praise service, overcoming the inherent problems of age, gender, ethnicity, or other characteristics that might hinder participation in any or all of these religious contexts offline.

This kind of freedom, however, can have its challenges from the vantage point of traditional offline religion. The ability to create multiple digital religious identities raises the question of which one, if any, is the authentic religious identity. At no point does online technology require us to create a unified identity. Rather, it revels in—and almost mandates—the fragmentation of our identities and increasingly few of us even think about the fact that this is the case. My identity in one app need not be the same as in another. Identities in fact to some degree are always fluid and fragmented, and digital technology allows us to decide how best to parse out these parts of ourselves intentionally. Although many postmodernist scholars would not see this as a problem, most religious groups would. When an avatar undergoes the ritual of baptism in order to join a virtual Christian community, does that virtual ritual count in the parallel offline Christian community? For most religious groups, the answer would be no. And yet, the experience and identity of belonging are real for that individual. So again, what is the authentic identity and who gets to determine that?

Digital religious identities also can skew our religious experience. If we wish to display only a partial identity during participation in an online religious ritual or as part of a community—for example, let's say a woman wants to participate in a male-only religious ritual—she can do so. We can even become fully integrated into a digital religious community. But this experience generates what Turkle (1995, 236) calls the "Disneyland Effect," in which the simulated experience becomes taken for granted as the real experience. Of course, this is very much what makes digital religion so interesting . . . our digital religious experiences are both real and yet not so real. Furthermore, it raises the question of whose assessment of digital religious identities and experiences are authoritative. Is it the individual themselves, or is it the offline religious community and its leaders who make that call? The impact of digital technology on the construction of an individual's spiritual identity requires us to challenge our assumptions about what a religious identity ought to look like and how it should develop.

Religious Authority Online

A third set of issues that digital religion raises has to do with the nature of religious authority. As Brasher (2004, x), observes regarding access to the Internet and the information available online, "Those who possess the means and skill to access it will have so much information at their disposal that they can challenge the expertise of professionals, and flaunt the jurisdictions of recognized [religious] authorities." If there has been a common theme in how people view the Internet, it is the observation that it promotes a democratic leveling of people, groups, and ideas.

Religious movements like Heaven's Gate (which remains an active site online, despite the tragic mass suicide of its members in 1997) and movements that were thought to be long extinct, such as worship of the ancient Sumerian goddess Inanna (http://inanna.virtualave.net/inannashrine.html), both find a place online, as does the Vatican (www.vatican.va), Muslims (www.islamonline.net, an extensive site), and many other more familiar religious groups. When we consider this online religious diversity, it is important for us to remember that there is no privileged access for some religious groups over others, nor is there a means for ensuring that only certain approaches or ideas within a religious group are expressed online. So, while the Vatican may maintain a site to promote official, orthodox teachings of the Roman Catholic Church, many other Catholic sites exist that reinterpret or challenge those teachings or reject them outright. In turn, Vatican officials can counter the information that is on these sites, but they cannot control the existence of the information. This is what we mean by "democratic leveling." For some, this inherent capacity to circulate divergent religious ideas and to challenge official ones is the great strength of digital religion. For some religious leaders, however, the Internet is seen as posing a substantial challenge to their authority.

Take for example the emergence of the "kosher" cell phone. When cell phone technology expanded, Orthodox Jewish Rabbis, in Israel and the U.S., believed iPhones to be spiritually dangerous to their communities (Rashi 2013). Campbell (2011) observed that these religious leaders opposed the ways that digital technology gave individuals too much moral freedom, undermining the authority of community standards and traditions. In the U.S., leaders' fears also included concern that it would enable women to more easily work away from home. As a result, Israeli rabbis launched an offensive against internet use, formally banning it for Orthodox Jews in 1999, a move matched in Orthodox communities outside of Israel. Initially, bans like this covered all internet use, though eventually the rabbis helped orchestrate the establishment of kosher phones. These phones have mechanisms which limit the user from browsing and downloading material deemed to be inappropriate. Concerns have been expressed by leaders of many other religious traditions as well. What links them all together is the fear of religious leaders that the easy accessibility to alternative spiritual ideas will undermine the legitimacy of official beliefs and practices, leading individual believers to question or even abandon their faith traditions altogether (Cheong 2013).

Yet, despite fears that the Internet can free users to explore differing religious beliefs and practices that are independent of existing religious authorities, religious leaders, rather than fleeing from the Internet, have come to use this technology to reinforce their own authority. Consequently, the Vatican's website isn't simply one among many, but rather, as the authoritative voice of the Catholic Church, it is likely to be the first (and possibly only) place that anyone seeking Catholic teachings about any theological, social, or political subject might go. By controlling the information on their own websites, religious leaders can use the Internet to circulate the precise messages they wish to convey to the world.

But the problems posed by digital religion are about more than access to information about diverse religious teachings. Digital technology also poses a challenge to the ability of religious groups to control or limit access to religious rituals. Some religions do not wish to allow anyone to have full access to all the rites that are central to religious practice. They allow only people who have been initiated into full membership in the faith community to participate. These groups may structure their websites in a way that maintains their own hierarchical authority.

For example, people who wish to join the group of ancient Egyptian worshipers that is based in Chicago must go through an extensive online initiation course to become full members. The application requires the consent of a person's family member or guardian for individuals who are under 18, who are married, or who have a caregiver (Krogh and Pillifant 2004). Only those who successfully complete this process receive the password that allows them to join the live broadcasts of the Egyptian rituals. So, as this example shows, while users have free access to some websites, technology also exists to limit access—another way to preserve religious authority.

In sum, the spread of new forms of digital technology force religious groups to adopt some level of online presence. They may not all use this technology for the same purposes or to the same extent, but they feel the pressure to create room for their understanding of the sacred online. Moreover, cyberspace is equally open to disseminating information on traditional beliefs and practices as it is to new beliefs and practices, so traditional orthodox belief and practice is not inevitably doomed by the new technology. Yet it is equally important to note that the Internet is not a blank canvas that has no impact on the religious traditions it presents. The structure of social media itself puts constraints on how core ideas and messages are communicated, which by definition changes the content of those ideas and messages. Brasher (2004, xii) argues,

> As they have attempted to make themselves at home in the social space of the Internet, religious organizations have had to define themselves in a menu-driven, protocol-determined space where images reign. Overt multiplicity, messy answers, and explicit contradictions work against web site aesthetics. Engaging with the Internet can propel religious organizations toward reductionism, minimizing diversity, complexity, and the unknowns that add spice and texture to a traditional heritage. Official religious web sites tend to present the tradition as a harmonic, unified singularity, and suppress dissent. Alternative opinions need not apply.

Once the "Disneyland Effect" kicks in, religious organizations may feel pressure to conform their real-time rituals and community gatherings to approximate the experience that participants find online. Bunt (2000) found that Islamic sites have to look "appropriate" in terms of the graphics that they display and the links that connect viewers to high-profile sites. Anthropologists have also found this effect in religions that formerly required people's physical presence and participation at gathering places but that are now taking advantage of the legitimacy and authenticity bestowed by adopting "televisual styles" that resonate with the tastes of the local population. As one study of Candomble, an Afro-Brazilian spirit-possession religious tradition, noted: "One's mother, neighbors, and colleagues from work will definitely be more impressed when a celebration marking an important moment in one's religious life 'almost looks like TV'" (Van de Port 2006, 457). And so, as in the early days of television:

> People soon wanted the production quality and professionalism of radio and television to be exhibited in *local* worship events. Rather than participants in a faith community, people started to think of themselves as an audience and began acting like observers at worship.
>
> (Brasher 2004, 16)

But today, the divides between audience and performer, follower and leader, and even consumer and producer are blurred or made irrelevant by social media (Musa and Ahmadu 2012, 71). As we already observed in our discussion of digital religious identities, digital technology has opened the possibility for the amalgamation of diverse religious beliefs, practices, identities, and experiences like never before. While religious leaders and individual believers striving to maintain the homogeneity and authenticity of their traditions may try to limit or ban the use of social media, it is so much a part of everyday life and the religious practice of believers around the world that more and more religious groups are adapting themselves to it. How digital technology will continue to change the religious landscape and how religion will continue to impact social media is one of the exciting areas for exploration.

What's in a Megachurch?

In addition to finding the sacred online, some Christians have embraced another new context for Christian belief and practice at "big-box" churches, also known as megachurches. This label, hinting at similarities to places like Costco and Wal-Mart, reflects the sheer size and scope of the congregations in these religious ministries. Since the first edition of this book, the number of megachurches in the United States has increased from 1250 to nearly 1750 (Thumma and Travis 2007; Bird and Thumma 2020).

This finding itself tells us two important facts about the phenomenon of these types of congregations. First, the label "megachurch" is almost exclusively limited to Protestant congregations. Most of these congregations could be categorized broadly as evangelical Protestant, and it is often assumed megachurches are non-denominational, but approximately 60% of these congregations belong to a particular denomination (See Table 3.2).

Table 3.2 Denominational Affiliation of Megachurches in the United States

Affiliation	Percentage
Nondenominational	40.0%
Southern Baptist	16.0
Baptist (Unspecified)	7.0
Assemblies of God	6.0
Christian	5.0
Calvary Chapel	4.0
Calvary Chapel	4.0
United Methodist	2.0
Other denominations (each ≤1.0%)	20.0%

Source: Hartford Institute for Religion Research (2020).

Second, a megachurch, by definition, has a minimum of 2000 attendees on any given Sunday morning, with an average attendance of 4092 people, but an average total membership of 5982 adults in 2020 (Bird and Thumma 2020, 3). It is important to know these distinguishing features because many Roman Catholic congregations may count thousands of members belonging to their geographical parish, though they do not typically attend in such high numbers on a weekly basis.

The work of Scott Thummaand his colleagues, Dave Travis and Warren Bird (2005, 2007), examining these churches remains some of the most extensive research on the subject and provides an important foundation for more recent follow-up surveys of these churches (Bird and Thumma 2020). It helps us understand these types of congregations and how they are shaping and being shaped by the American religious landscape. (See also Ellingson 2007.) Because so much of what most of us think we know about these churches comes from media sources that focus on the financial or sexual scandals that have beset a few of their leaders or the political views of at most a small handful of pastors from these churches, our ideas are incomplete at best or totally inaccurate at worst. Let's look at some of the recent data that Bird and Thumma (2020) provide on these congregations.

Megachurches are found all over the United States, though they tend to cluster in some unsurprising regions, notably in the South and Midwest. About 70% of all these churches are in the southern Sunbelt, a region that extends from Maryland south to Florida, west to Texas, north to Oklahoma and Missouri, and back east to Kentucky and West Virginia. California, Texas, Florida, and Georgia have the highest concentrations of these churches. The Hartford Institute for Religion Research (2020) reports that most megachurches are suburban. They are established around rapidly growing urban areas such as Los Angeles, Dallas, Atlanta, Orlando, and Phoenix.

Bird and Thumma (2020, 5) report that three-quarters of megachurches have experienced explosive growth in members since 2015. Growth has come in several ways. Many of these churches have expanded through the launch of satellite churches. Almost 70% of megachurches are multi-site. Almost half of megachurches (47%) started branch locations since 2015 (up from 22%) and 48% helped to start a new congregation (up from 18%)! Although these churches attract thousands in any given week, very few attract such huge numbers all at once. More commonly, megachurches have several services that are sometimes radically different in style or emphasis, to accommodate those who attend.

Megachurches are perhaps best known for their diversity in contemporary worship forms and styles (Thumma et al. 2005, 22). Most of these congregations use praise bands as their music source, with 94% using drums, 93% using electric guitars or bass guitars, and 84% using pianos "always" or at least "often" during their services. Ninety-five percent of these congregations use visual projection equipment as well. Yet there are a few megachurches that use more traditional forms of worship, including hymns, structured readings from the Bible, communion rituals, and recitations of creeds. What makes megachurches unique is their willingness to experiment with innovative worship styles and change what they do as needed. Moreover, because many of these churches have multiple services, it is possible for one megachurch to include a quieter and more formal traditional service, a rock-and-roll-style service, and many other variations, each targeting the different tastes and aesthetics of a subset of the congregation. Regardless of which type of service they attend, most people characterized their church as filled with a sense of God's presence (53%), inspirational (52%), joyful (50%), and exciting (43%) (Thumma and Travis 2007, 151).

Contrary to cultural stereotypes of the type of people who attend megachurches, Bird and Thumma (2020) found that people from a wide range of social backgrounds attend services at these churches and that their diversity is increasing all the time. (See Table 3.3.) Though most adults (72%) in megachurches are White, Bird and Thumma (2020, 38) report that more than half (58%) of all megachurches are now multiracial, meaning that 20% or more of the congregation belongs to a different racial group than the majority of churchgoers. This number is more than

Table 3.3 Percent of Megachurches by Congregational Characteristics

	% of Regularly Attending Adults
College graduates	56%
Female	56%
Over age 35	53%
Recent Immigrants	5%
Persons with Special Needs	4%

Source: Bird and Thumma (2020, 31).

double the percent of multiracial megachurches in 2000 and due in a significant to the ways these congregations have intentionally worked to create welcoming and inclusive environments. In general, though, approximately 11% of megachurch members are African American, while 10% are Hispanic or Latino(a) and 4% are Asian. Membership also tends to be younger, with almost half of the regular participants being 34 or younger, and only 15% being over 65 (Bird and Thumma 2020, 29). While they don't provide data, Thumma and Travis (2007) and Bird and Thumma (2020) both note that megachurches attract adults from a wide range of income levels and occupations. In their 2020 sample of 582 megachurches, Bird and Thumma found approximately 56% of adults in these churches are college graduates. In 2010, most adults were still new to these congregations, having joined in the previous five years. Today however, 65% of adults have been members for more than five years. The people who attend these churches, then, are no longer just drawing younger people as in years past, but they are still drawing more from relatively well-educated. While they may be becoming more diverse racially, megachurch members are not on the margins of American society.

Can You Have Community in a Megachurch?

Let us consider the meaning of *community* in the new religious context of a megachurch. Whereas digital religion presents the challenge of being in community while sitting at home alone, belonging to a church with several thousand members raises the question of how all those people ever have the chance to interact in such a way that they feel tied together as a spiritual community. In fact, megachurches do an excellent job of creating a sense of community, according to surveys of the people who attend their services. In their initial report, Thumma et al. (2005, 7) found that 72% of individuals who attended megachurches agreed that their church was "like a close-knit family." Other familiar aspects of community life abound as well; people who attend report having close friends at church, knowing as many or more people at their megachurch as they did when they attended churches with smaller congregations, and feeling cared about (Thumma and Travis 2007, 46). The question remains: How exactly do these churches make this happen?

One of the central ways that megachurches help develop this sense of family and community is to use small groups. Forming small groups has been a dominant way to build relationships, facilitate spiritual growth, and develop outreach activities in American congregations over the last few decades (Wuthnow 1994). Megachurches have taken this structure and run with it. Sometimes these small groups are designed to incorporate newcomers into the church by having them join an informal group to discuss the previous week's service and message. Other groups are designed to further members' spiritual development through prayer and Bible study. Still other groups cover a wide range of church-related activities and secular pursuits. Whatever their focus, megachurch pastors create these extensive networks of small groups to "make the big church small" (Thomas and Jardine 1994, 277). Bird and Thumma's (2020, 34) survey of megachurches found an average of 45% of adult participants were involved in a small group of some kind and that their involvement was directly correlated to other important aspects of church life. For instance, congregations with more people involved in small groups reported that they also had more people volunteering at church and recruiting new people to the church. Bird and Thumma also found that small groups encourage overall church growth, more frequent church attendance, and greater engagement with community service work. Small groups are at the heart of these churches' mission and strategy for growth and spiritual vitality.

The feeling of community is also maintained in megachurches through a variety of other means. First, these churches rely on families and friends to invite new people to attend a service at the church. These informal ties also help newcomers feel comfortable in the otherwise overwhelming context of the services. In addition, in some of these congregations, as Thumma and Travis (2007) observed in their early research, the ushers intentionally keep track of the individuals who sit in particular sections of the church week after week. While this practice may seem a bit like taking attendance, it also ensures that individuals who visit the church feel looked after and cared about. Being recognized by an usher can be extremely refreshing to people who, in the process of church shopping, often felt invisible; they believe that someone in the congregation cared enough to make them feel like they belonged.

In addition to attentive ushers, megachurches use an extensive staff of paid and unpaid people to make sure that the services and programs of the church are successfully conducted. Megachurches typically have an average of 20 full-time, paid leaders and 9 part-time leaders. In addition to leaders, these churches have, on average, 22 full-time and 15 part-time administrative staff. Volunteers are also crucial to the operation of these churches. Thumma et al. (2005, 10) found that, again on average, these churches have 284 volunteers who work five hours a week or more. Working or volunteering are additional opportunities for building community among those who attend megachurches. Newcomers are quickly connected to the congregation through small groups, volunteer opportunities, new member classes, or, in some cases, assignment to a formal "mentor." (See Table 3.4.)

By intentionally attracting visitors to their churches and keeping them as members of the congregation, not only do megachurches continue to experience amazing growth, but they also provide people with new forms of spiritual community. It is important to keep in mind, however, that megachurches cannot sustain themselves purely by their size and the entertainment value they offer to their audiences week by week. Their size alone is intimidating and potentially alienating. Building community in these churches requires them to incorporate many old-fashioned pre-pandemic patterns for interaction—handshakes, meal-sharing, intimate relationships in small groups,

Table 3.4 Percent of Megachurches Reporting Activities to Attract and Keep Members

Invitation to participate in a fellowship or other small group	88%
Orientation classes for new members	78
Support for adults with special needs	87
Invitation to volunteer for service in congregation or community	69
Designated people to extend hospitality, invitations for meals	58
Follow-up visits by clergy, lay leaders, or members	52
Other activities	22
No planned procedures or activities	3%

Source: Thumma et al. (2005, 13), Bird and Thumma (2020, 11).

and opportunities to work shoulder-to-shoulder on outreach projects. That they seem to have been successful is a testament to the continued importance of sustained personal interaction to maximize feelings of belonging and social support.

To sum up, just as Internet technology is shaping what the practice of religion looks like, megachurches, too, are having a profound impact on the American religious landscape. Megachurches are not the end of traditional Christianity expressed through small local congregations, but they certainly are affecting what a Christian congregation looks like and how it worships. Megachurches continue to attract the attention of young, suburban professionals because they provide them with practical ways to develop their faith and to experience the sacred. In doing so, megachurches make use of multimedia and contemporary music in ways that clearly resonate with the wider cultural shifts in American society. Formality, tradition, liturgy, and denominational heritage have become increasingly foreign to new generations of Americans.

But megachurches do not just create one more niche in the religious landscape for those who enjoy their evangelical and nondenominational cultural forms. Congregations of many types and traditions are feeling the cultural pressure that the megachurch phenomenon creates. In a 2007 study of the impact of megachurch styles and aesthetics on a set of Lutheran churches in southern California, Stephen Ellingson argues quite forcefully that there is a sense of crisis among traditional congregations that has its roots in the success of megachurches. The argument begins with the premise that people neither understand nor own the denominational traditions of their churches. Consequently, membership decline, especially among mainline Protestants, is facilitated by the churches' reluctance to change and update their worship styles to attract new and younger potential members. If congregations want to thrive in the 21st century, they should adopt contemporary worship, an emphasis on emotion and experience, and above all, minimize formality and tradition. In a word, they should become as much like megachurches as possible. What is remarkable about the churches in Ellingson's study is that more often than not, church leaders made changes to worship and programs as a result of receiving these messages secondhand, in materials circulated and presented by "experts," not as a result of any direct and consistent reflection on either the internal dynamics of the congregations themselves or on the dynamics of the churches' own communities.

What we see happening with megachurches then is twofold. On one hand, megachurches represent yet another adaptation of religion to the cultural changes that are occurring in the rest of American society. They intentionally seek to reach a specific audience with their largely evangelical and nondenominational forms of the Christian message. As such, megachurches have been incredibly successful in developing new methods for carrying out the basic function of religion to build community. On the other hand, megachurches introduce new pressures onto other types of congregations that push them to adopt similar forms of organization and worship, while simultaneously—and often unwittingly—causing these churches to change their traditions and theology as well. In short, megachurches are "colonizing" mainline Protestantism (Ellingson 2007, 178). For congregations that follow the megachurch models, there is no way to go back to older forms of tradition and the order of earlier times. Megachurches clearly meet the spiritual needs of many contemporary American Christians. They also force all others to become more aware of how they live out their respective traditions in a postmodern, consumer-driven, tradition-averse world.

Other New Forms and Contexts for Religious Community

Religious beliefs and practices in the 21st century continue to be a blend of tradition and innovation. Although many believers use technology to experience the sacred—either online or through megachurch multimedia events—others see these forms of religious enterprise as alienating, cold, and lacking humanity. In the contemporary world, growing numbers of people seem to be on quests for experiences of the sacred and now more than ever are likely to describe themselves as "spiritual but not religious." In fact, more than a quarter of Americans (27%) define themselves that way (Pew Research Center 2017b). This number is up from 19% in 2012. British sociologists have characterized this state of affairs as a "believing, not belonging" culture (Davie 1994). Today, pushed recently by the COVID pandemic, there is a strong market for books, consumer goods, and services designed to help us on our spiritual quest. What are sometimes classed as New Age shops sell crystals, incense, and other tools for touching the divine in ourselves and in nature. Christian bookstores, too, offer devotional books, candles, angel statues, and DVDs to aid one's personal spiritual growth. The *New York Times* reported on an increasing number of people seeking out "spiritual directors" who help people connect to the divine, however they define that (Cooper 2021). And there has been a veritable explosion of wellness centers offering yoga classes, massages, and aromatherapies (for people and sometimes for pets, too). While these kinds of shops are not new, their expansion into a multibillion-dollar industry that transcends religious and denominational boundaries *is* new (Roof 1999). Moreover, the recent increase in demand for renewable energy and organic food is also tapping into a concern for nature that borders on the spiritual and, occasionally, on the formally religious. Of interest here is the degree to which these shops and centers are providing people with alternative ways to pursue their individual spiritual journeys, paths that do not require people to associate with an organization, have a religious identity, or formally believe in God in order for them to engage the sacred.

For the purposes of this discussion, we are limiting our focus to beliefs and practices that we will term *alternative spiritualities*, meaning that they do not represent traditional religious beliefs and practices that one might find in a congregational setting. We choose not to call them New Age beliefs and practices because that oversimplifies them. Alternative spirituality encompasses two broad categories of beliefs and practices (Glendinning and Bruce 2006; Sointu and Woodhead 2008). The first category centers on the collective sets of beliefs and practices that revolve around divination. These include belief in and use of horoscopes and astrology, tarot cards, psychic readings, channeling (a practice in which a "channeler" either speaks with spirits and relays their messages to others or has his or her body taken over by a spirit, who then speaks directly through the channeler), and other practices. The second category addresses the wide range of beliefs and practices regarding personal health and wellness. These include, but are not limited to, holistic and alternative medicines and therapies, massage, yoga, diets, and aromatherapies. What links all of these things together is their overarching focus on personal enlightenment and growth (Bader et al. 2017).

The research that has been done on these types of beliefs and practices finds that alternative spiritualities are about consumer choice *par excellence*. Individuals assemble their own sets of beliefs and practices, aided increasingly by digital technology, that they find personally meaningful and instrumental. Consequently, alternative spiritualities function as religious supermarkets, where individuals borrow at will from any and all spiritual traditions from the past and present (Houtman and Aupers 2007, 306). Alternative spiritualities commonly draw on selected beliefs and rituals from Eastern religions like Hinduism and Buddhism and indigenous religious traditions of Native Americans (Jenkins 2004; Mears and Ellison 2000; Roof 1999). They provide a highly individualistic means of encountering the sacred by maintaining a core emphasis on the central aspects of identity and community: healthy and authentic relationships, especially with one's own body. Roof (1998) notes that in many of these new forms of spirituality, community and relationship building includes the fostering of human relationships with not just other people but with all of nature.

Houtman and Aupers (2007, 307) argue that at the center of all alternative spiritualities is the "belief that in the deepest layers of the self the 'divine spark' is still smoldering, waiting to be stirred up, and succeed the socialized self." Humans are socialized to live inauthentic lives, structured by the impersonal and dysfunctional institutions that dominate contemporary society. The Internet could be seen as a contributor to this socialization because it allows us to live through our fragmented, online selves instead of being a whole person all the time. Alternative spiritualities often also represent a rejection both of traditional forms of religion (especially Christianity) and Western scientific rationality. Individuals who embrace these alternative spiritual practices are on quests to find their whole authentic selves again. And while an individually focused quest seems to contradict the very basis for community, a common thread links these practices: the belief that developing an authentic self happens in relationships with others, not apart from them (Houtman and Aupers 2007; Sointu and Woodhead 2008).

But who follows these kinds of alternative spiritual practices? This is a difficult question to answer because to date, most sociological studies of alternative spiritually have relied on qualitative, narrative, and life history data to describe what it means to be a part of this group. Survey research simply provides correlations between specific beliefs (such as beliefs in Angels) with demographic characteristics like race, gender, or educational level (Goode 2011; Bader et al. 2017). Also, because there is no single set of unifying beliefs and practices that links everyone in this group, most statistical data simply reflect a wide range of questions that cover the basic areas of divination and wellbeing. For example, Bader et al. (2017, 42) analyzed the Baylor Religion Survey data to examine Americans' beliefs in things related to the paranormal. Individuals were asked whether they believed in astrology, communication with the dead, the power of dreams to predict the future, etc. Responses ranged from 18% of people in the survey believed in astrology, fortune-telling, and other means of predicting the future to 25.6% who believe that the living and dead can communicate to 60.9% who believe dreams can foretell the future. This is consistent with earlier findings by the Gallup Poll (2001, 2005). Table 3.5 reports the percentage of Americans who responded positively about these things in 2001, compared with the percentage in a similar study conducted in 1990. In 2005, in a follow-up survey, still a full 25% of Americans reported beliefs in astrology, 21% believe that it is possible to communicate mentally with the dead, and another 21% believe in witches (Gallop Poll 2005).

Overall, though belief in these phenomena has varied in recent years, belief continues to be strong. The Pew Research Center estimates that six in ten Americans hold beliefs in at least one of these areas (Gecewicz 2018). While findings over the last several decades consistently show that it is younger people, women, African and Hispanic Americans, and the less-well educated who are most likely to hold New Age beliefs, the reality is that significant numbers of men and those with higher levels of education do so as well (Bader et al. 2017; Glendinning and Bruce 2006). It may surprise you to learn that these beliefs are also not just held by those outside of traditional religion. Significant numbers of American Christians do as well! The Pew Research Center found 70% of Roman Catholics, 72% of Black Protestants, and 67% of Establishment Protestants reported believing in at least one of the following: that spiritual energy can be located in physical things, in

Table 3.5 Percentage of Americans Who Held Alternative Spiritual Beliefs, 1990, 2001, and 2005

	1990	2001	2005
Power of human mind to heal the body	46	54	–
Communication with someone who has died	18	28	21
Astrology	25	28	25
Reincarnation	21	25	–
Channeling	11	15	–
ESP	49	50	–
Mental telepathy	36	36	–

Source: Gallup Poll (2001).

psychics, in reincarnation, or in astrology. Although as a group Evangelical Christians are less likely than other Christians to report holding such beliefs, 47% of Evangelicals held at least one of these four beliefs (Gecewicz 2018).

Despite the wide range in context for these studies, alternative spirituality, as represented in various beliefs and practices related to divination and well-being, is a small but growing segment of the spiritual landscape. Yet there is no easy way to pull together these kinds of beliefs in a single creed for alternative spirituality, making it even more difficult to generalize anything about individuals who follow it. An additional challenge is the fact that many people who use aromatherapies, massage, meditation, or even astrology do *not* see a spiritual dimension to these activities. For example, a participant in a Native American sweat lodge ceremony may participate not to connect with anything spiritual but only to clear his or her mind and body of stress, as one might in a steam room in a gym. Often, the "suppliers," the people who conduct the ceremonies, read the tarot cards, give the massages, or mix the herbal remedies see a spiritual dimension in these activities, but that doesn't mean that the consumers who utilize or pay for them share these beliefs.

Many people in the mainstream religious realm see alternative spiritualities, at best, as techniques to hoodwink people who are seeking a spiritually easy way out. Wuthnow (1998), in addressing this rush to individualized forms of spirituality, argues that the spiritual realm works for people in the contemporary world because it remains on the margins of daily life and demands little of us; it doesn't require us to do anything uncomfortable, which by definition is likely to be inauthentic. But there must be more to these practices than an easy way out of the obligations of more traditional religious belief and practice. The development of an authentic inner life by using practices that focus on the body and mind—as well as building healthier relationships with others and with nature—clearly resonates with a generation of people who are confronting the damaged and dysfunctional links between themselves and others and between themselves and the natural world. Roof (1999) suggests that even congregations within the mainstream of the American religious landscape have moved to incorporate the ethic if not the actual practice of personal wellness techniques and recovery therapies. For example, some congregations offer sessions on "centering prayer" that focus on personal development, while others offer 12-step groups in the format of Alcoholics Anonymous. In addition, many groups are created within congregations to help young people, old people, men, women, gays, businesspeople, members, and nonmembers fit the traditions of that religious practice to their own personal and professional needs and life experiences. Alternative spiritualities continue to represent an adaptation to new social and cultural dynamics that are separate from conventional religion, but collectively they are also contributing to the changing dynamics within the beliefs and practices of religious groups.

Concluding Thoughts

In this chapter, we have seen the new ways that religion and religious organizations are adapting to technological and cultural shifts in our society. As with all such shifts, these changes may be frightening for some and may be considered long overdue by others. Nevertheless, we must appreciate how the forces of social change and cultural adaptation, regardless of their sources, are neither completely benign nor entirely threatening to older expressions of religious belief, practice, and experiences. It is clear that change can be disruptive. It calls into question longstanding beliefs and ways of doing things. Change creates confusion and frustration among those who don't believe that it is good. Change also can result in conflict, hostility, and the possibility of denominational or congregational break-up. People whose religious traditions are being picked over and used out of their original context—like many Native Americans—may disagree over who has the authority to determine when, how, and by whom religious beliefs and practices may be used.

At the same time, however, the kinds of changes we have discussed here can force religious groups to reflect on how best to make their traditions relevant to the world and people of today. As we saw in our discussion of digital religion, the Internet can resurrect long-dead religious beliefs and practices as well as forming and disseminating new ones. The development of new forms of religious organization—such as megachurches—puts pressure on all other religious groups to re-evaluate and modify their practices. Religion in our world constantly evolves and adapts, even though from our own individual perspective our own pre-pandemic traditions may appear to have always remained the same. Few believers can say that in the post-pandemic world, of course. It is essential for us to keep an open, but critical, mind about the long-term impacts of these religious adaptations in order to fully understand the causes, content, and consequences of all forms of religious change.

Suggested Reading

Bader, Christopher D. Joseph O. Baker, and F. Carson Mencken. 2017. *Paranormal America: Ghost Encounters, UFO Sightings, Bigfoot Hunts, and Other Curiosities in Religion and Culture*, 2nd Edition. New York: New York University Press.

Brasher, Brenda E. 2004. *Give Me That Online Religion*. New Brunswick, NJ: Rutgers University Press.

Campbell, Heidi A. (ed.). 2013. *Digital Religion: Understanding Religious Practice in New Media Worlds*. New York: Routledge.

Davie, Grace. 1994. *Religion in Britain Since 1945: Believing Without Belonging*. Oxford: Blackwell Publishers.

Ellingson, Stephen. 2007. *The Megachurch and the Mainline: Remaking Religious Tradition in the Twenty-First Century*. Chicago: University of Chicago Press.

Grant, August E., Amanda F. C. Sturgill, Chiung Hwang Chen, and Daniel A. Stout (eds.). 2019. *Religion Online: How Digital Technology is Changing the Way We Worship and Pray*. Denver: Praeger.

Sointu, Eeva, and Linda Woodhead. 2008. "Spirituality, Gender, and Expressive Selfhood." *Journal for the Scientific Study of Religion* 47(2): 259–276.

Thumma, Scott, and Dave Travis. 2007. *Beyond Megachurch Myths*. San Francisco: Josey-Bass Publishers.

Section II

The Shape and Politics of Religion

4 Can't We All Just Get Along?

Cohesion and Conflict in Religion

1 How does religion help create social cohesion?
2 How is cohesion related to conflict?
3 What are the functions of conflict for cohesion?
4 Why do people of different faiths sometimes get along and sometimes not?

Sicily. If you have heard of it, it's most likely in conjunction with La Cosa Nostra, more commonly known as the Mafia. But of course, Sicily is much more. An island state of Italy that is situated at the mainland's southern tip, Sicily is in many ways a world unto its own.

Almost all of its approximately 5 million citizens are Catholic, and Catholicism is steeped into the culture and daily life of Sicilians. It has dominated life on this island for nearly 1000 years. Religion is of vital importance here. This does not mean that everyone regularly attends Mass. Not everyone does. But Catholicism does permeate almost every aspect of society, including day-to-day activities, art and architecture, the way that people relate to one another, town celebrations, and pronouncements by heads of state. Nearly every town, no matter how small, has at least one Catholic church, and usually the town is organized around its main or original church. Holidays are more appropriately labeled Holy Days, as they typically center on celebrations of patron saints or other religious festivities. As one observer of Sicilian culture wrote:

> Almost all public places are adorned with crucifixes upon their walls, and most Sicilian homes contain pictures of saints, statues, and other relics. Each town and city has its own patron saint, and the feast days are marked by gaudy processions through the streets with marching bands and displays of fireworks.
>
> (Wikipedia 2008)

The Catholic religion in Sicily serves important social cohesion functions. Part of being Sicilian is being Catholic. It shapes Sicilians' life experiences, gives them meaning and purpose, influences family life, provides the contours of the yearly calendar, and provides norms, values, and key rituals that help solidify people's sense of belonging in their communities and in the company of a higher power.

But what about those Mafiosi who are supposed to have such influence on the island? (One of the authors was told by a Sicilian professor who specializes in studying the Mafia that as of 2010, over 80% of the businesses in Sicily pay "protection" money to the Mafia.) Are they Catholic?

In name, almost always. But in practice? Well, it is true that they often attend Mass, respect religious traditions, and contribute money to support religious festivals and churches. They show respect for priests, and part of their code is never to disturb or kill a priest, for they view themselves as men of honor and consider things related to God to be of a higher order than even the Mafia. To some extent, religion and culture have merged in Sicily, and some of the ideas of the Mafia are part of the practice of Sicilian Catholicism.

DOI: 10.4324/9781003182108-6

And what do the people of Sicily who are not part of the Mafia (the large majority of Sicilians) think of the Mafia? Many Sicilians either tolerate or outwardly support Mafia members—often out of fear, sometimes out of respect for the order and other advantages that they bring. When questioned by outsiders, Sicilians frequently deny that any such organization exists.

But Father Giuseppe Puglisi (pronounced "Pool-yee-zee") was different. Though he was a native of Sicily, he did not respect the Mafia. In fact, he thought they were decidedly anti-Christian. Like most Sicilians, he was born to working-class parents and grew up working-class. He entered seminary at the young age of 16 and then served in a country Sicilian parish that was affected by a bloody vendetta.

He had seen the violence and fear that the Mafia wrought upon Sicilians. He had also noticed how they infiltrated so many aspects of Sicilian life, including, in his view, the very understanding and practices of Catholicism. Although the Mafia members were baptized in the Catholic Church and were practicing members in good standing, in Father Puglisi's eyes they were decidedly pagan, a holdover from pre-Christian times.

Father Puglisi felt that it was his Christian duty to God and his flock to resist the Mafia. The Mafia fenced stolen goods, sold drugs, engaged in extensive extortion, controlled construction and other industries, and heavily influenced politics. (Just two years before this chapter was written, the governor of Sicily was indicted for himself being a Mafioso.) But even worse, according to Father Puglisi, the Mafia eroded civic and social life in Sicily and compromised the authentic practice of Catholicism. After centuries of experience with the Mafia, Sicilians had become cynical about political effectiveness and trustworthiness and had come to misunderstand aspects of their faith. In fact, they had become apathetic. Those who tried to change things only suffered at the hands of the Mafia's "men of honor."

When Father Puglisi was assigned as the parish priest in one of the poor sections of Sicily's largest city, Palermo, he decided that enough was enough, and he worked to effect change. He was outspoken about the evils of the Mafia. He taught his parishioners to resist their ways and to overcome apathy. He focused mostly on the children, wanting them to have a new and better Sicily. He taught them to take hold of their faith and use it to resist the Mafia by refusing to collaborate with them, buy their fenced goods, admire them, take or sell their drugs, or participate in traditional religious celebrations that were largely paid for by the local Mafia members. He encouraged them to see the Mafia for who they really were and to engage in alternative, more authentic Catholic practices, such as the Stations of the Cross. Father Puglisi refused the money and gifts that the Mafia offered him—even those from members of his own parish. He decried their practices from the pulpit, and he worked tirelessly to support the people of his parish in resisting the Mafia.

For these reasons, Father Puglisi was revered, loved, and respected by many people. He was brave, bold, and fully Sicilian, in the best sense. He was a role model. On his 56th birthday he spent the day not sleeping, eating treats, or opening presents, but rather doing his daily round of pastoral duties—visiting families in his parish, conducting two weddings, and hosting a conference with parents who were having their babies baptized. That evening, he returned home and stepped out of his car, only to be confronted by a man with a gun equipped with a silencer.

When Father Puglisi saw the man, he simply said, "I was expecting you." The man then violated the code of honor, put the gun to Father Puglisi's head, and shot the beloved priest to death.

Four years later, the killer was arrested. He was a low-level Mafioso and a practicing Catholic who had been baptized in the parish where Father Puglisi ministered. The man had been ordered to "take out" the priest by Mafia bosses, who were also practicing Catholics baptized in the local parishes.

During this time, there had been a particularly violent period of Mafia activity that included the murders of high-ranking officials, deadly bomb explosions, blown-up bridges, and bloodstained streets. But the murder of a priest caused a huge outcry. Massive crowds followed his funeral procession. The Pope came to Sicily and spoke about Father Puglisi, calling him a witness to true Christianity. Later, Father Puglisi was recognized as a martyr for the faith. And Sicilians united themselves even more around their Catholic faith, a faith now increasingly defined as one that was different from the one practiced by the Mafia members. (The story of Father Puglisi was taken largely from Cunningham 2002.)

We tell the story to introduce the topics of this chapter—social cohesion and social conflict, and their intimately related nature. Sicily, like many places, is a land of contrasts. It is more thoroughly infused by one religion than are most modern societies, and Catholicism produces a strong social cohesion among Sicilians. It serves to bring people together and infuse their lives with order and meaning at the individual and family level, at the parish level, at the community level, and at the national level.

But in a somewhat unique way, this religious conformity and resulting social cohesion is threatened by the continued presence of fellow Catholics—the Mafia—who have defined an alternative way of understanding and practicing Catholicism. Some people might consider them to be misguided, offenders of the faith, or even heretics. Conversely, the Mafia would view the behavior of more traditional Catholics as acceptable, so long as they did not interfere with Mafia activities. When they do interfere, they then are misguided, offenders, or heretics.

Thus, in the midst of centuries-old social cohesion exists centuries-old internal religious conflict. Non-Mafia members respond to the conflict by calling the Mafia Christian heretics, attempting to excommunicate them, and uniting around the faith and especially around religious leaders. Mafia members respond by attempting to buy favors, trying to compromise and change the faith, and using terror and murder. These differing responses heighten social cohesion on both sides. Conflict has the effect of actually strengthening the boundaries and group identity of conflicting parties.

Such is the way of social and religious life. Cohesion and conflict are two sides of the same coin. They need and feed on each other.

Some people use the fact that religion can lead to conflict as evidence that religions are false. This conclusion is premised on the assumption that conflict is negative. But it need not be. For example, in the case of Father Puglisi and the Mafia, he could have chosen peace (give in to the Mafia's version of the faith) over justice, but he viewed justice—and the subsequent need for conflict—as a higher religious goal than the avoidance of conflict. This chapter will explore these ideas further.

Getting Personal

Have you ever had disagreements or even arguments over religion or spirituality with others, perhaps with family members, friends, or even people you don't know well? If so, what have the disagreements been about? Stop and think about these disagreements for a moment and then summarize them in the accompanying box that follows. If you have never had any disagreements over religion or spirituality, you can write "none."

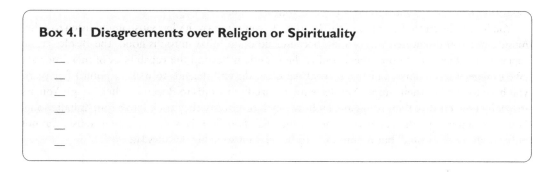

Box 4.1 Disagreements over Religion or Spirituality

—

—

—

—

—

—

If you have had disagreements over religion or spirituality, do you see any themes to those disagreements? If you have never had disagreements over religion, why do you think you have not, and why do you think others do have such disagreements?

Our interactions with other people are characterized by agreement and disagreement, cohesion and conflict. Sometimes you get along with your best friend, and sometimes you don't, perhaps occasionally to the degree that you stop talking to each other for a while, or even stop being best friends. One of the issues on which you might disagree with friends is religion. In the contemporary United States, we mostly *don't* talk about religion in public. Certain topics are considered to be too volatile to be discussed in polite company—religion, politics, race, and the like. But among close friends, such social taboos can be loosened, and you may, one late night in the dorm, get into a discussion of religious views. You might be surprised to learn the "crazy stuff" that other people believe. Perhaps your discussion will turn more into heated debate, with some people questioning and others defending certain religious views. Or perhaps you'll mostly agree with one another and instead talk about the "crazy views" of others who are not in the room.

In subsequent sections, we explore why people sometimes have disagreements over religion, while at other times they seem perfectly able to coexist. As part of this discussion, we consider whether religious conflict is only about religion.

Religion and Social Cohesion

In many societies, including that of the United States, religion is considered to be a private affair, a set of convictions that an individual holds or rejects by choice. But one of the first sociologists, Emile Durkheim, demonstrated that, to a great extent, religion is a social affair. He analyzed what he considered to be the most primitive of religions—totemism—and then broadened his theory to apply to all religions. Durkheim concluded that whatever else religion is, it is *the worship of the group*. By this phrase, he meant that religion contributes to the cohesion of the group and expresses its unity through shared norms and values, rituals enacting these norms and values, and consequences for heresy (such as ex-communication or even death). Rituals incorporate members into the group by reminding them of the meaning and obligations of being part of the group.

Thus, according to Durkheim, religion is symbolically and literally the worship of the group, because people experience the group to be a power above and beyond the individual. Religious beliefs are collective representations; that is, group-held beliefs expressing something vital about the group itself and reaffirming the group's shared meanings and core beliefs. Participation in religious worship can dissolve boundaries between people and unify them if only for a brief time during which their entire focus is beyond themselves, on a unified object of devotion.

It is vital for you to grasp what Durkheim is saying here, so we will consider an extended example. Think of your favorite musical group of all time. We will use the Beatles (because favorite groups change with the times, we use the most favorite, bestselling group of all time), but in the discussion that follows you should substitute your favorite.

You love to listen to the music of the Beatles. As you often say, it's less satisfying to listen to other music since you discovered the Beatles, because, although other music is good, the Beatles are so superior that they are almost otherworldly; their music is beyond the capabilities of mere mortals. (We exaggerate, of course, but this is what we often do with friends to make a point!) For years, you have listened to their music. You have memorized the words to dozens of their songs. You are struck by how creative their songs are, by how much originality they pack into a four-minute song. You are enamored by the cohesive genius of the "Fab Four." Truly, you think, their music was not only far ahead of its time, but it continues to be relevant so many decades later.

Then you hear news that is almost too good to be true. The remaining Beatles are going to reunite for a five-city U.S. tour, and one of those cities is yours. You call your close friends, who are your close friends in part because they also love the Beatles, and you tell them the news. After shouts of joy, you all agree that no matter what it takes, you are going to the concert. Tickets go on sale in three days, and you use the time until then to plot your strategy for getting the money that you will need and for getting online to order the tickets as soon as they are available. At 12:01 A.M. on Thursday night, with your friends by your side, you are online requesting four tickets (one each for you and your three friends). You are successful, and though the tickets cost you $500 apiece, you have no doubt that it will be more than worth it. You got great seats, and it is going to be a grand experience!

The two-month wait for the big day is the longest two months in the history of humanity. (OK, so we exaggerate yet again.) Days go by slowly, weeks drag on. But you are driven by the anticipation of the big night. You and your friends make plans for how you will get to the arena, what time you will leave, who is driving, and what you will wear.

Finally, the big day arrives. You don't sleep much the night before because you are too excited. The hours of the big day go by in a blur. You go to class, but your professor sounds like one of the adults in a Charlie Brown TV special, blah blah blah. You can't wait to get back home and get dressed for the big show. And finally, that time comes. You rush home, planning out exactly what you will do to be ready by 4 P.M., when your friends are due to arrive.

And arrive they do. In fact, since they are as excited as you, they actually are all at your place by 3:50 P.M. You all are smiling broadly, feeling a bit jumpy, and raring to go. You pack into the car, and head off to the restaurant. The food is good, the company even better. You laugh together, talking about what you will do if Paul McCartney happens to call you up on stage.

You are all glad when you have finished eating and can finally head to the arena. You have to pay $40 to park, but you don't even care. This is THE CONCERT, and mere money is not going to get in the way of your enjoyment. After parking, you walk the five blocks to the arena. Clearly, about 20,000 other fans wanted to get there early as well, because the parking lots are already overflowing, and you share the walk to the arena with the many thousands of other people going to the same place.

The presence of all of these other Beatles fans only increases your excitement. All the fans with their Beatles shirts and banners, some even sporting classic early 1960s Beatles haircuts. Into the arena you all flow, and wow, you see it, the stage where the Beatles will be tonight, after the warm-up band. Oh, warm-up bands, why do they bother, you came to see the Beatles!

The wait for the show to start is excruciating. You are so excited that you are beside yourself. The arena is loaded with the anticipation of the 23,000 people who are packed into it (the building only officially holds 19,000). Finally, a local radio DJ comes out on stage and says "Hello [your city name here]!" The arena erupts, for all of you know that this signifies the start of the show. After the DJ makes some introductory comments, he announces the warm-up band, and they are greeted with ear-splitting applause. They play seven songs. They are good, really good. You enjoy their music, but to be honest, you can't wait until they are done.

The warm-up band finishes. You are told that there will be a 20-minute intermission, and the house lights come up. Ugh, so close yet so far. You wait, and wait, and wait. Finally, the house lights flicker. A cheer rises up. Then the house lights go down; it is completely dark. The cheers grow louder, deeper, as if from the people's souls. From the darkness, a light show begins on stage, pulsating like your heart.

And then, after all the waiting, all the anticipation, and all the planning, there before your eyes appear the Beatles. They rise up in unison from under the stage, with Ringo Starr playing an opening drum beat to a familiar song, the others waving at you, yes, you could swear they are waving at you. The arena is beyond loud. Thunder is shaking the place. You are screaming as loud as you can, but you cannot even hear yourself. You don't care; this is unbelievable.

As the first song begins, the moment and all the anticipation catch up with you. You feel short of breath and weak in the knees, almost as if you are going to faint. Fortunately, you do not, and the music is in full force. There they are in front of you, so close you can almost touch them. Paul McCartney is singing now in that golden voice. That voice and that music, it is driving right down to your core. You have never quite felt this way before. The experience is almost mystical. After the first two songs, Paul McCartney finally talks, greeting all of you, telling you that they all intend to have an amazing time together. This is not just a concert, he says. We are here to change the world, and you are the world changers. Yes, yes, yes.

The concert is like a dream. You are so focused on the band, on the music, on the message, and on the sea of humanity all celebrating together. Ringo Starr later gives an impassioned talk about bringing the world together in unity. He says that you are part of the generation that will solve one of the world's greatest problems; he asks everyone who has a cell phone to hold it up, illuminated. Knowing that this moment was coming, all 23,000 people are ready. In unison, they wave their lighted cell phones, swaying gently together, back and forth. The Beatles are up onstage doing the same. Then they begin to sing one of their all-time classics, while all the people in the audience continue to sway with lighted cell phones held high. This moment is so amazing, your heart feels too big. Life's problems, at least for this moment in time, don't matter. You feel alive, wholly and completely. You feel an attachment to the other people in the arena that you cannot explain. This night is one that you will never forget.

What happened to you at this concert is what Durkheim says happens in religious worship. Even though at a concert you are with thousands of people you don't know, during that time you can feel as one, your individuality melted away as you surrender to the power of the group, all eyes and hearts fixed on the same object of devotion. If such social cohesion can happen at a concert, imagine the power that a religion can generate when it brings together people who may indeed know one another, when there are clear objects of devotion, when people gather to acknowledge and celebrate what they believe and who they are. The next time the Pope or the Dalai Lama takes a trip, watch the massive crowds, the throngs of humanity pressing to get a glimpse. It will make the Beatles reunion concert seem like mere child's play.

A few years ago, we interviewed several hundred Americans about their religious faith. We sat in their homes and asked them many questions, including, toward the end of the interview, "What if you were to just give up your faith, just chuck it and live without it?" People were dismayed by the question. They either could not imagine such a thing, or if they could, they thought it would make them despondent. One woman literally started crying at the thought. Why, we asked them, is the idea of living without faith so hard to imagine? The answer was that, to these people, their faiths were not just something they believed or did. Rather, religion was who they were (both their individual and social identity), it gave them purpose and meaning, and it united them with fellow believers. To "just chuck their faith" was like throwing away their lives.

So we see the power of religion for social cohesion. But this view assumes that, as in Sicily, nearly everyone in a community is of the same faith. In reality, large modern societies are highly diverse and include all types of religions and spiritualities, as well as believers, agnostics, and athe-ists. Take the United States, for example. Sure, there are lots of Christians, though they are divided among Roman Catholics, members of the Greek Orthodox church, and Protestants. But there are also followers of all the other world faiths. What is more, so many alternative spiritualist faiths—Rastafarianism, EST, the use of crystals—exist in the country that it is difficult even for scholars who are studying such phenomena full time to keep up. And an increasing percentage of Americans claim to be agnostic, atheist, or simply not to care about religion.

How can a nation be united amidst such diversity? Enter what scholars call Civil Religion. If you have never heard the term before, you might think that it means "polite religion." You are not that far off: Although the term *civil* refers to the public sphere of a nation, the religion that is developed for that level must be "polite," as we will see.

Scholars define Civil Religion as "any set of beliefs and rituals, related to the past, present, and/ or future of a people ('nation'), which are understood in some transcendental fashion" (Hammond 1974, 171). Civil Religion, like any religion, stirs a sense of awe and sentiment within its followers. All U.S. presidents refer to a generic God. (We don't know to what God they are referring specifically, but it is to a being or force spelled with a capital letter.) This God is thought to have special concern for the United States and is repeatedly asked to bless the nation. It is expected that God will want to do this, for the nation is thought to embody all that this God desires for humans: democracy, individual freedom and liberty, and the pursuit of happiness and economic gain.

Civil Religion in the United States has its objects of devotion, such as the flag (never let it touch the ground, never fly it upside down, put it at half-mast when tragedy strikes, fold it with military care if you are taking it down), the national anthem (put your hand on your heart, remove your hat, and focus on the flag while singing it), and the Constitution (revere this document as the Holy Book of Civil Religion, the final arbiter of Right and Wrong). It has its ordained theologians or religious scholars who decipher what the Holy Book is meant to say: judges, especially the Supreme Court. (They are almost supreme beings—the most learned among us of the Civil Religion; they are appointed for life, wear religious-style robes, are rarely seen except when they are hearing cases, and sit at the Civil Religion's version of the judgment seat.) The ultimate leader of Civil Religion is the elected president, who is charged with bringing us together under the power of this religion. The ultimate leader is both a prophet—challenging people to dream bigger and be better—and a priest—supporting people in times of trouble, encouraging them that God is on their side and will impart blessings as long as they stay true to the Civil Religion.

To see Civil Religion as it is enacted by its ultimate leader, the president, read the words of former president Barack Obama (2008) excerpted from his historic November 4, 2008, presidential election acceptance speech:

> [W]e have never been just a collection of individuals or a collection of Red States and Blue States, we are—and always will be—the United States of America. It's the answer that led [people] . . . to put their hands on the arc of history and bend it once more toward the hope of a better day. . . . [You proved that] a government of the people, by the people and for the people has not perished from this Earth. . . . [Yet] even as we celebrate tonight, we know the challenges that tomorrow will bring are the greatest of our lifetime. . . . The road ahead will be long. Our climb will be steep. We may not get there in one year or even one term, but America, I have never been more hopeful than I am tonight that we will get there. I promise you—we as a people will get there. . . . [We need] a new spirit of service, a new spirit of sacrifice. So let us summon a new spirit of patriotism, of service, of responsibility where each of us resolves to pitch in and work harder and look after not only ourselves, but each other. . . . In this country, we rise or fall as one nation, as one people . . . the true strength of our nation comes from . . . the enduring power of our ideals—democracy, liberty, opportunity, and unyielding hope. . . . Our union can be perfected. . . . This is our chance to answer that call. This is our moment. . . . [We] reaffirm that fundamental truth—that out of many, we are one. . . . [We] respond with that timeless creed that sums up the spirit of a people: Yes We Can. . . . God bless you, and may God bless the United States of America.

Notice that in his acceptance speech, President-elect Obama, like all presidents before him, speaks in lofty terms and frequently refers to ideals. He especially emphasizes that, although we are diverse, we are one people, united under the principles in which we all believe (the Civil Religion values). Empowered by our unity, we share a can-do spirit. Yes, we will face tough times (the prophetic voice), but we will emerge victorious because we are unified and we stand for what is good, true, and right (the priestly voice). And may America's God bless us, God's people and God's nation, as we go forth toward Nirvana ("Our union can be perfected").

Professor John Carlson notes that "Presidential inaugurations serve as the high holiday of our American civil religion" (2021). Analyzing the inauguration speech of Joe Biden, Carlson shows the strong use of civil religion that the new incoming high holy priest of the faith shares with the nation. Biden focuses on what unifies us (a must in the true practice of the civil religion), saying early on, "Today we celebrate the triumph not of a candidate, but of a cause, the cause of democracy," asking Americans, "What are the common objects we love, that define us as Americans? I think I know. Opportunity. Security. Liberty. Dignity. Respect. Honor. And yes, the truth." Biden goes on to say, "May this be the story that guides us. . . . The story that inspires us and the story that tells the ages yet to come that we answered the call of history" (www.nbcnews.com/think/opinion/biden-s-inaugural-speech-called-americans-embrace-civil-religion-what-ncna1255084). Over and over again in his speech, President Biden calls for and stresses unity, unity even if we disagree. And as all U.S Presidents do, he ends his speech: "May God bless America."

Thus, religion serves a powerful social cohesion function. When almost everyone belongs to the same religion, as in Sicily, religion is a social glue that is infused in the totality of life. When there is religious diversity within a nation, the nation often creates a new religion that we have called Civil Religion to broadly incorporate all persons, regardless of their faith tradition.

If we think of religion—even Civil Religion—as a cultural resource that we selectively use and appropriate, then we see how it can also lead to conflict with others who have a different interpretation of the same faith, a different faith, or no faith at all. Just as important, the more socially cohesive a religious group is, the more vigorously that group will defend its beliefs, practices, and ways of life against threats. Religious conflict, then, can arise out of religious cohesion. We now turn to the topic of this conflict.

Religion and Social Conflict

In his book *Religion and Social Conflict*, Lee (1964, 3) opens with a now-classic statement: "The society without conflict is a dead society. Hence the most peaceful place in the world, in terms of the absence of conflict, is a graveyard."

Outside a graveyard, humans have conflict, including religious conflict. It is our task as sociologists to better understand where, when, and why conflict occurs, and we seek to do that briefly in this section. But before we do, take a moment to identify three religious conflicts that you know of (not the personal disagreements you identified early in the chapter, but religious conflicts involving groups of people). If you cannot think of any off the top of your head, search the Internet, using keywords such as "religious conflict." Write three conflicts in the accompanying box.

Box 4.2 Religious Conflicts

1.
2.
3.

To help us understand these conflicts, let's draw on a core tool of sociologists, the sociological imagination (Mills 1959). The sociological imagination distinguishes between personal troubles (my friend and I had a disagreement over religion) and social problems (people from religious group A and religious group B often kill each other). Personal troubles involve a few isolated individuals and probably can be explained simply by the personalities of the people involved, but when whole groups clash, looking at the characteristics of individuals will not explain the conflict.

The sociological imagination understands that all individuals are embedded within groups, which are embedded in larger societies, which are themselves embedded in a specific time in history. The Hatfields and McCoys feuded not just because of what was occurring between them at the time, but because it had been their long history to do so. Part of the identity of each of these clans was to dislike the other. If either group stopped the feud, it would have risked a complete loss of identity.

As you review the three religious conflicts that you identified, can you use the sociological imagination to explain why the conflicts occur? That is, explain the conflicts without resorting to explanations involving the characteristics of individuals. What do you come up with?

Let us first classify the types of religious conflict and then examine why each may occur:

1 Conflict between religious groups (between, say, Buddhists and Zoroastrians)
2 Conflict within a religious group (Catholicism in Sicily, for example)
3 Conflict between a religious group and the larger society (Mormons once believed that it is permissible for a man to marry more than one woman, but the larger society did not)
4 Conflict between religious group and a nonreligious group or sector (Fundamentalist Christians object to the teaching of evolution in public schools, while public schools attempt to avoid religious particularism)

If you examine the three specific religious conflicts that you wrote down, they should fit into at least one of the preceding four categories. (If they don't, you have come up with a new category of conflict!)

To consider why religious conflict occurs, let's first think about why conflict in general occurs. On the surface, it seems simple: People and groups conflict because they disagree. Fair enough. But why do they disagree? Because they don't see eye to eye, you might say, or because they have different perspectives, or because one group is trampling on another group. OK, we grant you that. But we really aren't getting very far here. It is sort of like telling someone you are from Cokato, Minnesota. "Where is that?" the person will ask, to which you reply, "Six miles east of Dassel." "Where is Dassel?" to which you reply, "Six miles west of Cokato." All true, but not that helpful.

Let's go back to our original explanation for conflict: "People and groups disagree." But we know for sure that not all disagreements lead to conflict. We may disagree with another person's religion, or with all religion, but that does not mean that we necessarily engage in conflict with those who follow other religions. Religious conflict, then, can be better defined as *groups or individuals acting against resistors, in an attempt either to preserve or to change religious beliefs, rituals, or ways of being.* (See, for example, Marty 1964; Weber 1947.) Notice that according to this definition, action is required, and that "it takes at least two to tango." If the other group simply gives in or doesn't care, there is no conflict. Also, one set of actors is seeking a goal that is in opposition to the goal of another set of actors, and they care enough to engage in conflict.

There are two additional aspects of religious conflict. The first aspect, noted earlier, is that the social cohesion of religion on one side of the coin implies social conflict on the other side of the coin. Connected to, and elaborating on, this "two-sides-of-the-same-coin" concept is that conflict has several functions for social and religious life. At least as far back as the early 1900s, scholars have noted that conflict can have positive aspects. But it was Lewis Coser's 1956 book, *The Functions of*

Social Conflict, that developed this idea fully. According to his work—and subsequently supported by hundreds of studies—conflict between groups serves several positive functions:

1 *Clarifies boundaries*. A Hindu fully understands what it means to be Hindu only by knowing what a Hindu is not (the boundaries). This understanding is best achieved through conflict with non-Hindus, because it forces Hindus to clearly define who is in the group and who is not.
2 *Solidifies identity*. Conflict helps to firm and deepen group identity. If groups are going to be challenged or to challenge another group, they will continue to do so only insofar as they understand who they are in relation to other groups. Thus, if Hindus are conflicting with Sikhs, not only are the boundaries between the two religious groups sharpened, but both groups come to see their individual and group identities as being intimately tied, respectively, to being Hindu and being Sikh.
3 *Increases social cohesion*. We have come full circle, or in keeping with our metaphor, we have turned the coin again. Cohesion fuels conflict, and conflict fuels cohesion. You may fight with your sibling and berate each other mercilessly, but let some outsider attack your sibling, and bam: You rise to your sibling's defense. External conflict increases internal cohesion.
4 *Strengthens ideological solidarity and participation*. This is a fancy way of saying that conflict with outside groups also means that the members of a religious group come to think more alike. External conflict leads them to gain a greater clarity about what they believe and value, and again, these values become clear markers of being a member of the group. Another important benefit of conflict for a group is that it increases participation as people rise to the defense of their group.
5 *Augments resource mobilization*. Groups in conflict can do more than groups that are not in conflict. They get more donations of money or goods, members devote more time to the group, and members are more willing to sacrifice for the good of the group and to overcome the enemy.

In terms of social cohesion within religious groups, then, it is in a group's best interest to conflict with outside groups, though that is not nice to say in polite company. Accordingly, it is unfortunate, but asking people to love the whole world and all that is in it just doesn't work very well for building group strength. Of course, it could work if the world was engaged in conflict with aliens from another planet or some other type of outsider group.

Perhaps these benefits of conflict are why if we wish to maintain social cohesion and group strength, we can never be without conflict of some sort. As Emile Durkheim wrote in a famous example, imagine an isolated monastery full of completely devoted monks who are solidly committed to their faith, each following the hundreds of rules set forth by the abbot, each fully devoted to their object of worship. What seems to outsiders like the slightest deviation—hair a half-inch too long, praying for 3 hours and 58 minutes instead of the expected 4 hours, wearing a garment that is light-brown instead of medium-brown—would be met with great moral outrage and considered to be a clear violation of the group's way of life. And if some monks decided not to correct their moral violation, but instead began to claim that it is OK to wear light-brown garments, internal conflict would result. If it continued long enough with no clear resolution (neither side gives in nor is able to impose its will on the other group), the groups would split into two monasteries. In short, if there is no conflict from without, conflict from within will arise. (Think of those Catholics in Sicily who tolerate the Mafia version of the religion and those who oppose them.)

Internal religious conflict can arise over any number of issues: acceptable musical styles, traditional versus modern worship, clergy/laity battles, male versus female rights and behaviors, generational differences, the number of parking spaces that are available, whether men must grow beards to worship properly, or how short women's skirts may be. The list goes on, but you get the point.

If conflict has so many positive functions and is almost inevitable, why don't we see even more religious conflict, especially violent religious conflict? Here are a few reasons. First, as Wuthnow (2005) finds in his book on the challenges of religious diversity, people actually know very little about religions other than their own. They know that religion X is different from their own religion Y, but they don't really know much detail beyond that. Insofar as they do not know details, they do not feel threatened, and their religious understandings are not challenged. To put it bluntly, often there is no religious conflict because people don't much care what others are doing or believing. They are busy enough dealing with the conflicts within their own group.

Religious conflict *does* happen when one religious group's way of life impinges upon another group, be it religious or not. But full-scale violence is usually avoided because there are typically other avenues for dealing with the conflict and because the continued existence of the conflict actually benefits the group. (See the five positive functions of conflict listed previously.)

Sociologically, there is another reason that extreme levels of conflict between religious groups are limited. In most societies, social diversity is a reality. People occupy multiple roles, move in several spheres (religious, work, neighborhood, school, etc.), and maintain social relationships across several groups. Suppose that a religious group is in conflict with public schools, claiming that the schools teach secular humanism and are anti-God. A number of public-school teachers are probably members of the religious group. It will be hard for these members to engage in an extreme level of conflict both with their employer and their peers. They will seek to moderate the conflict.

Hence, the more groups are cross-cut with the same members, typically the less likely it is that severe conflict will occur (Blau and Schwartz 1984; McGuire 1997). The biggest trouble—conflict that results in bloodshed—tends to occur when there are concentrations of roles. When members of religious group A all tend to be lower-class, to share the same ethnicity, and to live on the west side, while members of religious group B tend to be upper-class, to share a different ethnicity than members of religious group A, and to live on the east side of town, there may be tremendous religious conflicts. In fact, any sort of conflict between groups can be at the same time a religious conflict, a class conflict, an ethnic conflict, and a regional conflict. Because religion may be a sacred marker that accentuates and stands for all the divisions between groups (Hanf 1994, 202), many conflicts labeled as religious conflicts may not really be about religion.

To learn more about such occurrences, research the Internet and read about the conflict that existed among Bosnians, Croats, and Serbs (or the conflicts in Rwanda or the Sudan). The ostensibly religious conflict among the Bosnians, Croats, and Serbs led to the deaths of thousands, the slaughter of families, and the disruption of life for many years. But were differences in religion really the basis of the conflict? You might also investigate the centuries-long conflict between Protestants and Catholics in Northern Ireland. The conflict is much more than a religious conflict.

Can't We all Just Get Along?

Can't we all just get along? No, we cannot, and yes, we can. The irony is that both statements are true. Religious groups need social cohesion to survive and thrive, but strongly cohesive groups often conflict with other groups. And the conflict actually has positive effects for the internal cohesion of the group.

Civil Religion is the attempt on the part of diverse nations to create a religion that overarches the particular views of the religious *and* the nonreligious people in the country. Such a religion is necessary, it seems, to take individuals beyond mere loyalty to the specific groups to which they belong and to create cohesion and commitment to the nation. But the Civil Religion that strengthens internal national unity becomes, at the same time, a basis for conflict with other nations. Whether we talk about it explicitly or not, America's Civil Religion distinguishes the United States, setting us up as different from other nations in our relationship to a sacred order. Our Civil

Religion establishes group boundaries and feeds conflicts with those viewed as outsiders, including other nations.

Some religious groups, admirably, attempt to be nonexclusive and open to all, lowering their boundaries, regardless of their religious beliefs. This doesn't work so well, because it makes it difficult to have clear boundaries, clear identities, and strong membership commitment, unless, of course, the group is in conflict with other groups, such as religious groups, which think that the first group's approach is heresy or not religion at all. In such a case, being "open and accepting" becomes an identity, boundaries are drawn to delineate the group from the intolerant groups, and membership commitment rises in defense of their views.

But when the boundaries are drawn, this open and accepting group is no longer open and accepting of all people, just other people who share its views. Such is the irony of social and religious life. In later chapters we will use some of this knowledge to understand fundamentalist movements and even religious violence. It will become clearer how the tension between religious cohesion and religious conflict plays out: Yes, we can all get along, and no, we cannot.

Suggested Reading

Coser, Lewis. A. 1956. *The Functions of Social Conflict*. Glencoe, IL: The Free Press.

Durkheim, Emile. [1915] 1965. *Elementary Forms of Religious Life*. Translated by J. W. Swain. New York: Free Press.

Wuthnow, Robert. 2005. *America and the Challenges of Religious Diversity*. Princeton, NJ: Princeton University Press.

5 News Flash

God's Not Dead (and Neither is the Goddess!)

1 Have contemporary societies become more secular over time?
2 What does religious vitality mean? What does a religiously vital society look like?
3 Is it possible for individuals to be more religious while their societies become less so?

Once upon a time, many say, society was *religious*. Now, unfortunately some would say, it is *secular*. Once religion informed and shaped all parts of our lives—education, family life, work, politics, and health care were all infused with religious meaning. Now, the story goes, religion is confined to Sunday mornings, and we largely forget our religion the rest of the week. Purported evidence of this decline abounds. More people used to attend religious services regularly. More people used to believe in and practice their particular religion's teaching every day. And, most importantly, religious organizations and leaders enjoyed a higher level of respect and authority within communities. In short, the past, it is assumed, was a "Golden Age of Faith."

And now, just look around and see what is happening. In many sectors, attendance at religious services is declining. Individuals feel less bound by a particular religion's strictures. Instead they assemble their own mix of beliefs and practices to suit themselves and their lifestyles, like "Sheila," whom we introduced in Chapter 2 (from Bellah et al. 1985). Others flat-out reject all religion and sometimes proudly announce their atheism at family gatherings or all over social media. Religious leaders are increasingly viewed with suspicion and ridicule because, while they require their members to obey their teachings and give money to support their enterprises, they themselves are found guilty of abuse and immoral conduct. Perhaps worst of all is the attitude, shared by many, that religious groups and their leaders are out of touch with contemporary life. For the religiously inclined, the sense that the world is changing and leaving religion behind causes great concern: Will religion lose its social significance and eventually disappear, or should the faithful be working to try to re-establish religion's prominence in social life?

Sociologists, too, wonder about the future of religion. For years, they have observed a shift away from what once seemed like a more religiously dominated world. For example, public education in the U.S. once explicitly taught a Protestant morality, but now religion instruction has been removed from public schools. Hospitals, once run as religious charities, are increasingly run as for-profit organizations with no religious ties whatsoever. And, as you may have noticed, many people get testy when religion comes up in political debates, as if faith had no role to play in support of or opposition to government policies, while others seem to be working to ensconce their religious beliefs and social teachings into law.

To account for the changing role of religion in society, and especially for its apparent decline in importance, sociologists developed *secularization theory*. Secularization theory links the decline of religion with the rise of some other important qualities of modern societies, especially rationality, bureaucratization, and impersonality. These qualities are byproducts of some big social changes, including the development and expansion of a capitalist economic structure, the rise of democratic

DOI: 10.4324/9781003182108-7

political systems run by bureaucrats, and the dominance of a cultural view of the world that is based in scientific rationality. The consequences for religion have been significant. Sociologist Max Weber argued that the modern world has been "disenchanted": The magic and the mystery once present in everyday life have vanished, replaced by a cold-hearted rationality that emphasizes efficiency and calculability. Religion, once the glue that held people's worlds together and a force that exerted authority over almost all aspects of people's lives, fell by the wayside. Or so the story goes.

But let's not be too hasty! Over the last two decades, sociologists of religion have also observed amazing changes in the religious sphere and in the vitality of it. They point out that despite the fact that the United States is among the most economically, technologically, and militarily advanced nations on earth, it also has among the highest reported levels of belief in God. Pretty clearly, the forces of capitalism, bureaucratization, and science did not pass us by, but somehow religion survives. Some denominations are seeing more success than others, however. While more liberal denominations have noted declines in membership, conservative Christian churches are seeing surges in attendance. As we already observed in Chapter 1, the market for religious products is huge and shows no signs of slowing down; it's a multibillion-dollar-a-year industry producing books, films, clothing, jewelry, diets, holistic healing techniques, and many, many other goods and services, all consumed by a public that is seemingly ravenous for all things religious and spiritual.

Worldwide, religion remains a strong force despite the spread of technological advances and economic development. In the Southern Hemisphere, Christianity and Islam together continue to attract millions of followers, even as those societies undergo dramatic economic change. Moreover, around the world, the rise of fundamentalism attracts millions of people to strict and decidedly antimodern religious beliefs and practices. Recall, for example, the suicide bombings and terrorist attacks around the world that are committed by religiously motivated extremists of many faiths. Religious teachings continue to be used to criminalize LGBTQ people, to limit roles for women in the public sphere, and to maintain traditional culture against secular influences seen to emanate from Europe and the U.S. Is religion on the decline? Hardly—indeed, the situation seems to be quite the reverse.

The question of whether contemporary societies have become more secular is thus a controversial one and answering it really depends on how we define *secularization* and how we see it working. But the question's flip side—explaining cases of strong religious vitality—cannot be overlooked, either. It's a conundrum only if you think, as some sociologists do, that religious vitality is the *opposite* of secularization. Here we argue, in line with other sociologists, that, in many of their forms, secularization and religious vitality are related, not in opposing, but in complementary ways. Finally, toward the end of this chapter, we will bring both sides of these debates together and examine the paradox of living in an increasingly secular, yet religiously vital and vibrant world.

Will the Real Secularization Theory Please Stand Up?

Secularization theory has been a central way of thinking about what has happened and is still happening to religion in our world ever since Max Weber first posited his theory about the emergence of the industrial society. Modernity was spurred on by the development of a capitalist economy that was founded on making as much money as possible, as well as the expansion of state structures that were based on legal and impersonal regulations and relationships. Together, these twin institutions, capitalism and the bureaucratic state, played key roles in making society less clearly "religious." Weber and others after him argued that religion would be increasingly marginalized as society became more dominated by scientific thinking and discovery. This theory resulted from a cost-benefit mentality rooted in capitalism and the modern state, which controlled all other social institutions (the economy, health care, education, media, and even family) through a complex bureaucratic structure of regulations intended to ensure the efficient operation of society as a whole.

In short, religion was no longer the institution controlling education, health care, or much else outside of the religious sphere. Religious explanations for sickness, a variety of natural phenomena, and even the origins of the universe gave way to scientific theories that were based on scientific evidence collected through research. After stripping away these religious explanations and meanings from everyday life, we are left with a world that is rational, impersonal, and bureaucratic, lacking the "enchantments" and mysteries of life in the premodern world. The bottom line is that Weber and other social theorists simply assumed that religion and modernity were antithetical; logically, then, as the forces of modernization increase, religion's power and influence must decrease.

Since Weber's time, other social scientists took for granted that religion was in decline. Some went so far as to suggest that it would disappear completely. Peter Berger put the matter quite succinctly:

> As there is a secularization of society and culture, so is there a secularization of consciousness. Put simply, this means that the modern West has produced an increasing number of individuals who look upon the world and their own lives without the benefit of religious interpretations.
>
> (1967, 107–108)

In other words, fewer and fewer of us think about our lives, friends, food, work, and other aspects of our existence as needing—much less *having*—religious significance. So, there's a vicious circle here. Religions lose their influence in society, causing fewer people to think and act religiously, which in turn further undermines religion's influence, until it basically disappears (Stark 1999; Tschannen 1991).

Then again, maybe these experts were all a little premature in predicting religion's disappearance. Over the last two decades, in the face of conservative religious resurgences worldwide, as well as the continuation of traditional religious beliefs and practices and the explosion of "holistic and alternative spiritualities," sociologists of religion have rejected this simplistic version of secularization. Nevertheless, an ongoing debate has raged, largely unchanged since we published the first edition of this book, about whether, given a rejection of secularization as the "death of religion," secularization theory as a whole has outlived its relevance as a way to understand religion today.

On one side of the debate loom the challengers and their case studies: Jeffrey Hadden, Rodney Stark, Roger Finke, William Bainbridge, and even secularization's former advocate, Peter Berger, among others. All these experts contend that religion is alive and well and will continue to be so, given the extensive data that show continued commitment to beliefs in God, adherence to the Bible, the practice of prayer, and so on. The United States remains the prime example used to counter secularization theory (Voas and Chaves 2016). Stark (1999) hoped to put the final nail in the intellectual coffin of secularization with the declaration that it should "Rest In Peace" and that it is high time we, as students of religion, get over it and move on.

On the other side of the debate are those who continue to want to rescue secularization theory from its detractors: Steve Bruce, Karel Dobbelaere, Mark Chaves, Peter Beyer, David Yamane, David Voas, and a host of others who do research on secularization and religious vitality with data from North America and Western and Eastern Europe. Unlike earlier theorists, they don't believe that religion will go away completely. Instead, they focus on the declining power of religion at a societal level. They share an understanding of secularization as fundamentally a *descriptive* term that characterizes the forces at work shaping entire societies and the world as a whole, rather than a predictive one that hypothesizes some inevitable future for the religious beliefs and behaviors of individuals.

Dobbelaere (1999) builds his argument on an understanding that in modern society, institutions are differentiated according to the functions they serve for society as a whole. This idea has been long connected to the work of Emile Durkheim, about whom you read in Chapter 1. As modern societies develop, their institutions become ever more specialized and develop their own unique cultures, with their own norms, values, language, and mechanisms for operating (Luhman 1989). Societies' institutions become more independent from one another while simultaneously remaining integrated through the operations, regulations, and policies of the bureaucratic state.

What does all of this have to do with religion? Dobbelaere argues that this process is precisely the way that secularization takes place. Secularization, according to Dobbelaere (1999, 232), is "a process by which the overarching and transcendent religious system of old is being reduced in a modern functionally differentiated society to a subsystem alongside other subsystems, losing in this process its overarching claims over the other subsystems." In other words, society develops a separate "religious" arena. As its own subsystem within society, religion freely develops its own unique forms of organizations, values, and ways of doing things. This is just another way to say that it develops its own *culture* and *subcultures*. But the cultural forms of religion are distinct from those of the economy, the state, science, law, and other institutions. Consequently, what may hold true and make sense in the religious sphere in terms of values, norms, and language does not necessarily hold true or make sense in the economic realm, in science, in education, or in medicine.

For instance, many religions value charity and encourage their followers to give selflessly of their resources. Yet if you, as a CEO, walked into a meeting of shareholders of a transnational corporation and suggested increasing the wages and benefits of employees worldwide because your religious faith requires economic justice for workers, or if you announced that you planned to accept a smaller profit margin for the company for the same reason, we may safely assume that you would be laughed out of the room and quickly become unemployed as a result. Similarly, when the owners of companies like Hobby Lobby and Chick-Fil-A took explicit stands to deny employee access to contraceptives though their health insurance or supported organizations that opposed LGBTQ rights based on their religious convictions, they should not have been surprised at negative public reactions and calls for boycotts of these businesses from those who supported these things.

The impact of this secularization process on religion is tremendous. Once religion has been separated into its own sphere of influence, separate from the state, which now governs and represents many different social groups, then religious rules—even the ones that at one time were widely accepted as universal—can no longer be used to regulate behavior for an entire society. So, for example, while one person's religious tradition may forbid marriage between individuals of the same sex, the use of birth control, the drinking of alcohol, or the eating of pork, such regulations can be applicable only *within* the religious group; prohibitions against these behaviors cannot be made into law if the larger society includes many people who view such behaviors as acceptable. Even in contemporary Middle Eastern societies where civil law is based on Muslim religious law, only selective religious laws are enforced by the governments. Highly religious Muslim states—despite the prohibition on these behaviors in Islam—tend to leave economic behavior (like accumulating profit, earning money from interest, and allowing wealth to concentrate in the hands of a few) relatively unregulated, but may highly regulate gender roles and sexual behavior. Why does this happen? It's because these nations are all dependent for their economic well-being on continued participation in the capitalist world economy, an economy that is based on the accumulation of profit, the earning of interest, and the concentration of wealth, all of which stem from decidedly secular motives.

Chaves (1994) and Yamane (1997) simplify Dobbelaere's ideas by arguing that secularization is best understood in terms of the declining scope of religious authority, shrinking to cover only matters of faith rather than also covering economics, education, politics, or health care. Chaves and others perform a threefold test for the decline of religious authority, measuring its decline at the societal, organizational, and individual levels. (See also Dobbelaere 1999.)

At the *societal* level, secularization refers to a general decline in religious authority over other social institutions and an increasing indifference by governments to favoring religion generally

(Brown 2019). Empirically, cross-national data support the idea that political secularization especially has been increasing over the last century. Governments increasingly are adopting a neutral or impartial position regarding religious groups. This doesn't mean that religious groups can't still attempt to influence governments to enact laws and policies aligned with religious ideas, but overall instances where this happens do not fundamentally change the secularizing trends. As noted previously, societal or political secularization underscores that religion is becoming one institution among many and no longer maintains any privileged place over other institutions, especially government, in its values, norms, or directives for how best to create the "good" society.

Think about what this means for religion in practical terms. In the spring of 2008, Pope Benedict XVI, the former head of the Roman Catholic Church, set out new doctrines that expanded the scope of what the Church considered to be mortal sins, meaning that they were serious violations of the Ten Commandments and other central Biblical teachings. Among the new sins added to the list of mortal sins were ruining the environment, carrying out morally debatable scientific experiments, allowing genetic manipulations that alter DNA or compromise embryos, and perpetrating injustices that cause poverty or the excessive accumulation of wealth in the hands of a few. These became official doctrines of the Church, violations of which are supposedly punished by consignment to hell. Yet despite this new exposition of religious authority over the economy and the scientific world, the practical consequences of the doctrines are nonexistent for anyone who is not Catholic. The Pope has no real authority to regulate the operations of capitalism or the scientific community. He can speak and make pronouncements, but whether individual businesspeople or scientists pay attention is completely up to them.

Think about marriage for a minute. Many of us imagine a classic marriage ceremony as a religious event because it is held in a church or synagogue and presided over by clergy. However, in Christian terms, such a ceremony is more properly called "matrimony," and some denominations consider it to be a sacrament. Marriage, however, is a civil event based on legal definitions. It occurs not when vows are made in church or blessings are pronounced, but when the legal document is signed by two individuals in the presence of witnesses. This is why every minister in the United States, regardless of religion, at the end of the ceremony says, "In the name of the state of . . . , I now pronounce you husband and wife." Notice that it is not the religious authority of the minister that creates the marriage, but the intention of the two people involved and their legal act according to the laws of the particular state. In many European nations, all couples get married in a registry office and then some go on to have a separate religious ceremony to bless the union at another time. Is this societal-level secularization? Most definitely, it is. Not only does the example of *matrimony* versus *marriage* illustrate a real differentiation between the powers of religion and those of the government, but it also illustrates that it is the state that has the greater authority. Any couple married by the state is legally married; however, a couple that participates only in a religious ceremony without fulfilling state requirements would not be considered legally married.

At the *organizational* level, secularization occurs at the level of religious organizations themselves (Chaves 1994; Dobbelaere 1999; Luckmann 1967). In this sense, secularization refers to internal changes occurring within religious groups that change how they look and how they operate, changes that make them look and act more like other organizations. Schools, churches, social service agencies, and hospitals all look and act like businesses. Their internal structures and cultures begin to resemble one another. Karl Marx made this argument years ago, of course, when he argued that this homogenization was due to the spread of capitalism, which eventually forces all other institutions into a dependent relationship with it, even so far as to impart its language, norms, and values to them.

But what does this mean in religious terms and how is it related to secularization? The increasing diversity of modern society creates religious markets in which religious groups compete for members. Such competition means that the groups need to appeal to religious consumers, who now have many different options to meet their spiritual needs, much in the same way that competing businesses all want to attract your attention and dollars by appealing to your needs and wants. This pressure leads to a change in religious groups' messages, which suggests that each group's members are "customers" who must be pleased and placated rather than expected to obey the authority of the minister or the religious tradition itself. As we saw when we discussed the phenomenon of megachurches, these internal changes mean that attending religious services begins to have a lot in common with activities like going to the mall, enjoying a grande latte at a Starbucks, or attending a rock concert.

Further evidence of internal secularization lies in the fact that religious leadership is increasingly left to lay people rather than clergy. A democratization of religious authority has emerged in Roman Catholic congregations, driven in part by the decreasing numbers of clergy. This is occurring in some Establishment Protestant and Evangelical congregations, too. Ministers now ask people to call them Bob or Jane, instead of Reverend or Pastor or Father, and to "like" them on social media, as a way to make people feel more comfortable by assuring them that religious leaders are "just people" like them. Likewise, buzzwords from the business world become more common among religious groups that try to find "best practices," to "assess outcomes" of programs and ministries, and to exercise "due diligence" in hiring and appointing new leaders. Outside programs and charities are expected to provide accountability by reporting back to congregations that support them. Any new project requires conversations with "stakeholders." And so it goes. The language and culture of the business world, including concepts such as return on investments, investor confidence, outcomes assessment, and customer/client satisfaction, become the cultural forms of religious organizations, even those which were founded on the principles of giving without expecting anything in return, following the golden rule, and caring selflessly for the poor, widows, and orphans.

Finally, at the *individual* level, as we begin to see from these examples, secularization can have an impact on the authority of religious leaders, doctrines, and traditions, affecting what individuals actually believe and what they do when it comes to their individual faith. This is the most problematic dimension to secularization for the sociologists who reject this theory. These scholars counter that if *society* is becoming more secular, then there must be an increase in the numbers of people who call themselves atheists accompanied by an overall decline in religious belief and practice among *individuals*, an expectation that seems to fly in the face of evidence, at least in countries like the United States, that individuals still report high levels of religious belief and practice . . . or does it (Stark 2015; Voas and Chaves 2016)?

In the last ten years, and in the wake of the COVID pandemic, more research suggests a growing indifference to religious belief and practice at the level of individuals, though not necessarily an increase in atheists, supporting the argument that yes, individuals in Western societies are more secular (Kasselstrand 2019). Longitudinal data increasingly show a decline in American religiosity measured in terms of such things as belief in God, church attendance, and the importance of religion to one's life (Voas and Chaves 2016). As we discussed earlier, evidence has shown clear religious identity and affiliation continues to give way to the growth of religious Nones, and growing numbers of young people do not use religion to provide meaning to their lives (Hout and Fischer 2014; Swenson 2014).

These trends in turn are yielding ever greater divides in values and personal religiosity between the religious and the non-religious (Wilkins-LaFlamme 2017). Furthering divisions between the religious and the non-religious are also demographic shifts evident in Europe and in the United States between older generations and the young. Voas and Chaves (2016) show clear declining trends in various measures of religiosity among younger cohorts. What they suggest, supported by Bruce (2016), is that the basis of religious decline at the individual level is spurred by the fact that each successive generation is less exposed to religion and therefore more indifferent to it than the one before. A recent Gallup poll report confirms this pattern among Americans, fewer of whom report holding a religious identity or attend religious services (Jones 2021). Over time, due to this generational shift, one can expect older, more religious cohorts to die, leaving fewer religious cohorts behind them. As you can see in Figure 5.1, the overall trend demonstrates such a decline.

Even among the religious, belief and practice can exist quite apart, and in many different forms, from the ones that are considered "orthodox" by religious leaders and organizations, suggesting we should think about individual-level secularization as more than just an all-or-nothing game. Survey data suggest that there are wide gaps between the official teachings of religious groups and the day-to-day attitudes and behaviors of their members. Think about the following examples: "My priest and church doctrine forbid me as a good Roman Catholic from using various forms of birth control, yet I still use them." Or this:

> "I believe in God, yet can be quite happy thinking about God in the form of Jesus, Allah, Jehovah, Krishna, or even as the Goddess on occasion, all the while happily attending my own traditional Protestant church, which rejects the idea that God is reflected in any form other than Jesus Christ."

As in the past, believers today mix and match their religious symbols and images in as many ways as they wish. Linda Woodhead has argued that these shifts are especially evident in the way that women in the United States and Europe increasingly are disaffected from religious traditions that do not support them in their contemporary roles as professionals and do not help them balance their work and home lives, leaving them to move into new forms of spirituality that will help them cope with these experiences (Sointu and Woodhead 2008; Woodhead 2008). We'll revisit this situation in Chapter 8.

Over time, the religious marketplace has become one in which individuals, rather than clergy, official doctrine, or traditions, set the terms of beliefs and practices. Phillips (2004, 149) points to these shifts as clear consequences of secularization in spite of the development of an active and competitive religious marketplace: "Excommunications no longer incur public stigma. Defectors and apostates can't be fined, flogged, or banished. In this setting, churches only exert influence over those who freely offer their allegiance."

In any case, it is important to understand that there is a great deal of variation in the ways that secularization unfolds, if it in fact does so, in local communities, nations, and regions of the world. Even though some people take clear sides in the secularization debate, nothing about these processes is simple or straightforward. As Chaves (1994, 752) notes, "secularization occurs, or not, as the result of social and political conflicts between those social actors who would enhance or

	1998–2000	2008–2010	2018–2020	Change since 1998–2000
	%	%	%	pct. pts.
Traditionalists (born before 1946)	77	73	66	−11
Baby boomers (born 1946–1964)	67	63	58	−9
Generation X (born 1965–1980)	62	57	50	−12
Millennials (born 1981–1996)	n/a	51	36	n/a

Figure 5.1 Changes in Church Membership by Generation, Over Time

Source: Gallup Poll (2001).

Note: Given that Gallup's polls are based on the 18+ U.S. adult population, the 1980–2000 period would have included only a small proportion of the millennial generation, and the 2018–2020 period includes only a small proportion of Generation Z (born after 1996).

maintain religion's social significance and those who would reduce it." What is significant about Chaves' point is that, in good sociological fashion, the outcome of any social process, including that of secularization, is never fixed or inevitable. Real people, acting in concrete times and places, make real differences in how these processes play out. In this sense, even as some aspects of our world are becoming more secular, religious groups and individuals remain vital forces in it.

Religious Vitality in the United States and Abroad

So far, our discussion seems to support one side of the secularization debate, leading us to agree with secularization proponents. But while structural changes in the world continue to affect religious authority, as this chapter's title suggests, neither God nor the Goddess—whether new or old, singular or multiple—is dead. Religious belief, practice, and experience remain an important presence in the lives of much of the world's population and in the world's geopolitical order. Sociologists use the concept of *religious vitality* to describe the level of religious activity in a community, nation, or region of the world. In much of the work done in this field, religious vitality and secularization are pitted as opposing sets of concepts. However, we will argue that these terms are describing sometimes related, but separate, phenomena. Now that we know something about the effects of secularization on religion, what exactly does a religiously vital society look like, what forces drive this vitality, and how does religious vitality vary around the world?

Religious vitality has been examined by researchers using a wide variety of quantitative, statistical measures. Typically, questions about people's beliefs, sense of belonging, and religious and spiritual practice, and the role of religion in the public arena, have all been used to define vitality. Let's look again at data from the Pew study of religion in the United States. This recent survey of 35,000 Americans reveals that there is an active religious market with several hundred different Christian denominations, as we discussed in Chapter 2. In this market, we see evidence of people switching their membership among religious groups over their lives. The Pew Research Center (2015c) found that 34% of respondents had left the religious tradition in which they were raised for either another tradition or none at all, a six percent increase since 2007. The study report notes that switching to become religiously unaffiliated, one of the religious "Nones," accounts for the growth of this group.

> Nearly one-in-five American adults (18%) were raised in a religion and are now unaffiliated, compared with just 4% who have moved in the other direction. In other words, for every person who has left the unaffiliated and now identifies with a religious group more than four people have joined the ranks of the religious "Nones."
>
> (Pew Research Center 2015c, 34)

Today, overall, 76% (down from 84% in 2010) of Americans belong to some religious faith tradition, out of which 70.4% belong to Christian traditions (Jones 2021; Pew Research Center 2015c). Compare these statistics with those describing religiosity in a country like Great Britain, where church membership has dropped to 7% of the population, or France, where only 5% of the population are practicing Catholics (Swenson 2014, 197)! Despite declining numbers, the U.S. population maintains a higher level of religiously affiliated people than many other nations, and worldwide, numbers of Christians and Muslims will continue to grow (see Table 5.1).

Vitality is about more than affiliation and membership, both of which can disguise the decidedly nonreligious lives of those who belong to religious groups in name only. Let's consider what people actually do and what they believe. While there are many measures of religious belief and practice that we could examine, let us for the moment consider some key questions that are often asked on surveys about religion, to measure church attendance, prayer, belief in God, and belief in an afterlife. According to the Pew Research Center (2015d), approximately 50% of Americans report

Table 5.1   Size and Projected Growth of Major Religious Groups, 2015 2060

	Projected 2015 population	% of world population in 2015	Projected 2060 population	% of world population in 2060	Population growth 2015–2060
Christians	2,276,250,000	31.2	3,054,460,000	31.8	778,210,000
Muslims	1,752,620,000	24.1	2,987,390,000	31.1	1,234,770,000
Unaffiliated	1,165,020,000	16.0	1,202,300,000	12.5	37,280,000
Hindus	1,099,110,000	15.1	1,392,900,000	14.5	293,790,000
Buddhists	499,380,000	6.9	461,980,000	4.8	−37,400,000
Folk Religions	418,280,000	5.7	440,950,000	4.6	22,670,000
Other Religions	59,710,000	0.8	59,410,000	0.6	−290,000
Jews	14,270,000	0.2	16,370,000	0.2	2,100,000
World	7,284,640,000	100.0	9,615,760,000	100.0	2,331,120,000

Source: Pew Research Center demographic projections.

attending religious services once or twice a month or more, and 36% report attending services at least once a week. Fifty-five percent report praying at least once a day and 78% of their respondents considered religion to be an important part of their life.

As noted previously, studies of religious vitality in Europe return much different results on these kinds of measures. For instance, Need and Evans (2001, 237) found that, among church members in Orthodox Eastern European nations, 31.8% of Romanians, 26.8% of Ukrainians, 16.3% of Bulgarians, and 11.0% of Russians attended church more than once a month. In Catholic countries of Eastern Europe, the findings were higher, but only Poland was close to the figures for the United States, with 76.6% attending services more than once a month. In other countries, 44.2% of Slovakians, 34.8% of Lithuanians, 23.8% of Hungarians, and 17.6% of Czechs reported attending church more than once a month.

Fewer studies have collected these types of survey data from nations in Africa, Asia, and Central and South America, so we don't know as much about how beliefs and practices vary there, but we do know that Christianity is vibrant in the developing world in ways that leave our ideas of vitality in the north in the dust (Jenkins 2002). Among Christians in the global South, religious vitality is manifested through the active adaptation of Christian beliefs and practices, the literal reading of the Bible, religious healing, spiritual conflict and warfare, prophecy, and social justice, all woven together with a wide variety of traditional beliefs and rituals that are indigenous to Africa, Asia, and Central and South America, including polygamy, divination, animal sacrifices, and the veneration of one's ancestors. While religion ultimately always adapts itself to new conditions and cultures, globally Christianity is vital precisely because it is creating entirely new forms of faith and practice that meet the needs of the millions of believers in the Southern Hemisphere.

Vitality as a Product of Religious Market Forces

But what force drives the religious vitality of a community, a nation, or even a whole region of the world? Social scientists point to various factors that help to make a location religiously vital. Recently, market-based (sometimes called "rational choice") models of religious vitality have received a lot of attention, both good and bad. In these models, religious groups are a part of a big religious market that is subject to the same basic principles as any other economic market. You may have heard about how "supply and demand" and competition drive a capitalist economy. Market models of religion assume that religious groups are in competition with each other. Each church, temple, and synagogue have a supply of "religious goods and services," and they compete with one another for "customers" (us!) who demand different things to meet their religious needs. Think about all the religious groups in your hometown. Market models of religion assume that all the congregations in your town are fighting it out to gain your business and to keep your loyalty by offering you what they think you want from your religion.

Chaves et al. (1994) summarize three forces that shape how religion marketplaces work:

1   The more free the religious market is from state regulation, the more services religious groups will provide and the higher the quality of these services will be.

Okay, let's explain this a bit. Many Americans think that state-controlled businesses and industries provide worse service than privately owned ones. In a religious context, this same principle means that the more independent a church is, the more it will work hard to provide you with the best religious goods possible. Why? Because this group doesn't want you to get your religious goods somewhere else, so it is motivated!

2   The more individuals are required to invest their time and energy in their sector of the religious market, the more they will feel that they have some control over it, which in turn will lead to higher levels of individual participation.

Let's unpack this one, too. How many of you have parents who assume that if you have to work and pay for your education on your own, it will be more valuable to you and you'll do your best at it? Religious markets work the same way. The higher the cost of "religious goods" in terms of time, effort, and money, the more likely the consumers will value their religion and participate in it. Low-cost, low-effort religion doesn't give people any reason to participate.

3   The more open and free the religious market is overall, the more varieties of religious belief and practice will develop to meet the needs of religious consumers.

Again, we'll borrow economic ideas and apply them to religion. Just as the free-market system is assumed to encourage people to start new businesses and find better, more efficient ways to do things, a free religious market allows new religious ideas and groups to appear to meet the needs of the religious consumers. Religious consumers choose to affiliate with particular religious groups where the benefits—spiritual or practical—outweigh the costs of belonging. Now, time and place matter here. The religious marketplace in Indianapolis is not the same as the one in Los Angeles, Des Moines, or Bridgeport, much less London, Mumbai, or Kinshasa, so there will be some variety in the groups that are competing and what each group is offering, but you get the idea.

Market models have also been used to illustrate vitality at an organizational level. Rodney Stark, Roger Finke, and other scholars are particularly well known for their works, which provide evidence that congregational vitality is rooted in the diversity, competition, and the degree of regulation in the religious market of a particular community. Although we don't have room to cover the many different pieces of data that are employed to support rational-choice models of religious vitality, one study in particular stands out. Finke and Stark (2000) studied changes in congregational growth and vitality among United Methodists in the California-Nevada Conference. Their study was not designed specifically to test the rational-choice approach, but their work illustrates how it operates at an organization level. In short, they examined how the tension between a congregation and the dominant culture shaped its overall vitality. They found that a new generation of more evangelically minded pastors in the United Methodist Church were affiliating themselves with church movements that sought to return the church to a more traditional position on a variety of theological and social issues, such as the authority of the Bible, the divinity of Christ, and the source of salvation being uniquely belief in Jesus. Simultaneously, these ministers were outspoken against inequalities that were based on gender and race, and were in favor of increasing support for the poor. Other ministers were operating in reverse, decreasing the tension between their congregations and the surrounding culture by relativizing their stances on these traditional beliefs. Finke and Stark found that, as a consequence of increasing the relative "costs" to belong, the high-tension congregations witnessed overall increases in the levels of membership, expenditures, and attendance figures, compared with those of congregations that pursued positions that were in lower tension with the dominant culture. Apparently, high-tension congregations carve out a niche in the religious market that increases their distinctiveness and appeal over their competitors.

It is important to keep in mind that, like secularization theory, market model theory is not universally accepted. The majority of studies that use market models have faced many challenges to their ideas and the data that they use to try to support them (Beyer 1997; Phillips 2004). One criticism of market models is based on their focus on Christianity in the Northern Hemisphere, with data taken from the United States, Canada, and Europe. Most of these studies examine competition between religious groups in principally Christian religious markets and make assumptions about forms of religious participation as individual measures of vitality that make sense only in the context of Christianity. For example, there is a strong bias in American Christianity to determine religious commitment and devotion on the basis of the beliefs that people hold. As we noted in Chapter 2, many other religions do not assess devotion or orthodoxy on the basis of what you *believe*, but rather what you *do*. It is difficult to know whether the market models make any sense at all if applied in other societies or to other religious markets that include Muslims, Hindus, Sikhs, or other religious groups. Only a 1994 study by Chaves, Schraeder, and Sprindys demonstrates that these supply-side approaches to religious vitality are applicable to religions other than Christianity. Their study examined the impact of state regulation of religion on the rate at which Muslims make their required once-in-a-lifetime pilgrimage to Mecca.

Of course, other approaches to explaining religious vitality can be found in the sociological literature. Smith (1998), in his study of American Evangelicals, favors the spirit of a market model but does not embrace all of its language or implications. Smith offers a *subcultural identity* approach to religious vitality, broken down into two arguments about religious persistence and religious strength. Smith's claim about religious persistence is as follows: "Religion survives and can thrive in pluralistic, modern society by embedding itself in subcultures that offer satisfying morally-orienting collective identities, which provide adherents meaning and belonging" (118). In other words, religious groups are subcultures. Most people interact with, befriend, and marry people from religious groups that are similar to their own, as we discussed earlier. This tendency creates a group context that allows people to believe and do things that wouldn't make sense to the majority of people in society. The group continues to reassure believers that their ideas make sense, even when it seems like everything else in the world says they don't. Belief in miracles from St. Jude, belief in a six-day creation as described in the Bible, the practice of sacrificing animals as offerings to gods, the belief that crystals can heal you, the practice of washing in the Ganges River in India to remove past sin and bad karma—these are all beliefs and behaviors that a variety of the world's religions have embraced. However, unless you belong to a group that thinks these things make sense, your reaction to hearing about them probably includes disbelief, confusion, and perhaps even revulsion or ridicule. This is Smith's point. Even the most seemingly outrageous ideas and behaviors—those which seem the least in step with life in 21st-century America—will never be in danger from the forces of secularization so long as there is a group that believes them.

As for the strength of any particular religious tradition in a religiously diverse society, Smith goes on to state that "those religious groups will be relatively stronger which better possess and employ the cultural tools needed to create both clear distinction from and significant engagement with other relevant out groups, short of becoming genuinely countercultural" (118–119). In his analysis, religious vitality is driven by the basic human need to create a sense of meaning about the world and to reinforce feelings of belonging to some group of like-minded people within a society that is made of many different groups with many different beliefs, values, and ways of acting. Because individuals actively seek to have these needs met, religious pluralism itself allows many religious groups to emerge to meet them. In the case of American Evangelicalism, the evangelical subculture reinforces a distinct religious identity that is built around evangelical theology and religious practice. What makes Smith's approach an improvement on pure market models of religious vitality is that it is not necessary to think either that religion is in decline or that it is totally alive and growing in contemporary societies like the United States. Rather than forcing us to choose one over the other, it allows us to consider that perhaps both things are happening at the same time.

Secular Yet Religiously Vital?

So the final question remains: Is it possible for people in society to be more religious while their societies overall become less so? This is the paradoxical position of religion in the 21st century. Since 2001, most North Americans and Europeans have been bombarded with the many ways that religion remains a vital and not always positive force in the world at large. For many of us, even the most devout, this comes as something of a surprise, because religion in countries like the United States, even in its most visible, seemingly public forms, remains largely a personal matter. Religion is in fact separate from the work of government, capitalism, science, health care, and other social institutions. In countries in Africa, Central and South America, Asia, and the Middle East, such a separation is inconceivable. Religion there is an active force that is involved in all aspects of social life. Then why, in so many of the debates among the scholars mentioned in this chapter, does there seem to be a desire to declare once and for all that the world is secularizing or that religion is alive and well? There seems to be little appreciation that these two alternative descriptions of what's happening to religion in our world are not mutually exclusive; rather they are parallel and complementary.

Those who study religion, especially proponents of religious vitality and religious market models, find it difficult to embrace this nuanced approach. To speak of religious authority declining and of religion differentiating into its own separate sphere of influence seems to carry with it the need to say that this is not a good thing or that religion will inevitably die or fade away. Many students of religion carry with them a set of normative assumptions about the roles religion *should* play in the social world—or that they, as persons of faith themselves, wish it to play. So, to save religion from the fate that some scholars incorrectly believe is predicted by secularization theory, they focus on how vibrant and innovative *the religious sphere* itself seems to be. They focus also on religion's engagement with secular institutions, portraying this as the final word on religion's continued vitality in this postmodern and distinctly nonsecular age (Finke 1992). We argue, however, that we must understand religion in our world in all of its complex and paradoxical reality.

So we are back where we started with the trends of secularization. From the beginning, Wilson (1982) and others have asserted that, although secularization proceeds at the societal level, it is not inevitable that most individuals will relinquish their interest in religion, their beliefs, or their religious practices. Thanks to globalization, religious markets in many North American and European contexts have become increasingly diverse, but this diversity alone does not automatically translate into religious vitality (Voas et al. 2002). All the same—as we have already noted—a great deal of evidence exists for continued higher (though declining) levels of religious participation in the United States, as well as evidence that points to continued low levels of religious participation in Western and Eastern European nations. In both cases, immigration from the global South has played a significant role in maintaining high levels of religious participation (Bruce 2016).

Yet rational-choice theorists argue that pluralism and diversity in religious markets force religious groups to actively compete for members by improving and changing their religious products to achieve greater appeal to a portion of religious consumers, as if an unregulated religious marketplace makes all religious choices available to all religious consumers. While some religious consumers might feel that they have choices about which groups to join, many other believers in the United States and abroad would disagree that they had or have much choice in their religion. Think about your own case here. What does it mean to have a religious "choice"? If you belong to a particular religion, could you really just decide that you like another one better and make the change? Probably few of us would be able to say yes to that. We grow up in particular religious traditions that are connected to our race, our ethnicity, our social class, and any number of other factors. We can't or don't easily jump ship from one religion to another, one day being a devoted Pentecostal and the next being a Buddhist. So what does having a "choice" mean here? Likewise, recent data from around the world demonstrates that if people leave their religions, they are more likely to join the ranks of the unaffiliated, the Nones, rather than join another group.

Another problem with the rational-choice approach is that it assumes that all religious groups are operating more or less on equal footing and simply need to make the right pitch to consumers to increase their membership. But this is not how most religious groups gain or lose members at the local level. People join or leave religious groups when the transitional costs are lowest. For instance, a Christian is more likely to switch among types of congregations and even denominations within the same religion, than to switch to a different religion altogether. Likewise, even within an open religious market, we do not find Jews, Muslims, Hindus, Buddhists, or any other types of religious shoppers switching among religious traditions.

The religious sphere's own setting of cultural limits on the range of choices that are available in the religious market is also the source of its vitality. Contemporary religion, segregated into its own sphere of influence and authority, gives rise to innovation and reflexivity in order to meet the needs of new generations of would-be believers. As we saw in Chapter 3, religious groups carefully watch changing cultural currents and modify both the messages and the media that they use to communicate to meet the stated or imagined needs of religious believers. This scenario is, of course, radically different from that of a fixed religious market in which traditions are, to a certain extent, frozen and cannot be changed. It is also a response to the "shopper," "seeker," or "questing" approaches to social life taken by individuals in the modern, differentiated social world. Today, within structured limits, we try to maximize the numbers and varieties of choices that we have available to meet our needs. Olson (1993, 35) describes us "moderns" in the following way:

> The very forces of modernization that disrupt the homogeneity of preindustrial community simultaneously give moderns greater control over the construction of their personal networks, control that can be used to rebuild networks of shared identity. The difference between contemporary subcultures and the preindustrial community lie in the greater freedom of moderns to choose which elements of their identity they will emphasize in the construction of their personal networks and the degree of their involvement in subcultures based on those identities. Moderns are freer to shape their personal networks and thus their own identity.

The implication for religion is clear. Today's believers are freer (not totally free, however) to make some choices in the religious market, to join groups that fit their needs and experience, to leave them again when their needs are not met or they experience life changes, and to assess religious groups with the full fervor of consumerism—trying to get the best spiritual bang for the buck. But for more and more people, religion is losing its significance, polarizing society still further into religious and non-religious camps.

Such an approach also underscores the shifting authority of religious traditions and their leaders. Although an individual may choose to worship in a particular way, to behave in proscribed ways or not, and to hold to or reject the doctrines of a faith tradition, now—unlike in times past—the individual believer is in a position to pick and ·choose what beliefs, behaviors, and experiences work best. The individual need not embrace the totality of the tradition or recognize the authority of religious leaders to dictate how that person's faith should shape his or her attitudes and behaviors. Evangelical women selectively interpret the pronouncements of their ministers on the roles of women in the household (Beaman 1999). Highly educated and politically liberal Protestants in the United States increasingly "believe without belonging," when faced with a growing cultural association between being religious and being conservative (Hout and Fischer 2002). And, as Roof (1999, 85) found in his survey of baby boomers, "one third of the respondents agreed that 'people have God within them, so churches aren't really necessary' . . . Even 13 percent of born-again Christians agreed!" Roof (1999, 110) goes on to say, "People now take a more active role in shaping the meaning systems by which they live and must themselves determine how to respond to this widening range of suppliers, all contending with one another in creating symbolic worlds." Couple the declining legitimacy of religious authority over the everyday lives of believers with high levels of commitment to classic forms of religious expression and many new forms of spirituality, and one sees the paradox: secular yet vital. It is important to note that, as stated by Chaves (1994), the decline and institutional segregation of religious authority does not occur without some resistance on the part of those who have an interest in maintaining some religious control over society. The process of secularization, therefore, may provoke political movements to restore the presence and power of religious authority. In many ways, as we consider the entry of clergy and people of faith into politics over the last three decades, we can see the rationale for such an argument. Hunter (1989), in his hotly debated but important book *Culture Wars*, argues that, as a result of the liberalizing forces of government, the economy, and the media, special-interest groups, religious denominations, and political parties have realigned themselves in opposition to these "secularizing" forces. Consequently, a cultural divide has emerged and has prompted the familiar battles over abortion, gay rights, education, government funding of the arts, and a host of other issues. In these conflicts, religious actors figure prominently on both sides of the divide, but as in the case of any conflict, much depends on who can gain the most resources and who has the backing of more people. As Hunter (1989, 158) observes:

> This conflict is 'about' the uses of symbols, the uses of language, and the right to impose discrediting labels upon those who would dissent. It is ultimately a struggle over the right to define the way things are and the way things should be. It is therefore more of a struggle to determine who is stronger, which alliance has the institutional resources capable of sustaining a particular definition of reality against the wishes of those who would project an alternative view of the world.

For those whose world views and values are threatened by any perceived decline in religious authority, the only alternative is to organize and fight back against the sources of those threats in whatever form they take: societal, organizational, or individual.

Hunter's thesis has been contested since he published it, but other scholars have examined these same forces in local community contexts. Demerath and Williams (1992, 202) illustrate the push-pull relationship between the forces of secularization and those of what they call "sacralization." They suggest that secularizing forces can and do provoke sacralizing reactions in ways that may even give the sacralizing side political victories. For example, in Springfield, Massachusetts, it became clear that, although in many ways religion is no longer a driving political force in the city, it still has significant effects. Clergy and coalitions of various religious groups push for a variety of political changes in the city. Sometimes, these political engagements support liberal causes such as funding in the city for low-income neighborhoods, and sometimes they support more conservative ones like limiting abortion access in the city and shifting sex education in schools toward abstinence. However, even though these victories for the forces of sacralization certainly seem to reflect religious vitality and resurgence, Demerath and Williams describe the victories as fundamentally limited, short-term gains in the face of long-term losses of religious authority in local communities. Religious victory over individual political issues is not the same as victory in reinstating the power of religious organizations and leaders over the moral order of a community as a whole and worldwide, evidence for any mass resacralization is tepid at best (Brown 2019).

Of course, in recent years, we have witnessed the transformation of these local sacralizing movements into more extreme forms of global religious political activism. Branches of Christianity, Islam, and other religions form fundamentalist movements around the world. These movements arise partly in response to the secularizing forces of global capitalism, global political and military forces, and, perhaps most significantly, the introduction of American and European cultural practices that threaten traditional ways of life and values. Lechner (1991, 1114) states this directly: "No fundamentalism without (prior) secularization." As paradoxical as it sounds, religious vitality and declining religious authority go hand in hand though they are creating an ever more polarized world. We will look in more detail at religious polarization and how it unfolds around the world in the next chapter.

Suggested Reading

Bruce, Steve. 2011. *Secularization: In Defense of an Unfashionable Theory*. New York: Oxford University Press.

Bruce, Steve. 2016. "The Sociology of Late Secularization: Social Divisions and Religiosity." *British Journal of Sociology* 67(4): 613–631.

Chaves, Mark. 1994. "Secularization as Declining Religious Authority." *Social Forces* 72(3): 749–774.

Finke, Roger, and Rodney Stark. 2006. *The Churching of America, 1776–2005*. New Brunswick, NJ: Rutgers University Press.

Jenkins, Philip. 2002. *The Next Christendom: The Coming of Global Christianity*. New York: Oxford University Press.

Roof, Wade Clark. 1999. *Spiritual Marketplace: Baby Boomers and the Remaking of American Religion*. Princeton: Princeton University Press.

Stark, Rodney. 1999. "Secularization, R.I.P." *Sociology of Religion* 60(3): 249–274.

Stark, Rodney. 2015. *Triumph of the Faith*. Wilmington, DE: ISI Books.

Swatos, William H., Jr., and Kevin J. Christiano. 1999. "Secularization Theory: The Course of a Concept." *Sociology of Religion* 60(3): 209–228.

Voas, David, and Mark Chaves. 2016. "Is the United States a Counterexample to the Secularization Thesis?" *American Journal of Sociology* 121(5): 1517–1556.

Woodhead, Linda. 2008. "Gendering Secularization Theory." *Social Compass* 55(2): 189–195.

6 **The Fight for Survival**

Religious Polarization and the Shrinking Middle

1 What is religious polarization?
2 Is it increasing and why?
3 What are the consequences of religious polarization?
4 How can it be addressed?

Let's eavesdrop on two dorm room conversations. They are actually happening simultaneously in the same building. In each conversation to which we are listening are seven students, making for a couple of crowded dorm rooms.

ROOM 347:

Can you believe there are still people who are not only religious, but they actually make decisions based on their religious beliefs?

It's mind-boggling. Just yesterday, I was talking to Adriana, and she said something like, "Same-sex sexual relationships are wrong; the Bible is absolutely clear in that teaching. On this secular campus, we never learn that reality." I mean seriously, these people have views from the Stone Age.

I personally am sick of these religious nuts. They don't think; they just follow the dribble their power-hungry leaders tell them. Why are they bothering with college? They aren't willing to learn. We are here to expand our minds; they're here to shut that down.

My prof was saying in class this morning that at least in the United States, White religious people overwhelmingly vote Republican and have shaped much of the party's platform. I find it offensive and disgusting. Have they never heard of the separation of church and state?

Yay, it's the religious zealots in this country that oppose a women's right to choose, that want prayer in schools, that want our political system to basically be a theocracy, and who are out-and-out racists.

Don't they know it's the modern age? Religion is superstition, period. We have advanced so far beyond that crap. Who are these people? What is wrong with them?

I can understand why some older people—who grew up in a different era—might believe that ?#*! But people our age? It's got to stop. Let me say it clearly: they need to be stopped!

ROOM 527:

To be a believer and attend this school is so hard. People are straight-up in your face opposed to our beliefs.

So much for the supposed open-mindedness and tolerance they claim to be about. Apparently, if we are defined as intolerant, that gives them license to be intolerant toward us.

I am shocked at how secular this campus is, even when so many of us are God followers. We're invisible, our views and perspectives not only don't matter; they don't exist, at least to the secular profs and students here.

DOI: 10.4324/9781003182108-8

I cannot believe how their secular views lead to such God violating beliefs. They think abortion is a right. I mean they actually believe that. How is killing the most defenseless of all human beings a right? It is straight-up wickedness, the result of the warped minds attempting to find truth apart from God.

I hear you. And they not only believe such insane things, they vote to get them the law of the land, attempting to snuff out not only babies' lives, but even God their Creator.

They run the Democratic Party. They run our school boards. They run our governments. They run the academy. Say the wrong thing, and they cancel you. You're kicked out of school, you lose your job, you are exiled. My church family warned me that when I came here, I would see how secularists seek to kill and destroy us believers. They can't stand us, because truth be told, we pierce their consciences.

Agreed. Deep down, they know they are on a wrong path. It is our call to stand strong, to represent the truth, to fight for God. We are the generation that must stand tall and resist the secularists, the haters of God and Truth.

Have you ever been part of such discussions? If so, chances are you have only been part of one of these, the one that aligns with what you already believe. And chances are you pretty much only hang out with people who think a lot like you, whether in person or virtually.

Such is the focus of this chapter. Different from the past, in the U.S. and in many other nations, we are becoming increasingly polarized religiously. Interestingly, while we will explore some polarization occurring within religion, the main polarization shaking Western nations is the increasingly vitriolic, high-stakes competition between the religious and the secularists. Both groups have their fundamentalists, those arguing there is one truth and any deviation from it is heresy. Such views, in today's world, are no longer just in the realm of religion. Oddly, secular movements have all the same trappings, complete with sins, absolute beliefs that must be adhered to, and prescribed right and wrong practices.

Religious Polarization and its Rise

Have you ever attempted to hold two magnets together? Some attract, some repel. Which will occur depends on the pole. Magnets have either a north pole or a south pole. Put a north pole with a south pole, and they attract. Put two north poles or two south poles together and they repel, violently if you force them too close to each other.

When we talk about religious polarization, the concept is similar. We are talking about groups of people and organizations moving to one pole or another, thus moving further away from each other. If and when they attempt to come together, they increasingly repel each other, sometimes violently. As we will explore, such processes have very real consequences for our lives. But before we get to those consequences, let's try to understand what is happening and why.

There is a false lore which persists generation after generation. That lore is this: in the past everyone was religious, and in turn, no one was secular. Even a brief reading of history will quickly dispel this myth, yet the myth persists.

Partly this myth persists because it serves well both today's religious and today's non-religious. For the former group, it provides a goal to return to, a time when life was believed to be better, and the ancestors were truly faithful. For the latter group, it provides a convenient "straw man" to suggest that in the past times were oppressive, and we must break free from the bonds of religion to think and do as we want. The old days were backwards, and they were religious, so religion is backwards, they argue.

Where people get confused is in the difference between what people believed and did, and what societies were officially. It is true that many—though certainly not all—societies in the past were officially religious, almost always having an official state religion. In that sense, such societies were religious. What does not follow and is not true is that because of that reality, every citizen in the nation was religious. Always there was a tremendous range, from the highly devout to the sacrilegious, the non-believers, and the non-practitioners. Even those charged with overseeing a nation's religious apparatus could be irreligious.

We discuss this myth because it contributes to the religious polarization we are witnessing in so many parts of the globe. In true sociological fashion, this polarization is contextual. That is, it can only occur under certain social conditions and certain assumptions.

Religious polarization has at least two meanings. It is important to know each. The first to arise was polarization *between* religious people. Societies always change—new technologies, climate changes, inventions, political changes, economic shifts. The list goes on. Some religious people believe that their religion must also change with the times. They often are called religious progressives or religious modernists. Other religious people believe that their faith is timeless. No matter the changes occurring in society, the teachings and principles of the faith remain unchanging. They are often called religious conservatives, or fundamentalists.

Note well this process, because in your lifetime, you will see it occur too. Cultural, political, economic, and social change occur—what is often called modernization. No matter how hip you are today, if you stay as you are, you will not be hip in ten years. Things change fast. Either we change with the times, or the next generation of hip folks can and will see you as a dinosaur of a previous era.

For example, think about clothing fashion. What looks good? What is "in"? No matter your answer, in ten years that same answer will be wrong, as defined by most everyone. You would be accused of being "so 2020s." And that is taken as a bad thing. In most Western cultures, which unthinkingly view most any change as progress, if you don't change, you are not progressive; that is, you are from an older (read "worse" or "backward" or "quaint but naïve") era. A novelty you may be, but not someone to be taken seriously.

Religion exists in a social context, and that context in at least the Western world (though increasingly everywhere) are societies which view modernization as inevitable, necessary, an improvement over previous times, and thus good. So what are the religious to do?

Shall they attempt to modernize their faith, keeping pace with other changes in society? For instance, if society were to decide prayer is unhealthy, and were to label those who pray as "at risk" of mental health instability and "suffering from delusions," should the religious adapt and stop talking overtly about prayer and praying less in their daily lives? Or should they resist the larger society and continue stressing the importance of prayer for the religiously faithful?

It is a real dilemma. Religious progressives would argue that to stay "relevant" their religion needs to focus less on prayer and more on something else, perhaps in providing more counselors to meet people's needs. Religious conservatives would argue that society itself is "delusional" or at least misguided, and of course they should not change. Religious teachings and practices are true, regardless of the social context.

Around 1870, the United States was beginning to be a world economic leader, shifting quickly from an agrarian economy to the "industrial leader." People were moving from farms to cities to work in factories. More people were going on to graduate high school and even go to college. With these shifts, beliefs and norms of the larger society were changing. Between 1870 to about 1925, when this massive shift happened (1920 was the first time in U.S. history that the majority of people lived in cities, about the same time that women secured the right to vote), Christianity—by far the dominant religion of Americans—saw a massive splintering.

Based on this discussion, can you guess what occurred? Without looking below, how do you think Christianity splintered and polarized?

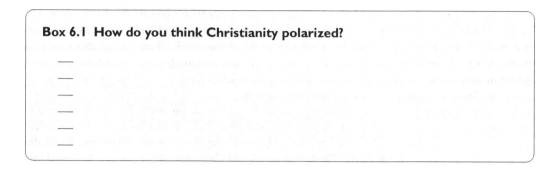

Box 6.1 How do you think Christianity polarized?

—
—
—
—
—
—

Let's focus just on White American Christians (the complexity of race in the U.S. means different racial groups, even of the same religion, experienced the modernizing world in very different ways). Some White Christians thought their religion must adapt to the changing times. These "progressives" argued that their faith must talk less about heaven and hell, and less about personal salvation, and instead more about advocating for workers' rights, about social sin, about adapting to an urban context, and related changes. They not only argued this, but they also actually changed their beliefs and practices. These folks came to be called religious liberals or progressives.

But a sizable group of White Christians across the nation pushed back. Not only should such changes as those suggested and practiced by the religious progressives not occur, they argued, but Christians must double down and reaffirm the very fundamentals of the Christian faith. In fact, a series of important pamphlets called "The Fundamentals: A Testimony of the Truth" were published between 1910 and 1915 to clarify for Christians what the fundamental, nonnegotiable beliefs and practices were. These folks thus came to be labeled as fundamentalists. As religious historian Marsden (1980, 4) noted, "fundamentalism was a loose, diverse, and changing federation of cobelligerents united by their fierce opposition to modernist attempts to bring Christianity into line with modern thought."

What we see here is an early, yet very real-life example of religious polarization. White American Christians, though not agreeing on everything, largely held similar beliefs and overall views of their faith and the world. Aggressive modernization and seismic economic and social upheavals changed that (beginning of course with the period leading up to and the actual Civil War). Faced with this reality, religious polarization ensued. Some modernized their faith to be "in line with modern thought," while others resisted and pushed back.

So what is religious polarization? We can find at least nine different definitions (Bramson et al. 2017), such as the degree of attitudinal disagreement, the degree of difference in practices, and the level of diversity in a population. But what all definitions of religious polarization have in common is the shrinking of the middle (Dilmaghani 2020). In religious polarization, people and organizations move to the extremes, separating from each other. So we can define religious polarization as *the process by which a common, shared middle understanding of religion evaporates while divergent, more extreme understandings of the religion swell.* And key to understanding this process is that it occurs not because of something inherent in religion, but because of changes occurring outside it; that is, because of something inherent in society, namely that it changes.

A quick example to illustrate: For many decades there was little talk about abortion within religious communities. American Christians largely understood it as something not to do, as against the faith, but it wasn't a huge topic. Abortion was illegal, so if it happened, it was done in secret. But then society changed. A lawsuit made its way to the Supreme Court and in 1972, the court declared abortion legal.

Society "changed its opinion." Now it was an open issue that religious communities had to address. And you can guess from our discussion thus far what happened. Sociologist Evans (2002) was able to track opinion data from 1972, the year of the changed law, all the way to about the year 2000. He found during this period that Christians were polarized on the issue. Mainline Protestants (those in denominations that tend toward adapting to societal changes) and evangelical Protestants (those in denominations that tend toward preserving the faith as it has been) diverged in seismic fashion over this nearly thirty-year period. Mainline Protestants became much more supportive of abortion as acceptable for most any reason. Evangelical Protestants, already against abortion, actually became less supportive of abortion over time. Hence the rapidly growing divergence. Evans also found a growing divergence between Black Protestants and Catholics. What is more, he found that within these traditions, there was increasing polarization, where for instance some Catholics were becoming more supportive of abortion choice for women and others more supportive of protecting the child, causing riffs even within faith traditions such as Catholicism.

Fast-forward to the 2020s. Abortion remains a heated topic nationally, driven in part by the religious schisms on the issue. When Texas passed a law significantly curtailing the legality of abortion, people on both main sides of the issue across the country either celebrated or were seething. The case was brought to the Supreme Court in expedited fashion, attempting to block the law on the grounds that the law itself was illegal because it violated the 1972 national law. The Supreme Court voted in a majority ruling to allow the Texas law to stand. Religious folks represent both sides, each believing they are correct in their view and each appalled at the other side.

So here we have our example. A societal change in a law back in 1972 forced religious people to grapple with the topic of abortion. And it has led to growing polarization, not only on this issue, but as we will see, on a whole host of issues, which has resulted in the intense polarization we witness a half century and more later.

Let us now consider an even bigger polarization, one that we can see across Western nations, and one that again is sociologically driven. By that we mean what we are about to discuss is not due to particular personalities of people, but to social factors that lead to choices having to be made and positions having to be taken. And the end result is polarization.

The second type of religious polarization, which has surpassed the initial internal religious polarization in terms of global impact, is the polarization *between the religious and the secular*. Increasingly, we are witnessing the dissolution of a religious left, because they are either leaving religion altogether to join the ranks of the secular, or because they are being replaced by younger cohorts who from the start of their adulthood reject organized religion altogether (the students in Room 342 at the beginning of this chapter). Meanwhile, conservative religious people are consolidating their conservativeness, and becoming more resistant to secular people and organizations attempting to force them to adopt secular ways (the students in Room 527 at the beginning of this chapter).

As nations secularize—an ever-reduced role for religion and more people rejecting religion altogether—we find that religious polarization increases and intensifies within those nations (see Wilkins-Laflamme 2017 for a review). Perhaps this seems odd at first, but when the ranks of the non-religious swell, when laws and norms begin to change to favor the non-religious, and when the religious feel the loss of the faith around them, they are understandably threatened. And they understandably seek to preserve their faith.

But this is utterly abhorrent to secular people. They find such people offensive and view them as standing in the way of progress, where progress is defined as something like a religion-free society where individual freedom is maximized, at least for those adopting the correct perspective. If religion is to exist, it must be done privately, quietly, and have no impact on public society whatsoever.

And what an offense such a perspective is to many religious people. Religion, sociologically speaking, may be personal, but always it is also communal. It is practiced together. And religion, taken seriously, always has implications for how people live their lives, such as how we educate, what laws we pass, what family is, and what we view as right and wrong. To be told—or even worse, to be forced—to retreat into a pretend world of "private religion" that has no real-world or public implications is abhorrent to the faithful. It is not viewed as possible.

And so the polarization spirals. But we must understand again the sociological reasons it does. When we have a highly homogenous society, we of course don't have much polarization. Most people view the world the same and largely agree on things like the role of religion.

Perhaps less obviously, though, is that when we have highly diverse societies—variation by religion, race, class, region, occupation, interests, politics and more—we also have less polarization. The reason? There are too many differences, too many different groups, too many cross-cutting interests of people for them to polarize from each other. Who should you hate? Who is your enemy? It is simply too complicated and time-absorbing. The famous French Enlightenment philosopher Voltaire (1694–1778), who was for a time exiled to England, put it this way: "If there were only one religion in England there would be danger of despotism, if there were two they would cut each other's throats, but there are thirty, and they live in peace and happiness." ([1733] 1980, 41).

Research hundreds of years later validates Voltaire's observation. Scholars Lu and Xiaozhoa (2020) argue that polarization occurs when there are relatively few groups and is most extreme when there are but two dominant groups. Heclo (2007) concludes that the American colonies were so diverse religiously that no particular group could keep up with persecuting the others. Growing polarization in the U.S. and in many Western countries is ironically not due to diversity of beliefs and views, but to *the increasing consolidation of diversity sorted into but a few groups.*

Most especially in current times, religious polarization is due to the rise of secularism, pitting the religious against the secular. Indeed, research studying the amount of polarization that exists in nations across the globe finds that religious polarization is strongest in the most secularized nations, and interestingly, in nations with a Catholic heritage. In Catholic countries, the research finds, polarization stems from anti-religious fervency. In secular countries, polarization stems from religious fervency (Ribberink et al. 2018). The British scholar Bruce (2000, 117) wrote, polarization and:

> [f]undamentalism [are] the rational response of traditionally religious peoples to social, political and economic changes that downgrade and constrain the role of religion in the public world . . . fundamentalists have not exaggerated the extent to which modern cultures threaten what they hold dear.

Thus, most everywhere that we see the rise of secularism and modernism, we also see the rise of fundamentalist religion and increased polarization. The struggle is over essentially all of life, from the macro (policies, laws, elections, national identities, holidays) to the meso (institutions, like the family, and organizations, such as schools), to the micro (everyday beliefs, interactions, norms, and practices). Because these struggles involve so much of life and are so far-ranging, those engaged in the struggle begin to consolidate in other arenas. White conservative Christians become overwhelmingly Republican; secular liberals become overwhelmingly Democrat. In so doing, the political becomes intertwined with and shapes the religious, and vice versa. And the end result is less diversity and even more polarization. The religious and the secular begin reacting and counter-reacting to actions and views perceived present in the other group (Putnam and Campbell 2010). The stakes become ever greater, and the battle begins to be viewed in cosmic terms, where groups are battling for the "soul of the nation" and the "future of our children" and even the "survival of humankind."

Consequences

So what? So what if we are growing more religiously polarized across Western nations?

If you stop for a moment in your reading of this chapter to reflect, do any possible consequences of this polarization come to mind? Go ahead and put down one or two that come to mind. Feel free to guess. You can then compare your responses to what scholars have found.

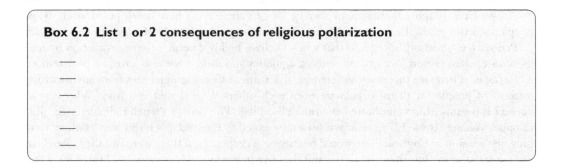

Box 6.2 List 1 or 2 consequences of religious polarization

Some of the consequences we can likely guess, but others we really only could see by using sociological theory and then testing the theory with data.

As religious polarization increases, groups feel increasingly *threatened*. This process leads to heightened *social tensions*, and we find that we get *consolidation of different spheres* of life (for example, religion and political party begin to merge, social attitudes and voting behavior become more sharply divergent across the groups).

Not surprisingly, *hostility* between the groups ratchets up significantly. We have then a clear case of *intergroup conflict*. Now think back to what we learned about the positive functions of intergroup conflict for each group internally (Chapter 4). We learned that such conflict strengthens the boundaries of the group. It is much clearer what the group is and who is in the group. As such, intergroup conflict solidifies group identity, offering its members clarity and a clear sense of importance from that identity. The members thus increase in social cohesion. A common enemy helps unite them behind a common purpose and minimizes any within-group differences, which pale in comparison to the difference with the outgroup enemy.

As a result, ideological solidarity and overall participation in the group is strengthened. People unite behind a common purpose and increase their participation in the attempt to achieve that purpose. Finally, then, we find that this leads to increased mobilization of people and resources to defend the group's identity and battle the outgroup, the enemy attempting to squelch the group's way of life. People are more and more willing to donate money, commit time and expertise, and sacrifice other goals for the good of the group.

Wow, that is a lot. And all these positive functions for the ingroup stemming from intergroup conflict can, it turns out, lead to some very real problems too, for at this point, mutual *prejudice and hatred* increase between groups. They react and counter-react to each other's actual or perceived moves, raising the stakes ultimately to a cosmic level. It is here that we can see the first outbreaks of *violence* (see review in Lu and Xiaozhoa 2020; also Migheli 2019). It might be just a few at first engaging in a physical fight, or in online bullying or cyberattacks. But it increases over time as the stakes continue to increase, each group seeing the battle as life and death for their group.

Across the globe, we have seen the rise of what then follows: *terrorist attacks*. As a scholar of religious violence, Mark Juergensmeyer, in this groundbreaking work *Terror in the Mind of God* (2003), studied terrorism and religious violence across the globe. He concluded that the confrontation between religion and secularism is increasingly framed as a cosmic war resulting in one group winning, and the other being annihilated. Secularism seeks to destroy religion or shove it to the dark backrooms, never to be seen again in public. Religious groups seek to restore their position at the center of public consciousness and want to minimize or end secularism.

Ultimately, Juergensmeyer claims that religious violence is theater. It is used to dramatize the conditions and views of the group. This "performance violence" is used to bring attention to a cause, buttressed on both sides (religious or secular) by moral absolutism. In this sense, then, religious fundamentalists battle secular fundamentalists. Importantly, such violence is heightened in nations where religion is regulated and controlled by the government (Iannaccone 1997).

At the extreme, *armed conflict* can occur (Basedau et al. 2011), and even civil war. These outcomes are more likely in non-democratic societies. One study found that as the level of polarization increases, so too does *human death* (Migheli 2019). It is hard to fathom a more severe consequence.

But still there are others, and they are not necessarily what your average person on the street might think would be consequences of religious polarization. Migheli (2019) found that as religious polarization increases, the level of *financial satisfaction* of its citizens *decreases*. Put another way, increased polarization means that at any given level of income, people will be less satisfied with their financial position and feel more financially insecure.

Sociologist Samuel Perry, in an article (2022) reviewing the implications of polarization, draws our attention to other vital consequences. We witness *social capital losses*: less trust between people across groups, less overall social interaction, more suspicion of others, greater anger levels, more stress, and more anxiety in social situations. All this adds up to the findings of scholars Lu and Xiaozhoa (2020). Based on a massive study of nearly 70,000 people across 51 nations, they found that as religious polarization increases, the *health* of its citizens *declines*. In this sense, everyone is losing as each group battles for victory. Interestingly, these researchers found that when societies were highly diverse with lots of different groups, citizens of those nations on average had better health. Truly, religious polarization itself, with just a few groups (the loss of diversity and pluralism), is unhealthy.

And still the consequences of religious polarization continue. Perry (2022) also cites literature finding that we get *political gridlock and collective ineffectiveness*, such as increased governmental partisanship (there can be no compromise), and less overall work getting done in the halls of Congress. And this leads to the *erosion of democracy* itself. Democracy is threatened and challenged, stretched thin, pushed to its limits, as each side seeks victory over the enemy through total control or takeover. As Perry (2022, 22) concludes: "political elites are moving toward extremes, the American public is increasingly sorted along partisan and ideological lines, and Americans increasingly distrust one another and democracy. Always in combination with other social factors like race and class, religious identities, beliefs, behaviors, and institutions are deeply implicated in these growing divides."

Finally, amidst all of these consequences, the *economic growth* of polarized nations is *negatively impacted*. Overall investment declines, government expenditures shrink or are directed in non-logical ways, and the growing probability and reality of violence interrupts supply chains and economic life (Montalvo and Reynal-Querol 2000).

A Conversation

Clearly, increasing religious polarization, especially when that polarization is between the religious and the secular, isn't pretty. It is costly, harmful, and destructive. One of the earliest prognosticators that the U.S. could find itself in such a reality was a sociologist of religion and culture, James Davidson Hunter. He has published books with such ominous titles as *Culture Wars*, *The Death of Character*, and *Before the Shooting Begins*.

A few months prior to the writing of this chapter, he did an interview with the magazine *Politico*. The article, written by journalist Zack Stanton (2021), is condensed and abbreviated here, to give you insight into an eye-opening interaction in real time from a world-class scholar on the topic of this chapter. Do note as you read this piece that what we call religious polarization Hunter will refer to as a culture war. That is because in sociology, religion often falls under the category of culture. Let's peek in now on the conversation.

In 1991, with America gripped by a struggle between an increasingly liberal secular society that pushed for change and a conservative opposition that rooted its worldview in divine scripture, James Davison Hunter wrote a book and titled it with a phrase for what he saw playing out in America's fights over abortion, gay rights, religion in public schools and the like: "Culture Wars."

Hunter, a 30-something sociologist at the University of Virginia, didn't invent the term, but his book vaulted it into the public conversation, and within a few years it was being used as shorthand for cultural flashpoints with political ramifications. He hoped that by calling attention to the dynamic, he'd help America "come to terms with the unfolding conflict" and, perhaps, defuse some of the tensions he saw bubbling.

Instead, 30 years later, Hunter sees America as having doubled down on the "war" part—with the culture wars expanding from issues of religion and family culture to take over politics almost totally, creating a dangerous sense of winner-take-all conflict over the future of the country.

"Democracy, in my view, is an agreement that we will not kill each other over our differences, but instead we'll talk through those differences. And part of what's troubling is that I'm beginning to see signs of the justification for violence," says Hunter, noting the insurrection on January 6, when a mob of extremist supporters of Donald Trump stormed the U.S. Capitol in an attempt to overthrow the results of the 2020 election. "Culture wars always precede shooting wars. They don't *necessarily* lead to a shooting war, but you never have a shooting war without a culture war prior to it, because culture provides the justifications for violence."

"The earlier culture war really was about secularization, and positions were tied to theologies and justified on the basis of theologies," says Hunter. "That's no longer the case. You rarely see people on the right rooting their positions within a biblical theology or ecclesiastical tradition. [Nowadays,] it is a position that is mainly rooted in fear of extinction."

In 1991, politics still seemed like a vehicle through which we might resolve divisive cultural issues; now, politics is primarily fueled by division on those issues, with leaders gaining power by inflaming resentments on mask-wearing, or transgender students competing in athletics, or invocations of "cancel culture," or whether it's OK to teach that many of the Founding Fathers had racist beliefs. And this reality—that the culture war has colonized American politics—is troubling precisely because of an observation Hunter made in 1991 about the difference he saw between political issues and culture war fights: "On political matters, one can compromise; on matters of ultimate moral truth, one cannot."

To sort through it all, POLITICO Magazine spoke with Hunter on the phone late last week. A condensed transcript of that conversation is below, edited for length and clarity.

The changes you looked at in "Culture Wars" had largely happened over the 30 years prior—basically since the early 1960s, with the civil rights movement, sexual revolution, the gay rights movement, women's lib and the backlashes that followed. It's now 30 years since that book came out. How has the culture war changed in that time?

An important demographic and institutional structural shift took place [in recent decades]. Modern higher education has always been a carrier of the Enlightenment, and, in that sense, a carrier of secularization. What happened in the post-World War II period was a massive expansion of higher education and the knowledge-based economy. And with that came a larger cultural shift: What used to be the province of intellectuals now became the province of anyone who had access to higher education, and higher education became one of the gates through which the move to middle-class or upper middle-class life was made.

With that came profound cultural change. The '60s revolution and the political, cultural and sexual protests at the time essentially became institutionalized, and it challenged fundamental notions of what was right, decent, good, fair and so on. And in a way, what you had in the late 1970s into the '80s and '90s was a reaction *against* the challenge represented by that structural change. Conservatives—especially conservative Christians, whether Catholic or Protestant—found themselves on the defensive against progressive notions of family structure, "family values," sexuality; abortion was a—or maybe *the*—critical issue.

Conservatives see this as an existential threat. That's an important phrase: They see it as an *existential threat* to their way of life, to the things that they hold sacred. So while the earlier culture war really was about secularization, and positions were tied to theologies and justified on the basis of theologies, that's no longer the case. You rarely see people on the right rooting their positions within a biblical theology or ecclesiastical tradition. [Nowadays,] it is a position that is mainly rooted in fear of extinction.

I talk about this sense of a struggle for one's very existence, for a way of life; this is *exactly* the language that is also used on the left, but in a much more therapeutic way. When you hear people say that, for instance, conservatives' very existence on this college campus is "a *threat* to my existence" as a trans person or gay person, the stakes—for them—seem ultimate.

There's a passage you wrote 30 years ago that seems relevant to this point: "We subtly slip into thinking of the controversies debated as political rather than cultural in nature. On political matters, one can compromise; on matters of ultimate moral truth, one cannot. This is why the full range of issues today seems interminable."

I kind of like that sentence. *[Laughs]* I would put it this way: Culture, by its very nature, is hegemonic. It seeks to colonize; it seeks to envelop in its totality. The root of the word "culture" is Latin: "cultus." It's about what is sacred to us. And what is sacred to us tends to be universalizing. The very nature of the sacred is that it is special; it can't be broached.

You hear this all the time. The very idea of treating your opponents with civility is a *betrayal*. How can you be civil to people who threaten your very existence? It highlights the point that culture is hegemonic: You can compromise with politics and policy, but if politics and policy are a proxy for culture, there's just no way.

The book that I followed "Culture Wars" with was called "Before the Shooting Begins: Searching for Democracy in America's Culture War." And the argument I made was that culture wars always precede shooting wars. They don't *necessarily* lead to a shooting war, but you never have a shooting war without a culture war prior to it, because culture provides the justifications for violence. And I think that's where we are. The climatological indications are pretty worrisome.

What would it look like to actually reckon with that issue, culturally?

Well, I'm going to sound really old-fashioned here, but I think that this work takes a long time and it's hard. I think you talk through the conflicts. Don't ignore them; don't pretend that they don't exist. And whatever you do, don't just simply impose your view on anyone else. You *have to* talk them through. It's the long, hard work of education.

The whole point of civil society, at a sociological level, is to provide mediating institutions to stand between the individual and the state, or the individual and the economy. They're at their best when they are doing just that: They are mediating, they are educating. I know that argument is part of the "old" liberal consensus view, the "old" rules of public discourse. But the alternatives are violence. And I think we are getting to that point.

The Future

In this chapter, we have explored the important concept of religious polarization, a phenomenon we are witnessing expanding across the globe, becoming more deeply conflictual, entrenched, and dangerous.

Sociology can be accused (at times rightly) of simply identifying problems and explaining why they are problems but offering no path forward. In the earlier conversation, Professor Hunter offers the beginnings of a path forward. The problem is not that the solution is incorrect; the problem is that it entails people actually following the proscribed path. Too many people, too many organizations, and too many leaders want to play to the extreme, constantly upping the ante and making the "game" a winner-take-all battle.

In a democracy, whether from the left or the right, that approach is always wrong. Democracy is the agreement to discuss, to find places of compromise, to find ways for multiple groups with multiple understandings of reality to peacefully live their lives as they believe to be right.

Let's take marriage to make this tangible. Many people believe, often due to religious reasons and teachings, that marriage is between one man and one woman. Many others believe marriage should be for any two people (eventually, we suppose, a movement will push either to define marriage beyond two people or to end marriage altogether, but we leave that discussion to a future generation).

If we take seriously democracy, as defined earlier, if a law is to exist that defines marriage as between any two people (this can be negotiated, of course), what we cannot do is then force every organization and every person to believe and practice that version of marriage.

Doing so is clearly trampling upon one group in favor of another. If people want the right to marry legally in the eyes of the government, as long as they can do so, they have their freedom. Forcing religious congregations or religious believers to support or participate in such unions, which they have the right to believe are wrong, is unacceptable. Conversely, for those who see religious marriage as between a man and a woman, what a government defines marriage as need not be an assault on religious marriage. Smart, advanced people can find ways to allow groups with different views to co-exist. Is it messy? Of course, but so what. We love a challenge.

Can you be a leader who helps us create a nation that allows room for pluralism? Can you be part of generation willing to break the cycle of polarization we find ourselves in? Believe us when we say we are rooting for you. We need you.

Suggested Reading

Hunter, James Davidson. 2007. *Before the Shooting Begins: Searching for Democracy in America's Culture War*. New York: Free Press.

Juergensmeyer, Mark. 2003. *Terror in the Mind of God: The Global Rise of Religious Violence*, 3rd Edition. Berkeley: University of California Press.

Lu, Yun, and Yang Y. Xiaozhoa. 2020. "The Two Faces of Diversity: The Relationships between Religious Polarization, Religious Fractionalization, and Self-Rated Health." *Journal of Health and Social Behavior* 61(1): 79–95.

Ribberink, Egbert, Peter Achterberg, and Dick Houtman. 2018. "Religious Polarization: Contesting Religion in Secularized Western European Countries." *Journal of Contemporary American Religion* 33(2): 209–227.

7 Divine Rights and Fighting the Power

How Can Religion Simultaneously Block and Encourage Social Change?

1 Does religion inevitably help to keep things the same?
2 Is there a link between religion and forms of social inequality?
3 Many religions believe in justice. Can religion help to bring it about?
4 What factors limit the ability of religion to bring about change?

Think back to any course you've taken in history, especially any that dealt with Europe. You may remember that before the 19th century in Europe, and somewhat later in preindustrial societies elsewhere in the world, the wielding of power by rulers in most human societies was justified by linking the ruler to the sacred forces of the universe. Chiefs, kings, nobles, and other leaders ruled because they were chosen by the gods to do so.

In Christian Europe, North Africa, and the Middle East, this approach to the intersection of religion and secular political power had its roots in the Christian New Testament. In his letter to the Romans, St. Paul states:

> Let every person be subject to the governing authorities. For there is no authority except from God, and those that exist have been instituted by God. There he who resists the authorities resists what God has appointed, and those who resist will incur judgment.
>
> (Romans 13:1–2)

Almost 400 years later, Saint Augustine of Hippo argued in his work *The City of God* that God has instituted the authority of civil governments, even when they seem to be acting contrary to or in an antagonistic way toward the Church. It was not for another 1200 years that "divine right theory" took on a more extreme form when a French bishop, Jacques-Bénigne Bossuet, argued that kings, whether they ruled well or poorly, were accountable only to God and consequently that their actions could not be questioned or opposed. Wow! It doesn't get much clearer than that. Rulers can do what they want because God has put them in charge. They rule. We obey. For any of us to challenge government is to challenge God. We'll give you a minute to let that sink in!

While you may have learned about divine right theory before, you might not know that similar ideas exist in other religious traditions. In some Islamic traditions, for example, the ideal and only appropriate political structure is a theocracy, literally "the rule of God," which does not separate secular and religious authority at all. Allah rules through human representatives whose task is to enact laws that reflect Allah's will (Usman 1998).

Almost 2000 years ago, as the result of Chinese military conflicts that replaced the *Shang* dynasty with the *Zhou* dynasty, a new political philosophy called the *t'ien ming*, or "Mandate of Heaven," gained prominence to make legitimate the authority of the *Zhou* military victors. Like its parallels in Christian and Muslim history, the Mandate of Heaven requires those who rule to do so in ways

DOI: 10.4324/9781003182108-9

that support the welfare of the people with justice and wisdom. As long as a ruler does this, Heaven mandates that they and their family will remain in power for generations. However, unlike the situation in Christianity or Islam, the Mandate of Heaven could be removed from a ruler's dynasty if the ruler did not take care of the people or was unjust. This is quite a difference from Christian versions of divine right theory. In China, you had to be a "good" ruler. You had to make sure your people were happy, and that society worked well overall. If you didn't do this, you were in trouble. You would lose your Mandate. In such cases, the people are free to oppose and rebel against unjust rulers, and it is in fact their duty to do so. Japan's rulers also had a Mandate to rule, but their Mandate originated in the belief that the rulers were the direct descendants of the goddess of the sun (Hane 1991).

In all these examples, religious beliefs and practices helped to maintain the political and economic power structures of the societies in which they were used. One of the key observations that early social theorists made about religion as a social institution was that religion functioned specifically to support the status quo of society in political, economic, and cultural terms. In other words, religion was always "conservative" in the sense that its operations conserved society or kept society from changing.

From a sociological perspective, religion's conservative nature has important implications for understanding how power and inequality operate in a specific society. On the macrosocietal level, religion can maintain the power of individuals or groups through beliefs like the divine right of kings or the Mandate of Heaven. On the microsocietal level, it teaches individuals to accept the structure of society as it exists, even when the structure has negative consequences for the majority of people. Anyone who questioned the power structure in any of its forms or operations throughout history could be put in prison, tortured, or even killed for challenging the divinely ordained order of things. Yet, over the last century and a half, we have witnessed religious leaders and ordinary believers using their faith as the basis for challenging the power structures of societies around the world. From the antislavery and early labor movements of the 19th century to the Civil Rights movement of the 1960s, in the anti-colonial movements around the world, in the pro-life movement, and many other social movements, in all these events religious beliefs, practices, leaders, and organizations find roles in challenging the status quo. In this chapter, we will explore some of the classic theoretical statements about religion and social change that help explain why religion so often seems only to support the status quo. We will also look at insights from the study of social movements to see under what conditions religion can become a force for social change, what it brings to these kinds of social struggles, and what the consequences are of religiously motivated activism for both the religious traditions and the society in question.

Classic Observations About Religion and Social Change

Because many of the early social theorists were interested in the changes that were occurring in Europe and North America due to industrialization and the changing landscapes of politics following the French and American Revolutions, their observations and thoughts about the role that religious groups and people play in society must be understood with that social context in mind. In Chapter 1, for instance, we briefly discussed Karl Marx's famous statement that "religion is the opium of the people." Of all his statements in the thousands of pages that he wrote, this is one of the most memorable, and many people either strongly oppose it or agree with it. But people rarely consider why it made sense for him to write this statement in 1843.

As a result of capitalist expansion in the 19th century, European—and later American—industrialization was restructuring the social class system. The old system of feudalism, in which the kings, queens, lords, and ladies ruled and the peasants worked, was being replaced. Industrialization brought about a new system of social classes with capitalist employers, who owned most of society's productive property, including land and the new factories, and also controlled all the profits that their businesses earned. An industrial working class labored in these new factories for starvation wages, an arrangement that some outspoken labor advocates called "wage slavery." Now you may be thinking: "Hold it. What about the middle class?" We will grant that, at this time in history there were some people—such as small shopkeepers, blacksmiths, and farmers—who were neither employers nor workers. But the large, significant middle class that you may be thinking of didn't come into existence until more than a century later.

Now let's get back to religion. Supporting the status quo of this new capitalist system with its extremes of wealth and poverty were Christian congregations of all types. Religion supported these new forms of class inequality more often through its silence than in formal statements like the divine right theory. Although the negative results of industrialization, like hunger, disease, chronic unemployment, and threats of revolution were all around them, most religious leaders never said much about them. Those problems were economic issues, after all, and ministers were supposed to worry about people's souls, not their jobs. Religious leaders encouraged church members to live good Christian lives by being obedient to religious teachings and to see the dynamics of the world as part of the spiritual battle between good and evil, righteousness and sin, and God and the devil. Ministers usually observed that wealth and poverty simply expressed the social differences given to each person by God in which people receive the legitimate result of their intelligence and labor. Wealth and poverty were just part of the natural order. (The poor, after all, were always to be with us.) Ministers also implied—or directly stated—that wealthy people demonstrated more moral behavior than did the poor, who were assumed to be poor because they wasted what little money they had on alcohol and tobacco. But most of all, the significance of religious support for the capitalist system was the manner in which it diverted the attention of the working classes and the poor away from the real-world social causes and the lived experiences of their poverty. When religious messages addressed economic inequality, they did so in a way that patted the wealthy on the back for their right living and gave the poor hope that they would go to heaven after they died, where there would be no death, hunger, mourning, or pain, provided that they endured these inevitable trials here on earth and remained obedient to their church's teachings.

This was the historical context, then, when Marx dismissed religion from playing any positive part in changing society, especially through efforts to alleviate economic or any other form of injustice. Religion diverts attention *away* from practical conflicts between the powerful and powerless, rich and poor, and bosses and workers in the realm of capitalist production and directs it *toward* a mystified struggle between good and evil on some abstract, spiritual plane. But Marx also understood that religion was something that was attractive to exploited or oppressed peoples because it provided some degree of actual comfort and solace to those whose lives were painful. By likening religion to opium, a drug that numbs and deadens pain, Marx underscores the real and material nature of the suffering and oppression that drives people to seek relief in religion. The problem, as Marx saw it, was that instead of diagnosing the true cause of the suffering (capitalism) and encouraging those who were oppressed to fight back and end it, religion links suffering to otherworldly, and therefore false, causes (sin, the devil, God's wrath, hell), telling them to be passive and patient and wait for change in heaven.

For further evidence in support of this position, consider the many ways that religion in the 20th century, up to our own time, has supported a variety of economic, political, racial, and sexual expressions of inequality. In the days of the American Civil Rights movement, White clergy regularly preached about the Biblical basis for the system of racial segregation in the American South. Well-known ministers such as Reverend Jerry Falwell, who later went on to found the Moral Majority, and Dr. W. A. Criswell, one-time pastor of the largest Southern Baptist congregation in the country, which was located in Dallas, preached against any attempt to integrate American society and condemned those who supported integration as working against God himself (Freeman

2007). Other ministers tried to support the basic equality of Southern Blacks as children of God while simultaneously defending segregation as a theological reality. For example, Smith (1950, 15, 28), a Southern Evangelist with his own radio program, tried to defend both the rights of African Americans *and* segregation. In preaching on the Radio Bible Hour in 1950 from Del Rio, Texas, Smith argued:

> If America turns from God's answer, and fails to keep her RACES PURE by SEGREGATION, there will be neither WHITE nor NEGRO race remaining. But SHE WILL TURN INTO A NEGROID RACE OF PEOPLE! . . . God wants the races to be BLACK, YELLOW, or WHITE, like He intended them to be. He does not delight in a mixture. We all want pure food and have PURE FOOD LAWS. We want purity in our worship and medicine. Why not have it in our RACES?

But as we noted before, religion does not always work to legitimatize the status quo in such obvious and extreme ways. Most clergy in Northern Ireland, for example, rarely speak out about the sectarian violence that continues between Protestants and Catholics there; instead, they shy away from generating bad feelings and conflict among their parishioners (McAllister 1998). Silence on these issues is another way in which religion acts as an agent of social control.

Marx's critique of religion as a conservative social force was picked up by later generations of social theorists and reformers who challenged religious groups on many issues, including their support of slavery, colonialism, segregation, male domination and privilege in society, and discrimination on the basis of sexuality and gender.

Approximately 80 years after Marx, Max Weber built a more nuanced argument about religion, power, and inequality that introduced the concept of *theodicy*. For Weber, as modern society became more bureaucratic and rational, its culture increasingly raised questions about "causes and effects" and "means and ends." If I do X, then Y will result. Or, put in a different way, if I want to achieve Y, then I ought to do X. People act on the basis of the meanings that they give their actions (things they want to do or know they ought to want to do) and also act as a result of their interests in achieving certain outcomes. But life is not that simple.

Many times, we do all the right things and yet do not achieve what we expect or are told we ought to achieve as a result. Students study hard and still fail exams. Employees put in long hours and sweat only to have their wages cut or to be fired. A poor nation in the developing world builds a McDonald's in their capital city to be just like countries in Europe or North America, yet the country remains poor and marginal. In each of these cases, there is a discrepancy between behavior and its results. In religious terms, this problem can be summed up as "Why do bad things happen to good people?" "Why do the good die young?" or even the words of Jesus himself when he says, "My God, my God, why have you forsaken me?" What Weber (1967 [1922]) observed is that people's individual experiences of the inequalities of modern life—inequalities that are based on class, prestige, and political power—create discrepancies in what people believe. Why do the poor, who follow their mandated religious beliefs and practices devotedly, remain poor, living lives of hardship, hunger, and sickness; while the rich, who seem to violate many religious teachings, end up living lives of comfort? It just doesn't make sense.

Box 7.1 Theodicy

A concept used by Max Weber to explain systems of belief that help to explain human suffering, inequalities, sickness, and other negative aspects of human life and society.

Into the gap between what we believe should happen and what actually does happen in our experience step theodicies. Theodicies explain why these discrepancies exist at all—especially the ones that result from the widespread misfortunes of whole groups of people—and help us to resolve them in our minds. It is important to realize that, because not every social group in society experiences these negative consequences in the same way, different forms of theodicies emerge to help explain various groups' experiences. Theodicies of *suffering* are the religious beliefs that help the lower classes of society come to terms with why they are poor, powerless, or otherwise marginalized in society, and what they can do—if anything—to gain some degree of redemption. Weber observes (Gerth and Mills 1964, 275):

> One can explain suffering and injustice by referring to individual sin committed in a former life (the migration of souls), to the guilt of ancestors, which is avenged down to the third and fourth generation, or—the most principled—to the wickedness of all creatures *per se*. As compensatory promises, one can refer to the hopes of the individual for a better life in the future in this world (transmigration of souls) or to hopes for the successors (Messianic realm), or to a better life in the hereafter (paradise).

Regardless of the specific causes and solutions that a particular poor person's religious tradition identifies, a theodicy of suffering helps explain why things are the way they are in the lives of those who are at the margins of society.

In contrast to the theodicies that are developed to explain the lives of the poor, there are theodicies for those in power that explain the gaps between these people and other groups ranking below them in society. For the elite, theodicies of *dominance* answer the difficult question of why their lives are so full of resources while others have so little:

> Strata in solid possession of social honor and power usually tend to fashion their status-legend in such a way as to claim a special and intrinsic quality of their own, usually a quality of blood; their sense of dignity feeds on their actual or alleged being. (Gerth and Mills 1964, 276)

In religious terms, the elite believe that they have been blessed by God or the gods. Frequently, the possession of great resources comes linked with the ethical responsibility to use these resources in the service of others and society as a whole. Religious teachings that mandate acts of charity and outreach to the poor and needy become more central among the elite. Moreover, instead of placing an emphasis on guilt and sin—either one's own or one's ancestors'—a theodicy of dominance affirms the ways of life enjoyed by the elite as evidence of righteous living or as a lifestyle to be upheld. You may remember that we talked about a similar concept in Chapter 2. Members of the Indian Brahman caste who fulfill their responsibilities as elites in society expect to enjoy continuing good fortunes in future lives.

The importance of Weber's theodicies is that they link religious beliefs and practices to specific social groups. Theodicies recognize that even when people all belong to the same religion they may worship differently from one another, their theologies and beliefs may emphasize different things and in some cases be radically different, and they may experience the sacred in different ways. Now, Weber did not want us to think that religious beliefs were inevitable reflections of economic class differences or that they supported only the interests of the privileged, as Marx's formulations did. However, Weber did acknowledge that religion has the potential both to support the status quo of inequality and to challenge it at specific times and in specific places in history.

Weber's ideas about religion also laid the groundwork for contemporary studies of religion and social change. Incorporated in the theoretical links he made between theodicies and different class and status groups is the idea that religion, especially for the non-privileged, can be the basis for expressing those groups' frustrations and resentments at the injustices they experience. Unlike

Marx, Weber held that the theodicies of the poor or lower classes were not always a drug to comfort and divert them. Instead, their theodicies could encourage them to work to try to change their world. Theodicies of suffering, Weber observed, also bring with them the idea that the religion of the poor includes "a special mission," an "ethical imperative," and a " 'task' placed before them by God," to bring the social order back in line with the divine will by prophetic social action in this world. As we will see, religious beliefs and practices include prophetic calls for social and economic justice in this world, not just promises that it will exist in the next. Throughout history, religion has played a role in maintaining the existing structure of society and has also given birth to a wide range of social movements and reform efforts that have literally changed the world.

The Lessons from Studying Social Movements

Much of the sociological work on religion, forms of economic and social inequality, and social change has been based on the two perspectives provided by Karl Marx and Max Weber. Many studies conducted during the 20th century tried to address the theoretical binary of "religion as opiate" versus "religion as mobilizer." The study of social movement activism has produced a great deal of evidence to demonstrate that the relationship between religion and social change is never "either/or." It is always "both/and." Religion provides a set of resources that are important to all efforts to create social change.

Christian Smith's *Disruptive Religion* represents a rare attempt by a sociologist to systematically categorize all the possible resources available from religious institutions that are significant for social movement activism, though other scholars focus on subsets of these resources (1996a, 9). (See Table 7.2.) In all, Smith notes 21 separate "religious assets" that make up six basic types of resources, which are useful for activism, some obvious and others less so. Religious resources are divided into motivational, organizational, identity-constructing, social and geographical positioning, privileged legitimacy, and institutional self-interest.

Among the most important assets that religion can bring to social movements is a reason or motivation for a person to participate in the movement and put himself or herself at risk in fighting for social change. The idea that justice and freedom are God's will for humans here on earth, so fighting for these causes is a moral commandment, not only gets people to act, but also provides strength and courage, rooted in the sacred, that allows participants to face police brutality, jail, torture, and even death for the cause of justice. For example, religious teachings that mandate social and economic justice, paired with stories from sacred texts, are powerful means to motivate people to action (Gutterman 2005; Swarts 2008). In one example, a Muslim environmental activist affiliated with the Muslim Green Team in California clearly sees her activism as rooted in the Qur'an:

> There are verses in the Qur'an—the world around us, od refers to it as a miracle, a sign. But he uses the same Arabic word . . . for the environment . . . we should also be respecting it. It's also sacred and divine. It's also a creation of God. . . . You've heard on the news, the burning of the Qur'an, Muslims get mad, right? I mean, it's our sacred text. We should also be upset when the environment is being destroyed. . . . It's also a miracle of God.

> (quoted in Hancock 2015, 51)

On the basis of these teachings, religious leaders also have the authority to tell their members what to do—which causes they should support and which they should oppose. Sometimes this authority can also be used to challenge or even condemn people in power when they are perceived to be violating a religion's moral teachings (deviance-monitoring), such as when U.S. Catholic Bishops advanced a policy in 2021 to deny access to the Eucharist to Catholic politicians, in this case President Joe Biden, who did not support church teachings that opposed abortion. Similarly, though in a manner that was more opposed to protest, Patriarch Kirill, head of the Russian Orthodox Church, condemned the 2011 mass demonstrations against election fraud in Russia, citing that protesters were in opposition to Orthodox Church teachings and God's truth, thereby throwing the religious authority of the Church behind the government (Sweet 2015).

Music, songs, and personal testimonies can also motivate people to fight back in spite of the dangers they are likely to encounter in doing so (Gutman 1966; Halker 1991; Mirola 2003a). Among other religious resources that Smith noted are useful for social activism are financial support, meeting space, access to computers and copiers for communicating information and making flyers and leaflets, and established organizational networks that link local congregations to national and international religious bodies. During the Occupy Movement that began in 2011, Trinity Episcopal Church on Wall Street, which was at the epicenter of the Occupy Wall Street protests in New York City, initially provided space for meetings, electricity, toilets, and food and shelter for protesters (Cloke et al. 2016). Sharing a religious tradition, even at the most universal level where people are simply Muslims or Christians or even just religious believers, often can get them to work together for a common cause in a way that no other shared identity could (Yukich and Braunstein 2014; Ng and Fulda 2017; Delehanty 2018).

The Emergence of Religious Activism

So, now you know something about the complex ways that religion simultaneously can inhibit and empower social activism. But now a new question emerges: "What conditions shape whether any particular religious tradition will generate activism for social change and whether it will maintain the status quo?"

Box 7.2 Religious Resources That Are Available for Social Movements (Smith 1996a)

I **Transcendent Motivation Assets**
   A Legitimation for protest rooted in the ultimate or sacred
   B Moral imperatives for love, justice, peace, freedom, and equality
   C Powerfully motivating icons, rituals, songs, testimonies, and oratory
   D Ideologies demanding self-discipline, sacrifice, and altruism
   E Legitimation of organizational and strategic-tactical flexibility

II **Organizational Assets**
   A Trained and experienced leadership
   B Financial resources
   C Congregated participants and solidarity incentives
   D Preexisting communication channels
   E Preexisting authority structures and deviance-monitoring mechanisms
   F Enterprise tools
   G "Movement midwives"

III **Shared-Identity Assets**
   A Common identification among gathered strangers
   B Shared superidentities nationally and internationally
   C Unifying identity against outside threats

IV **Social and Geographic Positioning**
   A Geographical dispersion
   B Social diffusion and cross-cutting associations
   C Transnational organizational linkages

V **Privileged Legitimacy**
   A Political legitimacy in public opinion
   B The protection of religion as a last "open space"

VI **Institutional Self-interest**
   A Institutional resistance to state encroachment

Let's think about the answer to this in two ways. First, we need to explore this question from the standpoint of religious groups and congregations themselves, what we might call "religious activism." For them, the question is best reframed to address those occasions when whole denominations or religious groups engage in social and political change efforts or movements. Familiar evidence for this can be seen today in the pro-life movement, in which evangelical Protestants, Roman Catholics, and many congregations from socially conservative religions have mobilized their resources to call for greater regulation of abortion procedures and to attempt to overturn *Roe v. Wade*, the Supreme Court case that made abortion legal in the United States.

A less familiar example comes from the ways in which congregations in countries like Poland and East Germany became the organizational base for their respective national movements to end the Soviet-backed socialist government in their countries. In 1989, every Monday night, thousands of people gathered at the Church of Saint Nicholai in the East German city of Leipzig for prayer services that were also political demonstrations led by Pastor Friedrich Magirius. In these, as well as many other instances, congregations and their leaders have mobilized around a wide variety of social changes. But the question remains: Why does this seem to happen around some social changes but not others?

Of course, one key reason this happens comes back to the content of these religious groups' theologies and their histories of social and political engagement. Congregations will not become politically involved overnight. Most religious traditions have theological understandings of secular politics and social change that shape whether the members of these groups will make efforts to try to change aspects of the secular world. Many fundamentalist Christian congregations, for instance, believe that the world is too sinful to be changed for the better. Such an approach leads them to retreat from contact with the world and to focus on holy living while waiting for Jesus to return, destroy this world, and create a new one. Many U.S. Evangelical and mainline Protestant religious groups have had more open social theologies that go back to the fight to end slavery in the American South and earlier still, to battles for freedom of religion and for the separation of church and state following the Revolutionary War (Smith 1998). Today, mainline Protestants and Roman Catholics who were radicalized by the Civil Rights movement of the 1950s and 1960s continue to be more engaged than members of some other denominations in fights around racial equality, poverty, employment, and many other related issues. Black Pentecostal clergy and congregations that have not been engaged in political activism are increasingly drawing on their own racial and religious histories to mold new ways of generating congregationally based activism (McRoberts 1999). Consequently, when a new issue comes along, such as immigrant rights or neighborhood development, these types of congregations can draw from their tradition of beliefs and practices and apply those ideas to the new issue (Craig 1992; Wuthnow 1988).

But a historical tradition of activism is not enough to predict whether or not religion will become a force for social change. A classic 1942 study by Liston Pope examined the role of local churches in shaping labor reforms in the textile mills of Gastonia, North Carolina, in the 1930s. In their introduction to the study, Peterson and Demerath (1942, xxxii–xl) argue that five principal conditions shape the likelihood that religious groups will become forces for social change. (See Box 7.3.) These include the type of issue itself and how the congregation's members feel about it, the degree of actual congregational involvement, the structure of the denomination, the level from which a religious group is calling for involvement, and the background of the minister.

Of course, not all social issues engage religious groups equally. In our own recent history, we have seen that issues related to gender and sexuality generate great interest and concern in congregations from many religions. Issues related to life and death, such as abortion, war, the death penalty, stem cell research, and euthanasia all have mobilized religious groups to work politically in both support of and in opposition to them. But think for a minute about environmental activism, the anti-globalization, or anti-nuclear power movements. Religious groups or leaders do not figure as prominently in these social movements. We'd be wrong to think that religious groups are unconcerned about these movements and their causes, or even that they have not taken stands or worked politically either to support or oppose any goals of these movements. Yet it is rare for entire religious organizations with their members to participate in social activism around these issues.

However, as Peterson and Demerath suggest, the more frequently and deeply members of churches do get involved with such issues, the more likely it will be for the religious group or denomination as a whole to do so. A clear example of this tendency is the environmental movement or the global justice movement focused on global economic inequality. Until recently, it was rare to hear religious leaders speaking out about environmental degradation or the need to expand conservation efforts. Likewise, until the Occupy movement popularized the elite economic 1% versus the remaining 99%, talk of Biblical views of wealth disparities were few and far between.

Box 7.3 Factors Influencing Religion to Become a Force in Social Change Movements

1 The type of issue and the degree of congregational interest and commitment to it
2 The extent of congregation members' involvement in social issues
3 The governing structure of the congregation and/or denomination
4 The level of the religious organization's hierarchy from which a statement is issued
5 The background characteristics of the religious leaders in congregations

Source: Robinson (1987, 53).

1 A preponderantly religious world view among revolutionary classes
2 Theology at odds with the existing social order
3 Clergy closely associated with revolutionary classes
4 Revolutionary classes united in a single religion
5 Revolutionary classes' religion different from the religion of the dominant class
6 Alternative organizational structures and political access not available

Source: Robinson (1987, 53).

Today, because so many more people have become motivated to protect the environment as well as working to reduce economic disparities around the world, many faith groups are more visible in these movements and have developed new theologies and policies to address them (Hancock 2015; Smith and Smythe 2017). When we get to Chapter 14, you'll see how this happened among Evangelical and other Christian groups.

More important than the issues that attract the interest and activism of religious groups, though, is the internal political structure of the religious group. Religious groups have different kinds of decision-making and governing structures. Some groups are hierarchical with formal pronouncements about what members of a faith ought to do or think about issues being handed down from those with authority at the top of the organization. For instance, the Roman Catholic Church has issued "encyclicals" and other formal statements from the Pope regarding the Church's position on various social issues. In 1891, Pope Leo XIII released *Rerum Novarum*, "On the Condition of Workers," in which he officially called on all Catholics to support the labor movement's efforts to achieve collective bargaining rights, living wages, shorter hours, and other reforms. The encyclical also formally permitted Catholics to join labor unions. Likewise, in 1968, Pope Paul VI issued his encyclical, *Humanae Vitae*, which became a contemporary basis for Roman Catholic involvement with the pro-life movement. But not every religious group is hierarchical. Some are arranged so that each member has a say or a vote in making decisions or crafting policies. In these cases, whether a religious group becomes involved in social change, and whether the group works for or against change, rests solely with the congregation itself. When James Wood studied which types of church-governing structures were most likely to support national civil rights policy *as churches*, he found that those with hierarchical structures were most likely to do so and those with more congregational (member-based) structures were least likely to do so (Wood 1970). The reason for this finding has to do with the way the political structure of the denomination or congregation buffers clergy who wish to take action on an issue from a disapproving or apathetic congregation. In a hierarchical structure, a minister's authority to openly engage social and political issues is recognized, even if church members disapprove of the involvement. In a congregational structure, because the minister serves at the will of the congregation, disapproving members of such congregations can "veto" a minister's wish to become publicly involved in any particular social issue by threatening to rescind that minister's call to lead them.

Of course, decisions by those at the top of a religious structure to take a political stand on some issue—regardless of the governing structure of local congregations—may not result in local congregations actually doing so. For instance, the national governing bodies of many mainline Protestant denominations have issued statements calling on members and local congregations to actively work for economic justice around the world by supporting campaigns for a higher minimum wage, the right to organize unions, and employer-provided health care and other benefits. However, as Pope (1942) and others have demonstrated, just because the leaders of a denomination call people to action doesn't mean that they will actually work for these issues locally. When the national Episcopal Church voted to approve the ordination of female priests, some local congregations and regional dioceses simply ignored the issue, and a few continue to do so to the present day. The point here is that the further removed an official call for social action or involvement is from local members of religious groups and their concerns, the less likely these religious pronouncements in support of change are to translate into action.

Finally, whether a religious group will engage in social activism depends to a great extent on the characteristics and background of the group's religious leaders. As Peterson and Demerath (1942, xxxvii) observed, the level of activity is related to a minister's age, the minister's social status (in the sense of prominence), the amount and quality of his or her education, the location of the congregation (rural, urban, or suburban) a minister serves and whether he or she was brought up in these areas, and whether the minister has "tenure" or some degree of protection from members who disagree with him or her. Younger ministers, those with more personal social prominence in their background, those with university educations (as opposed to a Bible college training), and those from more urban and cosmopolitan backgrounds all are more likely, as Peterson and Demerath said in 1942, "to be more independent and more adventuresome" when it comes to working for social and political change in their communities. Similar patterns have been found among today's clergy.

Using data from the first wave of the National Congregations Study in 1998, several sets of researchers found relationships between education or social class and clergy social activism. Among Evangelical clergy, the amount of education had no effect, but among mainline Protestants and Black Protestant clergy, higher education was associated with the clergy being more politically engaged (McDaniel 2003; Guth et al. 2003; Smidt et al. 2003). The higher the social class, the more likely clergy were to support social- and gender-related public issues while remaining neutral on or opposing issues that touched on economic justice. This finding reflects a long-standing effect of how class mediates religious convictions for making the world a better place, which has appeared in many studies of religion and social reform (Hart 1992; McCloud and Mirola 2008; Olson 2000).

Race and gender also play roles in shaping clergy activism. As a group, Black clergy are theologically conservative but can be politically liberal and are more likely to be politically engaged on many other issues besides theology (Olson 2000). In her study of 10 Black churches in Philadelphia, Day (2001, 184) found that Black pastors were in positions in their communities where almost daily they had to "confront the urban policies of city, state, and federal agencies as well as banking, commercial, and philanthropic communities . . . Once again, if the Black Church doesn't do it, who will?" Swarts (2008) notes that urban congregations, especially Black Protestant, mainline Protestant, and Roman Catholic churches, are among the few organizations that remain in many inner cities across the country. Their location makes them prime candidates for institutions to work on social activism, especially on poverty, housing, and urban development issues, because they witness the economic and political forces that cause these problems on a daily basis.

Women clergy are more likely to express their interest in political engagement as a living out of their religious convictions. However, there is still a debate about whether women ministers are more actively engaged than their male counterparts. Laura Olson's 2000 study of Milwaukee Protestant clergy included four women pastors. She found that the three women serving in mainline Protestant churches felt unable to be vocal about or personally involved with political issues because of pressure from their congregations to avoid these issues. The single woman she interviewed who served a Black Protestant congregation, in contrast, addressed political issues in her preaching and in her ministerial role, although she was neither personally nor practically involved with political efforts to change the conditions of life in her inner-city neighborhood because those efforts were not the focus of the senior male pastor in the congregation.

When Activists Get Religion

Examining what factors push religious groups from within to work for social change is only one part of the story. Secular social movements and their organizations often attempt to mobilize religious resources. In these cases, movements see benefit in building coalitions with congregations or religious individuals in communities to tap their resources. While social movements seeking support from religious groups see benefits in forging these associations, they are not trying to make their movements "religious." More often, they are trying to use religion to gain the support of a religious general public, to build solidarity within their movement when activists themselves hold strong religious values, or to appeal to individuals or groups in power to grant their desired changes or reforms.

Robinson (1987) outlined a set of conditions that shape the likelihood that religion will become a tool for social movement activism in the way we have described. (See Table 7.2.) Although Robinson was interested in revolutionary movements that were aimed at radical national and political change specifically, it is useful to think about these conditions as they apply to less extreme forms of social movements. Two of these conditions focus on the religious beliefs of the groups mobilizing for social change.

Robinson argues that religion is likely to be used as a source for social movement resources when movement participants themselves maintain a view of reality that is specifically rooted in religious tradition and when these participants also share the same religious tradition. In other words, religion is important when there is a shared religious culture among the people who are fighting for change. For example, Southern Black churches have been the cornerstones of community life for African Americans since the end of slavery. Because African Americans in the South joined a rather small number of different Protestant denominations, they tend to share a similar religious culture that ultimately made the interweaving of the civil rights message with religious ideas logical and fairly straightforward for the movement. Today, it is still true that any social movement that seeks to engage the African American community must first gain the approval of Black churches and their clergy (Swarts 2008; Wood 2002).

But sharing a similar religious culture with potential supporters is not in itself a sufficient basis for movements to "get religion." Robinson also noted that the beliefs and practices of a religious group must truly oppose the ones that the social movement is opposing. Because the elite often use religion to justify their power, those who are trying to challenge elite power may be suspicious of people who are religious. However, when alternative religious beliefs link God's will, themes of justice, and liberation to legitimatize a movement's critique of the existing social order and the need for concrete social reform—and even radical change—religion will become revolutionary. *Theologies of liberation*, constructed by religious activists living among the poor in developing countries, provided oppressed groups in these places with a foundation for their resistance and reform efforts. These beliefs became alternatives that allowed marginalized and poor people to reject other religious beliefs that would have kept them in their place. Furthermore, this distinct separation between the religious beliefs of the groups who are fighting for change and those of the group with power becomes another way to reinforce the "us versus them" distinction between groups in conflict. The groups that are fighting for change ("us") have God on our side, are Right, are Good, are fighting for Justice, and will eventually be victorious, while their opponents ("them") by definition are Wrong, are Evil, are Unjust, and will eventually lose.

Religion also is likely to play a role in social movements when religious leaders themselves, in their personal lives, have close ties to movement participants. These ties may emerge from *physical proximity*, in which participants of a social movement are members of their congregations, or when clergy witness the objective conditions that affect movement participants, such as unemployment, hunger, disease, poverty, or military repression. Both of these conditions were obtained when Roman Catholic priests and nuns stood up for the poor and indigenous peoples throughout Latin America after directly experiencing their living conditions (Lernoux 1982). This closeness may also emerge when religious leaders are members of the group fighting for social change and would benefit directly from its success.

Finally, Robinson argues that in order for religion to be seen as a practical resource for social change, movement participants must lack alternative resources, organizations, and means for generating social change. Religious resources, in other words, often are the only ones available. But let's be clear about this. We are not saying that religion is a choice of last resort. For groups that lack access to political, economic, and other sorts of power, using religion not only makes sense for the reasons we have noted, but it is one of the only resources available to support a mass movement. An examination of the many social movements around the world in history confirms that groups fighting for social changes are also systematically denied access to political power, economic resources, media resources, and just about any other set of resources. In these cases, religious resources become, at least initially, the only ones available to support social activism. Congregations become political-organizing locations because they are the one physical space where movement participants can gather free from observation by the powerful. The collection plate on Sunday mornings becomes the means for collecting scarce finances among the poor. Sermons call for social change in practical terms that are supported by religious teachings, symbols, and traditions. When some groups in society are blocked from using formal mechanisms to achieve social change, or when those in power resist the change that the public demands, religion is likely to enter the struggle as a force for change.

But more than anything else, movement activists see religion as a strategic source of resources apart from the fact of the activists holding religious worldviews or lacking access to the political process. Movements "get religion" because they believe that doing so can and will help them win the tangible goal of social change.

Any Limits of Religion's Influence on Change?

In a word, yes. It's important to know about the conditions that turn religion into a force for social change or open up religious resources as tools for secular social movements. However, believers and activists alike sometimes assume that religion is without limits in its abilities to change the world once it is mobilized to do so. Nevertheless, the histories of many social movements include a subtext that hints at the structural challenges that limit the powers of religious groups and leaders once they become part of social movements.

Religious beliefs themselves can be an obstacle to mobilizing groups for change. Though many religious traditions have social teachings regarding justice, equality, and fairness with which most people would agree, these same groups also have beliefs with which many, especially activists from secular organizations, would disagree. For example, Roman Catholics have a strong tradition supporting peace and social justice and consequently often appear in movements focused on those types of issues. But Catholic teaching that opposes abortion or recognition of same-sex marriages can be equally central. Since Roman Catholicism teaches that all the beliefs of the church are absolute and not open to compromise, this combination of teachings can pose a potential problem for movements that seek the support of Catholics. Activists who are working to alleviate poverty, hunger, or war may see Catholics as easy allies because of their peace and justice traditions. But—and here's the key—what happens to movement unity and cooperation when those same activists also want to fight for LGBTQ+ rights, abortion rights, or population control (see for instance Smith and Smythe 2017)? For non-Catholics and for many non-religious secular activists, all of these issues are clear social justice issues, but Catholics may see them as violations of their Church's teachings on family, marriage, and the life of the unborn, making religion more a divisive force in building social movement coalitions. This example illustrates how the process of building movement relationships and coalitions that are religiously diverse or that bring together religious and nonreligious activists can break down over religious beliefs, dividing a movement before it even begins to mobilize the unity it needs to achieve its goals.

Religion's impact on and within social movement activism is further limited by the characteristics of the religious activists themselves. Differences among these activists in class, race, gender, neighborhood, and even official roles within the religious group can disrupt the ability of religion to create a united front to achieve change. Social class divides between, say, different groups of religious activists, or movement leaders and the rank-and-file members, can create conflict with movements. Middle-class churchgoers often come from religious and class cultures that are more reserved and that emphasize respectability, while parishioners who are working-class, poor, and members of minority cultures are often accustomed to being more emotionally involved in church services. For example, they may be accustomed to "call and response" services in which congregations shout out their agreement with the minister's or other leader's statements. It can be difficult for members of these two different types of churchgoers to join forces to verbally challenge the elite. In a 2008 study of congregation-based community organizing, Swarts recounts an event hosted by the Saint Louis-based Metropolitan Churches United. A state senator's aide at the event was booed by 2500 church members, most of whom were poor, for not being prepared to discuss a piece of legislation that was the focus of the meeting. The priest who was chairing the meeting allowed the booing to go on. In hindsight, the priest felt badly about allowing the aide to be booed. Swarts (2008, 10) notes, "The priest's understanding of Christian behavior influenced his etiquette of contention: he was reluctant to polarize the conflict and cast the aide as an opponent. But to his organizers, the moment of empowering the disempowered enacted a higher justice." Class differences in forms of contention and disagreement vary widely, leading to intra-movement divides between middle-class leaders and rank-and-file participants or their working-class counterparts.

Likewise, participants in the Occupy Wall Street Movement, although initially supported theologically and practically by the clergy and lay leadership of Trinity Episcopal Church-Wall Street, faced a radical shift in that support when they wished to move their camp to an empty lot owned by the church. The clergy and the Vestry, which is the governing board of lay church members, decided that it would not be appropriate to allow this, calling the proposal "wrong, unsafe, unhealthy, and potentially injurious" (quoted in Cloke et al. 2016, 503). Just imagine it—Trinity Wall Street, one of the largest real estate owners in the city, owning close to six million square feet of property in Manhattan, moves from embracing Occupy to rejecting it because the economic and political demands of support got too high. Trinity Wall Street as a wealthy, land-owning parish is a part of the religious and economic "1%" and as such, due to their changed position on Occupy, went from being an ally to a target. "Occupy Trinity Church Wall Street" was a focused protest of the church's actions with close to 60 people sleeping on the church steps as a "sleep-in" protest surrounded by signs that asked: "Who Would Jesus Prosecute?" and "Trinity Church: Real Estate Company or Church?" (Cloke et al. 2016, 503). Gaining the support of wealthy people (religious or not) can bring needed financial resources and media attention to a social movement. Yet, class divides between those same wealthy people and the middle class, working-class, or poor participants in social movements can disrupt resource mobilization and coalition-building, as well as achieving desired goals.

Differences in race and ethnicity also can undermine religiously based activism. White congregations and religious leaders on the whole think about social justice and how to achieve it differently from the ways that African American congregations do. White conservative Protestants along with many other types of Christians in the United States, for example, tend to focus on individual rather than structural factors in their understanding of social inequalities. This goes hand in hand with America's historic ideological legacy of rugged individualism (Delahanty 2018). If a person is poor, they believe that the solution is to improve the person's skills and abilities and to limit any individual behavior or morality that may be blocking them from achieving economic well-being (Emerson and Smith 2000). In African American congregations, individuals are more likely to take a structural or policy approach to addressing social problems, focusing less on the individual and more on the economic and political policies that maintain inequalities. African American congregations are also more likely to be involved in local neighborhood issues, community issues, and civil rights activities. Racial differences can play out as religious leaders and their congregations decide what kinds of movements for change "make sense."

Gender differences also can cause controversy, especially with regard to the leadership of social movements. For example, women ministers from Black and mainline Protestant congregations and women rabbis from Jewish congregations may not be recognized as legitimate religious leaders by other clergy or by conservative Protestant or Roman Catholic activists (Olson 2000).

Religion is also limited in its ability to mobilize mass movements when religious and secular activists work in the same social movement organizations and must agree to strategies and tactics for action. Sociologists who study social movement activism observe that the unique cultures of religious groups do not always work well with the cultures of other social change groups, such as unions, political parties, or secular community organizing groups like the Association of Community Organizations for Reform, more commonly called ACORN (Rose 2000; Simmons 1994; Smith 1996b; Swarts 2008; Wood 2002). Religious groups tend to enter social movement activism and coalitions with less focus on top-down decision-making and action within hierarchies and more focus on building inclusiveness, supporting equality, allowing democratic participation, and operating by consensus (Delehanty 2018; Krull 2020). Unions, political parties, and other similar groups with whom these religious groups may partner are hierarchical organizations whose leaders tend to determine the strategies and tactics and whose rank-and-file members are expected to carry them out. Religious groups may want to focus on process and on building consensus before taking action, whereas secular groups want to act quickly. Religious activists see their role as building and extending a moral force for change that requires strong relationships. Secular activists are more likely to focus on doing what is necessary to win. These fundamental differences in group process and culture can breed frustration and alienation between would-be allies.

But it is not just a religious versus secular divide that can disrupt social movement coalitions. Differences among religious activists themselves can create tension and undermine protest activities. In her study of more liberal Protestant congregational social justice activism aimed at "expanding the social safety net" in North Carolina in 2013, Krull (2020) identifies tensions within liberal congregations committed to inclusivity. How should religious activists who claim to welcome and embrace everyone approach social protest activities that target oppositional groups or individuals? For example, should a progressive, left-leaning congregation or religious individual, committed to both social justice and inclusion, participate in protest activities that specifically target police officers in the case of the Black Lives Matter movement or men in #Metoo or Trump-era Republican politicians who supported dismantling social welfare, environmental protection, or immigrant rights? Can one still be "inclusive" while morally or practically demonizing others? Maybe you can, but then maybe not. These are not easy questions to answer, and speak to how holding to seemingly straightforward religious beliefs about equality and inclusion can constrain as well as empower activism.

Tactical decisions for how best to achieve movement goals can also be a source of division for religious activists in social movements (Smith 1996b). When a social movement uses more aggressive tactics, religious activists often are less willing to engage, even when the tactics are used in the heat of intense conflicts. In William A. Mirola's study of church-labor coalitions in the 1995 strike of 2500 newspaper employees against the *Detroit News* and *Detroit Free Press*, religious leaders and lay supporters were extremely put off by the use of derogatory and profane language on picket lines, in conflicts with replacement workers, and with the police (2003b, 455). One religious activist noted,

> We had a hard time in being involved in some of the union face-offs where the Teamsters would show up with slingshots and hide behind one another and zap the guards. We were trying to make a public impression that the guards were acting out, which they were, and expose it, but not this sleight of hand thing, where you are doing the same bullshit but you're just exposing the opposition. We'd like to see a consistent ethic across the board.

Conflicting definitions of what constitute appropriate or legitimate forms of protest between congregation-based and secular participants in a social movement can undermine their ability to work together. Perceptions that tactics have "gone too far" can bring a halt to religiously motivated activism (Cousineau 1998). Religious activists often withdraw from these conflicts under such circumstances. Secular activists may learn from the experience that religious resources are more trouble than they are worth to organize and may be reticent to build coalitions with congregations in future conflicts.

Concluding Thoughts

In this chapter, we have explored the complex ways that religion works to maintain the structures of power and inequality in the social world. We also have explored how religion can challenge those structures and work to change them. Because religion so often emphasizes the importance of order, harmony, patience, meekness, and service, religious leaders and their teachings have consciously and unconsciously helped to support the powerful. The teachings tell members of society who are on the bottom rungs of the social ladder to obey their rulers and to be content with their current circumstances, perhaps awaiting a better world in the afterlife. In more extreme cases, clergy support the political and economic elite with their silence because they benefit from the patronage of those with power. Yet we have also seen that, under certain circumstances, religion generates and supports movements for change. It mobilizes people to be willing to risk what little they have, including their lives, to fight for an end to inequality, exploitation, oppression, military rule, and a host of other social injustices.

Religion is never simply on one side or the other of social conflicts. More often than not, we see religion on both sides simultaneously. The same beliefs, rituals, traditions, and leaders are deployed in the interests of both those with power *and* their challengers. While sociology helps us to understand why religion can both motivate and hinder social changes in our world, it also helps us to consider the unintended consequences of religious activism for religious groups and for secular social movements that try to mobilize religious resources. It may seem as though religion should be an obvious source of resources for social movements, but instead the legacy of social movement successes and failures underscores the need for movements to be aware of the challenges that the involvement of religion can bring to a movement. Likewise, religious leaders are wary of being used by secular movements for the resources that they may provide. If you are a member of a religious group that has become involved in social activism, or if you are an activist for a secular cause considering whether or not to try to mobilize religious resources to achieve your goal, be aware that religion is always both a conserving and a transforming force in social life. But whether religion exerts more of a conserving or more or a transforming force will depend on both the religious and political context in which it operates.

Suggested Reading

Braunstein, Ruth. 2017. *Prophets and Patriots: Faith in Democracy Across the Political Divide.* Berkeley, CA: University of California Press.

Braunstein, Ruth, Todd Nicholas Fuist, and Rhys H. Williams. 2017. *Religion and Progressive Activism: New Stories about Faith and Politics.* New York: NYU Press.

Hart, Stephen. 1992. *What Does the Lord Require: How American Christians Think about Economic Justice.* New Brunswick: Rutgers University Press.

Morris, Aldon. 1984. *The Origins of the Civil Rights Movement.* New York: Free Press.

Munson, Ziad. 2008. *The Making of Pro-Life Activists.* Chicago: University of Chicago Press.

Smith, Christian. 1996a. *Disruptive Religion: The Force of Faith in Social Movement Activism*. New Brunswick, NJ: Rutgers University Press.

Swarts, Heidi J. 2008. *Organizing Urban America: Secular and Faith-based Progressive Movements*. Minneapolis: University of Minnesota Press.

Wiktorowicz, Quintan (ed.). 2004. *Islamic Activism: A Social Movement Theory Approach*. Bloomington, IN: Indiana University Press.

Wood, Richard L., and Brad R. Fulton. 2015. *A Shared Future: Faith-based Organizing for Racial and Ethical Democracy*. Chicago: University of Chicago Press.

Wuthnow, Robert, and John H. Evans. 2002. *The Quiet Hand of God: Faith-based Activism and the Public Role of Mainline Protestantism*. Berkeley, CA: University of California Press.

Section III
Religion, Identity, and Social Inequalities

8 What are God's Pronouns?

Does Religion Work Differently for Men, Women, and Trans Persons?

1 Is religion a woman's institution?
2 What roles do religion play in shaping gender relations in society?
3 Does religion change when women are in charge?
4 How do non-binary people negotiate the cisgendered world of religion?

In July 2008, the bishops of the Church of England made a historic decision. After many years of debate, they voted to allow women to become bishops, a position that was previously denied to women even though they could serve as priests and deacons. Now, depending on your point of view and your religious tradition, this decision is either the biggest non-news event of the year or something that is revolutionary—and not necessarily in a good way. Since that time, societies around the world have grappled with the appropriate roles of women and men in every social institution, including religion. Much of what religious groups are being forced to confront is the steady growth in awareness of and efforts to rectify the economic, political, and social inequalities faced by women in a world still built to reinforce men's privilege and power. As women make gains in the economic and political spheres, similar gains are far slower to emerge in families and faith communities.

Changes in how we think about gender and religion are also being furthered by the increased visibility of people who don't fit the simplistic binary of male and female. Trans, or non-binary, people also are present and active in faith communities that continue to talk and act as if they don't exist; or worse, they work to punish them in efforts to force them back into a cisgender binary of male and female. Around the world, trans people, like Nur Sajat, a young Muslim trans woman from Malaysia who wore a hijab to a prayer service, face charges of "insulting Islam," for wearing clothing that is out of keeping with their biological sex (Beech and Azmi 2021). In this case, this trans woman was assaulted, groped, and arrested before she was released, after which she fled Malaysia and went to Australia, where she felt more secure as a trans Muslim woman.

Gender, as well as sexuality, which we explore in the next chapter, and the conflicts over them seem to be central to many religious groups. Some religious groups make efforts to reinforce clear boundaries in the division of labor between men's and women's roles in the congregation and in the home. So for example, Evangelical Christian groups like Promise Keepers help men stay focused on their God-given responsibilities as husbands and fathers. In Muslim circles, women debate the practice of wearing the hijab. To some non-Muslims, this veil is a symbol of women's second-class status in Islam. Others counter that the veil frees women from Western cultural pressures regarding their appearance and that it empowers women. There is no consensus in sight. Debates over the role of women as religious leaders also continue. Can women lead worship services, as men do? Can they fully participate in all religious rituals? And how do any of these issues impact trans or non-binary believers?

DOI: 10.4324/9781003182108-11

But before we go any further in attempting to answer these questions, let's define some terms. In Box 8.1, we include some basic, perhaps familiar, definitions at the start of this chapter simply because we need to be clear about the analytic differences between terms such as "sex" and "gender," as well as others that you may not be as familiar with like "gender-binary" and "genderfluid" (Sumerau and Cragun 2015a, 2). Often the term "gender" brings to mind women and their issues, as if gender is only about women. But gender refers to men's issues, too. Furthermore, everyone faces pressure to conform to society's binary gender roles, and men, women, and trans persons are affected by disparities that arise out of social relationships and structures build around a binary (or "cis-") gender regime. So, in order to understand the complexities of religion and gender, in the United States and worldwide, we must examine how religion shapes—and is shaped in turn by—the experiences of men *and* women *and* those who identify as trans or nonbinary.

Box 8.1 Now, in Case You Have Forgotten:

Sex:	*The biological and anatomical categories of being male or female.*
Gender:	*The binary social categories of what it means to be a male or female in a particular society in specific times and places. A person's gender is not always identical to that person's sex.*
Gender binary	*The social and biological classification of sex and gender into two distinct oppositional forms of masculine and feminine selfhood.*
Gender Roles:	*Society's "scripts" or expectations for how those classified as males and females are supposed to behave, how they should look, what their attitudes should be, what jobs are appropriate for them, and so on.*
Gender Identity:	*How an individual identifies his or her own gender as male, female, or something in between.*
Transgender	*An umbrella term referring to all people living within, between, and/or beyond the gender binary, which may also be used to denote an individual's gender identity.*
Cisgender	*An umbrella term referring to people who conform to the gender binary by interpreting their gender identity as congruent with the sex they were assigned by society.*
Genderfluid	*An identity referring to people who reject gender labels, and live as women, men, neither, and/or both in varied situations over their lives.*

Gender is more than just an identity. It is also institutionalized in society as a "regime" or structure of power and privilege referred to as "patriarchy." Patriarchy is a system in which cisgender men enjoy the privileges and control the resources of the society. They make the decisions. They set the policies. It's a man's world. Within patriarchy, certain gender roles, behaviors, attitudes, and experiences are defined as normal or "divinely ordained." For example, within patriarchy, men are expected to be heads of the household, women and children are expected to be obedient, boys must be adventurous, and girls must be nurturing. Those who do not adhere to these norms or who do not behave or believe as they are expected to do within the gender binary scripts are seen as "others" (or outsiders). A man who stays home with his children, a woman who makes the family's financial decisions, girls who play football, and boys who love Broadway musicals or want to wear makeup and skirts sometimes are identified as "different," sometimes "sinful," or just plain "weird." Remember, within patriarchy, gender roles are constraining for *both* cisgender men and women. Those who fall outside this norm—trans or genderfluid people—are marginalized, derided, and viewed as immoral. As we will explore further, religion plays a central role in the support and maintenance of patriarchy. It reinforces power differences and inequalities between men and women and trans people. But it's never quite that simple. Religion is also a force for resistance, social change, and empowerment. We should expect religion to be a part of the story of how society is changing with respect to gender.

But Isn't A Woman's Place in ... Religion?

If sociologists concur on anything about the relationship between gender and religion, it's that women often are more active in religion than men. Certainly in countries like the United States and other areas of North and South America, more women than men belong to religious organizations, women attend religious services more, religion is more important to women and their identities, and women engage in religious behaviors like praying more than men (Pew Research Center 2016). Of course, this pattern does not always hold true. Outside of the U.S., studies reveal that among Orthodox Jews (especially in Israel) and Muslims around the world, men have higher rates of religious participation in many instances than do women.

According to the Pew Research Center (2014, 69), in the United States, women make up more than half (55%) of all Christian groups, 59% of Black Protestants, 65% of Jehovah's Witnesses, and 55% of Establishment Protestants and Evangelicals. (See Figure 8.1.) More women than men also espouse "alternative" spiritualities, especially New Age, neo-pagan, and holistic spiritualities (Woodhead 2008). Jenkins (2006) argues that women also have played a key role in the spread of Christianity worldwide. They are converts themselves, but they are also channels through which entire families are brought into Christian communities in Asia, Africa, and Central and South America. Men do predominate in the several major non-Christian religions in the United States: Judaism, Islam, and Hinduism. But men also are more likely than women to claim no religious affiliation; 57% of those with no affiliation, the "Nones," are men. Even more striking, men make up about two-thirds of those who say they are agnostic and those who are atheist.

Among Christians, women attend church more regularly and they pray more often (Schnabel 2015). Religion is also more important to the lives of women than men in the U.S. (See Figures 8.2–8.4.) For several major non-Christian groups—Jews, Muslims, and Hindus especially—men sometimes surpass women on some, though not all, of these measures.

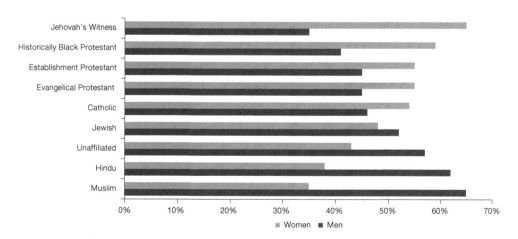

Figure 8.1 Gender Distribution Among Major U.S. Religious Traditions, 2014

Source: Pew Research Center 2014, 69.

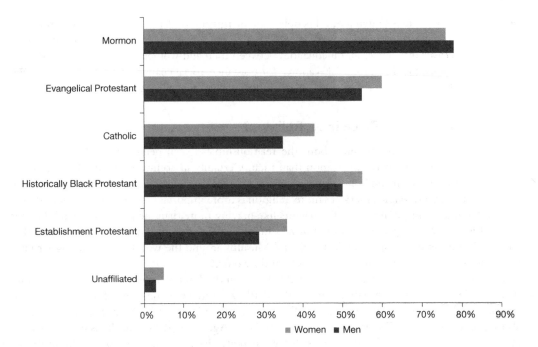

Figure 8.2 Gender Differences in Worship Service Attendance Among Major U.S. Religious Traditions, 2014

Source: Pew Research Center 2014, 273.

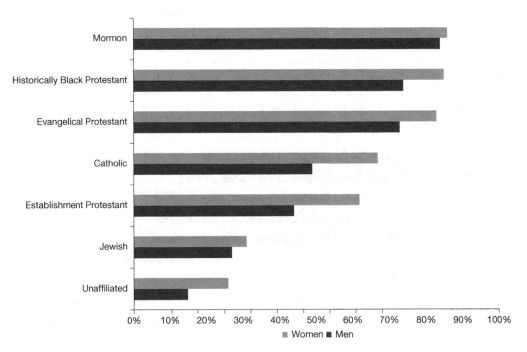

Figure 8.3 Gender Differences in Daily Prayer Among Major U.S. Religious Traditions, 2014

Source: Pew Research Center 2014, 280.

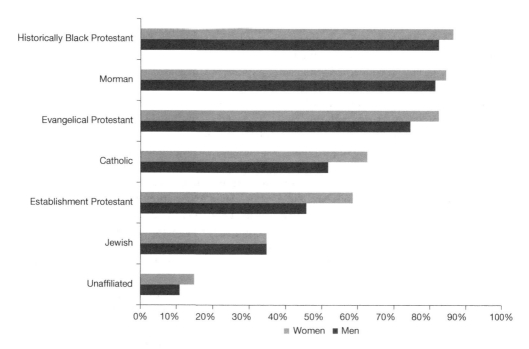

Figure 8.4 Gender Differences in Importance of Religion to Life Among Major U.S. Religious Traditions, 2014
Source: Pew Research Center 2014, 246.

Similar patterns continue to be shown around the world. In almost a third of 192 countries, women are more likely than men to claim a religious affiliation, including in China, Australia, Brazil, South Africa, and Mexico, among others (Pew Research Center 2016, 7). Women around the world pray daily and view religion as important to their lives as well. Differences only appear in comparing Muslim countries like Iran, Iraq, Indonesia, Egypt, and Algeria, as well as Israel, with its majority of Orthodox Jews, to predominantly Christian ones when it comes to attending religious services (Schnabel et al. 2018).

So why does it seem that women are more religious than men on so many dimensions and across so many different traditions? This is not a new question. In the 19th century, Christian clergy bemoaned how few men were in their churches. One study of Methodists in upstate New York in the early 1800s found that the focus on the spiritual rather than on the practicalities of business deterred most men from joining and participating (Johnson 1989). Most men at this time, especially men from the upper and middle classes, resisted any attempt by religious or any other authorities to limit their personal freedom. Consequently, some clergy tried to create environments that would appeal to a more "masculine" audience. Late in the 19th century, for example, the Men and Religion Forward Movement was organized to address the religious dimensions of masculinity and fatherhood in a manner that would bring men back to church (Curtis 1991).

A century later, the head coach for the University of Colorado turned his vision for "a revival among Christian men who were willing to take a stand for God in their marriages, families, churches, and communities" into a movement known as Promise Keepers. Their first conference in 1991 drew 4200 participants to address the question: "Where are the men?" (Promise Keepers 2008). This group remains strong among evangelical men.

In the past, some scholars argued that women were naturally more emotionally expressive, nurturing, willing to meet others' needs before their own, and more inclined to build and maintain relationships. In contrast, men were naturally less emotional and more instrumental, more aggressive and active, and more concerned with accomplishing practical tasks. Thus, the reasoning went, women were better suited to the comforting and community building aspects of religion. Take, for example, Christianity, which places high value on taking care of the needy, engaging in self-sacrifice, and being in solidarity with others. It sometimes seems literally made for women! (Or, at the very least, made for patriarchy's image of the ideal woman.) Sociologists are, however, suspicious of attributing social behaviors to inborn traits. We question the assumption that these traits are fixed orientations arising out of inborn differences between men and women. Is it not just as likely that religion shapes the identities of men and women to feature such distinctions in traits? Or more likely still that different religious traditions have different gendered expectations for how men and women are expected to behave and different incentives to encourage them to do so (Schnabel et al. 2018)?

Women's disproportionate commitment to religion is especially perplexing because most contemporary religious traditions around the world continue to embrace doctrines and practices that *reinforce* the inferior status of women. Let us examine in brief several examples of such doctrines and practices.

In the sacred texts of the Torah, women are ritually and socially inferior to men. In the Ten Commandments, a man's wife is listed as a piece of property that others are forbidden to covet (Exodus 20:17). The same chapter of the Old Testament notes that a man may sell a daughter as a slave . . . and the text does not read "if" but "when" he does so (Exodus 21:7)! Jewish women, who were considered ritually unclean during menstruation, were segregated during this time to prevent them from touching others and making them unclean (Leviticus 15:19–24). Women also were segregated after giving birth to a child. The duration of the segregation was based on the sex of the child. If a woman gave birth to a boy, she was considered unclean for 40 days. During that time, she couldn't touch anything holy or enter the sanctuary. But if she had a girl, she was unclean for 80 days (Leviticus 12:1–8). Although not many Jews embrace these rules today, they still shape the patriarchal nature of Orthodox and Hasidic Judaism (Avishai 2008). For example, in contemporary Orthodox Judaism, women must be seated apart from men, they cannot lead services, and they are not counted as part of a *minyan*, a minimum of 10 male adults who must be present in order to conduct public services.

The Christian New Testament also contains passages that relegate women to subordinate positions in society and church. In his writings to Christians throughout the Roman Empire, Paul laid out a clear gender hierarchy: The head of a woman is her husband (I Corinthians 11:3) and women were created for men (I Corinthians 11:8). He taught that

> The women should keep silence in the churches. For they are not permitted to speak, but should be subordinate, as even the law says. If there is anything they desire to know, let them ask their husbands at home. For it is shameful for a woman to speak in church.
>
> (I Corinthians 14:34–35)

Paul also reminds wives to "be subject to your husbands, as to the Lord," and he writes that "wives also be subject in everything to their husbands" and advises, "let the wife see that she respects her husband." (Ephesians 5: 21–33). In his first letter to Timothy, Paul writes,

> Let a woman learn in silence with all submissiveness. I permit no woman to teach or to have authority over men; she is to keep silent. For Adam was formed first, then Eve; and Adam was not deceived, but the woman was deceived and became a transgressor.
>
> (1 Timothy 2:11–14)

He encourages Titus to train "young women to love their husbands and children, to be sensible, chaste, domestic, kind, and submissive to their husbands" (Titus 2:4–5). These are a small sample of Christian teachings related to women, though hardly the only ones.

Some feminist scholars argue that Jesus never supported these subordinate roles for women. To the contrary, Jesus treated women in a more egalitarian way, especially given the cultural norms of the day. In addition, historical evidence suggests that women held positions of prominence in the first millennium of Christianity as abbesses. An abbess was the female head of a community of nuns and had full authority over the running of her nunnery. The medieval church was, nonetheless, a strictly patriarchal institution. Even today, there is not much change in some denominations. Among Catholics, "women cannot be priests, so the argument goes, not because of any lack of appropriate skills or ability, but because their femaleness makes it impossible for them to resemble Christ in the Eucharist" (Chaves 1997, 88). Similar arguments are put forward by some Protestant denominations.

Islamic expectations regarding gender roles also reflect Qu'ranic mandates regarding the submission of women to men, especially in marriage. Among the verses that are the most challenging is 4:34. In this section, men are given authority over women and are permitted to strike them if they resist their husband's authority.

> Men are in charge of women by [right of] what Allah has given one over the other and what they spend [for maintenance] from their wealth. So righteous women are devoutly obedient, guarding in [the husband's] absence what Allah would have them guard. But those [wives] from whom you fear arrogance—[first] advise them; [then if they persist], forsake them in bed; and [finally], strike them. But if they obey you [once more], seek no means against them. Indeed, Allah is ever Exalted and Grand.

Other verses in the Qu'ran also reflect this image of a sexual hierarchy between women and men (Hidayatullah 2014; Rinaldo 2019).

Buddhism's principles have also been used to undermine the position of women. Buddhism teaches that there are "five impediments" to reaching enlightenment: desire, anger, drowsiness, restlessness and remorse, and doubt. In most Buddhist traditions, these impediments confront men and women alike. In some branches, however, especially in Japan, these impediments are understood to apply *especially* to women, who by their very nature are burdened with these obstacles. No matter what they do, women will not be able to reach enlightenment.

Changing Gender Roles, Changing Relationships to Religion

Despite historic religious teachings involving gender that seem to leave little room for reinterpretation, men, women, and trans persons in almost all traditions continue to renegotiate gender roles and their understandings of masculinity and femininity in the contemporary world. Religion often plays a substantial role in this process. Sometimes these teachings are the authority against which people rebel, such as when cisgender and trans men and women outright reject religious authority during their sorting out of appropriate gender roles. Other people hold to traditional religious teachings about gender in the face of secular trends toward equal treatment and access to leadership and other social resources for men and women. Some people fall in the middle between these two positions. They attempt to modify traditional religious beliefs and practices for themselves to accommodate a more equitable distribution of power in their personal relationships, but often comply with rather than reject the beliefs and practices altogether.

This is a fourth option too in that other men, women, and trans persons move to new religious movements and alternative spiritual practices that hold gender equality and options for gender fluidity as key tenets. In a world where "religion" is often understood to mean intellectual belief and practices that exist in cisgender male experience, these cis- and trans person's spiritual practices sometimes fly below the radar. That is, sometimes they do not count as "real." Consider Susan Starr Sered's (1994, quoted in Woodhead 2007, 565) comparative study of religious groups in which women predominate:

> Women's religions tend to be characterized by greater concern for this-worldly matters including bodily and emotional wellbeing (health and healing) and the quality of intimate and family relationships, and to be more centered around home, food preparation and sometimes the natural world.

But because the concrete expression of women's spirituality compared with men's spirituality tends to involve New Age, neo-pagan, and holistic health and wellbeing practices, they are routinely subsumed under the categories of "folklore," "superstition," "syncretism," "heresy," or simply "ladies' auxiliary," but not considered to be *real* or legitimate expressions of religion (Sered 1994, 286 quoted in Woodhead 2007, 565). Negotiating religious and gender identities individually or collectively remains a complicated business!

One important point that we must keep in mind when we think about these issues is that men, women, and trans persons of faith are active agents within their faith traditions and must be seen as that. This is true even when it seems that the only logical response of cisgender women or trans persons is to reject their faith traditions because of the ways they explicitly and implicitly reinforce broader gender-based power inequalities. Men, women, and trans persons, regardless of how they negotiate the cisgendered way religion operates, are almost always trying to be true to their faith and live as authentically faithful people within their tradition.

Burke (2012) identifies several approaches to how men, women, and trans persons have been seen to negotiate gender-traditional religious traditions in which they find themselves. Because many Establishment Protestant groups have worked toward creating a more inclusive religious culture within their denominations, sociologists who study the question of agency more often focus on Evangelical Protestant groups, Roman Catholics, Mormons, Orthodox Jews, and Muslims. It is within these traditions that religious teaching and practice most clearly reinforce a strict traditional cisgender-based religious culture. This culture, regardless of the specific tradition, is built upon the following key points (Sumerau et al. 2016, 294):

- There are only two genders, male and female, in the world.
- Men and women were created (by a male creator-god) to fulfill different and unequal roles in the home and the religious community and these roles are part of the divine plan for the world.
- More specifically, men are divinely ordained to be leaders and to hold authority in domestic relationships and in religion, while women are to remain obedient to men's authority as wives and mothers.
- Any deviance from these points, either in principle or reality, should be rejected and punished.

These ideological principles are institutionalized in every facet of cisgender-traditional religions, reinforcing patriarchal power in religion and in society more broadly. However, men, women, and trans persons still don't passively embrace them. They actively confront the gendered power inequalities they face "in the small, ceaseless, real-time interactions between individuals" as they construct religious and gender identities within their faith traditions (Woodhead 2007, 551).

Let's think about those men, women, and trans persons who seem on the surface to just *comply* or go along with their faith tradition's gender role expectations. Why do you think women and trans people today specifically would want to go along with a tradition that explicitly marginalizes them? Often, going along means living up to the teachings of one's faith against the countervailing force of a secular society that does not share these beliefs. Mary, an evangelical traditionalist who was a respondent in Beaman's (1999, 28) study of evangelical women, embodies this approach. She recounts her ideas about men's and women's roles:

> I feel that the man should have a stronger, how should I put it? . . . well, he's the leader in the home and I just feel that . . . I know in some homes a wife can balance the checkbook much better than the husband can, and so I think those things, I'm not saying he has to be the head of everything. But I think when it comes to . . . well, like buying a new car—I want a certain kind, and he feels another kind would be more for our budget and more economical, so I think his word has to be the final word.

In the case of Mormon women, in which church teaching underscores that gender roles are eternal and carry on in the afterlife when men and women become divine mothers and fathers/gods and goddesses for eternity. They are not just earthly expectations that apply to this world alone. Margaret Nadauld, General President of the LDS's Young Women organization, reminded women that (quoted in Sumerau and Cragun 2015b, 57):

> The divine light you carry within your soul is inherited from God because you are His daughter. Part of the light which makes you so magnificent is the blessing of womanhood. What a wonderful thing it is for you to know that you are female, feminine characteristics are an endowment from God. Our latter-day prophets teach that "gender is an essential characteristic of individual premortal, mortal, and eternal identity and purpose."

Mormon women embrace their roles as the way to demonstrate authentic womanhood within the Latter-Day Saints tradition. Kane (2018) observed that LDS women in her study found a great deal of personal empowerment through their observance of the elaborate rituals that invested them as "priestesses." Although these women were limited by male leaders in what they were actually allowed to do ritually within the LDS Church—and it is important to note that they were quite vocal about their frustrations at these limits—these women still embraced these rituals as ways to be devout Mormons.

Men are no less active in constructing their religious and gender identities within these gender-traditional contexts. Like the women discussed earlier, faith is an important dimension of masculinity and manhood. In Griffith and Cornish's (2018, 84) study of African American men, religion was a central theme in how these men defined themselves *as men*:

> A man is God-fearing. A man is a protector, a provider, a man is kind but stern. A man has principles, has a core set of qualities that he believes in, which is defined by his faith, his moral conviction, and by his character. A man motivates his family, his household. A man secures his family and his household as well as himself and a man is defined by his intentions and his intentions, whatever those intentions are, blaze a trail.

Even gay men, worshipping within the context of an LGBT church can still hold ideas of masculinity and manhood that reinforce a divide between "real" men and women, trans persons, or gay men who don't express their masculinity in stereotypical ways. In J.E. Sumerau's study of how men in an LGBT church construct their masculine identity in ways that offset the stigma of homosexuality, a new male pastor in the church made it his priority to construct a clearly heteronormative, cisgender identity for the gay men in the congregation. Sumerau (2012, 471) recounts that in his first sermon, the pastor told the congregation:

> We all know how others try to clobber us gay guys by saying we're antifamily or irresponsible children who only want to play. Well, we know different, and part of our job as men is to show the world we are good providers and leaders in our communities.

Martin, one of the members of this church, echoed a variation of the gender-binary so commonly expressed in religions that embrace traditional notions of gender.

> I think people need to be honest with themselves. We're all born gay or straight. We all know this. God doesn't mention other options in the Bible, and why should we expect otherwise? The point is to find a partner, a companion, a lover, and how are you supposed to do that playing both sides of the field? It seems weird to associate with the bisexuals, and poly-whatevers in politics. It makes the rest of us look like freaks.

Cisgender women and men embrace traditional gender roles and practices as ways to reflect their religious identities as well as using their religious beliefs and practices as a way to signal their gender identities.

Although it may be surprising that transgender people remain committed to religious traditions that openly reject them and their experience as non-binary persons, they do! In a rare study of Muslim transgender people in Iran, you can see a foundational belief that being seen by others to be a devoted Muslim was key to social and spiritual acceptance (Heidari et al. 2021). One Iranian trans man noted that:

> I try to say my prayer on time and speak to God, so I could believe that even if all my family, because of my difference with other people whom they know, does not like me, God favors me with open arms since he understands me and knows me well.

Another trans woman told her interviewer that she goes to the mosque and has made new friends there. As a consequence, her family has become more tolerant because they now see her as a "normal person who can communicate with people" (Heidari et al. 2021, 423). Another trans man found more acceptance as the result of going to the mosque with his mother:

> I live in a small town. My mother is a Qu'ran reciter and a sharia teacher. But others accept me just because of her. I often participate with her in Qu'ran teaching sessions. People have seen me next to her, so they have changed their opinion about me.

As the young trans women from Malaysia whose experiences we presented earlier reported in her interview with the *New York Times*, faithfully observing Muslim traditions related to women was what it meant to her to be a devout Muslim as a trans women.

In religious contexts where men, women, and trans persons comply with traditional beliefs about proper gender roles, this compliance should not be considered to be some form of "false consciousness," in which women like Mary or the trans men and women in Iran are blinded by their faith to the gender inequalities within their religions or societies. Instead, clear-cut traditional roles and devotion to these beliefs and rituals provide an alternative to the confusion, complexity, and frustration that women face when they juggle domestic duties, a career, and community life.

In *The New Faces of Christianity*, Philip Jenkins makes a similar point. He notes that North Americans or European Christians might see the decision to follow traditional roles as an uncritical acceptance of Biblical texts. But these roles may actually protect women who regularly face the prospects of rape, incest, sexual abuse, and abandonment in patriarchal societies. Literal readings of the Bible provide women with the means to regulate men's behavior, especially within homes and extended families. Biblical literalism also allows women to use the many powerful women in the Bible as examples for their own roles in their families and their communities.

But complying is not the only way men, women, and trans persons negotiate the intersections of gender and religion in their lives. Active *resistance* is another approach that women and trans persons especially demonstrate in gender-traditional religious traditions. Resistance is demonstrated anytime cisgender women and trans persons do not comply with formal teachings of their tradition regarding gender roles and expectations. Sometimes resistance is demonstrated when people *exit* their traditions and either join religious groups that are more welcoming and have a culture built around gender equity or they become one of the unaffiliated or Nones. Take the example of Katherine, a female professor at a local university, interviewed as part of a study of how Roman Catholic women create their gender identities (Ecklund 2005, 142). She saw no way to balance her ideas about gender equity in society with church doctrine.

> The doctrinal things about Catholicism that made it not worth it for me to struggle in the Catholic Church were related to a lot of issues surrounding misogyny. I found their position on birth control indefensible. . . . I chose a profession that was strongly male-dominated. I didn't need that crap in Church as well. . . . I don't know where you go except out of the Church in some way.

Similarly, trans persons, who probably face the most serious obstacles to change in gender-traditional faiths, often resist through exiting more frequently than cisgender women. One genderfluid person recounted an experience as a young (still cisgender) man in the Mormon church and identified a time when they were put in a position over an adult woman (Sumerau et al. 2018, 442).

> I as a 16-year-old was "the presiding priesthood member" at some relief society functions because the bishop who was there had to leave . . . The experience jarred me because I KNEW the relief society president (a woman) was the one really in charge but the bishop still felt the need to pull me out and send me to sit in on the lesson so there was a "priesthood authority" there . . . but the fact that a child was "in charge" was one of the experiences that led me from the church.

Kazi, a trans Muslim, also left their faith tradition behind for reasons specifically related to being trans (Darwin 2020, 200):

> I don't feel comfortable going to mosques. I do not pray for that reason, 'cause I don't know how I should be praying as someone who is nonbinary.

But exiting is an extreme strategy adopted most often when individuals see no hope of changing or being able to challenge their tradition's gender ideology.

Those who oppose or wish to change gender-traditional faiths find ways to "do" their faith and their gender differently from within both through their positions within congregations and in their everyday relationships. In this way, men and women are *empowered* to create their own religious and gender identities in ways that seem to simultaneously embrace and challenge official religious teachings.

Most faith traditions create gender-segregated environments and formal groups for education and service. These groups in turn allow men and women to meet and interact with others. Men can confront the disconnects between official teachings regarding masculinity and male authority and their lived experiences with women in everyday life. Women in turn can meet free of male supervision and direct control to discuss their disconnects and frustrations with the gender dynamics idealized in their faith traditions.

For centuries, Catholic women's religious orders have provided a space where women were educated, held positions of some power, and escaped the traditional social pressures to be wives and mothers. Until recently, these women were also heads of healthcare facilities and hospitals, principals of schools, and university presidents. Nevertheless, these women, living in communities, found opportunities to voice their frustrations and commitment to gender equality without leaving the Church. Take, for example, the expression of collective frustration by Sister Clare, a participant in a study of Canadian women's religion and feminism (Gervais 2012, 394):

> The thing that drove me nuts was the bishop coming in to supervise our chapter. Can you imagine? That only ended after Vatican II. It's like we couldn't be trusted . . . the worst one was . . . not dealing with the sense of belonging [as a woman] in all those years. That was quite painful. . . . I couldn't function. All these Jesuit priests coming to give retreats. . . . I was so angry! I mean just the thought we couldn't do it ourselves.

Other Sisters shared similar feelings of marginalization in this study, and yet they also expressed how the community itself and finding positions where their skills were valued counterbalanced those frustrations. Sisters Loretta, Collette, and Carmen all express similar themes (Gervais 2012, 398–399):

> I just know in my heart of hearts I belong to this Church. I don't believe in all the things that it does or is doing. And I don't believe in patriarchy and all that stuff. But there is something in the church that is for me. . . . I love the Church. I don't love all the things they are doing . . . hopefully we can make a change you know by plugging away little by little.
>
> This is a mistake I believe in the Catholic Church to be anti-women. So I try to do what I can to not be pulled down by it, but to be fully alive. . . . I don't feel called to leave the Catholic Church so I seek out the parts of the church that are not hung up on patriarchy and hierarchy. . . . I seek out a parish where they welcome female homilists . . . who are not ordained.
>
> Part of that frustration was resolved by my community allowing me to go into pastoral work and being in pastoral work, I did everything; I was the pastor of that parish de facto rather than de jure, in everything except the administration of the sacraments and offering the Mass.

Today, though dwindling in numbers, Catholic religious women use their unique positions in the Church to empower themselves in unique ways that also push the boundaries of traditional gender roles and expectations.

Women's groups in Evangelical churches are another venue that can empower women to interact on their own terms and develop social bonds. Evangelical women may work together through organizations such as Women's Ministries Unlimited (Assemblies of God), Wesleyan Women, Women's Aglow International, and Women's Missionary Union (Southern Baptist), among many others. These contexts also provide opportunities for women to discuss and debate Biblical texts and religious teachings about gender roles. Research shows that there is only a loose relationship between believing church teachings and conforming to them completely in daily life. Consider, for example, the Southern Baptist women in Pevey et al.'s (1996) study of the Ladies Bible Class at the Shady Grove Baptist Church. While these women know and accept Southern Baptist teachings about a wife's duty to submit to her husband, they also claim a fair amount of independence in their marriages. One of them, Susie, definitively described her relationship with her husband:

I'm not afraid to speak up and I mean I am [a] very assertive woman and so it wouldn't bother me to be pretty adamant, you know if I felt really strong about something. And of course I would. I think that I could prevail upon [my husband] if I felt [a decision] was not in his best interests. . . . And he will have to listen to me. You know we're a team.

Another woman in the group, Ruth, explains that her willingness to submit to her husband is due to their unique relationship, not to a decision to follow Biblical principles:

A lot of my willingness to [submit] is his personality and how confident I am in our relationship and I don't know that I'd necessarily do that with someone else. . . . I don't know if I would be willing to take that submissive role in another situation, even though I think the Bible very strongly says that is our role.

Thus, religion can become a means of empowerment for women from other faith traditions as well. Jewish women, in both Orthodox Judaism and in Reform and other branches of the tradition, find ways to use the traditional practices of their faith as a way to empower themselves as women. For instance, Orthodox women use the practice of *niddah*, a time of ritual segregation during their menstrual period in which they can have no physical contact (not even by passing objects directly to them) with their husbands, after which they must have a ritual bath to symbolize their cleansing after their period is over (Avishai 2008). Although Orthodox women do express frustration with the demands of the ritual, they also embrace it as a time for themselves, free from marital demands, as well as a time to build deeper interpersonal communication with their husbands when other forms of contact are forbidden. What can be seen as an outdated ritual which marginalizes women's physical experiences also empowers these women to be in tune with their bodies and with their marriages in a very intentional way.

In Darwin's (2018) study of Jewish women in Conservative, Reform, and Reconstructionism traditions, the traditionally male practice of wearing a *kippah*, or small skullcap, is used as a way to symbolize their faith but also to end the gender-segregated nature of the practice. The women in this study are not just trying to break with or resist tradition here. They are actively trying to reclaim the tradition for themselves and future generations of women who will follow them. What is interesting is that these women did their best to make wearing a *kippah* different from their male counterparts. In some cases, they chose different fabrics or materials for them; in other instances, they had *kippahs* in different colors and patterns that could then match the clothes they were wearing. *Kippahs* empower women in this tradition because wearing them does not carry the same cisgender cultural baggage that wigs and headscarves do in Judaism.

Muslim women similarly use their gender-segregated environments and social roles in order to empower themselves. Prickett (2015) observed and interviewed African American Muslim women doing just this in their local mosque. Although women occupy a separate space from men for services and daily prayer, they used this separation to create meaningful opportunities for worship and prayer for themselves. They ensured men did not block their views of the Imam during the services, even if that meant the men had to squeeze into their overcrowded space. They ensured other women did not use their cell phones or let their children run around unsupervised during services, and made sure the men spoke up so they could hear appropriately. In other instances, women worked to create new spaces, including women's bathrooms, in the mosque and ensured the men were not allowed to use them.

Now while the experiences of these women do demonstrate a level of empowerment, there are also limits to how far they can push the boundaries of traditional gender roles without pushback from male leaders, and more often from other women. The Jewish women who wear *kippahs* reported being yelled at by their rabbis for wearing them, were stalked and shouted at, and have had them ripped off their heads by those who opposed women wearing them (Darwin 2018). Catholic religious women are publicly reprimanded for using gender-inclusive language in worship settings (Gervais 2012). Mormon women find themselves denied access to ritual roles for questioning specific gender traditions in the church, such as being required to go through a "covenant of obedience" ritual that included being compared to Eve, who is understood to be the first woman who was to submit to her husband Adam (Kane 2018). Others are directed to be counseled by men and to spend more time in prayer and scripture reading in order for their gender-related questioning to go away. In almost all religious traditions, those who challenge formal teachings too much also face "excommunication" or being kicked out entirely. Trans persons face similar sanctions simply for existing. Sumerau and Craygun (2015a) found trans people were ridiculed, had their gender identity associated with evil and the devil, were sent to therapy, and also were kicked out of their congregations. All of this points out that negotiating religious and gender identities in a way that is personally empowering is not simply something one is free to do without limits. All challenges to the cisgendered world of religion brings risk of sanctions to ensure superficial conformity if not personal compliance.

Finally, women, men, and trans persons often find their way from gender-traditional faith traditions to others that are more egalitarian or those that replace a cisgendered, male orientation with a female one, like Wicca and other neopagan traditions. In these religions, women identify with the Goddess, Her power, and Nature, and they reject the worship of a supreme male God who is separate from the natural world, as in the Judeo-Christian tradition (Christ 2007). These women (and some men who also follow this religious tradition) challenge what they believe to be the root cause of women's oppression and of environmental degradation: separating the divine from the physical world on which all life depends and not seeing the natural world as sacred (Griffin 1995).

Men who follow these religious movements also use the beliefs as a way to critique men's traditional gender roles. In Neitz's (2005, 270) study of Goddess movements, practitioners see their beliefs and practices as liberating for men as well as women. One woman she interviewed expressed it this way:

> Patriarchy is just as crippling for men as for women. It's just that most men don't understand that. They are in a gilded cage, so they think it's a nice cage. The men who are in the Craft (Wicca) are aware that it's a cage . . . and they are trying to find a way out. . . . There are men now who are trying, for their own reasons—for their own healing, for their own sense of wholeness. I know men who feel that they have been robbed of having a feminine half, and being told culturally that any kind of female behavior was wrong for them, and they are reclaiming their right to have a feminine side. But they are also now freer to find an expression for their masculine energy that makes them feel comfortable and find an expression for their female energy that is more balances and more true to themselves.

Wicca and growth of a diverse neopagan religious sector provides a collective basis for both men, women, and trans persons to challenge and reshape existing gender roles. The growth and visibility of these religious traditions have also empowered those who belong to them to organize politically for religious and social change.

Religion is integrally tied to the structures of power and privilege that shape the lives of both men, women, and trans persons. These structures are changing, however. As they change, individuals are finding new ways to redefine gender identities, often drawing on religion for guidance. For all of us, "doing religion" is interconnected with "doing gender." In looking at the experiences of people of faith, it is important to remember that coming to grips with the process of defining your gender identity may mean holding on to an older form of identity, creating a new one, or fighting politically for wholesale changes in the roles of cisgender and nonbinary men and women in the broader society.

Does Religion Change When Women are in Charge?

More than 20 Christian denominations permit women to be ministers. Some have ordained women since the early 1800s. Others have only allowed women to be clergy within the last 10 or 20 years. Interestingly, several large conservative Evangelical groups, such as the Church of the Nazarene and Assemblies of God, have been ordaining women for over 75 years or more, while more liberal Establishment Protestant groups, like the Lutherans and Episcopalians, only began ordaining women in the 1970s.

Data on women clergy in the United States are scant. We do know that women made up approximately 34% of all Protestant seminary students in 2019 and composed 30% of those who were specifically pursuing a Master of Divinity degree. Women also make up just about 25% of all full-time faculty members in seminaries (Association of Theological Schools 2021). In specific denominations, the number of ordained women continues to grow. They make up 32% of clergy and 28% of bishops in the United Methodist Church. In the Episcopal church, they compose 38% of all active clergy and 20.6% of bishops. In contrast, Rowell (2003) noted that less than 3% of Nazarene clergy were women, a drop from 20% in 1908. Within Judaism, approximately 20% of all non-Orthodox rabbis are women. And although women are not officially permitted to be priests in the Catholic Church, Catholic women carry out many leadership roles in local parishes as "pastors," and women make up 80% of lay ecclesial ministers.

There is evidence of occupational segregation by gender in religious organizations. In a study of Episcopal clergy, Nesbitt (1993) found that women were more likely to be segregated into positions as "permanent deacons," which focus on community service and outreach. Such positions are often unpaid, so the women who fill them often also work full-time jobs. In 2015, Nesbitt reported that women who were newly ordained as priests in the Episcopal Church were still more likely to take jobs as "associate" priests rather than to head a congregation entirely on their own, compared to their male counterparts (Nesbitt 2016). More recent studies continue to find that women clergy are more likely than men to hold part-time and non-congregational clergy positions (Scheifer and Miller 2017). Women are also more likely to lead congregations that are smaller, that are located in rural areas, and that operate with smaller budgets (Campbell-Reed 2019). Some scholars have described the obstacles that women face in advancing to high-profile, high-prestige leadership positions in the church as a "stained-glass ceiling." And while women clergy are almost earning the same as men on average (93 cents/$1), the explanation continues to point to a stagnation of men's wages that have allowed women to catch up and close the wage gap, rather than women genuinely receiving higher salaries at the same rate as men.

As is also the case with women in other male-dominated career fields, women holding clergy roles still face daily obstacles to carrying out their ministries. This remains in clear opposition to having women in formal leadership roles that can play out explicitly or implicitly. In Christian contexts, women clergy in some denominations must cope with parishioners who actively refuse to recognize their authority to administer sacraments like communion. Other women report facing congregational cultures that verbally accept women in leadership but patronize, belittle, ignore, or criticize them in ways that would not happen to a man (Robbins and Greene 2018). Candice, an Anglican priest interviewed as part of a study of clergywomen in England, did not expect such challenges (Greene and Robbins 2015, 413):

> It was a real culture shock to move from working in education to moving to working in the Church . . . the expectation that I would know my place . . . and not get above myself. So I went from being very

confident about my role and my abilities to being quite kind of puzzled, hurt, angry, confused about the sort of different expectations about ordination and being a woman. . . . I remember there was a really significant appointment made to one of the parishes . . . And it was made without consultation (with me) and then when I said what I thought and why I thought it, it was made very clear that that wasn't my place.

Women also face pressures based on their appearance, the content of their sermons, and assumptions that they should still take on tasks like making the coffee or running Sunday School. And when the ceremonial clothing used in religious rituals that have been made with men's bodies in mind don't fit women clergy, it underscores that perhaps women don't "fit" as clergy either (Page 2014).

Many sociologists wonder whether women lead congregations differently than men. Research suggests that women do exercise their power as ministers differently than men do. Wallace (1993) found that, among Catholic congregational leaders, women were more likely to use collaboration and men were more likely to use hierarchical power to get things done. That is, female pastors focus more on building relationships with other laypeople and on using their knowledge and abilities to help lead, whereas men rely more on the authority of their positions. Women leaders also have different priorities for the social focus of the church. Wallace found that female clergy are often more liberal on issues such as abortion rights or gay rights. They are also more likely to be more engaged with broader issues of peace and social justice.

But the pressures on women clergy go beyond the job itself. Sometimes these pressures shape the content of their ministries as well. For example, Olson (2000) argues that, despite their personal political views, women find it more difficult to exercise moral authority as clergy in the political arena within their communities. The uphill battle simply to become a minister within a congregation is draining. Encouraging a congregation to engage in community-based political action can be an important form of outreach for a religious leader, but it is also often risky: Political action is needed precisely in the areas where there is resistance to change. Put together, these challenges represent a substantial barrier blocking many women clergy from pushing their congregations toward community-based social activism. Olson's interviews of four female clergy in Milwaukee revealed that three of them had strong personal political convictions but were not politically engaged as clergy. One African American female pastor preached about the importance of political engagement. She was limited from becoming more politically engaged herself, however, because "the senior (male) pastor of her church stressed day-to-day survival issues, rather than politics, as the top priority for his staff" (40).

Again, we see that power structures are inherent both in religious organizations and in society's gender roles. But patriarchy is not just built on abstract ideas about gender roles. It is perpetuated but also challenged through the formal roles and personal relationships of men, women, and trans persons within religion as well as outside of it.

Challenging and Transforming Religious Ideas About Gender

Gender, gender identity, and religious identity intersect in ways that are mutually reinforcing, but they can often conflict with one another. These conflicts occur at the institutional level and also within individuals. Once again, religion matters here. As you have seen in many of the stories in this chapter, people actively engage with religion to construct religious and gender identities that make sense to them and meet their needs. We expect that American men, women, and trans persons will continue to both embrace some forms of organized religion and reject or work to change others as they negotiate today's changing gender roles. And in parts of the world where religion relegates women to subordinate positions, we should expect that women will continue to draw on religion to cope with these realities as well as to fight to change them. And as we will see in the next chapter, it plays a vital role in determining the treatment of gay men, lesbian women, and other sexual minorities in society as well.

Further Reading

Bagley, Kate, and Kathleen McIntosh (eds.). 2007. *Women's Studies in Religion: A Multicultural Reader.* Upper Saddle River, NJ: Prentice Hall Publishers.

Beaman, Lori. 1999. *Shared Beliefs, Different Lives: Women's Identities in Evangelical Context.* St. Louis: Chalice Press.

Brown Zikmund, Barbara Adair, T. Lummis, and Patricia M. Y. Chang. 1998. *Clergy Women: An Uphill Calling.* Louisville: Westminster John Knox Press.

Hartman, Harriet, and Moshe Hartman. 2009. *Gender and American Jews: Patterns in Work, Education and Family in Contemporary Life.* Waltham, MA: Brandeis University Press.

Mahmood, Saba. 2005. *Politics of Piety: The Islamic Revival and the Feminist Subject.* Chicago: University of Chicago Press.

Manning, Christel. 1999. *God Gave Us the Right: Conservative Catholic, Evangelical Protestant, and Orthodox Jewish Women Grapple with Feminism.* New Brunswick, NJ: Rutgers University Press.

Nesbitt, Paula D. 1997. *Feminization of the Clergy: Organizational and Occupational Perspectives.* New York: Oxford University Press.

Scott, Joan. 2009. *The Politics of the Veil.* Princeton NJ: Princeton University Press.

Sered, Susan Starr. 1994. *Priestess, Mother, Sacred Sister. Religions Dominated by Women.* New York: Oxford University Press.

Sumerau, J. E., Ryan T. Cragun, and Lain A. B. Mathers. 2016. "Contemporary Religion and the Cisgendering of Reality." *Social Currents* 3: 293–311.

Wilcox, W. Bradford. 2004. *Soft Patriarchs, New Men: How Christianity Shapes Fathers and Husbands.* Chicago: University of Chicago Press.

Zagano, Phyllis. 2011. *Women & Catholicism: Gender, Communion, and Authority.* New York: Palgrave Macmillan.

Adam, Eve, and Steve

How Changing Dynamics of Sexuality Challenge and Transform Religion

1   Sex, sex, sex . . . why does it always seem to come back to sex?
2   Are people around the world thinking differently about sexuality today?
3   What do religious groups say about sexual orientation and why does it matter?
4   How do LGBTQ+ individuals think about religion and spirituality?
5   Can the roles of trans individuals, gay men, lesbian women, and those with other non-binary sexual identities in society change in the absence of a concurrent change in religion?

In the last chapter, we discussed the interplay of religion and gender, but closely related to the battles over women's and men's roles in religion and society are the even more explosive battles over how religion should address the changing roles of LGBTQ+ people in contemporary society. In no way should we think about sexuality as a separate arena from gender, as they are too tightly intertwined. In fact, sociological research on the intersection of religion and sexuality does demonstrate a clear link between acceptance of LGBTQ+ individuals as members and leaders in congregations and support for egalitarian gender roles and gender equity in leadership (Whitehead 2014). How religious or spiritual people think about sexuality, especially LGBTQ+ rights and full participation in all aspects of society, remains tied to how they think about gender.

So let's return to the Anglican Church once more to begin to think about these battles over sexual orientation and sexual identities to provide some groundwork for thinking about how much things have changed since the early 2000s. In 2003, delegates (bishops, priests, and laypeople) to the General Convention of the American Episcopal Church voted to approve the consecration of the Right Reverend Gene Robinson as the new Bishop of New Hampshire. We hear you yawning, "So what?" Well, Bishop Gene Robinson, who now has retired, was an openly gay man, and many Anglicans around the world (then and now) rejected the idea that openly gay men and lesbian women can serve in any position in the Church. American Episcopalians, on the other hand, refused to change their minds and retract Bishop Robinson's appointment. The result of this stance in those first years of the 21st century prompted Anglican leaders around the world to call for the censure of the American Church for what they believed to be outright heresy. Episcopal proponents of gay and lesbian acceptance, however, saw this international Anglican condemnation as rooted in ignorance which should be dismissed as irrelevant to life in the American Church today.

Fast-forward ten years or so, and by comparison the world has changed in a revolutionary way when it comes to religion and sexuality. In the United States, same-sex couples are allowed to marry in every state. Access to this legal right has given LGBTQ+ couples access to the benefits long enjoyed by heterosexual couples in the areas of taxes, parenting, healthcare, and inheritance. The prohibitions on gays and lesbians serving openly in the military were overturned in 2010. Trans people were formally permitted to serve in the military in 2016, and though repealed under the Trump presidency, they were again allowed to serve once President Biden repealed the Exclusion act. More and more companies have banned discrimination based on sexual orientation and

DOI: 10.4324/9781003182108-12

gender identity, and LGBTQ+ citizens are more visible in every sector of American life than ever before. These remarkable changes are mirrored in other countries as well. Across many countries in the Global North and some in the Global South, one can identify the rising visibility and access to civil rights and leadership for non-heterosexuals. These social changes have provoked parallel changes but also backlashes in the religious realm as congregations began to embrace, or even more emphatically reject, non-heterosexual persons and relationships.

No matter what, the subject of sex and sexuality doesn't go away. Just read the news. Coverage of religion continues to involve conversations about sexuality. Sometimes it may seem that some American religious groups have made negotiating (in supportive or oppositional ways) the complexities of human sexual identities and relationships—between men and women, women and women, and men and men—a centerpiece of their theological, political, and cultural missions. At the same time, somewhat ironically, believers bemoan that so much attention is focused on the issue of sexuality. They want to know: "What about other vital issues like racism, poverty, or climate change?"

While these other issues are also important, conflicts over sexuality seem to be central to many religious groups. As you'll see in this chapter, Christian, Jewish, and Muslim groups around the world are confronting shifts in our understanding of human sexuality, especially as gay, lesbian, bisexual, and transgendered people and relationships become more visible and are increasingly given legal recognition, inside and outside religious groups.

But once again, as we start some difficult conversations about sexuality and religion, it is important to define our terms. In Box 9.1, we include some basic, perhaps familiar, definitions simply because we need to be clear about the analytic differences between terms such as "sexual orientation" and "sexual identity." The concept of sexuality encompasses the full range of sexual identities and orientations that can only be understood in the context of a larger social system. We should never think of sexual identity and orientation as only a "gay thing." If we do, we miss the bigger picture of how the experiences of the sexual identities of everyone, straight people, gay people, and people whose sexuality and sexual identities are fluid and nonbinary, are defined and limited by religion.

In this chapter, we explore the intersections of religion and sexuality in the United States and worldwide. Sociologists have especially focused on the construction of the religious and sexual identities of LGBTQ+ people in the face of openness and inclusion encountered in some religious traditions, as well as continued overt or more subtle condemnation in others.

Box 9.1 Now, in Case You Were Wondering

Sexuality: *The totality of categories that individual societies construct around our bodies' sensual feelings, desires, fantasies, behaviors, and emotions.*

Sexual Orientation: *How society defines specific sets of feelings, desires, fantasies, behaviors, and emotions to express what is expected from particular sexual categories.*

Sexual Identity: *How an individual identifies his or her own sexuality, as a man, woman, or something in between (sexually fluid), possessing unique sets of sexual feelings, desires, fantasies, behaviors, and emotions.*

But as is the case with gender, sexuality is about more than just identities. Sexuality itself represents both power and privilege. To consider power and privilege in the realm of sexuality requires us to understand heterosexism. Heterosexism works in the same way that patriarchy does for men and women. Heterosexism is a system in which heterosexuals enjoy the privileges and control of social resources. Heterosexism posits male-female sexual relations as "normal," and those who fall outside this norm—those of gays and lesbians, bisexuals, single people, even polygamists—are marginalized, derided, and viewed as odd. Heterosexism ensures it's a straight people's world. Religion has been an important prop for heterosexism because it reinforces power differences and inequalities between heterosexuals and gay, lesbian, bisexual, and transgendered people. Religion remains a principal weapon in keeping same-sex sexuality and relationships illegal around the world, consequently denying LGBTQ+ individuals equal access to political and social rights. Until recently, most faith traditions permitted only heterosexual couples to marry and consequently acted as a significant barrier to legal marriage for same-sex couples. It would be silly to try to understand heterosexism without including religion and to examine religion today without thinking about heterosexism. Now let's move on to look at how people around the world (religious or not) think about sexuality today.

Our Evolving Thinking About Sexuality

Given how contentious sexuality issues are today in the United States and around the globe, you might think it safe to assume that sexuality was always at the forefront of religious controversy over the millennia, but this isn't really the case at all. Let's take a minute to think about the past. Historically and cross-culturally, societies have not divided human sexuality into heterosexuality and homosexuality. These terms developed in the early 20th century as clinical psychological labels. Behaviors associated with these labels existed, of course. But people were not organized into significant social and political groups on the basis of "who they partnered with." Instead, for most of human history, the social meaning of sexual behavior has focused on procreation within family units to ensure that people had children, and attitudes about sex were shaped by that context.

In the premodern world, men and women were obligated to reproduce to maintain the extended family as an economic and political unit. Among elite members of society, women's sexual behavior was highly controlled. Virgin daughters were valuable to their families because they could be given in marriage as part of political treaties, to connect two already powerful families, and to build a family's economic wealth (Boswell 1994). For elite men, things were different. Their sexual behavior was less tightly controlled. Although the broader society might discourage promiscuity, men could have sex with women, other men, girls, boys, and servants, just as long as they produced male heirs with their wives—heirs who could inherit family property and keep political power in the family. For people who did not have political power or wealth, sexual behavior was much less tightly controlled. Peasants might enter into a common-law marriage, but the relationship was local and informal, not a concern of the church or the state.

Prior to the modern era, people developed gender identities, for sure, but there were no distinct *sexual* identities for people to claim. Especially in North America and Europe, men and women often identify themselves as "straight," "gay," "lesbian," "bisexual," or "transgendered" (as we know, today others identify as nonbinary or genderfluid as well). The development of these identities has prompted new forms of political, psychological, and religious regulation. In her analysis of homosexual behavior prior to World War II, Vaid (1995, 39) points out that widespread "public morality campaigns, police crackdowns on homosexual solicitation, and increased enforcement of criminal laws" were a backlash against what was perceived to be "sexual anarchy" in the 1890s and early 1900s. In that era, gays and lesbians were pressured to remain invisible on the fringe of social life.

If we speed ahead in time to the present day, attitudes about homosexuality have changed drastically. In the U.S., Western Europe, and in other parts of the world, people's attitudes about same-sex sexual orientations, non-heterosexual sexual identities, and same-sex marriage have been slowly shifting and become more accepting. In 2007, five years after the Pew Research Center (Poushter and Kent 2020) began asking questions about the acceptability of homosexuality, just under half (49%) of people in the U.S. thought homosexuality should be accepted by society. In 2020, the percent of people agreeing with that statement had increased to 72%. In Figure 9.1, you can see that more and more people report believing that homosexuality should be accepted in countries as diverse as Mexico, India, Japan, and South Africa.

In almost every country, acceptance of homosexuality is also shaped by several key demographic variables. It may be no surprise to you to consider that younger people, women, those with more education, and those with higher incomes are more likely to believe that society should accept homosexuality than older people, men, and those with less education and lower income (Poushter and Kent 2020).

If we look at overall support for same-sex marriage, we see a similar pattern of growing acceptance. In 2004, most (60%) Americans opposed marriage rights for LGBTQ+ people. Ten years later, same-sex marriage was legal in every state, and by 2019, 60% of Americans supported it. That's a big turnaround in attitudes in a very short time! As with more general attitudes about homosexuality, demographic patterns in who supports and who opposes same-sex marriage are much the same. The young, women, and those with better education are all more likely to support same-sex marriage (Fingerhut 2016; Pew Research Center 2019).

While the data certainly shows that more people worldwide support the idea that homosexuality should be accepted by society, there are also parts of the world that remain staunchly opposed. Table 9.1 shows the extremes. Among the top nations where people remain the most opposed to accepting LGBTQ+ people in society are all countries in Africa, the Middle East, Eastern Europe and Russia, as well as South Asia (see also Janssen and Scheepers 2019). The demographic factors

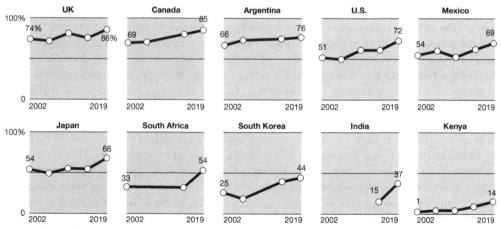

Rising acceptance of homosexuality by people in many countries around the world over the past two decades

% who say homosexuality should be accepted by society

Note: Only countries with double-digit increases from firtst survey year to 2019 shown. For more details, see Appendix A. Source. Spring 2019 Global Attitudes Survey. Q31.

PEW RESEARCH CENTER

Figure 9.1 Rates of Acceptance of Homosexuality in Selected Countries

Source: Poushter and Kent 2020.

Table 9.1 Highest and Lowest Rates of Global Acceptance of Homosexuality, 2019.

	Should be Accepted	Should not be Accepted
Sweden	94%	5%
Netherlands	92	8
Spain	89	10
France	86	11
United Kingdom	86	11
Nigeria	7	91
Lebanon	13	85
Kenya	14	83
Indonesia	9	80
Russia	14	74

Source: Poushter and Kent 2020.

we noted earlier within these countries continue to reinforce opposition, but so do factors like support for ideologically right-leaning politics, low levels of education, lack of internet access, whether or not homosexuality is legal in a country, or whether a country has signed the U.N. Declaration on Human Rights, Sexual Orientation, and Gender Identity (Jackle and Wenzelburger 2015; Ying and Peng 2018).

Religious Perspectives on Non-heterosexual Sexualities

Of course, religion remains a distinctive factor in shaping attitudes about homosexuality and same-sex marriage around the world. This makes sense, as religion remains one of the last institutional sources of sexual regulation. You should keep in mind, however, that most faith traditions didn't make explicit statements about homosexuality or same-sex marriage until very recently. Prohibitions on non-heterosexual relationships were based on statements in various sacred texts.

In the Jewish and Christian traditions, seven Biblical references are used to justify opposition to sexual behavior that is oriented toward others of one's own sex. In the story of Sodom and Gomorrah, God sends two angels to Sodom to see whether it is as wicked as its reputation suggests. When the people of Sodom try to gang-rape the angels, God destroys the city. This tale is traditionally used to show "what God thinks" of homosexuality (Genesis 19:1–28). Other Biblical references include injunctions from the Torah that "You shall not lie with a male as with a woman; it is an abomination" (Leviticus 18:22), that "If a man lies with a male as with a woman, both of them have committed an abomination; they shall be put to death, their blood is upon them" (Leviticus 20:13); and, presumably to address "drag" in the ancient world, "A woman shall not wear anything that pertains to a man, nor shall a man put on a woman's garment; for whoever does these things is an abomination to the Lord your God" (Deuteronomy 22:5). In the New Testament, Paul refers three times to what is presumably homosexuality:

> For this reason God gave them up to dishonorable passions. Their women exchanged natural relations for unnatural, and the men likewise gave up natural relations with women and were consumed with passion for one another, men committing shameless acts with men and receiving in their own persons the due penalty for their error.
>
> (Romans 1:26–28)

Do you not know that the unrighteous will not inherit the kingdom of God? Do not be deceived; neither the immoral, not idolaters, nor adulterers, nor sexual perverts [traditionally translated as "homosexuals"], nor thieves, nor the greedy, nor drunkards, nor revilers, nor robbers will inherit the kingdom of God.

(I Corinthians 6:9–10)

Understand this, that the law is not laid down for the just but for the lawless and disobedient, for the ungodly and sinners, for the unholy and profane, for murderers of fathers and murderers of mothers, immoral persons, sodomites, kidnappers, liars, perjurers, and whatever else is contrary to sound doctrine.

(I Timothy 1:9–10)

These verses have been used repeatedly to argue that being Christian is incompatible with being gay or lesbian. In turn, this has reinforced a religiously based sexual ideology that privileges heterosexuality.

Many non-Christian traditions also condemn alternative sexual behavior. Islamic texts resemble those of Christianity and Judaism in their rejection of homosexual behavior as inherently immoral. The Qur'an and the Hadith, a collection of actions and teachings attributed to Muhammad, both contain condemnations of sexual relationships between men (with almost no references to women):

We also sent Lut: He said to his people: "Do ye commit lewdness such as no people in creation (ever) committed before you? For ye practice your lusts on men in preference to women: ye are indeed a people transgressing beyond bounds.

(Qur'an 7:80–81)

What! Of all creatures do ye come unto the males, and leave the wives your Lord created for you? Nay, but ye are forward folk.

(Qur'an 26:165)

The Hadith recommends that men who engage in homosexual behavior be punished by death. In contrast to the Christian, Jewish, and Muslim scriptures, it is interesting to note that the sacred texts of Hinduism and Buddhism do not contain prohibitions on same-sex sexual relationships.

How religious groups and their members thought and spoke about sexuality began to change in the middle of the 20th century. In 1943, the Quakers issued the first formal denominational statement on the "problem" of homosexuality (Cragun et al. 2015). Several decades later, in the 1970s, many Christian denominations found themselves in the (sometimes awkward) position of needing to talk about sex in ways that weren't necessary in the past. It was at this point, as the gay and lesbian rights movement was growing, that denominations developed official policies and taught more directly about sexual behavior of all kinds, and other faith traditions followed (Wilcox 2003).

Remember our discussion of the controversy over consecration of the Rt. Reverend Gene Robinson at the start of this chapter? Consider how different things are now, at least in the U.S. Episcopal Church. If you look the Church's webpage, here is the statement that now appears (Episcopal Church 2021):

In the first century, Jesus of Nazareth inspired a movement. A community of people whose lives were centered on Jesus Christ and committed to living the way of God's unconditional, unselfish, sacrificial, and redemptive love. As Episcopalians, we believe in a loving, liberating, and life-giving God: Father, Son, and Holy Spirit.

We believe in following the teachings of Jesus Christ, whose life, death and resurrection saved the world.

> We have a legacy of inclusion, aspiring to tell and exemplify God's love for every human being; women and men serve as bishops, priests, and deacons in our church. Laypeople and clergy cooperate as leaders at all levels of our church. Leadership is a gift from God and can be expressed by all people in our church, regardless of gender, sexual identity or orientation.
>
> We believe that God loves us all—no exceptions.

Similar statements can be found on other Establishment Protestant websites, such as those of the United Church of Christ/Disciples of Christ. Other Christian denominations, like the United Methodist Church, welcome LGBTQ+ persons based on their sexual orientation and publicly oppose all forms of discrimination against them. However, the United Methodist Church still maintains that all sexual behavior outside the bounds of heterosexual marriage is incompatible with Christian teaching.

The Roman Catholic Church maintains a similar position to United Methodists. The Church teaches while there is nothing inherently sinful about *being* homosexual, any same-sex sexual *behavior* is a mortal sin. So too is sexual activity outside of heterosexual marriage. But in 2013, Pope Francis, in response to questions about the stance of the Church on gay rights, asked, "Who am I to judge?" Pope Francis, in contrast to his predecessors, has supported welcoming LGBTQ+ persons into the Church. This focus on treating LGBTQ+ persons with dignity led a subset of U.S. Catholic Bishops to issue a statement entitled "God Is On Your Side" in 2021, in support of LGBTQ+ youth and calling for LGBTQ+ persons to be treated with respect, compassion, and sensitivity (Povoledo and Graham 2021). However, despite this seemingly increasing focus on inclusivity, the Vatican has made it clear that in no way could same-sex marriages be understood as equivalent to heterosexual marriages, either socially or spiritually. Other Christian traditions continue to argue likewise.

One of the most extreme cases of a church opposing any acceptance of gay rights is the Westboro Baptist Church in Topeka, Kansas. It was headed by the Reverend Fred Phelps, who died in 2014; he and his family members who made up the congregation of this small Baptist church were notorious for publicly proclaiming that "God Hates Fags" and that the United States was doomed for its acceptance of homosexuality. Phelps was infamous for organizing antigay demonstrations during gay and lesbian pride celebrations and at the funerals of celebrities who had died from AIDS. Phelps and his followers protested at the memorial service held for Matthew Shepard, the gay University of Wyoming student who in 1998 was brutally beaten and left to die hanging on a barbed-wire fence along a country road. Although most conservative Christians in the U.S. would distance themselves from Phelps and his actions, they nonetheless concur that expressions of sexuality other than heterosexuality are morally wrong and should be formally opposed. Some Christian and Muslim clergy in parts of Africa and Asia, however, would agree with Phelps, going so far as to call for LGBTQ+ persons to be killed, based on those verses in the Bible and Qu'ran we talked about earlier.

But official statements opposing acceptance of LGBTQ+ people issued by religious authorities seem to be disconnected from the evolving attitudes of the members of these faith communities. A recent Pew Research Center survey asked respondents whether they thought homosexuality was acceptable or whether it should be discouraged by society. (See Table 9.2.) In 2007, only about 50% of the 35,500 respondents surveyed felt that homosexuality was acceptable but by 2014, it was 62%. And while support for or opposition to homosexuality in society continues to break down along religious lines, a general pattern of growing support is evident in every denominational and religious grouping. Establishment Protestants and Catholics were most supportive of public acceptance of homosexuality; 66% and 70% of them, respectively, said that it should be accepted by society. Among other Protestant groups, Evangelicals were the group where members were less likely to believe homosexuality should be accepted (36%), but even this represents a 10% change

Table 9.2 Differences in Attitudes about Acceptance of Homosexuality by Religious Affiliation 2007–2014.

Total Population	2007	2014
	50.0%	62.0%
Protestant	38.0	48.0
Evangelical	26.0	36.0
Establishment	55.0	66.0
Historically Black	39.0	51.0
Roman Catholic	58.0	70.0
Mormon	24.0	36.0
Jehovah's Witness	12.0	16.0
Orthodox	48.0	62.0
Jewish	79.0	81.0
Muslim	38.0	45.0
Buddhist	82.0	88.0
Hindu	48.0	71.0
Unaffiliated	71.0	83.0
Atheist	80.0	94.0
Agnostic	83.0	94.0
Secular unaffiliated	74.0	83.0
Religious unaffiliated	59.0	70.0

Source: Pew Research Center 2014, 308.

from 2007! Black Protestants also have grown more accepting, with 51% reporting that they saw homosexuality as acceptable, up from 39% in 2007. Mormons, the Orthodox, and even Jehovah's Witnesses all show an increase in support for LGBTQ+ acceptance. The religiously-unaffiliated (83%) American Buddhists (88%) and Jews (76%) were the most accepting of it, while Muslims were the least accepting (45%).

In the years following the legalization of same-sex marriage, one can identify growing support from many religious groups and consistent opposition from others (see Table 9.3). In 2014, U.S. Evangelicals, Mormons, and Jehovah's Witnesses were the most likely to oppose marriage rights for same-sex couples. American Jews, Buddhists, Hindus, and the religiously unaffiliated were the most supportive of same-sex marriage. By 2019, the religiously unaffiliated (82%), Roman Catholics (64%), and Establishment Protestants (63%) all report believing that the legalization of same-sex marriage was good for society (Pew Research Center 2019, 68).

While support for homosexuality in general and same-sex marriage in particular has grown in the United States and elsewhere in the world, it is important to underscore that this support doesn't vary only based on religious identity. Religious beliefs and practices continue to be strong predictors of opposition to acceptance of LGBTQ+ people and relationships in society.

Let's first look at how religious beliefs and practices shaped opposition to homosexuality in the first decade of the 21st century (see Table 9.4).

You can see from the data in this table that a number of factors correlate with opposition to public acceptance of homosexuality: an absolute belief in a personal god, weekly attendance at religious services, daily prayer, and a strong sense of religious identity. Among Mormons and Evangelical

Table 9.3 Differences in Attitudes about Same-Sex Marriage by Religious Affiliation 2014.

Total Population	Favor	Oppose
	53.0%	39.0%
Protestant	39.0	53.0
Evangelical	28.0	64.0
Establishment	57.0	35.0
Historically Black	40.0	52.0
Roman Catholic	57.0	34.0
Mormon	26.0	68.0
Jehovah's Witness	14.0	76.0
Orthodox	54.0	41.0
Jewish	77.0	18.0
Muslim	42.0	52.0
Buddhist	84.0	13.0
Hindu	68.0	23.0
Unaffiliated	78.0	16.0
Atheist	92.0	4.0
Agnostic	91.0	6.0
Secular unaffiliated	80.0	14.0
Religious unaffiliated	61.0	30.0

Source: Pew Research Center 2014, 310.

Table 9.4 Impact of Religious Belief and Practices on Public Opposition to Homosexuality for Selected Groups, 2008.

Total	Attend weekly or more	Religion is very important	Pray at least daily	Absolute belief in personal God	
Total Population	40.0%	57.0%	52.0%	49.0%	51.0%
Protestant					
Evangelical	64.0	75.0	70.0	69.0	69.0
Establishment Protestant	34.0	44.0	42.0	39.0	39.0
Historically Black	46.0	54.0	49.0	49.0	50.0
Catholic	30.0	37.0	35.0	33.0	34.0
Mormon	68.0	76.0	75.0	74.0	71.0
Orthodox	76.0	57.0	47.0	48.0	44.0
Jewish	20.0	N/A	27.0	32.0	24.0

Source: Pew Forum on Religion and Public Life 2008, 94.

Christians, those who were most devout were also more likely to oppose homosexuality. Similar patterns hold for the other groups as well. Even among Jews, who have been among the most accepting of homosexuality, religious devotion increases the likelihood of opposition: Jews who reported praying at least once daily were four times as likely as other Jews to oppose public acceptance of homosexuality.

More recent studies underscore how these patterns continue. Study after study demonstrates that those who are the most devout, those for whom religion is important to their lives, those who attend services frequently, those who believe the Bible to be the literal word of God, and those who claim a religious fundamentalist identity are significantly more opposed to any acceptance of homosexuality and same-sex marriage (Ogland and Verona 2014; Perry 2015; Perry and Whitehead 2016; Sukhmani and Sinha 2016). In their analysis of how religious beliefs and practices shape opposition to homosexuality worldwide, Janssen and Scheepers (2019) identify all of these same factors as predictors of anti-homosexual public opinion.

LGBTQ+ persons of faith have faced more than just religiously-based public opinion as a challenge to their full equality within religious communities. As we saw in our discussion of women's roles within faith communities, religion institutions reinforce non-heterosexual bias by limiting leadership to heterosexuals. Some religious organizations prohibit openly gay and lesbian people from belonging to or holding positions of power in congregations. Establishment Protestant denominations, for example, continue to struggle to define appropriate institutional roles for openly gay and lesbian parishioners. The United Methodist General Conference passed a statement in 1984 that prohibits the ordination of gays and lesbians. In 2004, the church also formally prohibited the church from funding groups that are deemed to support or promote homosexuality (United Methodist Church 2004). These stances were reinforced at the General Conference in 2019, while recognizing that United Methodists do not all agree. Like the United Methodists, the Presbyterian Church (U.S.A.)'s *Book of Order* originally forbade the ordination of sexually active gays and lesbians (Presbyterian Church USA 2008). However, facing a denominational split, it adopted a resolution in 2006 that allows some presbyteries to opt out of this prohibition on the basis of the Church's Theological Task Force Report that concluded that "sexual orientation is not, in itself, a barrier to ordination" (Presbyterian Church USA 2006, 20). In 2018, the Church formally approved a resolution that committed itself to full inclusion of transgender, nonbinary, and people of all gender identities.

In contrast to the debates in Establishment Protestant denominations, most Evangelical denominations, the Roman Catholic Church, and Eastern Orthodox Churches prohibit openly gay people from being ordained. For Evangelicals, this is a nonissue because they follow a literal interpretation of the Bible and associate homosexuality with evil. In the rare cases in which an evangelical congregation supported gays and lesbians, the parent organization typically responded by expelling the congregation. In 1992, for instance, the North Carolina State Baptist Convention "disfellowshipped," or expelled, the Olin T. Binkley Memorial Baptist Church in Chapel Hill, North Carolina, for fully including LGBTQ+ members in the life of the congregation and for approving John Blevins, an openly gay man, to preach as a step toward ordination (Hartman 1996). Following this episode, the Southern Baptist Convention decreed that all Southern Baptist congregations were required to oppose homosexuality.

Roman Catholic policy also officially bars LGBTQ+ people from being ordained. In 2005, Pope Benedict XVI reaffirmed the Vatican's longstanding policy that homosexual men should not be admitted to seminaries even if they are celibate:

> [The Church] . . . cannot admit to the seminary or to holy orders those who practice homosexuality, present deep-seated homosexual tendencies or support the so-called "gay culture." Such persons, in fact,

find themselves in a situation that gravely hinders them from relating correctly to men and women. One must in no way overlook the negative consequences that can derive from the ordination of persons with deep-seated homosexual tendencies.

This ban also applies to religious orders.
Eastern Orthodox Churches have a similar policy:

The Orthodox Church believes that homosexuality should be treated by religion as a sinful failure . . . correction is called for. Homosexuals should be accorded the confidential medical and psychiatric facili-ties by which they can be helped to restore themselves to a self-respecting sexual identity that belongs to them by God's ordinance.

(Harakas 2005)

The effects of these ideologies are not limited to what happens *inside* congregations. They also drive political action by religious groups in broader society. As we have already discussed, the Roman Catholic Church does not permit the marriage of same-sex couples. This isn't just a question of church ceremonies, however. The Congregation for the Doctrine of the Faith (2003) remains clear:

In those situations where homosexual unions have been legally recognized or have been given the legal status and rights belonging to marriage, clear and emphatic opposition is a duty. One must refrain from any kind of formal cooperation in the enactment or application of such gravely unjust laws and, as far as possible, from material cooperation on the level of their application. In this area, everyone can exercise the right to conscientious objection . . . When legislation in favor of the recognition of homosexual unions is proposed for the first time in a legislative assembly the Catholic law-maker has a moral duty to express his opposition clearly and publicly and to vote against it. To vote in favor of a law so harmful to the common good is gravely immoral.

Why does *this* issue remain so important to conservative religionists today? Part of the answer lies in the central role of the Bible or other sacred texts as a source of moral authority. If we dismiss the Bible's rules on sexuality as being historically or culturally based and thus no longer applicable to today's society, rather than regarding them as universal and absolute, then what stops us from dismissing all its other rules and commandments in the same fashion? People who take a religiously conservative approach to sexuality argue that if the Bible isn't absolutely, literally true for all times and places, then maybe none of it is true. At what point do you draw the line? If we disregard the text's codes of conduct regarding sexual behavior, then why believe that the Bible's call to feed the hungry, not to kill, or not to steal are relevant in today's world either? Of course, as with efforts to promote gender equality, redefining sexual norms also challenges religious ideas about family, the structure of authority in marriage, and the raising of children. The point is that opposition to homosexuality, gay rights, or same-sex marriage is based on more than just ignorance or fear. Opponents are fighting for larger religious principles here, and despite legal same-sex marriage and increasing support for acceptance of LGBTQ+ people and their relationships, the fight over full inclusion in religious communities is far from over.

Negotiating LGBTQ+ Identities Within Religious Institutions

In the United States today, most religious groups and people fall somewhere between the extremes of opposition to and support for homosexuality. And within most religious groups, the debates have raged "over the heads of LGBT people themselves . . . despite the presence of a small number of very vocal LGBT activists" (Wilcox 2003, 44). Sociologists too often lose sight that non-heterosexual people are not just objects in these religious debates, but they are subjects who have their own ideas about what they see happening around them. What also is less often examined is the religious beliefs and practices of LGBTQ+ persons themselves—something we'd like to begin to correct here.

A 2020 report from the UCLA School of Law Williams Institute reported only about 46.7% of LGBTQ+ Americans were moderately or highly religious, and 53.3% were not religious at all (Cronron et al. 2020, 5–6). Using data from the Gallup Poll, this report defined being religious as a combination of how important these individuals said religion was to their lives and how often they went to religious services. Religious LGBTQ+ persons are more likely to be older, to be persons of color, and to have slightly lower levels of education and income than those LGBTQ+ persons who are not religious. Table 9.5 provides a glimpse at some of the religious beliefs and practices of gay men and lesbian women. As you can see, gays and lesbians are all significantly less likely to hold traditional religious beliefs, to see religion as important, attend services weekly, or to pray daily than straight people.

These findings also reinforce Darren E. Sherkat's 2017 study of the religious commitments of sexual minorities, in which he found LGBTQ+ people rejected religious identification and participated less than their straight counterparts.

Despite these higher rates of non-affiliation among LGBTQ+ people, a significant number of them remain tied to religious identities and communities. It is no surprise then to observe that religious groups and organizations have emerged, led by LGBTQ+ individuals, to meet the needs of other LGBTQ+ persons and to create a safe and inclusive sacred space for them to find a spiritual home. The Universal Fellowship of Metropolitan Community Churches (MCC) is a worldwide federation of over 200 churches and 43,000 members in more than 20 countries that serve the LGBTQ+ communities. A central part of the MCC mission is for the federation members to be "leaders in the world about the union of *spirituality* and *sexuality* by articulating our message and spreading it effectively" (United Federation of Metropolitan Community Churches 2005). Other groups that attempt to meet the spiritual needs of LGBTQ+ people within traditional denominations include Dignity (Roman Catholic), Integrity (Episcopal), Lutherans Concerned (ELCA Lutheran), the National Gay Pentecostal Alliance (Pentecostal), Affirmation (Latter-day Saints/Mormon), AXIOS (Orthodox), and al-Fatiha (Muslim) (Wilcox 2003).

What the continued presence of all of these groups points out is that for many LGBTQ+ people, there is some disconnect between being a person of faith in a traditional religious community *and* an openly lesbian, gay man, bisexual, or transgendered person. How do such people manage the tension between their religious and sexual identities? Ethnographic studies have explored how LGBTQ+ people make sense of their place in religious groups (e.g., Mahaffy 1996). Until recently,

Table 9.5 Gay, Lesbian, and Bisexual Persons' Religious Beliefs and Practices, 2019.

	Gay/Lesbian	Straight
Believe in God	77.0%	89.0%
Religion is Important	34.0	54.0
Scripture is Word of God	33.0	61.0
Attend services weekly	16.0	36.0
Pray Daily	41.0	56.0

Source: Schwadel and Sandstrom 2019.

there were few ways to negotiate these conflicting identities. One could remain silent about one's sexuality. One could actively attempt to change into a heterosexual person. Or one could compartmentalize the two identities, keeping them separate in daily life. Each of these approaches, however, "consolidates" heterosexist power and privilege (to borrow a term from Woodhead 2007). That is, these approaches maintain heterosexuality as the norm in the face of a rapidly changing culture. In Randal Schnoor's study of gay Jews (2006, 49), Saul, a traditional Jew, said,

> If I weren't Jewish, I might be out there fighting for gay rights, but my Jewish identity is far more important to me than my gay identity. And that's something I know right from [the start]. I did not want to allow my same-gender romantic orientation to affect my passion for Judaism and Jewish life and the Jewish people. I never wanted that to impinge on it, to steal time from it and to even affect it.

Schnoor reports that other respondents adopted an ultra-religious life to "purge" themselves of their homosexuality.

To integrate their religious and sexual identities, LGBTQ+ people often reinterpret the Bible verses and religious traditions that have been used to condemn gay people (Rodriguez and Ouellette 2000; Schnoor 2006; Thumma 1991; Wilcox 2003; Yip 1997). Historical and cultural analyses reframe the texts. So, for example, Paul's injunctions against same-sex activity are reinterpreted to refer to man-boy sexual contact, which was common in parts of the ancient world, or to the practice of temple prostitution. New meanings emerge from an examination of different translations of texts. And as we have already observed, the reality of living with an LGBTQ+ *identity* did not exist in the ancient world. Men and women who engaged in homosexual behavior had no language to describe this behavior as some kind of unique sexual identity. Sex was sex. People's sexual partners, when they had sex, and whether their behavior was okay or taboo depended on whether they were men or women, elites or peasants, free people or slaves. Each society in human history has had its own unique cultural norms for defining human sexuality. Consequently, gay rights advocates within religious groups argue that Biblical texts, like the ones we have cited, cannot be used to condemn contemporary sexual identities and behavior. Likewise, it would be wrong to say that an individual from the past, like the Greek philosopher Plato, was gay just because he engaged in sex with male students. Our cultural norms and the meaning of sex and sexual identities are just too different to be applied to people from earlier eras.

Such reinterpretation is nearly universal among religious LGBTQ+ individuals, especially those who are Christians. It mirrors Woodhead's (2007) tactical approach by ignoring or challenging the "sanctified" sexual order that is posited by official church teaching. Research shows that LGBTQ+ believers are more likely to alter their religious beliefs than their sexual identity in order to resolve the tension between the two. Mahaffy (1996, 397) notes that more than half of the lesbians in her study adjusted their religious views by "reading about other gay Christians' experiences, meeting other gay Christians, participating in therapy, recognizing that spirituality and religion are separate entities, and disregarding the portions of Scripture that are condemning while affirming beliefs and traditions that embrace homosexuals." Similar patterns have been reported among LGBTQ+ Seventh Day Adventists, Evangelicals, and Jews (Drumm 2005; Schnoor 2006; Thumma 1991).

It is important to keep in mind, however, that the religious identity-sexual identity relationship is not an all-or-nothing proposition for most LGBTQ+ people. Identities are fluid and context-specific, so how LGBTQ+ people experience themselves as both religious and sexual beings generates many different outcomes. In studies of LGBTQ+ students at two faith-based universities, Fuist (2016) and Wedow et al. (2017) certainly identify students who try to reconcile their religious and sexual identities in the ways we described earlier, but not all of them did. Figure 9.2 helps us think about the different ways LGBTQ+ people negotiate their identities.

	ACCEPT SEXUAL IDENTITY	REJECT SEXUAL IDENTITY
ACCEPT RELIGIOUS IDENTITY	Integrated Identity	Embattled Identity
REJECT RELIGIOUS IDENTITY	Liberated Identity	Disillusioned Identity

Figure 9.2 LGBT Identity Negotiation Types
Source: Wedow et al. 2017, 299.

Some students seemed to embrace their religious and sexual identities in a fully cohesive way (these students had an ***integrated identity***). As one lesbian student noted in an interview:

> It never occurred to be . . . that [being religious and a lesbian] would be a problem. I mean, I've had it shouted at me that I'm going to hell because I'm gay, but I'm from [a conservative area] (she laughs). But that never concerned me. I didn't think that was true. I just thought that those people were really closed-minded.
>
> (Fuist 2016, 779)

Others reject their religious identities, what Wedow et al. (2017) call a ***liberated identity***, or reject or at least distance themselves from their sexual identities (an ***embattled identity***). In the former case, students expressed their anger with their church's teachings on sexuality.

> It makes me really angry; I completely disagree, and I think it's just so wrong to say that you are allowed to be this way or whatever but you can't actually act on it. That definitely has a lot to do with [not identifying as Catholic anymore]. I'm not going to pretend to get along with a religion or a group of people that tell me that I can't be in a relationship because of something I never chose.
>
> (Wedow et al. 2017, 305)

In the latter case, LGBTQ+ people struggle emotionally and practically with what they believe to be two irreconcilable identities. One man, in yet another study of how Orthodox Jewish gay men cope with being both Orthodox and gay, makes the pain of living in secrecy clear:

> I fight the urge . . . every day and all day and I don't know how to stop the thoughts. . . . I keep thinking if this is the way I was born or this is a deviant behaviour I acquired during my life. . . . I keep trying to make up for this horrible sin. . . . I am actually waiting to get punished, even to die.
>
> (Itzhaky and Kissil 2015, 631)

Still others did both, rejecting or marginalizing both their religious and sexual selves (a ***disillusioned identity***). In this case, LGBTQ+ people give up after a fashion. Typically, they are caught in family, school, or church contexts which do not allow them to express integrated identities. As one student who was enrolled at a Catholic University expressed:

> I'm tired of it; whatever. It's just not worth the effort anymore, and I'll be graduating soon anyway. . . . It doesn't matter, because it doesn't matter for anyone. No one is going to change around here suddenly

just because I express my opinions . . . but I'll be out of here and I'll get to be somewhere after this that listens to me more hopefully.

(Wedow et al. 2017, 308–309)

The important point to remember is that group contexts and relationships with others in your social network both have an impact on how one juggles the multiple identities that make us, us (Fuist 2016). For religious LGBTQ+ people, it is possible to embrace differing sexual and religious identities despite formal teachings and policies of their religious communities. Likewise, congregations themselves, even in traditions that formally do not accept gays and lesbians, respond in fluid ways to the LGBTQ+ members in their midst (Whitehead 2017).

Outside of the boundaries of Christian traditions, LGBTQ+ people also negotiate their religious and sexual selves through what Woodhead calls "questing": the acceptance of the dominant (hetero)sexual order while simultaneously seeking an individual or group position within it that confers well-being (Woodhead 2007, 559). LGBTQ+ people who reject traditional organized religion have embraced New Age spirituality, neo-pagan traditions, and other forms of alternative spiritualities. Many lesbians have been attracted to the goddess-centered spirituality of Wicca and to other forms of neo-pagan religion. These traditions emphasize gender equality and balance as central themes (Neitz 2005). The use of magic and ritual to access spiritual power and social empowerment attract some LGBTQ+ individuals to a spiritual quest. Many LGBTQ+ Buddhists also engage in questing: Meditation and "practicing mindfulness and compassion in daily life . . . helps to stop the suffering of ourselves and of all beings" (Cadge 2005, 144).

In a more conventional form of questing, Savastano (2005) describes how gay Italian Catholic men in Newark, New Jersey, became devotees of Saint Gerard Maiella, a popular Saint among Southern Italian immigrants to the United States. Saint Gerard is the official patron saint of mothers, infertility, and childbirth, but gay followers recraft him as the patron of:

> fecundity—the fecundity of romantic and sexual relationships with all of the emotional, spiritual, and ·
> physical fulfillment such relationships can bring—and with a new and creative configuration of family
> that extends beyond traditional patriarchal family structure.
>
> (Savastano 2005, 184)

Gay devotees tap into the spiritual energy of Saint Gerard by participating in processions, prayers, novenas to the Saint, and an annual *fiesta* in Newark's Little Italy. In all these examples, the negotiation of religious and sexual identities takes place outside the confines of tradition religion.

Challenging and Transforming Religious Ideas About Sexuality

Sexual identities and religious identities still seem to conflict with one another today, despite all of the legal and social gains in acceptance for LGBTQ+ people and their relationships. These conflicts occur at the institutional level, but also within individuals. And religion matters here. Religion is still the main source of opposition to full equality for gays and lesbians and the acceptance of alternative sexualities, as well as playing a vital role in determining the treatment of LGBTQ+ people around the world.

As we have seen in this chapter, people actively engage religion to construct religious and sexual identities that make sense to them and meet their needs as whole human beings. The integration of gays and lesbians into mainstream American religion (or the failure to integrate them) has important implications for all Americans. Religion has historically been used to justify intolerance toward poor people, racial minorities, and women, and to deny them access to resources in religious groups and broader society. Today, religion is still used to deny gays and lesbians full inclusion in society. In some parts of the world, gays and lesbians are imprisoned and killed by governments that base their civil law on Biblical and Qu'ranic injunctions against homosexual activity, all with approval of religious authorities. Controversies about gender and sexuality in religion extend beyond the academic or theological realms. They are political: Conservative groups around the world rely on religion to maintain both the structures of patriarchy that we saw in Chapter 8 as well as heterosexual privilege, and yet religion also remains paramount to challenging and transforming them.

Further Reading

Boswell, John. 1980. *Christianity, Social Tolerance, and Homosexuality*. Chicago: University of Chicago Press.

Fetner, Tina. 2008. *How the Religious Right Shaped Lesbian and Gay Activism*. Minneapolis: University of Minnesota Press.

Frank, Gillian, Bethany Moreton, and Heather R. White. 2018. *Devotions and Desires: Histories of Sexuality and Religion in the Twentieth-Century United States*. Chapel Hill, NC: University of North Carolina Press.

Hartman, Keith. 1996. *Congregations in Conflict: The Battle over Homosexuality*. New Brunswick, NJ: Rutgers University Press.

Talvacchia, Kathleen T., Michael F. Pettinger, and Mark Larrimore. 2015. *Queer Christianities: Lived Religion in Transgressive Forms*. New York: New York University Press.

Thumma, Scott, and Edward R. Gray. 2005. *Gay Religion*. New York: Altamira Press.

Weiss, Meredith L., and Michael Bosia. 2013. *Global Homophobia: States, Movements, and the Politics of Oppression*. Urbana, IL: University of Illinois Press.

Wilcox, Melissa M. 2003. *Coming Out in Christianity: Religion, Identity, and Community*. Bloomington, IN: Indiana University Press.

10 Blessed are the Poor, Woe to the Rich, But What about the Middle?

Are There Class Differences in How Religion Works?

1 Does religion matter when thinking about social class?
2 What is class all about, anyway?
3 Are religious identities, beliefs, practices, and experiences different for believers from different classes?
4 Are there ways that religion might influence how the class structure works?

It doesn't take much effort when reading the sacred texts of many different religious traditions to encounter conversations about social class. Now, the texts themselves don't use that term exactly, but they do speak a lot about different categories of people based on their economic power in their particular societies. In the Hebrew Scriptures, for example, God rewards those who follow the Law with prosperity on one hand, but condemns the rich who oppress the poor on the other. The Prophet Jeremiah says that because the Hebrew king Josiah judged the cause of the poor and needy with justice and righteousness, "it was well" with him, but Josiah's son, the next king, "had eyes and heart only for dishonest gain" and for "practicing oppression," and as a result, God condemned him and so Jeremiah predicts, "with the burial of an ass he shall be buried and dragged and cast forth beyond the gates of Jerusalem" (Jeremiah 22:13–19). Much of the Hebrew Law itself speaks about requirements for faithful Jews to care for the poor, needy, and oppressed.

In the Christian New Testament, the story is much the same. Jesus, in the famous Sermon on the Mount, says "Blessed are you poor for yours is the Kingdom of Heaven" while simultaneously declaring, "but woe to you that are rich, for you have received your consolation" (Luke 6: 20, 24). He also spoke about it being easier for a camel to go through the eye of a needle than for a rich man to enter Heaven (Matthew 19:24). The parable of Lazarus and the rich man tells a similar story (Luke 16:19–31). Lazarus was a poor man, begging for crumbs from the rich man's table. The rich man had it all—food, wealth, power. Both men die and the rich man is consigned to hell while Lazarus goes to heaven. The moral of the story Jesus tells his followers was that the rich man had everything in this life, but because he neglected taking care of the poor man, he now was being punished while the poor man received all he needed.

In other religious traditions, such as Islam, the relations between the rich and poor are similarly portrayed. Those with wealth are required to contribute money to alleviate hunger and other economic needs of the poor. *Zakat*, one of the five Pillars of Islam, reflects this obligation for faithful Muslims. The Qu'ran (9: 60) notes:

> Alms are only for the poor and the needy, and those who collect them, and those whose hearts are to be reconciled, and to free the captives and the debtors, and for the cause of Allah, and (for) the wayfarer; a duty imposed by Allah. Allah is Knower, Wise.

DOI: 10.4324/9781003182108-13

And in case a wealthy person tried to exploit the poor and needy, the Qu'ran is equally clear: "And give to the orphans their properties and do not substitute the defective [of your own] for the good [of theirs]. And do not consume their properties into your own. Indeed, that is ever a great sin."

Hinduism also directs believers to take care of those who are poor and needy and in doing so, they acquire good karma. The Hindu Vedas, like other sacred texts, condemns the accumulation of wealth for its own sake. For example, in *Rig Veda* (10–177–6) we learn that:

> One may amass wealth with hundreds of hands but one should also distribute it with thousands of hands. If someone keeps all that he accumulates for himself and does not give it to others, the hoarded wealth will eventually prove to be the cause of ruin.

What should we make of all this? Well, even these few verses from a range of sacred texts show that believers in many traditions are called upon to address the inequalities of wealth and poverty that arise from class differences. Social class differences, in some form, clearly matter to many religions. That's all well and good, but a quick glance around the world shows us that economic inequalities are only getting more extreme despite the numbers of Christians, Muslims, Jews, and those from other faiths who are supposed to be doing something about it. So maybe the challenge isn't that religion doesn't talk about class, but rather that people from different social classes understand these texts and therefore live out their faith traditions in very different ways. The rich are different from the middle and working classes as well as the poor in their religious identities, beliefs, practices, and experiences. That's what this chapter is here to help you think about. But religion can be part of the story about how some people get to be (and stay) rich or poor as well. Before we go further down this road, let's step back and think more about social classes generally, what defines them, and how they work.

What are Social Classes, Anyway?

Thinking about social class can be a tricky business for anyone, including sociologists. In some countries, social class differences are clearly defined based on things like your job (and whether or not you even need one to live your life as you wish), how much money you earn (and how it's earned), your education, the language you speak, how you live, and sometimes even how you worship. In other countries, especially the United States, class is muddier. It isn't that the things we just named don't matter for determining one's social class position, but for many Americans, social class is invisible. Americans, rich and poor alike, often see themselves as all somewhere in a giant middle class. Sure, there are rich people, mostly understood to be celebrities and professional athletes, and there certainly are poor people, like those who depend on government economic support systems to make ends meet or who are the people standing on corners or at traffic intersections with signs asking passersby for any money they can spare. In between these extremes is everyone else. Whether you are a professional with an Ivy League education living in a multimillion-dollar home in the suburbs or you work as a delivery driver for Amazon or elsewhere in the service sector, lots of us seem to think of ourselves as middle-class. Of course, the Occupy movement of 2011 gave us a new way to think about social class differences: the 99% vs. the 1%. Yet even for those sympathetic to Occupy and its call for economic justice, the idea that there are significant economic, social, and cultural class divides in America (within both the 99% and the 1%) remains a hard idea to accept in a country still tied to the belief that if they work hard enough, anyone can be President.

If trying to think about how class shapes people's life experiences is tough, the idea that there are class differences *in religion* is even more challenging. Do rich people worship differently than poor people? Are there differences in religious beliefs and experiences even within the same religious tradition for people at different locations in the class structure? How sociologists think about religion and social class, and frankly, not all that many do, is our focus in this chapter, so get ready to confront some thought-provoking ideas. We will come back to these issues in a minute.

Let's start with the big picture: when sociologists talk about social class, what do they even mean? Good question! Social scientists have been debating definitions and meanings of social class for more than 100 years, maybe close to 200 if you go back to the time Karl Marx was first writing about it. Unfortunately, one of the biggest problems in thinking about religion and class is that we have not moved too far beyond the debates over what defines class or what separates one class from another. Unlike race or gender, which may seem to you to be easier to distinguish from one another, class categories are up for debate, defined and measured in multiple ways, none of which overlap to any great degree. Sadly, this has left many sociologists of religion to ignore entirely the class dimensions to the things they study, despite the theoretical importance of class to the social sciences overall! This also probably helps explain why the study of religion and social class remains an area that many sociologists feel we need to know more about, but very few actually incorporate into their work.

Now hold on for a crash course on social class. We can think about class in three different ways: objectively, subjectively, and relationally. First, social classes can be thought of as relatively distinct groups, organized into a hierarchy where the groups at the top have more social and (especially) economic power than those below them. This is an objective view of class because we can argue that the people in each class are similar in that their life experiences are shaped, both positively and negatively, by the different amount of power and privilege they have as a result of their class position. The outcomes of belonging to a particular social class, in terms of one's lived experiences, is what social scientists refer to as *life chances*, the opportunities and vulnerabilities faced by individuals based on the forms of power and social resources at their disposal. Life chances are shaped by the collective impact of many different aspects of one's social location, including gender, race, sexual orientation, and age. However, it is one's access to economic resources, such as income and wealth, central to social class differences, that plays a unique role in shaping an individual's advantages and disadvantages. Differing access to these resources also becomes the basis for the inclusion and exclusion of individuals into each class.

So for example, what makes me middle-class in an objective sense is not that I think of myself that way as much as the fact that I have a middle-class income and a modest amount of wealth (perhaps through having retirement investments, a savings account, or owning a home) and live in a manner these resources allow. A wealthy person or a poor one can still imagine themselves to be middle-class, but their life experiences will be objectively different from someone who is middle-class, bringing more opportunities in the case of the wealthy person or more vulnerabilities in the case of the poor person. To put it in simplistic terms, a six-or seven-figure income is objectively different than a four-or five-figure income in the kind of life it allows those who earn them to lead.

Since those of us who live in the United States don't live in a society with a traditional hereditary aristocracy, as you might have seen depicted on reruns of "Downton Abbey" or "The Crown," and as you still see in European societies with class boundaries fixed by birth, *socioeconomic status* is traditionally how American social scientists have defined social class in many social scientific surveys. Socioeconomic status is a quantitative index built on the combined effects of family income, educational level, and occupational prestige. The working assumption in using this concept is that the upper-class is characterized by high levels of income and education as well as holding occupations that have high status. Lower-class people have low levels of income and education and tend to hold jobs which bring low status. Between the two extremes, however, are classes that vary on all three measures. Imagine yourself as a university professor; you may have a high level of education and occupational prestige but earn an income that is on par with or even below some skilled working-class occupations. Or perhaps you are a plumber or carpenter. Women and men in these occupations may earn high incomes but have lower levels of education and occupational prestige. Such irregularities refer to what we call *status inconsistencies*. These examples show the challenges of using the components of socioeconomic status, alone or combined, as the only way to determine someone's social class position. Family income or educational level on their own can lead to misidentifying the position of individuals or families in the class structure. It isn't that they are not important distinguishing features of social class, but they don't do a good enough job as they don't include other important aspects of what helps define class.

Bourdieu (1986) provides a more nuanced way to think about social class by introducing us to the concept of *cultural capital*, a term you may be familiar with from other areas you've studied. This concept gives us a different, more *subjective*, way to think about class. Think about it this way: day to day, we don't see a person's "family income" or "educational level" or "occupational prestige" when we encounter them walking down the street or at a party. We do, however, see the style of their clothing, the kind of car they drive, the food they plan to buy in the grocery store check-out line, and we also hear their choice of words and accents. All of these are aspects of cultural capital.

At its most basic, cultural capital refers to what you know and how you know it. Now, Bourdieu argues that this is a distinct form of class power and works very differently from the economic power that comes with income and wealth. Social commentator Fussell (1983, 28) in his humorous examination of the American class structure, puts it this way: "money doesn't matter that much." For Bourdieu and Fussell, classes are differentiated from each other by the degree to which their cultures and lifestyles work to include those who share them and exclude others who don't. Class cultures include all of the social norms, values, and language that make people from the same class feel comfortable with each other while setting up a clear "you don't belong" dynamic for those who don't share them. In addition to what we've already mentioned, what you eat and how you eat it, what constitutes a desirable vacation as well as the number of them per year, where you live, how you decorate your home, whether you have access to health care, how you speak and the words you use, and on and on—all make up the behaviors and attitudes that are "normal" for people in each class. These kinds of things also separate one class from another.

Okay, we already can sense you are asking: "But doesn't all this come down to differences in taste or personal preference?" We have to say, sociologically, the answer is no. Those sociologists who study these subjective aspects to class argue that, more than just differences in taste, they are differences in the "physical markers of consumptive power" (Patillo 2008, 266). In other words, food, clothing, cars, art, and a wide array of other consumer goods provide clear class signals to others in ways that can unite or divide them. Because we are in the same class, we will learn to adopt shared tastes, not the other way around. And while our shared tastes make you and I feel like we have things in common, they also clearly separate those who don't. Subjectively, then, class is expressed not only in the physical cost involved in buying certain items over others, but also in the very choice itself of what we buy. An upper-middle-class person may purchase high-end clothing with designer labels, while a truly upper-class person may spend less money for a plainer, higher-quality but less ostentatious outfit that won't go out of fashion within a year or two. This probably accounts for why so many of us think that athletes or popular music or film celebrities must be upper-class. Just look at what they can buy or where they live or the cars they drive! You might think that shows like *Real Housewives of Beverly Hills* (or any other city, for that matter) must show us how the upper-class lives, right? Once again, the answer can only be no when we compare them with the more exclusive and largely invisible world of the really upper-classes. The consumer choices the celebrity "housewives" make are certainly made possible by their economic wealth, but these choices communicate to others further above them that, even with all their money, they still don't belong to the upper class.

Now, in addition to thinking about class in objective and subjective terms, it is important to take into account the relational aspects of social class. Up until now, we have really been talking about what separates one class from another. But social classes exist in relationships with each other, and these relationships are built into the fabric of every social institution. Class relations are operating all the time, even when we can't always see them. This idea is reflected in Marx's analysis of social class relations within the structure of capitalist society. The power and resources of the few at the top of the class structure is directly linked to the powerlessness and lack of resources of those below them. The rich are rich *because* the poor are poor! It's not an accident, Marx would say, because they are related. Around the world, the poor (or the working classes, in Marx's language) spend their lives working for employers (the upper class), who pay them only enough to get by while pocketing all the profits their work produces. The upper classes exploit the classes below them and stay at the top by doing so.

Class relations are always political things, as elites use their economic resources to get into public office, to fund political campaigns, and to lobby for legislation and social policy that favor their economic and social interests and oppose anything and anyone that hurts these interests. Elite access to political power is unavailable to most others, who in turn can only rely on the power of their numbers to pressure elites to pursue particular courses of action. At times, mass movements, such as the Occupy movement that we've talked about already, emerge to challenge the power of elite classes. The American labor movement, too, represents challenges from below, as workers have organized themselves through unions to fight for economic justice on the job and in society more broadly. Class relations are reflected in economics and politics and inevitably shape our life experiences, in good and not-so-good ways depending on our own class position, in every social institution, including religion.

So How Does Social Class Fit into the Study of Religion?

We are sure you must be thinking that all this talk about social class seems pretty far removed from religion, right? But don't be too sure. There are class differences in religion, just as we have seen racial and gender-based differences at work there too. Now, sociologists who look for links between religion and social class often try to find out how religious beliefs, behaviors, and experiences vary across different social class contexts. In other words, they want to know how the religious experiences of the upper classes, the middle classes, and the working classes and poor are similar or different from each other.

In theoretical terms, many of the underlying assumptions and approaches to the religion-class relationships were shaped by Marx's ideas of religion as a tool of class domination within capitalism and Weber's idea that religion both shapes and is shaped by class relations that we talked about in earlier chapters. In both cases, religious traditions in their theology and cultures reflects differing degrees of class power and powerlessness. For Marx, religion was the "opium of the masses," a system of beliefs that acts like a sedative that keeps the working classes passive in the face of exploitation while providing them with a promise of a better life in the next world. Marx's opiate metaphor is what's behind the old phrase "Pie in the sky, when you die." No matter how awful and oppressive your life is here on earth, when you get to Heaven or Paradise or wherever the good people go after they die, you will have everything you could ever want. For Weber, on the other hand, religion wasn't just about the rich oppressing the poor. Faith traditions provide people from different classes, Weber argued, with ethical beliefs and behavioral mandates that give meaning to their lives and shape their behavior in distinct ways. Religion also reinforced that whichever class you were in, elite, middle, working class, or poor, you were there for a reason. So, whether religion keeps the rich rich and poor poor or whether it shapes the beliefs and behaviors of people based on their social class positions, you should remember that most if not all early and contemporary studies of religion and class still return to these ideas.

As we talk about a little further on, sociological research in this area draws on both quantitative and qualitative data to illustrate how these class differences in religion work. Plenty of statistical studies, for example, identify distinct economic and educational differences in patterns of an array of religious beliefs, religious service participation, and many other religious practices and experiences. Sociologists also use statistics to show how people from different religious traditions and denominations, as well as an assortment of religious beliefs and activities shapes their views about income and wealth accumulation, educational attainment, and occupational choice.

But in addition to crunching numbers, other sociologists dig deep into how religion and class work together by conducting intensive interviews, observational studies, and even content analysis of religious preaching, music, and other symbols. These kinds of studies, unlike those based solely on statistical relationships, typically delve into the lived religious experiences of individuals from different classes as well as examining the ways in which different forms of religious expression are themselves shaped by distinct class cultures. A significant portion of this type of research examines how religion impacts the life and work experiences of those at the bottom of the class hierarchy, the working and nonworking poor. Here, the way that faith shapes how poor people view the challenges of their lives and their views of the larger society are particularly central concerns.

So, let's talk about these different kinds of studies in more detail first. By the numbers and by tradition, the wealthy tend to experience religion differently than the middle class, working classes, and the poor. Historical and contemporary studies in American religion highlight that wealthy people cluster in certain faith traditions and even in specific congregations within a community while middle class, working class, and poor people can be found in others. Perhaps the most prominent early study of class differences within Christian traditions was the work of Niebuhr ([1929]1987). Although Niebuhr was really analyzing Christian denominational differences in Europe following the Reformation, he made a distinction between the churches of the poor—or, in his language, the "disinherited"—and the churches of the middle class. Niebuhr discovered that the religious traditions of the richer and poorer social classes vary distinctly in terms of their denominational identities, their beliefs and worship styles, their organizational structures, as well as their ethical concerns. Wealthier people were to be found most often in Establishment Protestant denominations, while working-class and poor individuals more often belonged to what we would now identify as evangelical denominations. Then as now, the upper classes favor worship styles that we might call traditional—formal rituals, music, and language and their beliefs go along with the culture around them. In contrast, Niebuhr's poor preferred less-formal, more emotionally-driven, experiential religion where the beliefs often run counter to those of the dominant culture around them. In upper-class denominations, leaders are highly educated and exercise more formal authority, while in lower-class denominations, ministers often have less formal training and, while they have authority, the congregation shares in decision-making. In all of this, Niebuhr shows us a religious world where rich and poor lead very different religious lives.

Many classic studies of community life in towns and cities on the East Coast and the Midwest focused at least a portion of their attention on religion and class and confirm and also build off of Niebuhr's work (Warner and Lunt 1941; Lynd and Lynd 1929; Vidich and Bensman 1958). These studies identified similar class differences in religious affiliation as well as in beliefs, practices, organizational structures, and aesthetics as those in Niebuhr's work. In study after study, American elite in local communities belonged to Episcopal, Presbyterian, and Methodist congregations—Establishment Protestant traditions—underscoring that descriptive label, while the working classes clustered in Evangelical and Roman Catholic congregations. These patterns provide a basis for understanding the social distribution of religious traditions among differing social classes. It is clear from these older works as well as from more recent studies that these patterns have not changed in radical ways. Among Establishment Protestants, Episcopalians still speak of their "carriage trade" congregations; that is, their members who belong to the American old-money class that at one time would have been brought to services in fine carriages. Presbyterians and United Methodists also claim ties to the industrial and financial elite, as do American Jews. Evangelical and Black Protestant as well as Roman Catholic congregations still include an overrepresentation of the middle class and the working class compared to these other groups. In the case of Roman Catholics, this ongoing concentration is tied to the fact that now, as in the past, many Roman Catholic Americans were immigrants from Europe and more recently Central and South America.

But wait, we hear you say! That was then, but this is now and times have changed. Of course times have changed, but these patterns remain remarkably consistent. Smith and Faris (2005) provide what was the first in a series of contemporary research articles that revisited the relationships between religion and social class, at least in America. They used statistical analysis to examine data from the 1980s and 1990s, but what they found reinforced the patterns we have been talking about so far. Smith and Faris identified ongoing differences in income, in occupational status, and in education among different American religious groups. The same Christian denominations as well as Jews that long made up the Protestant Establishment still reflect the highest levels of earnings, educational attainment, and occupational prestige. American upper-class Christians were most likely to be found in Establishment Protestant churches, such as the Presbyterian Church, U.S.A., the Episcopal Church, and others that were theologically more liberal, but still were traditional in their worship styles and hierarchical in their organization, as was the case in those studies from almost 80 years ago.

This is still evident based on more recent research conducted by the Pew Research Center in 2014 (Masci 2016; Murphy 2016). Take a look at Table 10.1. It is fascinating to think that after decades, or even the better part of the last century, so much remains the same. Among Christians, Establishment Protestants in the United States remain at the top in terms of income and education. Although Table 10.1 only reports percentages for Episcopalians, similar patterns were found among other Establishment Protestant denominations like the Presbyterian Church (U.S.A), the United Methodist Church, and the United Church of Christ. American Jews, Hindus, and Muslims also report among the highest levels of income and education.

Table 10.1 Income and Educational Characteristics of Major Religious Categories, 2014.

	Earning > $100,000	Bachelor's Degree
Jewish	44%	59%
Hindu	36	77
Episcopal Church	30	56
Orthodox Christian	29	40
Muslim	20	39
Roman Catholic	19	26
Unaffiliated	17	24
Buddhist	13	47
Historically Black Protestants	9[a]	16[b]
Jehovah's Witness	4	12
National Average	19%	908

Source: Masci 2016; Murphy 2016.

[a] Percent averaged for Church of God in Christ and National Baptist Convention
[b] Percent averaged for African Methodist Episcopal (AME) Church, Church of God in Christ, and National Baptist Convention

As you drop down the class structure, you find people who are more likely to belong to Evangelical denominations like the Southern Baptists, Pentecostal and fundamentalist denominations, Jehovah's Witnesses, and Black Baptists. As in the past, these groups tend to be more religiously conservative and enjoy more informal and experiential worship styles. But what also remains true is that members of these religious groups have some of the lowest levels of economic, educational, and occupational resources. These findings continue to be identified by other sociologists as well (Davidson and Pyle 2011; Keister 2011; Coreno 2002).

Today we can also find the very poor and destitute who, while sometimes expressing a personal religious faith, often don't attend any congregation at all. This might surprise you and certainly would have surprised Karl Marx, who might have reasoned the people that most need religion to be that opiate to numb the pain of life would be people at the very bottom of the class structure. But that doesn't seem to be the case. The poor often don't show up at religious services because they are embarrassed by what people might think of them, or because they don't have any way to get to services, or some combination of these factors. Sullivan (2011), in *Living Faith: Everyday Religion and Mothers in Poverty*, interviewed single mothers living in poverty regarding the role of faith in their everyday life. These low-income women who are personally religiously devout frequently express their feeling that church attendance and participation reflects middle-class cultural norms that make them feel out of place. How people dress, how they talk, and their lifestyles all work to create boundaries for these women. Remember that congregations express their class differences through their organization and worship cultures, reinforcing social comfort or discomfort, which is inviting for those who share that culture and excludes those who don't.

But despite the consistency of these patterns, it probably is a good idea to ask critical questions about them. One important change to them that we can identify is that today, within local communities, it is more likely for individual congregations rather than entire denominations or religious traditions to be segregated by social class. Reimer's (2007) work on class diversity within congregations found that despite ongoing patterns of class differences between whole denominations, there is more class diversity within individual congregations themselves these days. But although there is more diversity, Reimer points out that the class divides still operate through the type of neighborhood location a congregation is in, by the worship style, architecture, and overall culture you find in it, and in the social and friendship networks operating in a congregation, which often follow class lines. Since American Jews report the highest levels of income, education, and occupational prestige, it wouldn't be a surprise to find their temples and synagogues reflecting a more homogenous class culture. Among U.S. Christians, if you go looking for them, you'll find upper-middle-class Roman Catholics, for example, attending a particular Catholic parish in a community, while middle- or working-class Catholics will attend others. Some upper-class Episcopalians and Presbyterians will gravitate to grand churches with traditional music with professional musicians and preaching from a highly educated minister, as opposed to working-class and poor Evangelicals and Black Protestants who might be found in a more ordinary church space where the music, preaching, and overall experience will be energetic and emotional. But whether your faith community meets in a cathedral, a temple, or a storefront, you are likely to make and maintain friendships and other social bonds with people like you, and shared class cultures will be a defining feature of them (Schwadel 2012). Congregations remain class-segregated places for most American Christians and Jews. Whether these patterns of class segregation hold for other religious groups—like Muslims, Hindus, or Buddhists—despite the high incomes and educations of Muslims and Hindus in the United States remains an area for further study.

If class differences are evident in which religious traditions people belong to, they are also evident in what they believe and how they practice their faith. We've borrowed some more data from the Pew Research Center's 2014 U.S. Religious Landscape Survey to show you. Unfortunately, their report only hints at class differences in religion by looking at the differences in some specific religious beliefs and practices based on whether a person has at least earned a bachelor's degree or whether they have completed less education than that. Check out Table 10.2.

Table 10.2 Educational Differences in Selected Religious Beliefs and Practices, 2014.

	<Bachelor's Degree	Bachelor's Degree
Belief in Heaven		
Establish. Protestant	84%	72%
Evangelical Protestant	89	84
Historically Black Protestant	93	92
Roman Catholic	86	83
Non-Christian Faiths	57	37
Belief in Hell		
Establish. Protestant	67	47
Evangelical Protestant	83	78
Historically Black Protestant	82	81
Roman Catholic	65	58
Non-Christian Faiths	40	23
Sacred Text is Word of God		
Establish. Protestant	69	49
Evangelical Protestant	88	89
Historically Black Protestant	86	82
Roman Catholic	68	58
Non-Christian Faiths	36	27
Worship Service Attendance		
Establish. Protestant	31	36
Evangelical Protestant	55	68
Historically Black Protestant	52	59
Roman Catholic	37	45
Non-Christian Faiths	22	22
Pray Daily or More Often		
Establish. Protestant	55	52
Evangelical Protestant	78	83
Historically Black Protestant	80	85
Roman Catholic	59	58
Non-Christian Faiths	46	37
Read Sacred Texts		
Establish. Protestant	31	28
Evangelical Protestant	61	68
Historically Black Protestant	60	64
Roman Catholic	26	23
Non-Christian Faiths	28	17

Source: Pew Research Center (2014).

Look at these first three: beliefs in heaven and hell as well as the belief that the Bible or Qu'ran or Torah or other sacred text is the Word of God. What do you notice? It is pretty obvious that in almost every category, believers with at least a college degree are less likely to believe these things. In a couple of cases, such as the belief that the sacred text is the word of God, there's not all that much difference among Evangelicals and Black Protestants. But otherwise, the differences are significant. While these specific beliefs may seem to be somewhat random and limited since they are only related to educational level, the differences that we see in the data is matched by many other studies built around income which point to the same patterns. Sociologists of religion identify that the higher the income and education a person has, the less likely they are to believe that the Bible is the literal word of God, that God is involved in a person's everyday life and has a specific plan for them, or that only one religion is true exclusively (Liu and Froese 2020; Schwadel 2011; Schieman 2010; Schieman et al. 2010; Mirola 2009).

Religious practices also can differ based on a person's social class position. Let's go back to Table 10.2 once more. We highlighted three frequent measures, attending services, praying, and reading sacred texts, to see the effects of educational attainment on these religious practices. Sure enough, we see some but not all of the same patterns, at least regarding who reads their sacred texts. Ironically, people without a college degree actually attend worship services less often that those with one. Evangelical and Black Protestants with bachelor's degrees are more likely to pray at least once a day and read the Bible compared to other groups. These findings underscore what Susan Sullivan found in her work on the religious practices of poor women that we talked about before. These women don't often attend church services for practical and personal reasons. But they do pray and look to God and the Bible for guidance in their everyday life. For low-income people with limited education, prayer especially becomes an important way to request help with money, material needs, and health concerns, as well as to call for help to deal with other problems in their everyday lives. Upper- and middle-class people attend services and pray too, of course. However, these practices reflect more of a taken-for-granted cultural practice—it's just what you're supposed to do for them. But for those on the bottom of the class hierarchy, prayer and faith are more significant as coping strategies when no other resources are available.

Class dynamics do more than simply shape the religious identities, beliefs, and practices of individuals. Class differences also influence how people of faith engage with community issues at the congregational level in ways other than through the effects of their individual-level income, education, or occupational status. The social class makeup of entire congregations shapes its group culture in ways that can encourage or hinder particular forms of outreach or civic participation of its members (Reimer 2007; Olson 2000; Wedam 2003; McRoberts 1999). High levels of civic engagement sometimes can be related to whether congregations are located in economically strapped neighborhoods or more well-off ones, where the pressing needs of the local environment spur congregations to action (Crawford and Olson 2003; Smith 2001). Among wealthier congregations, social class can work against community engagement though, where the divides between rich and poor are reinforced by geographic boundaries. Just as was the case in 19th century American communities, wealthier people often see a more limited role for congregations in terms of meeting the practical needs of disadvantaged people around them. Congregations are there to do charitable work and were supposed to address people's spiritual needs and sometimes to provide social services to help poor people, but have no role in trying to fix the economic issues in a community that creates the needs for help among the poor as a class in the first place (Mirola 2003b).

So far, we've identified about talked about social class patterns in religion. Before we wrap up, we should probably think about why they have stayed the same for so long. Does religion somehow play a role in keeping people in the social class positions they are born into? It is an interesting question to think about—maybe religion influences these class patterns by shaping how people think about things like getting an education or finding jobs that bring high salaries and wealth. Darnell and Sherkat (1997), for example, identified strong negative relationships between belonging to a conservative Protestant congregation and educational attainment. Young people from Evangelical and fundamentalist faith traditions report lower educational aspirations and are less likely to enroll in college preparatory courses than other young people. But why would that be so? These sociologists argue that growing up in more fundamentalist traditions limits the educational and occupational choices of young people because their religious cultures rule out certain options as inappropriate or incompatible with their religious beliefs. College preparatory courses in literature or history present ideas and materials from the dominant culture that are seen as corrupting and dangerous. A university education itself can be a threat to faith because it encourages a questioning of taken-for-granted ideas and beliefs. Young people from these traditions opt out of college, which can leave them economically and occupationally stuck at the lower end of the class structure. Once again, you might want to object to this idea as being no longer true now. But we still find that although there are more young people from fundamentalist traditions going to college, they tend to go to non-elite and faith-based schools where their beliefs are less likely to be challenged, but their occupational choices can still be limited (Schwadel 2016).

In contrast, there are ways that religion can reinforce economic power and position too. Keister (2011), in her work *Faith and Money*, reported that Establishment Protestants, Jews, and increasingly White Roman Catholics all demonstrate behaviors that support and reinforce wealth accumulation, such as maintaining small family sizes, aspiring to and completing high levels of education, and holding high-status occupations. The religious cultures of these traditions shape the values and decision-making opportunities for individual members in ways that keep them in high-socioeconomic-status positions. So what we see here is the process of class reproduction. Wealthier families are a part of faith traditions that encourage and support successive generations in making choices about their futures that tend to keep them in a better-off social position. Religion alone doesn't guarantee this, but it does contribute to the forces that keep well-off people well-off. In contrast, Evangelical and fundamentalist Protestants, Black Protestants, and Catholics of color operate within religious cultures that limit their access to social and economic resources, which in turn limits opportunities for upward mobility and wealth accumulation.

Concluding Thoughts

The study of religion and class remains a central feature to understanding the American religious landscape, but the relationship between the two is complex and often shows up in subtle ways. Religious groups remain divided in class terms economically as well as culturally. However, in this chapter, we've looked at how these divides shape the lived experiences of entire denominations, local congregations, and individual people of faith. But there is still a lot we don't know about how class works in religious contexts. As we have discussed in this chapter, ongoing changes in how income and wealth are distributed and also how changes to the education and occupational structures all will continue to impact the religious landscape of local communities, as well as the experiences of those who participate in economically advantaged congregations and those whose religious communities are less advantaged. We should also expect that social class differences and inequalities in American society and around the world will continue to be reproduced and transformed through the workings of religious groups. How exactly social class will impact religion and how religion will impact class needs further examination. Just remember that class matters! We cannot fully understand religion without understanding social class any more than we can fully understand social class without its religious dimensions.

Suggested Reading

Bruno, Robert A. 2008. *Justified by Work: Identity and the Meaning of Faith in Chicago's Working Class Churches.* Columbus: The Ohio State University Press.

Davidson, James D., and Ralph E. Pyle. 2011. *Ranking Faiths: Religious Stratification in America.* New York: Rowman & Littlefield.

Keister, Lisa A. 2011. *Faith and Money: How Religion Contributes to Wealth and Poverty.* New York: Cambridge University Press.

Lareau, Annette, and Dalton Conley (eds.). 2008. *Social Class: How Does It Work?* New York: Russell Sage Foundation.

McCloud, Sean, and William A. Mirola (eds.). 2009. *Religion and Class in America: Culture, History, and Politics.* Boston: Brill.

Moreton, Bethany. 2009. *To Serve God and Walmart: The Making of Christian Free Enterprise.* Cambridge, MA: Harvard University Press.

Sullivan, Susan Crawford. 2011. *Living Faith: Everyday Religion and Mothers in Poverty.* Chicago: University of Chicago Press.

11 Religion and Race

A Double-Edged Sword

Isaiah Jeong and Tryce Prince

1 In what ways is religion a source of harm or source of good?
2 Why should we study religion and race together?
3 How can religion be a source of inspiration to oppose wrongdoing and welcome others from different cultures and racial backgrounds?

You may recall the song "Imagine" by John Lennon (former member of the Beatles). In the song, he asked listeners to imagine a world without religion. What would such a world look like? Would it be a place where people lived freely without struggles and strife? Certainly, religion has been a great source of conflict and division across the world, and many today would share the sentiment behind this song. But is religion only good for creating divisions?

Martin Luther King Jr. and many members of marginalized communities have found religion to be a powerful, motivating source of liberation to combat oppression. In the U.S., John Lennon was asking us to imagine a world without religion because he viewed it as a source of oppression and death; decades earlier in India, Mahatma Gandhi was asking us to imagine a world of non-violence stemming directly from his profound religious devotion to Hinduism.

So which one is it? Is religion, as a force in society, oppressive or liberating? Does it hold people back or inspire them to great ends? To answer these questions, we must study the concepts of religion and race together. From the institution of chattel slavery (enslavement that is passed on to each generation without the possibility of earning freedom), the terrorizing of Black people, and the segregation of the races, to rise of the Black freedom struggle and contemporary accounts of White Christian nationalism, movements in society have positioned themselves along racial and religious lines. The intersections of religion and race have played a profound role in global history and continue to impact globally today. As such, we ask you to imagine with us how religion, when married to race, serves as a double-edged sword: it is both an immense source of oppression and an immense resource for liberation.

In short, let's explore together not just what religion and race are, but what they do when fixed together. We will present a brief snapshot of the story of religion and race. This is not meant to be comprehensive. Rather, we aim to paint an illustrative picture of how religion is racialized and race is spiritualized (Emerson et al. 2015). Now imagine with us.

The Sharp Side of Oppression

Religion and Race: Colonialism and Slavery

In telling the story of religion and race, we begin in the 15th century. During this time period, European nations sought to expand their political and economic network through the conquest of Africa. The expansion was also further justified based on religious reasons. Conquest allowed

DOI: 10.4324/9781003182108-14

the opportunity to spread the Christian message to non-Christians. One of the key characters in this time period was Prince Henry the Navigator, who explored the continent of Africa for the purposes of economic exploitation and to further advance Christianity. But this expansion was at the expense of the lives of Africans. In his journey to Guinea, Henry displaced, kidnapped, and enslaved hundreds from their homeland.

This history was recorded by Gomes Eanes de Zurara, a Portuguese chronicler who recorded major historical events for Prince Henry the Navigator (Jennings 2010). In one of Zurara's account, he chronicled a major slave auction that occurred in Portugal in 1444 after Henry's conquest. Although the construction of "race" was not officially coined during this time, there were racialized seeds present here. In describing this event, Zurara employed a framework of colorism, a spectrum that uses color to place a hierarchy. He described those who are "White" as fair-skinned and pleasing to look at; "mulattoes" (a person of mixed Black and White ancestry) as in-between; and Ethiopians or "Blacks" as ugly, deformed, and from the pits of hell (Jennings 2010, 23). Those with lighter skin were deemed more beautiful and those who were darker were unappealing. Note how Zurara's account did not exist in a vacuum but was occurring during a slave auction. To justify the enslavement, Black people were deemed inferior, were fit for conquest, and ready for shipment. The description of racial difference was coupled with an ascription of value.

The story of the auction is incomplete with just a racial analysis. Religion also took on a central role. Zurara viewed the enslavement of African peoples as destined by God (Jennings 2010). In the chronicler's eyes, God's will was for African people to be enslaved so the Portuguese could save their souls. Their enslavement, he believed, was their salvation. The slave auction even became ritualized. Zurara described how two African boys were offered as thanks and as an offering to God (Jennings 2010, 16). The conquest was successful, just as they believed God willed it to be. Through European colonialism, economic greed, religion, and slavery became inseparable ingredients. From the perspective of the colonizers, both religious and racial hierarchy became two sides of the same coin. People were categorized as superior and inferior; Christian and heathen; civil and savage (Fredrickson 1981, 7–12).

These justificatory beliefs were also preserved once the European colonizers landed on American shores. The European settlers embedded themselves in the place of Israel in the biblical narrative. They were the chosen people to conquer other lands and capture non-Christians. The enslavement and domination of both American Indians and African peoples were again using the Christian religion.

Known as America's earliest settlers, Puritans fled religious persecution in Europe, and desired to establish a society based on principles of religious liberty. Ironically, those who professed liberty were simultaneously restricting freedom from others. In the name of Christianity, many American Indian children were stripped from their families and were forced into schools, where White Christians sought to culturally and religiously assimilate the Indian children (Charles and Rah 2019, 333). This assimilation process was often inhumane. The children were abused, beaten, and punished for speaking their language and practicing their own culture. The children were invited to receive the Christian message under the condition that they would behave like White people. The assimilation process would not be complete without total religious and cultural domination. As the saying went, "kill the Indian, save the man" (Charles and Rah 2019, 325).

For many Puritans, how to incorporate the enslaved African people into the Christian religion became a thorny topic. Anglo-Christians were caught in a limbo because they saw the need to Christianize the slaves, but were afraid that the message of eternal liberty would equate to temporal freedom. To solve this problem, some clergy stated that Christianity was a liberating tool for spiritual souls, but not for the physical chains of servitude (Emerson and Smith 2000, 22–25). Anglo-Christians inhabited a sense of dualism: "spiritual equality with temporal inequality" (Emerson and Smith 2000, 23). In such a way, many Puritans would advocate for slavery, as it was seen as a convenient conduit for salvation.

The sentiment behind the separation of earthly and spiritual equality is further captured in an important historical artifact known as the Slave Bible. Originally published in 1807, it was a Bible that was specifically designated for evangelizing the slaves—with one caveat. It was like the other versions, but all the sections that would insinuate liberation were removed. Particularly, 90% of the Old Testament and 50% of the New Testament were completely omitted (Martin 2018). The slaveholding Christians shied away from the narrative of the Exodus. As Moses had liberated the Israelites from the slavery from the oppression of Egypt, the Christian masters were afraid that such narratives would give ideas for liberation among the slaves. Along with the central narratives of the Old Testament, many parts of the New Testament were also redacted. For instance, Galatians 3:28 (an epistle in the New Testament) reads, "There is neither Jew nor Gentile, neither slave nor free, nor is there male and female, for you are all one in Christ Jesus." Such passages were deleted that signified any sort of equality that was seen as a threat to the institution of slavery.

Religion played both a clear and complicated role in preserving racism in America. It was undeniably utilized to justify oppression and subjugation of both African people and Native American communities. Christianity was twisted to benefit the ideologies of the oppressors. The story of religion and race also demonstrates more nuance as well. As we will observe later in this chapter, the same Bible that was utilized (or withheld) for oppression will also serve as a source of liberation. While the slave-owners withheld the Exodus narrative to oppress, Black Christianity reclaimed the Exodus narrative in pursuit of liberation and equality in America. The collision of race and religion as a double-edge sword remains to be seen.

Religion and Race: From Passive Complicity to Active Participation

After slavery was abolished in 1865, the slaveholder's religion continued to preserve racism in society by offering no form of resistance to racialized violence against Black people. Instead, the overwhelming majority of White Christian churches were silent in the face of Black suffering. This silence represented what historian Jemar Tisby refers to as the legacy of White American Christians' 'complicity' in racism (Tisby 2019). To be complicit in racism is to compromise or accept racial injustice instead of challenging it on behalf of oppressed peoples. In the U.S., the legacy of the White Christian church is a legacy filled with racial compromise.

When the Civil War ended, Congress passed the Reconstruction Acts of 1867. These acts resulted in a military presence in the South and required the formerly confederate states (the southern states who failed to secede from the United States during the Civil War) to ratify the Fourteenth Amendment, which granted full citizenship and equal protection to Black Americans, in order to reenter the Union (Equal Justice Initiative 2020, 10). As a result, Black Americans experienced unprecedented social and political progress. In response, a large portion of the southern White population began organizing to resist progress by terrorizing the Black community. While it would be difficult to find a White church during this time that openly advocated for racial terror against Black people, it would be equally or even more difficult to find a White church community that publicly stood against it.

Historian Eric Foner helps put in perspective both the terror experienced by Black Americans, and the gravity of the White Christian churches' complicity. He labels the period of terror after the Civil War as unprecedented and unrivaled among civilizations in the Western hemisphere that abolished slavery in the 1800s (Foner 2014, 425). From 1868 to 1871, *at least* 400 Black Americans were lynched, and the justifications for these racial terror lynchings were often falsified (EJI 2020, 15). Black men were wrongly accused of sexual crimes against White women. These accusations were often the justification for White mob violence toward entire Black communities. Black women were raped and lynched, sometimes with their families watching. Both Black women and men experienced genital mutilation and castration.

There were often hundreds, and sometimes thousands, of spectators who attended racial terror lynchings. These incidents were heavily ritualistic—like a church service—and acted as a point of unity for the White community in a manner very similar to the unifying force of religion (Bailey and Snedker 2011). All this was done by White mobs in an effort to instill fear in the formerly enslaved and to preserve White dominance in the South. Despite having the ability to influence its members to resist racial terror, as seen in slavery and colonialism, White Christians remained complicit. It is important that we understand that racial terror lynchings were not isolated incidents. They were a widespread cultural practice that disproportionately affected both Black individuals and communities. According to the Equal Justice Initiative, an Alabama-based non-profit which documents the legacy of racial terror lynchings, Black victims outnumbered White victims 17 to 1 (EJI 2020, 27). In its work, the EJI has documented more than 4,400 racial terror lynchings of Black people in the United States between Reconstruction and World War II.

Mob violence was not the only action that southern White communities took. In the years following the Civil War, White leaders also resisted the progress of Black Americans politically. Multiple court cases challenging Reconstruction-era legislation were victorious in the Supreme Court. As a result of these rulings, the federal government officially lost its power to enforce the legislation created to protect Black Americans across the South. What emerged from these constitutional rewrites was a culture that combined both the religious and civic influences of the Confederacy. This culture is often referred to as the "religion of the lost cause," an unofficial civil religion White Southerners identified with to maintain the religious and political legacy of the Confederacy in the post-Civil War U.S. (Bailey 2011). These resistance movements help us see the lengths White Southerners were willing to go to in order to maintain White dominance. And arguably, no form of resistance was more effective than Jim Crow.

The system of segregation implemented in the South after Reconstruction is known as "Jim Crow"—a reference to a minstrel character that used racist caricatures of enslaved Black people. As a result, the public and private lives of Americans in the Southern states were forced to follow a strict color-line. This color-line also extended to religious communities, and local churches were overwhelmingly segregated. Even when Black people were a part of mostly White denominations, they were forced to gather in independent congregations or in Black-only sections in a predominantly White church—two practices which were used throughout American slavery. The independence and growing influence of Black-led organizations, denominations, and churches likely threatened the social, religious, economic, and political influence of White Christianity and increased the White mob violence seen during this time (Bailey 2011).

It could be assumed that our language of compromise and complicity is meant to communicate that White Christians were only passive actors during periods of racial violence and never took an active role in violence against Black people. This assumption, however, couldn't be further from the truth. While not all, many White Christians participated in racial terrorism and played an active role in the implementation and preservation of Jim Crow segregation in the South.

Well into the Civil Rights movement of the 1950s and 60s—commonly referred to as the "Black Freedom Struggle"—the White Christian church in America continued to preserve racial hierarchy and segregation in society. In response to *Brown v. Board of Education*—the U.S. Supreme Court ruling that found racially segregated public schools to be unconstitutional—White leaders across the country voiced their opposition to the ruling. To resist the legislation, they actively stoked the fears of their communities in a manner similar to the tactics used to justify racial terror lynchings decades before. For example, leaders in Mississippi believed that integration was the brainchild of those "advocating intermarriage between the races," which would eventually lead to the end of the White race "forever, never to return" (Lyon 2017, 14–15). It was also feared that the ruling would impact their private institutions as well. If integration succeeded in the schools, leaders argued, the churches would eventually be next. Their fears were confirmed almost a decade after

Brown v. Board. In 1963, students were led in part by civil rights leaders like Medgar Evers to stage a coordinated movement to integrate local White churches. It was the hope that their coordinated effort would challenge segregation and influence local White Christians to join their movement. As a result, the church became a key battleground in the fight against integration. White Christians used both their religious beliefs and social standing to preserve the practice of segregation in their communities.

Over the course of 10 months, activists attempted to gain entry in over twenty Catholic and Protestant churches, expecting to prick the consciences of their religious brethren and influence them to join the movement (Lyon 2017, 10). In response, local White leaders in Jackson organized a countermovement to "save these churches from integration" (Lyon 2017, 11). In the end, the activists realized that they could not depend on White churchgoers in Jackson to overcome segregation, and the campaign ended. The overwhelming majority of Jackson churches did not allow the groups to integrate their services, demonstrating both a social and theological failure on the part of the local White churches. Instead of joining the movement, local White churchgoers used their standing as both members of their churches and leaders in their community to resist integration.

Through these efforts, we see White Christians as *active* participants in upholding racial segregation rather than passive participants, or "people of their time" as they are commonly called. By recounting the efforts of Jackson's churches to preserve racial segregation and the Black activists' efforts to resist it, we are not simply restating historical facts for the purpose of telling a story. Instead, we wish to give you a clear example of the active strategies that White Christians across the South used for decades to preserve racial segregation. This helps us see the enduring link between a religious community's beliefs and their practices. The religious beliefs of the White community members in Jackson were not overshadowed by their political or social beliefs. Instead, all three were aligned with one another. We cannot emphasize this point enough: the religion of many of the White Christians who were active participants in preserving Jim Crow segregation did not convict them of any wrongdoing. In their minds, their political and social resistance to integration was a way to uphold their religious beliefs. White Christian churches in Jackson were not the only White church community to take an active role to preserve racial segregation. White Christians across the South and the United States used their religious beliefs and their social and political positions to preserve racial segregation and oppress Black people.

Other Side of the Sword: Liberation

Freedom Through the Slave Religion

We have detailed so far how religion has been utilized for gruesome and ugly purposes. But the story must not end here. Religion has been an immense source of oppression, but also a great catalyst for freedom. To see how this is so, let us turn our attention to examining the life of a former slave, who became an American legend.

The abolitionist Frederick Douglass was born around 1818. Born into slavery on a plantation in Maryland, Douglass had witnessed both psychological and physical terror on these plantations since he was young. In his autobiography, *Narrative of the Life of Frederick Douglass* ([1845] 1995), he narrated how his own aunt was stripped naked and beaten with a cow-skin whip until blood was dripping on the floor. Eventually, Douglass was transferred to a different home in Baltimore, where his road to liberation would gradually ensue. Interestingly, Douglass did not attribute his move to simply chance, but as a divine intervention and a favor from God. This was a common theme throughout Douglass's writings. He beautifully and masterfully interwove religious imagery not only to interpret his life, but also America's desolate condition.

In his new home in Baltimore, Douglass learned how to read and write under the guidance of Sophia Auld, the mistress of the home. Never having owned slaves before, Mrs. Auld initially saw the common humanity in Douglass, and she taught him the alphabet. Mr. Auld noticed that his wife was teaching Douglass how to read. He soon intervened and stopped Douglass's learning, as reading competency among the slaves could create possibilities for liberation. This provided an even stronger determination for Douglass to educate himself, and he gave poor boys in the local area bread in exchange for reading lessons. He also taught himself how to read by immersing himself in books and hymnals. His ability to read during this time would flower, crafting the rhetorical tools that would later provide scathing prophetic criticisms of America. It was also in his teenage years that he would convert to Christianity in his encounter with Black parishioners (Blight 2018).

After years of weathering abuse, and at times weekly whippings, Douglass eventually found a pathway to liberation by disguising himself as a sailor heading to Philadelphia, where there were growing anti-slavery sentiments. Soon after his liberation, Douglass rose to national prominence, becoming the face of the abolitionist movement and social reform as one of the most recognized faces in America.

However, Douglass was not like any other social reformer. His social justice was simultaneously deeply informed by his religious fervor. Douglass did not mince his words in critiquing the religion of Christianity. This was because some of his worst abusers were those who professed liberty in Jesus Christ. But he did not critique all religions, but instead the "slaveholding religion of this land" (Douglass [1845] 1995, 71). We encourage you to read the whole appendix in *Narrative*, but for now we leave you with a short excerpt of his words:

> [B]etween the Christianity of this land, and the Christianity of Christ, I recognize the widest possible difference—so wide, that to receive one as good, pure and holy, is of necessity to reject the other as bad, corrupt and wicked. To be the friend of the one, is of necessity to be the end of the other. I love the pure, peaceable, and impartial Christianity of Christ: I therefore hate the corrupt, slaveholding, women-whipping, cradle-plundering, partial and hypocritical Christianity of this land. Indeed, I can see no reason, but the most deceitful one, for calling the religion of this land Christianity. I look upon it as the climax of all misnomers, the boldest of all frauds, and the grossest of all libels.
>
> (Douglass [1845] 1995, 71)

Douglass critiqued the religious institution of slaveholding Christianity that taught the oppressive beliefs that shaped abusive behaviors. For him, American Christianity and the institution of slavery were so integral that they were like a well-blended dish: "the slave auctioneer's bell and the church going bell chime in with each other" (Douglass [1845] 1995, 72). Douglass utilized what he saw as authentic Christianity to critique the false Christianity that preserved the institution of slavery.

While religion had been an instrumental force in shaping colonialism, slavery, and Jim Crow, there were other streams within the religious tradition that saw Christianity as a great source of liberation. Douglass was not merely an exception. There were pockets within the slave community in the Antebellum South (the time period leading up to the Civil War) that applied Christianity to their particular contexts (Raboteau 2004). In these communities, the enslaved created a distinct ritualized religion, and unique set of beliefs and practices. The distinction of the slaveholding Christianity and the slave religion was not just a matter of having different rituals. While slaveholding Christianity oppressed, the slave religion liberated.

The spirituals sung by enslaved persons captured this sentiment in a way that was beautifully original to the American soil that drenched the Black experience in Christian themes. The spirituals elicit the emotions and words of the collective hope and liberation the disenfranchised community faced. Religious scholar Albert J. Raboteau states, "One person's sorrow or joy became everyone's through song. Singing the spirituals was therefore both intensely personal and vividly a communal experience" (Raboteau 2004, 246). While the reality of the institution of slavery attempted to suffocate the existence of the slaves, religion also provided a space for meaning and liberation.

In examining the words of classic spirituals, such as "O Mary Don't You Weep," one can readily feel the richness of the literary images as the ancient experience of the Bible was directly translated into the experience of the slaves. The same God who comforted Mary and the enslaved Israelites was present now in America, consoling the disenfranchised community. It was believed that God then was on the side of the oppressed—not the oppressor. Moreover, the lyrics served not only as a consolation but also a condemnation against the masters who represented the oppressive regime of Egypt: "Just as God fought on the side of his people Israel and destroyed Pharaoh's army before them, so he will fight for [their] deliverance" (Owens 1971, 57). The chattel slavery will abolish on this side of eternity just as there is liberation from Egypt's oppression.

Recall earlier in our story how the slave masters attempted to erase the Exodus narrative in the Slave Bible. But here, we see how the oppressed communities reclaimed the same narrative of the Exodus to proclaim liberation and consolation. Although the White masters would abuse the biblical text to justify enslavement, the slave religion fundamentally understood that the God of the Israelites gave them new status as the eternally liberated. The liberation did not merely reside in the realm of spiritual freedom as what their White masters commanded; it collapsed into the realm of temporal freedom—it demanded freedom in the here and now.

No one understood this better than the former runaway slave, Henry "Box" Brown (Blum 2016). Brown was a slave during the 19th century who wittingly planned his escape by traveling through a cartel box. In order to survive the 27-hour trek to Philadelphia, the destination of his liberation, he poked various holes in the box. The holes created airflow and provided light in the darkness (Blum 2016). Once the box reached the destination of freedom, Brown jumped out in elation, reciting Psalm 40: "I waited patiently on the Lord and He heard my prayer."

Whether it was Douglass or Brown, the slave masters tried to enclose them in a religious box and suffocate them through their diseased understanding of the Bible. But for Brown, "the box and its holes became part of the evidence of his resurrection" (Blum 2016, 88). It can be said that the slave religion poked holes through the understandings of the slaveholding Christianity (Blum 2016). The slave religion freed them from physical and spiritual claustrophobia. No matter how hard the White Christians tried to claim that the gospel had no liberating power to their temporal status, the slave religion simply was allergic to such understanding.

Religion and Race: Liberation Movements

The Civil Rights era is often heralded as a period of the golden synthesis between religion and race. Preserving the tradition of Frederick Douglass, who prophetically called out the injustices of America, many activists and scholars—including Anna Julia Cooper, Ida B. Wells-Barnett, W.E.B. Du Bois, Howard Thurman, and Martin Luther King Jr. —utilized religion as a source *to address societal ills*. In fact, historian Paul Harvey states, "It remains impossible to conceive the civil rights movement without placing Black Christianity at the center, for that is what empowered the rank and file who made the movement *move*" (Harvey 2016, 2).

One movement in particular used Black Christianity to "affirm the dignity, sacred personhood, creativity, and moral agency of Black people (Dorrien 2015, 38). Drawing on the Black social gospel, Black Americans responded to racial oppression and envisioned a new America that was based on equality and justice for all people. Early sociologists like Anna Julia Cooper and Ida B. Wells-Barnett—members of the Episcopal and African Methodist Episcopal faith traditions—helped provide a model for activism informed by the Black social gospel through their groundbreaking sociological works. In their scholarship, both Cooper ([1892] 1988) and Wells-Barnett (1895) examined the racial violence that occurred after the Civil War and called out the hypocrisy of White Christianity. Following both Cooper and Wells-Barnett, sociologist W.E.B. Du Bois ([1935] 2007) saw the institution of the Black church as an imaginative organization that would help America become a more racially just society. Together, Black sociologists helped to build and influence the Black social gospel that inspired the generation of leaders in the Black Freedom Struggle.

Like the slave religion of the South, central to the Black social gospel was the understanding that Jesus Christ was the source of both spiritual and physical freedom. Arguably no one person understood this freedom better than the pastor-theologian Howard Thurman, author of the book *Jesus and the Disinherited* (1949). The central question Thurman posed in this work is what does "the religion of Jesus" offer to those with their "backs against the wall"? (Thurman 1949, 3). The language of having one's back against the wall is how Thurman described the position of oppressed peoples in society. To help answer this question, Thurman made an effort to study religion "from the point of view of the needs of underprivileged peoples" (Harvey 2020, 86). His deep inquisition took him to India, where he would meet the face of the Indian independence movement: the lawyer and ethicist Mahatma Gandhi.

In their conversation, Gandhi and Thurman discussed the experiences of Black Americans, the Indian independence movement, and the complexities of nonviolence. Gandhi explained to Thurman that the philosophy of nonviolence found its ultimate meaning in "ahimsa," a teaching of Hinduism (Harvey 2020, 101). Ahimsa was a supernatural belief that one should not injure any living thing. Gandhi also saw the connections between ahimsa and Christianity's understanding of sacrificial love (Dorrien 2018). In ahimsa, Thurman found parallels to the radical love of Jesus Christ. While Thurman himself did not take an active role in leading the Black Freedom Movement, his teachings after his meeting with Gandhi informed Black America's own version of ahimsa, nonviolent direct action, which became the philosophy of the Black Freedom Struggle. Throughout the Black Freedom Struggle, Thurman would act as a mentor to its leaders, including King Jr., and provided them with spiritual and philosophical guidance (Harvey 2020, 15).

Through the Black social gospel and the philosophy of nonviolence, Martin Luther King Jr. found motivations for his social activism. Contemporary images of King depict him as a radical public intellectual and a social activist. But there was another side to King's portrait—he was also a reverend. King was deeply shaped by Christianity since childhood. Not only was he raised in the Baptist tradition, but his father was also a pastor and a close contemporary of Howard Thurman. King later enrolled in Morehouse College and graduated with a degree in sociology. King completed his graduate work at Crozer Theological Seminary and Boston University's School of Theology. Equipped with the tools of sociology and theology, King analyzed the problems that would challenge both the religious and non-religious communities to create a more equitable and just society.

At the same time King was enrolled at Boston, Howard Thurman was employed there as a professor in the School of Theology, where he delivered a number of sermons with King in attendance (Harvey 2020, 15). During his studies at Boston University, King was exposed to the nonviolent philosophy of Gandhi. Like Thurman before him, King also found parallels between Gandhi's nonviolent protest and the ways of Jesus Christ. These are the parallels that informed his own understanding of social activism. As King (King and Washington [1963] 1991) expressed in *The Letter from Birmingham Jail*: "Jesus Christ, was an extremist for love, truth and goodness, and thereby rose above his environment. Perhaps the South, the nation and the world are in dire need of creative extremists" (298).

King's call to treat every human being regardless of the color of their skin was rooted in his religious convictions called the *imago dei*, the Christian doctrine of the image of God that teaches that there is dignity in each human as a reflection of the divine. For King, however, it was not enough to just treat each human with dignity on a personal level. America had to confront, renew, and eradicate systems and institutions that created and preserved the conditions of inequality. King's gospel was not just a freedom in a spiritual sense that ensured security from eternal damnation; it was also a social liberation that confronted unjust systems. King challenged the three evils of society: evils of racism (White supremacy), evils of greed (economic inequality), and evils of war (global militarism). He believed each of these evils were deeply rooted in American structures and resulted in a violation of human dignity, and a desecration of the fellow image-bearers.

In response to the nightmare of the American project that was filled with racism, militarism, and poverty, King dreamed of an alternative beloved community. For King, the beloved community was a society that was built on justice, equality, and unity where each person was treated with the dignity imagined by the Christian scriptures. His hope was a society that carried the burdens of one another, as seen in a familial relationship. In his famous "I Have a Dream" speech, King (King and Washington [1963] 1991) would cite the Old Testament prophet Amos, "No, we are not satisfied, and we will not be satisfied until justice rolls down like water and righteousness like a mighty stream" (219). The beloved community was only to be achieved through a radical and revolutionary change, where justice was not just an isolated droplet but would wash the American soils anew.

King would never see America enter the promised land. He was not able to see his dream fulfilled as he was murdered in 1968. However, his death did not result in futility as it ignited various freedom struggles across the globe. As King provided a paradigm of religious fervor that addressed racial injustice, many religious leaders would pick up his mantle to continue his struggle for freedom and equality.

The death of one American prophet would resurrect another prophetic voice. A year after King's death, Cone (1969) published a book called *Black Theology and Black Power*, a foundational text in the Black liberation theology movement. Liberation theology arose to provide religion as a source to address the systemic and political injustice that was running rampant in society (Kim 2018), and found many influences in King's radical activism (Cone 1969).

Much of Cone's work grappled with how Christianity was both a great hindrance and enabler of liberative justice. In contrast to the oppressive Christianity of this land, Black liberation theology also preserved and carried on the religious spirit of the slave religion and Martin Luther King Jr. In its pronouncement of theology of liberation, many within this religious stream did not view religion as merely an opioid of the people, as Marx would articulate. But rather, it was a panacea—an actual way forward for the marginalized class and societal problems.

One of the most famous assertions that the theologian James Cone made was that *Jesus is Black* (Cone 1986). At first, this seems confusing! Was Jesus historically not a Palestinian Jew? When asserting Jesus's Blackness, however, Cone is not necessarily asserting a literal skin color. As Blackness is a political reality that captures the category of oppression, Blackness is not just a matter of pigmentation. Christ is Black in the sense that he was also a poor, oppressed Jew and therefore "involved in Black history, bringing out liberation from White oppressors" (Cone 2003, 47). Just as God liberated the Israelites from the Egyptian empire, Black liberation theology proclaimed that God is working here and now to bring out freedom of Black communities from the American empire. Historian Robin D.G. Kelley (2008) states, "Exodus provided Black people with a language to critique America's racist state and build a new nation, for its central theme wasn't escape but a new beginning" (17). Throughout American history, we have seen how many Christians tried to withhold this narrative of freedom from the disenfranchised communities, but they would not succeed. The religious imaginations of freedom and liberation that were found in Christianity served as a fuel for both King and Cone.

Liberation theology did not remain in geographic or intellectual siloes. Its liberative fire would eventually ignite around the world, whether in Latin America or South Korea. Each of these articulations of liberation was rooted in Jesus's radical way of living that also addressed the respective political struggles according to the needs of the community that saw no cultural bounds. Across the globe, when religion was used to justify oppression, it also provided a possibility of liberation: a double-edged sword.

Religion and Race: A Story Left Untold?

The central theme of this chapter was to understand the intersecting relationship between race and religion. When these two concepts collide, we have seen how they serve as a source of great oppression, but also liberation. We proposed to further nuance the story of religion and race, where it is often purely seen as social good or evil. To complicate this narrative, studying the processes of religion and race is a necessary task. Indeed, Christianity was central in its role of European colonialism and slavery. And many White Christians were also complicit in the face of injustice during the Civil Rights Movement. However, there were religious devotees, especially from marginalized voices, who participated in religious struggles to eradicate oppression in society. From Frederick Douglass, Anna Julia Cooper, and Ida B. Wells to Howard Thurman, Mahatma Gandhi, and Martin Luther King Jr., their formulation of justice stood upon the shoulders of religion.

The dynamic consideration of these two categories, which have often been neglected in sociological studies, not only demonstrates complexities but also relevancies in understanding today's American society. We are confronted with various movements that have positioned themselves along both racial and religious lines. Since the Black Freedom Struggle of the mid-20th century, arguably no time in American history has witnessed the amount of social activism as our contemporary society. In 2020, in response to the murders of Breonna Taylor, Ahmaud Arbery, and George Floyd, anti-Asian violence, and voter suppression, the United States witnessed one of the largest movements for racial justice in the nation's history. These cries for justice also found vitality in religious movements led by figures like William Barber II and the Poor People's Campaign, calling for a moral revival of the nation rooted in explicit religious convictions taking on the legacy of Martin Luther King Jr. We have also seen calls for Black and Asian solidarity from religious communities.

Calls for justice, however, were opposed by resistance movements also deeply rooted in religion. After months of nationwide organizing and protest in pursuit of a more just society, the results of the 2020 U.S. presidential election provided opposition groups with grounds to create a new lost-cause narrative centered around accusations of a rigged and falsified election. In January of 2021, a months-long propaganda campaign before and after the 2020 election reached a climax in the aftermath of the electoral college's certification of President Joe Biden's victory over former President Donald Trump. On Capitol Hill on January 6th, 2021, we witnessed a clear example of the cooperation of White Christian Nationalism and other White nationalist movements for the sake of mutual political gain. Sociologists define White Christian Nationalism as a political project which fuses a particular kind of Christianity (White Christianity) with American civic life. The White Christian nationalists who stormed the capitol viewed the success of their version of America as inextricably linked to the success of Christianity. In their eyes, the only hope to save America from the imminent threat of what they perceived to be anti-Christian forces was a rebellion. Alongside the streams of White nationalists present in Charlottesville, Virginia in 2017, White Christian Nationalists scaled the Capitol walls carrying crosses, the Christian flag, and "Jesus saves" signs—busting through doors and windows, attacking Capitol police officers along the way—to hold a prayer service in the chambers of the United States Congress, where they thanked their god for empowering them to save their Christian America.

Will the intersections of religion and race be utilized to exclude? Or will the two be utilized as a source of liberation to establish an inclusive society? We have asked you to imagine the story of religion and race in this chapter to see both the ugly and good. But the future of religion and race has yet to be imagined—it is a story left untold.

Further Reading

Cone, James H. 2011. *The Cross and the Lynching Tree*. Maryknoll, NY: Orbis Books.

Douglass, Frederick. [1845] 1995. *Narrative Life of Frederick Douglass*. Mineola, NY: Dover Publications.

Gorski, Philip S., and Samuel L. Perry. 2022. *The Flag and the Cross: White Christian Nationalism and the Threat to American Democracy*. New York: Oxford University Press.

Tisby, Jemar. 2019. *The Color of Compromise: The Truth about the American Church's Complicity in Racism*. Grand Rapids, MI: Zondervan.

12 Who Brought the Enchiladas to My Bar Mitzvah?

Immigration and Religious Change

1 What large-scale changes to U.S. religion have resulted from immigration?
2 What are the lessons of immigrants and religious change?
3 How does becoming religious help immigrants to become American?
4 Why do immigrants often become more religious after arriving in their new land?
5 How is religion transformed when it is transplanted from one place to another?

Migration is a frequent behavior among humans. Except when political laws or other obstacles limit or prevent the crossing of international boundaries, groups of people commonly travel and come into contact with other groups that are new to them. The United States is often known as a nation of immigrants; about 99% of its citizens came from or have ancestors from other nations. Immigration law has long shaped who may legally enter and stay in the United States.

Back in 1965, U.S. immigration law fundamentally changed. And those changes have dramatically altered the United States. Before 1965, immigration laws were racially biased to freeze the racial and ethnic diversity of the United States at 1890 levels. The goal was to make sure that diversity in the United States did not increase.

In the wake of the Civil Rights movement, immigration laws were changed to overcome the biased immigration system. The modifications that occurred in 1965 and subsequently have been designed to allow into the country immigrants who (1) increase economic productivity (usually meaning highly educated, highly skilled, or well-to-do people), (2) need refuge from nations that do not support the United States, or (3) are joining members of their immediate family who already reside in the country. No nation may issue more than 20,000 visas per year, but visas are no longer distributed in accordance with quotas that are based on nationality and race. Because family reunification is deemed so important, most visas that are granted to reunite immediate family members do not count against the 20,000 upper limit.

How have these changes in immigration law affected religion in the United States? While the vast majority of all voluntary immigrants prior to 1965 were from Europe and Canada (and nearly all were Christian or Jewish), the majority of immigrants since 1965 have been from Latin America, the Caribbean, Asia, Africa, and the Middle East. In 1900, the top countries of origin for immigrants were Italy, Russia, Hungary, Austria, and the United Kingdom—all European. In 2020, the top countries of origin were Mexico, India, China, the Philippines, and El Salvador. Clearly, none of these countries are European. About 1 million immigrants per year legally enter the United States. They and their children are diversifying the racial and ethnic composition of the nation and now account for most of its population growth.

Overarching Changes for Religion

This change in ethnic composition has led to important changes in the religious landscape in the United States and, ultimately, the rest of the world. Currently, about two out of every three

DOI: 10.4324/9781003182108-15

immigrants to the United States is Christian. But this fact masks important changes in the composition of the nation's religious peoples. First, the 65% of immigrants who are Christian are significantly fewer than the 82% of native-born Americans who claim a Christian identity. Within Christianity, immigrants—mainly Latino—are twice as likely to be Catholic as native-born Americans (42%, compared with 22%). In fact, Latino immigrants are estimated to account for 40% of all Catholics in the United States and are responsible for about 90% of the nation's growth in Catholics (Levitt 2007, 14 and 205). Clearly, the ethnic composition of American Catholicism is changing dramatically.

Additionally, most immigrant Christians who are not Latino end up in Evangelical Protestant churches. Usually these are ethnic-specific churches, but as we will see later, this pattern typically lasts only through the first generation, and later generations expand the ethnic composition of those with whom they worship. Tens of thousands of ethnic congregations exist across the United States. These multiracial, multiethnic congregations filled with immigrants appear to be increasing, and seminaries and divinity schools increasingly are populated by immigrants or their children. As with Catholicism, the immigrant effect on Evangelical Protestantism (and some mainline Protestant denominations) is profound and growing, so much so that the sociologist Warner (1998, 4) has said that the United States is witnessing a "de-Europeanization" of American Christianity.

Although the majority of immigrants to the United States are or become Christian, immigrants still are *four times* as likely as native-born Americans to claim a non-Judeo-Christian religion. As several scholars of immigrant religion have noted, these immigrants and their children worship in temples, mosques, gurdwaras, meditation centers, and storefronts; they have fiestas and religious carnivals; and they meet in homes (Ebaugh and Chafetz 2000; Zanfini 2020). Immigrants have been the driving force behind a fourfold increase in the number of adherents to non-Judeo-Christian religions in the United States since 1970. Although non-Judeo-Christian religions (such as Islam, Jainism, Buddhism, Hinduism, Sikhism, and Zoroastrianism) still account for only about 3% of Americans, this represents a substantial increase since 1970, when virtually no Americans belonged to these religions. By sheer numbers, then, immigrants are simultaneously transforming American Christianity and increasing religious pluralism (Eck 2001; Warner 1998).

On the surface, Judaism has been changed the least by the arrival of the tens of millions of new immigrants, because few of them enter as Jews or convert to Judaism. But Judaism, too, confronts the influence of new immigrants even if they are not Jewish. Both Jews and new immigrants are heavily concentrated in the nation's large urban areas, so they frequently come into contact with one another.

Religious Changes for Immigrants

The Story of Karen Chai Kim

Let's move beyond these large macro changes to explore why religion is of vital importance to so many immigrants to the United States, how their religion changes when they enter the country, and how they change their religions after arriving. Chen (2008, 201) ends her superb book about Taiwanese immigrants with the following words: "[I]mmigrants use religion to address problems of meaning, morality, identity, and belonging in the U.S. because Americans have given religion this sacred power. By becoming religious, immigrants become Americans." What does she mean?

We can understand what Chen means if we consider the story of Karen Chai Kim. Dr. Kim has a Ph.D. in sociology and has authored important works on immigration and religion (e.g., Chai 1998, 2001a, 2001b). She is also an immigrant herself. She has been kind enough to provide her religious autobiography for inclusion in this book. Her story, as well as that of her family, illustrates most of the lessons of immigration and religious change:

> I was born in Seoul, Korea, and moved to the United States with my family at the age of four. In Korea, religion had not played a major role in my parents' lives. My mother, Chae Hyun Chai, grew up with

no religious education and has no memory of ever attending a religious service as a child. My father, Soo Hyuk Chai, only recalls attending Christian church services with his sister and her friend as a young elementary-school student in order to receive the "free notebooks, pencils, and candy" given out during Christmastime.

My paternal grandmother, Young Sook Hong, actually converted to Christianity as a high-school student in Korea, even serving as a Sunday school teacher at her church. When she married Re Suk Chai, however, she adopted Buddhism, the religion of her husband's family. Her parents-in-law were very prominent members of their Buddhist temple, and, as their young daughter-in-law, Young Sook became very active herself. Despite her previous commitment to Christianity, Young Sook remained a devout Buddhist until the day that she died. She maintained an altar in her home and practiced daily devotions several times a day. It was well known among family members and friends that they were not to disturb or call upon Young Sook during certain hours of the day when she was saying her prayers. Both she and her husband Re Suk had Buddhist funerals in Korea. (For my family tree, see Figure 12.1.)

My maternal grandmother, Sung Nam Chang, came from a prominent Buddhist family that helped establish several temples. According to family lore, Sung Nam's wealthy parents had been so delighted with her birth that they even established a temple in her honor, and they prayed that she would live to be 100 years old. She has, in fact, reached the age of 100 and continues to reside in Seoul at this time. When Sung Nam married Jang Hun Lee, however, she also adopted the religious practices of her husband's family. The Lee family was not particularly religious, but they ascribed to Confucianism. Sung Nam did occasionally still visit Buddhist temples, especially after the passing of her husband, but she has never been a devout follower of any religion.

It was only after immigration to the United States that my parents began to practice religion regularly and with commitment. On one hand, it is not surprising that they eventually found themselves involved in a Korean ethnic Christian church, as the church has long been the most important social institution for Korean Americans. On the other hand, the experience of immigration is extremely difficult, and it is often during times of difficulty that people seek comfort and spiritual meaning.

As stated earlier, my mother, Chae Hyun Chai, grew up in a Confucian household and attended no religious services as a child. She was later introduced to Protestant Christianity when she attended Ewha Women's University, which had been founded by an American Methodist missionary. She remembers attending the mandatory courses on Christianity three times a week as a college student, but my mother had no interest in religion at the time. Similarly, my father, Soo Hyuk Chai, did not grow up attending regular religious services. Part of the reason that they were not particularly religious growing up was that religion was seen as ascribed by family association, and their family was considered Buddhist. The Buddhism that they subscribed to was not congregational (it was not expected that one regularly attend temple). It was just assumed that one was a Buddhist without having to attend regular services.

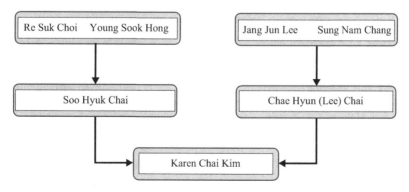

Figure 12.1 Karen Chai Kim's Family Tree

As a young child in New Jersey, I lived in a predominantly White neighborhood. Until my family moved to another neighborhood within the same town, my brother and I were two of the only three Asian children in school. It was quite a disorienting experience at first for my family and me, to not always be around Koreans.

After my family had been in the United States for about two years, my mother took my brother and me to a Korean Protestant church. We had been invited by a Korean acquaintance who attended the same college in Korea as my mother. A few weeks later, my father also attended the church with us. There we found many Koreans from back home. We made many new friends. This was a place for us.

But both of my parents were hesitant to convert to Christianity because they had been warned by family members in Korea not to give into the temptation to convert to Christianity, as many Korean immigrants before them had done. My father even carried around a small piece of paper that had been given to him by a Buddhist monk in Korea prior to immigration. The paper was a talisman meant to protect the family. Converting to another religion was seen as dishonoring one's ancestors and a bad omen for the entire family lineage.

Because of his family heritage, my father seriously wrestled with converting to Christianity. He called his mother, Young Sook, in Korea and asked what she thought about his possible conversion to Christianity. She replied, "Whatever religion you practice, do it with all your strength, and become the salt and light of the earth." She still remembered Bible verses from her days as a Christian girl. About a year later, my family and I were baptized, and my father burned the Buddhist talisman that he had carried around so faithfully for protection.

I have not always been "Karen." My birth name is Jung Won, and that is what I was called all my life, that is until we started attending Korean church. At Korean church, my parents noticed right away that all of the children in the Korean church used American names. Not wanting their children to feel left out, my parents immediately went about finding American names for my brother and me. My parents chose names that they thought sounded very American. My brother went from being Sung Do to "Walter," and I from Jung Won to "Karen." Perhaps ironically, for quite a while we only used our American names in Korean church. So, during the week, my brother and I were Sung Do and Jung Won, but at Korean church we were Walter and Karen.

My parents continued their involvement at the church and eventually received lay leader positions. After the church experienced a schism (a common occurrence in immigrant churches), my family switched to a smaller Korean church that was very close to our home. By this time, I was bored with church and only reluctantly attended. There was little youth programming, so I kept myself busy by teaching Sunday school.

When it came time for me to go away to Wellesley College in the Boston area, my parents were anxious about sending their daughter so far away from home. They remembered hosting a pastor from Boston who was once a guest speaker at our church. When we got to Boston, my parents met that pastor for dinner and requested that he look after me. They then dragged me to a church Bible study on my second day of college orientation. So, in the mind of my parents, the Korean church would serve as a connection for me to the local Korean community, and its members would be there for me should I need help. Although I was a reluctant member at first, it was at this church that I gained a greater understanding of Christianity. I attended this church for over a decade, and my involvement even guided my career.

I eventually decided to pursue a Ph.D. in sociology at Harvard University. Although I entered the program with the intention of studying Japanese society, I stumbled upon an announcement of a fellowship program for sociologists who wanted to conduct research on ethnic religious organizations. I applied for the fellowship and was selected for the New Ethnic Immigrant Congregations Project, headed by R. Stephen Warner. Through this fellowship, I began my study of the Korean Protestant Church in the United States.

While my family was very involved as Korean American Protestants, other relatives either maintained their Buddhist traditions or practiced Catholicism. As I pondered the religious differences within my own extended family, I wondered how my life might have been different had my family chosen to join a Buddhist temple or a Catholic church. When it came time for my dissertation research, I decided to expand my studies to examine Korean American Buddhists and Catholics. For over a year, I regularly attended services at a Boston-area Korean Catholic church and a Korean Buddhist temple, as well as my Korean Protestant church.

While I was growing up in the United States, the only time I saw a large group of Koreans was at church. The only context in which I saw Korean culture being celebrated was at church. Therefore, I realized that what I had come to consider as Korean culture was, in fact, *Protestant* Korean *American* culture. While I was doing my dissertation research, I saw that the celebrations of Korean holidays (such as New Year) were actually done quite differently across religions. Buddhists, for example, have no ban on traditional Korean traditions that are rooted in Shamanism. Korean Protestants, on the other hand, developed different ways of respecting elders while avoiding what they viewed as "idolatry" or "pagan" rituals. I even had to expand my Korean vocabulary, as I learned Buddhist and Catholic terms I had never heard before.

After I finished my dissertation, I met my husband Stanley Kim through church connections. Although we had never attended the same church or lived in the same city, we both knew the same pastor. Pastor Hoon Kyung Lee had been the pastor of my family's small Korean United Methodist Church in New Jersey. He then went on to become the senior pastor of one of the largest Korean churches in the country, located outside Detroit. Stanley's parents were active members of the church, and Reverend Lee decided to introduce Stanley and me to each other.

After we married, we attended Korean churches in Buffalo, New York, and Austin, Texas, for a number of years. Although we are both fluent in Korean, we are now much more proficient in English and prefer to worship in English. Therefore, we attended the English worship service at our Austin Korean church. However, when problems arose between the English ministry pastor and the senior pastor, the English ministry pastor was fired. This was done without consulting with or informing any of the English ministry lay leaders. The families in the English ministry were dismayed. They appreciated attending a Korean church and enjoyed fellowship with people from similar backgrounds while they maintained ties to the Korean ethnic community. I especially enjoyed being able to attend the same church as my parents (who had retired to Austin) for the first time since high school.

A common issue in Korean ethnic churches is the relationship between the Korean-speaking congregation and the English-speaking congregation. Differences in culture and lifestyle exist, as well in differences in beliefs about how churches should operate. Stanley and I enjoyed the Korean fellowship, but we also realized that the English ministry within a Korean ethnic church would always be treated as a branch of the "Sunday school," and the Korean ministry would always come first. Typically, the English ministry pastors in the Korean church are young—sometimes they are seminarians. We could live with this arrangement in our younger days, but we now had children of our own. How long could we remain in the ethnic church, relegated to the status of Sunday school students, even though we were grown adults?

The English ministry pastor who had been fired decided to start his own church in Austin, which a few families joined. Stanley and I did not feel a particular calling to establish a new church, but those few families wanted to support the pastor, whom they believed had served faithfully and had been wrongfully terminated. They worked hard in the new church for about 10 months, until the pastor realized that the church membership was dwindling and members were becoming burned out, and the church closed.

Stanley and I felt burned by our experience with Korean church in Austin, and we decided to take a break and attend a local church where I knew a few women from a community Bible study. The members are predominantly White, and there is a large Latino ministry. We had intended to "shop around" at different local churches, but our children love the Sunday school and insist on remaining at this church.

So, at the time of this writing, we are currently in limbo, hesitant to return to an ethnic church experience, enjoying more family time and the lack of required activities. On the other hand, we miss the fellowship that we had with other Korean American families like ourselves, and we wonder if our children would be happier regularly meeting with fellow Korean Americans. As parents, our priorities have changed, and we now are considering what type of church environment might be best for our children's spiritual and social growth. Stay tuned . . .

Karen Chai Kim's story contains many of the lessons of immigration and religious change that have been revealed in thousands of studies. Let's examine an even dozen of the most important lessons!

Lessons About Immigration and Religious Change

Lesson 1: Religion is often more important to immigrants in their new nation than it was in their old nation. Karen Chai Kim noted that her parents were not particularly religious in Korea. They were Buddhist, but this was largely in name only; they were expected to follow Buddhism to honor living relatives and ancestors. Religion was largely taken for granted, rather than being a consciously chosen identity. Dr. Kim's parents gave little thought to it. After they moved to the United States, however, several factors contributed to changing the importance of religion in their lives.

If you spend your whole life in one social environment, you do not perceive your life as one possible life among many, but simply as life. Rights and wrongs, family obligations, and traditions seemingly have always been there. But if you are uprooted from your taken-for-granted world and placed in another—with different rules, languages, foods, laws, worldviews, and ways of doing things—you will be faced with questions that you never before needed to ask: What is right, what is wrong? Who am I, how should I act, what should I think, who are my people?

Immigration can open up new opportunities, but it is also unsettling. Immigrants often become more religious in their new countries than they were in their home countries because they are trying to figure out their place in the new world. Immigration is, in the words of Smith (1978) a "theologizing experience." Immigrants often react to the alienation, confusion, and uncertainty of their new land by seeking the reassurance that religion can bring. Migration and the experience of displacement draw religious questions to the forefront and open people to change (e.g., see Chen 2008, 187). Religion can answer some of the questions that people have, and it can help them form connections with other people like themselves as they attempt to make sense of their new realities.

Lesson 2: The new religious groups that immigrants join tend to be organized into congregations. Some religions are organized around regular gatherings in congregations, where the faithful gather to worship, socialize, learn more about their religion, volunteer in the community, and so on. Congregations are important in Judaism and Christianity. But many other religions are not organized around congregational gatherings. Hinduism and Buddhism, for instance, are not congregationally based. Karen Chai Kim's parents did not regularly go to Buddhist temple in Korea not only because religion was not central to them, but because Buddhism is simply not congregationally based in Korea. You are not expected to regularly go to temple to be a good Buddhist. What is more, you do not go to temple to socialize, have lunch, or even learn about the Buddhist faith.

But something rather fascinating happens for immigrants who find religion in the United States. No matter what the religion is, the immigrants' religious life becomes congregationally based. In part, this is because U.S. law grants tax-exempt status to religious organizations. Thus, local houses of worship try to look something like congregations. But we also end up with *de facto* congregationalism because of religion's role in the United States. Local congregations serve multiple functions in this country: They are places to meet friends, find a mate, find community, make connections to get a job, and help the needy. Furthermore, they are run on the donations of those who attend, who also end up serving on committees and being appointed to positions to help run the congregations. So regardless of the religion, immigrants often find it advantageous to do as Americans do and to have their houses of worship serve these same functions. As Carolyn Chen noted earlier in the chapter, this is because "Americans have given religion this sacred power." As a result, people in the United States attend houses of worship "more frequently than any other nation at a comparable level of development" (Levitt 2007, 17).

Lesson 3: Immigrants are usually drawn to congregations by invitations from coethnics. Why did Karen Chai Kim and her family start attending a Korean Protestant church when her family was, by tradition, Buddhist? In their case, Karen's mother was invited by a fellow Korean. Why did she accept? According to the literature on these processes, she accepted either because she was repeatedly asked (immigrant Protestants in the United States overwhelmingly are evangelical, meaning in part that they emphasize proselytizing), or because she was experiencing a sense of alienation in the new land and wanted to take temporary refuge with fellow coethnics. Regardless of which reason was actually the case for Karen Chai Kim's mother, the general lesson for us is that first coethnics draw immigrants to religious congregations, and as we will see, this is especially the case when the religion in question is a majority religion in the United States (Protestant and Roman Catholic forms of Christianity).

Lesson 4: Religious involvement offers nonreligious benefits. Once immigrants begin attending congregations, they find many benefits that keep them there. Dr. Kim's mother found fellow Koreans, Korean children to play with her children, Korean food and Korean culture, and much more. She likely shared the newfound benefits with her husband, who soon agreed to also attend. Research shows that immigrants often end up in such congregations not for religious reasons but for the other benefits they find there. These congregations quickly become the central social institutions for immigrants. Let's listen to their words:

Here's a Vietnamese immigrant who was originally nonreligious but is now Christian:

> When my family came here, everything came through the Catholics . . . even before we came. . . . How could I forget this? They helped us with the documents, they helped us find housing, they found jobs for my mother and father, and they filled out the paperwork for us so that I and my two sisters could attend school. . . . At the very least, it was natural that their religion would make sense to me since I had no religion in Vietnam.
>
> (Ebaugh and Chafetz 2000, 38)

Here's a Sudanese immigrant, who is Muslim:

> The mosque helped us in the ghorba [the state of being away from home] and helped us get to know other Muslim people.
>
> (Abusharaf 1998, 98)

Here's a Korean immigrant who is Christian:

> When I came to Houston, I did not know a single person here. I had only about $200 in my pocket. As soon as I arrived, I went to a Korean church. . . . Soon, they found me a position in a restaurant that was operated by a church member. He allowed me to eat as much as I wanted and to sleep at the restaurant at night. . . . That's how I saved the money to start my . . . business. Later, when I opened my shop, many church members came . . . as customers.
>
> (Ebaugh and Chafetz 2000, 75)

Here's an Indian immigrant who is Hindu:

> OHM is like an extended family. It helps to alleviate problems—it helps in crisis management. There are many problems here—job related, domestic. Before OHM I had around 4 or 5 people to turn to, but

now I have around 20 families that I can trust. I have several close friends, and we call each other one or two times a week for personal conversation. . . . OHM also helps us in practical matters. We have doctors with different specializations from psychiatrists to cardiologists, engineers, accountants, businesspeople, scientists, and attorneys. So, whatever problem comes up, we have an expert who can help us.

(Kurien 1998, 49)

Here's a Nigerian immigrant who is now Christian:

I always go to the coffee and donuts after Mass to meet with any of the 20 families that are formally registered at St. Catherine's. . . . We try to get job opportunities available for our own group. Currently we have some working at [company X] and each time there are job openings they recommend each other for these positions.

(Sullivan 2000, 219)

We can see from these examples that the benefits of involvement in congregations include partaking in fellowship; maintaining ethnic traditions and ties with one's original culture; receiving aid in learning the new culture, educational and economic assistance and family support; finding a psychological and cultural refuge, as well as a social identity; receiving aid in navigating the immigration and naturalization system; and establishing and maintaining social connections. As this list suggests, the benefits are extensive. We could devote an entire book to what immigrants can gain through religious involvement (and several scholars have done so).

Lesson 5: Religious involvement offers religious benefits. Missing from the list of benefits in the previous lesson are the religious benefits that also accrue to immigrants. What makes a religious congregation different from other organizations is a transcendent locus of meaning (Christerson and Emerson 2003; Kniss and Numrich 2007; Lund 2020; Zanfani 2020). That is, religion offers people ways to understanding the world that go beyond this world. Why do we suffer? What is the meaning of our journey in life? What are we on earth for? All these are questions that religion can answer. Religion provides immigrants with ways to interpret their experiences that go beyond themselves and give their lives direction.

Although it is common for social scientists to focus on what religion provides socially for immigrants, we must not overlook the religious benefits of religion. Chen (2008, 186), like many other researchers, gathered data that revealed these benefits in her interviews of immigrants. For example, when she interviewed Taiwanese immigrant Mr. Hou, she asked him, "Was immigrating to the U.S. worth it?" His response was telling: "Life is harder for me here. I would be better off in Taiwan, I think. But here I found God." Another interviewee, Mr. Tang, a Buddhist, agrees that he has gained religious benefits from his migration. Life was fuller in Taiwan with his friends and family and the abundant social activities. But, he says, he would not have been "awakened" had he not come to the United States.

Lesson 6: Immigrants can become more American if they attend an ethnic congregation. Consider the following title of an article: "Becoming American by Becoming Hindu: Indian Americans Take Their Place at the Multicultural Table" (Kurien 1998). At first glance, the title of this article may puzzle you. How does one become American by becoming Hindu? For that matter, how does one become American by gathering with fellow immigrants in religious congregations? The answer has to do with the aid that fellow members of the congregation give to new members to help them integrate into American society by helping them find jobs and childcare, get access to information, learn English, and so on. Herberg (1955) wrote that while immigrants may be expected to eventually abandon their nationality and language, they were not expected to abandon their faith. Indeed, attending religious services is a way for immigrants to become more American and adapt to American society.

Karen Chai Kim was not "Karen" until she and her family began attending a Korean church. As she noted earlier, her birth name was Jung Won, but at the Korean church everyone gave their children American names. To help her fit into the new American context at the Korean church, Jung Won's parents gave her the American name Karen. Although at first she was called Karen only in the Korean church, she eventually adopted the new name as her identity and came to be called Karen by everyone. Ethnic religious congregations, then, actually facilitate the transformation of immigrants to Americans on multiple levels. In fact, Ecklund (2006) found that American Koreans who were attending a Korean church were in many ways more "Americanized" and concerned with being traditionally good Americans than Koreans who attended multiracial congregations.

Lesson 7: Religious involvement helps immigrants process the differences between their internal selves and their outward roles in their new lives. Congregations may experience conflict and change from time to time. Two recurring issues are the role of women in the church and generational struggles.

The American emphasis on the individual and the nuclear family leads most immigrants to question roles that they have taken for granted and to search for their "authentic selves" in the new land. Religious language and conversion experiences "are ways for men and women to work out the contradictions between traditional gender expectations and the realities of their lives in the U.S." (Chen 2008, 145). Women often carve out an identity that is not solely shaped by family roles, and men often assert a true self that is independent of their career status.

Generational issues are particularly common among children of immigrants (e.g., Chai 1998, 2001a). Karen Chai Kim alludes to her struggles with Korean church over the course of her life. Her sense that she is "less Korean" than are immigrants who came to this country as adults has led to much frustration and conflict in her life; we often see this pattern repeated among the American-born children of immigrants. These second-generation children are more integrated into American society than are their parents, they are often more fluent in English than in their parents' native language, they have fully adopted American ways of living, and they struggle with what they often view as the backward ways of their parents. These conflicts are played out in congregations—what language will be spoken, what customs followed, what level of deference will be shown to elders, and what religious beliefs and practices will be emphasized.

Lesson 8: Immigrants often return to theological foundations. The changes that religion brings to the lives of immigrants—a *de facto* congregational form of worship, many benefits from joining a congregation, greater interest in religion, and changing gender roles and generational relationships—are accompanied by another process—what Yang and Ebaugh (2001) call "returning to the theological foundations of the religion." The many changes we have discussed thus far need theological justifications in order for people to accept them. So, too, does practicing a particular form of religion amidst the religious and cultural diversity of the United States. Many immigrant religious leaders and members perceive these changes not as straying from the true faith, but returning to it, resurrecting the way that their religion was originally meant to be practiced. For example, Yang and Ebaugh (2001, 278) write:

> For many Muslim immigrants in our study, the evolution of the mosque from simply a place to pray to a center of social activity and learning means a reversion to the dynamic role the mosque was given in the days of Prophet Muhammad.

Yang and Ebaugh find this to be true for immigrants from a variety of religions and national origins. The vast religious changes they experience in their migration to the United States are perceived to be good, as they believe that they are returning to "true religion," their religion as it was intended to be.

Lesson 9: Religious majority/minority status matters. Examine Figure 12.2, which considers two variables: whether a particular religion is the majority or minority religion in immigrants' homeland, and whether it is a minority or majority religion in the United States. For illustrative purposes, the figure also lists a few examples of each.

Immigrants experience religion and their immigrant status differently, depending on the cell they inhabit in this chart, what Ebaugh and Chafetz (2000) describe as environmental opportunities and constraints. Those who are in Cells B and D are double minorities—living in a foreign land and members of a foreign religion. Those in Cell B have the additional constraint of having lost what was once a majority religious status. But there are some advantages for those in Cell B—they are driven to learn more about their faith so that they can explain, defend, or present it to others. As one Muslim immigrant noted, "The Americans are always asking, 'Why do you Muslims do this or that?' I feel like I am a representative of Islam . . . so I read more so I can know how to answer them." (Ebaugh and Chafetz 2000, 35) And consider this priest of a Greek Orthodox Church:

> The average Greek is forced to . . . understand . . . his/her faith, because we have so many denominations around us. . . . [B]ecause we are in America, we have to learn to back it up. . . . We do not have those [other faiths] in Greece; everyone is Orthodox. Here in Texas there are a lot of Baptists, so they say Orthodox? What is that? You have to be able to respond.
>
> (Ebaugh and Chafetz 2000, 34)

Immigrant congregations in Cells A and C find it difficult to recruit native-born Americans even if they wish to do so, because native-born individuals often have many congregational choices already. But immigrant congregations in Cells A and C do offer an attractive choice to fellow coethnics who are not specifically committed to a religion, because they can find fellowship in the context of joining the dominant religion of their new home. Conversely, immigrant congregations in Cells B and D often have more success in recruiting Americans because Americans have limited choices of minority religion congregations. At the same time, they may struggle to recruit coethnics who are religiously unaffiliated, because for these people, joining them means adopting a double minority status.

Lesson 10: Religion shapes immigrants' civic engagement. In many ways, the United States runs on volunteers. Religious congregations, soup kitchens, ethnic organizations, neighborhood associations, voter registration drives, Habitat for Humanity, and many other organizations are operated largely by volunteers and directed by a few paid staff. Most volunteer opportunities in the United States come via religious congregations, which have the people, the social organization, and, importantly, appeals to transcendent authority and purpose that can both motivate volunteering *and*

Majority Religion in Homeland		Minority Religion in Homeland	
Majority Religion in the United States	Minority Religion in the United States	Majority Religion in the United States	Minority Religion in the United States
A	B	C	D
Mexican Catholic	Vietnamese Buddhist	Chinese Protestant	Indian Jain
Cuban Catholic	Pakistani Muslim	Argentine Brethren	Zoroastrian
	Indian Hindu	Mexican Protestant	Iranian Jew

Figure 12.2 Majority and Minority Religion Status, by Location.

Source: Adapted from Table 1 in Ebaugh and Chafetz (2000, 32).

direct the type of volunteering. Studies find that different immigrant congregations volunteer in unique ways—some volunteer largely for the purpose of evangelism, while others volunteer largely to improve their communities. Some volunteer out of a personal feeling that volunteering is a good thing. Others volunteer because they believe that their religion requires it. Some focus their help only on coethnics, while others go beyond their own ethnic group. Why do these differences exist?

Two variables matter here—what we might think of as the means and the ends—and they shape religious orientations and engagement with the wider society. The first factor is the locus of moral authority. Moral authority "is concerned with the grounds for defining or evaluating ultimate ends" (Kniss and Numrich 2007, 38). How do we decide what is good, true, and worthy of pursuit? Moral authority provides such answers and direction. The locus of moral authority varies across religions. It ranges from the individual's reason or experience at one end to a collective tradition (a Holy Book or the teachings of a hierarchy, for example) at the other end.

The second factor of importance is the object of moral projects. Moral projects are the means by which we achieve the goals that moral authority has defined as good, true, and worth pursuing. Moral projects may attempt to maximize individual utility, or they may attempt to maximize the public good.

Figure 12.3 is a map of these two factors. For religious traditions in which the locus of authority is rooted in the individual, what is good, true, and worthy of pursuit varies across time, place, and person, and it must be determined by applying reasoning to the situation. With exceptions, of course, Buddhists, Hindus, Reformed Jews, and mainline Protestants tend to fall into the individual authority category. Conversely, for traditions in which the locus of authority is rooted in the collective, what is good, true, and worthy of pursuit is given by a transcendent absolute authority. Right and wrong are the same regardless of time, place, and person. Muslims, Conservative and Orthodox Jews, Catholics, and Evangelical Protestants tend to fall into the collectivist authority category.

The content of moral projects also varies by religious tradition. For traditions such as Hinduism, Buddhism, and Evangelical Protestantism, the individual is the moral project. That is, transformation of the individual is central to the purpose of the religion. For traditions such as Roman Catholicism, Islam, and Judaism, the collectivity or the community is the moral project. Transforming and ministering to the community of believers or of neighbors is the central purpose of the religion.

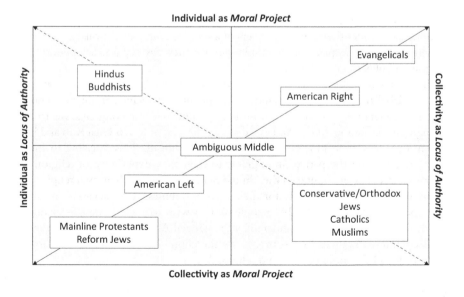

Figure 12.3 Moral Order Map

Source: Adapted from Kniss (2003) and Kniss and Numrich (2007, 39).

What does Figure 12.3 have to do with immigrants and volunteering? Studies repeatedly find that the combination of a person's faith tradition with respect to locus of moral authority and moral project, as well as whether the person is part of a majority or minority religion, shapes how much the person volunteers, what the focus and goals of that volunteering are, and to whom the volunteer work is directed (e.g., Chen 2008; Ebaugh and Chafetz 2000; Ecklund 2006; Foley and Hoge 2007; Kniss and Numrich 2007).

Immigrant Hindus and Buddhists tend to focus their volunteer activities on educating people about their faith. Because both these religions are minority faiths in the United States, immigrant followers are eager to spread the word and show that their religions need not be feared or seen as un-American. As a result, they take their message not just to members of their own ethnic community, but to native-born Americans as well. Immigrants in Evangelical Protestant churches also tend to devote a great portion of their volunteering to evangelism. Even when they volunteer for a community organization—a soup kitchen, for example—they typically bring an evangelical message to the event. Ecklund (2006) finds that immigrant Evangelical Protestant churches tend to focus their volunteering overwhelmingly on coethnics, especially immigrants from the same home nation. If immigrants or their children are members of racially mixed churches, though, they see their group as being broader than coethnics, and their volunteering efforts are often directed beyond their own ethnic group. Muslim and Catholic immigrants' volunteer work tends to focus on the community—for example, all other Muslims, regardless of ethnicity, or all people in the parish, including non-Catholics.

Thus, even if Muslim, Catholic, Evangelical Protestant, Jewish, Hindu, and Buddhist immigrants found themselves all working on building a Habitat for Humanity house (probably not likely for a variety of reasons), they would be there for very different reasons with different goals in mind. Religion, then, shapes the civic engagement of immigrants.

Lesson 11: Immigrants and their children become racialized (start to see themselves as members of a larger racial group). Immigrants come to the United States as Dominicans, Nigerians, Hmong, Mayans, Pakistanis, and so on. That is, they come as members of specific groups that share a common history and culture. The United States has a long tradition of turning ethnic peoples into racial peoples. For example, Chinese, Koreans, Japanese, Malaysians, Vietnamese, and so on become Asian; Nigerians, Bahamians, Sudanese, and Ethiopians become Black; Mexicans, Puerto Ricans, Salvadorans, and Cubans become Latino. Of course, immigrants and their children often continue to consider themselves members of a specific ethnic or national group. But in addition to (or in some cases, in place of) an ethnic identity, they develop a racial identity (for all sorts of reasons too complex to cover here).

What this means for ethnic congregations and immigrant religious identity is what Yang and Ebaugh (2001) label the "striving to include other peoples" principle. Immigrant churches, over time and across generations, often move from being ethnic-specific congregations to being race-specific congregations (Jeung 2005). And as we saw in the case of Karen Chai Kim and her husband and children, they may even move to multiracial congregations. This "striving to include other peoples" is a response on the part of immigrants to their new experience of religion and to the multicultural society they encounter in the United States. If they see their own religion as true and worthy, why should they keep it only for their own co-ethnics? The racialization process allows them to adopt a broader view of other people and to wish to include people of diverse ethnic backgrounds who are nonetheless considered by the general American public to be the same racial group. This openness and inclusiveness may move the church along its way to multiracial gatherings. (See Chapter 11 for more on race and religion.)

Lesson 12: Immigrants maintain contact with the religious culture in their countries of origin as they develop a new religious identity via transnationalism. When immigrants move to a new land, they do not lose all contact with their homeland. As Karen Chai Kim and her family were going through religious transformations, for example, they did so in dialogue with relatives who had remained in Korea. When they communicate with them, and particularly when they travel back to Korea for visits, they transmit new religious sensibilities back to their homeland, affecting people and organizations there. Transnationalism is the "the process by which immigrants forge and sustain multistranded relations that link together their societies of origin and settlement" (Basch et al. 1994, 7). Immigrants may be rooted in a particular place, but they also transcend borders. As sociologist Levitt (2007, 23) writes:

In some cases, the ties between migrants and non-migrants are so strong and widespread that migration also radically transforms the lives of individuals who stay home. . . . In response, the religious, social, and political groups they belong to also begin to operate across borders. Transnationalism means that the religious changes immigrants experience in the United States are communicated back to people and organizations in their homelands. One of the authors works with a Taiwanese immigrant who converted from atheism to Evangelical Protestantism in the United States. This man has taken several missionary trips back to Taiwan with his church (now pan-Asian), helping to establish congregations there, and his church helps fund the education of local pastors to lead these Taiwanese congregations. The influence is not just one-way. Taiwanese ideas and practices, in turn, influence religious practice in the United States. Gauging the full impact of transnationalism on religion has thus far proved elusive, but it is clear that it has an effect. And the increasing ease of travel and the vastly improved and cheaper forms of communication around the world mean that the impact of transnational influences may well increase.

Let's Conclude

Our exploration of a dozen lessons related to immigrants and religious change—as well as our earlier discussion of the significant changes that immigrants are having on religion in the United States—bring us to a few summary points. Religion is not transplanted unchanged from place to place. It is transformed in the process, just like the people involved (Kwon et al. 2001). The lessons discussed in this chapter help us to understand the basic contours of this religious change. Immigrants use religion to address issues of morality, meaning, identity, and belonging. In the process, immigrants become Americans. As Ebaugh and Chafetz (2000, 148) conclude, as long as immigrants come to the United States, they will create "vibrant religious institutions that simultaneously recreate for their members feelings of the homeland while helping them to adapt to their new land." And in the process, religious change will continue.

Suggested Reading

Ambrosini, Maurizio, Paola Bonizzoni, and Samuele Davide Molli. 2021. "How Religion Shapes Immigrants' Integration: The Case of Christian Migrant Churches in Italy." *Current Sociology* 69(6): 823–842.

Chen, Carolyn. 2008. *Getting Saved in America: Taiwanese Immigration and Religious Experience*. Princeton, NJ: Princeton University Press.

Ebaugh, Helen Rose, and Janet Saltman Chafetz. 2000. *Religion and the New Immigrants: Continuities and Adaptations in Immigrant Congregations*. Walnut Creek, CA: AltaMira Press.

Zanfrini, Laura (ed.). 2020. *Migrants and Religion: Paths, Issues, and Lenses*. Boston: Brill.

Section IV
More Big Questions

Section IV

More Unit Questions

13 The End of Days? Religion Meets Climate Change

1   What is our relationship with the environment, and how is that understanding shaped by religion?
2   How have religious groups' understandings of the environment changed over time?
3   Does religious affiliation affect how we see climate change, and whether we think we need to do something about it?
4   How might religion affect us, even if we ourselves are not believers?

Record-breaking heat waves. Destructive forest fires. Softening tundra. Melting glaciers and ice caps. Polar vortexes. Rising sea levels. More frequent and intense hurricanes. Deep drought in some places; historic floods in others. All around us, we see evidence of climate change. Scientists, activists, policy-makers and many others have sounded the alarm for over 40 years.

The Intergovernmental Panel on Climate Change (IPCC) has tracked climate change since 1988. Drawing on data from around the world, the IPCC has documented evidence of human impacts on the environment including changes in sea levels, extreme weather events, regional climate change, water cycle changes, and more. In the summer of 2021, the IPCC released its Sixth Assessment Report, which warned that "the scale of recent changes across the climate system as a whole and the present state of many aspects of the climate system are unprecedented over many centuries to many thousands of years," and "global surface temperature will continue to increase until at least the mid-century under all emissions scenarios considered" (Intergovernmental Panel on Climate Change 2021). Climate-wise, we are in new territory, and scientists fear that we will not be able to stop, much less reverse, global warming in the near future.

Environmentalism is a long-standing social movement and worldview that prioritizes care and preservation of the earth's natural environment: water, air, forests and other natural landscapes, and wildlife and animals' habitats. It encompasses beliefs that our fate is intertwined with that of the environment and that we have a responsibility to care for the earth and minimize our impact on it. It also includes behaviors that many of you may practice: "reducing, reusing, and recycling," conserving energy, reducing your carbon footprint, eating locally, and living sustainably, among others. In recent decades, climate change caused by humans has emerged as a pre-eminent environmental issue.

But what does religion have to do with environmentalism and climate change?

Historic Roots of Ecological Crisis?

No living thing—no plant, microbe, or animal—exists on this earth without having an impact on the natural world around it. Humans are no exception, as historian Lynn White argued in his 1967 *Science* article "The Historical Roots of Our Ecologic Crisis":

> Ever since man became a numerous species he has affected his environment notably. The hypothesis
> that his fire-drive method of hunting created the world's great grasslands and helped to exterminate the

DOI: 10.4324/9781003182108-17

monster mammals of the Pleistocene from much of the globe is plausible, if not proved. For 6 millennia at least, the banks of the lower Nile have been a human artifact rather than the swampy African jungle, which nature, apart from man, would have made it. . . . In many regions terracing or irrigation, overgrazing, the cutting of forests by Romans to build ships to fight Carthaginians or by Crusaders to solve the logistics problems of their expeditions, have profoundly changed some ecologies. . . . Quite unintentionally, changes in human ways often affect nonhuman nature.

(1203)

White goes on to argue that elements of Christianity as a worldview profoundly affected the beliefs, norms, and values of the modernizing Western world and that Christianity bears much responsibility for the environmental crises of the 20th and 21st centuries:

Christianity inherited from Judaism . . . a striking story of creation. By gradual stages a loving and all-powerful God had created light and darkness, the heavenly bodies, the earth and all its plants, animals, birds, and fishes. Finally, God had created Adam and, as an afterthought, Eve to keep man from being lonely. Man named all the animals, thus establishing his dominance over them. God planned all of this explicitly for man's benefit and rule: no item in the physical creation had any purpose save to serve man's purposes. . . . Especially in its Western form, Christianity is the most anthrocentric religion the world has seen.

(1205)

In short, White argued the Judeo-Christian creation story espouses a worldview of "mastery over nature" where humans are set apart from, and above, the natural world. The natural world exists for human use. In addition, humans are imbued with soul and consciousness, while nature is a lifeless set of resources to be taken and shaped as we wish. According to White, this worldview informed and drove technological development and scientific discovery from medieval Europe through the present. The Judeo-Christian worldview is thus implicated in the ecological problems that technology and science produce: excessive carbon emissions, climate change, ozone depletion, overpopulation, pollution, habitat destruction.

This essay was read and discussed widely. Checking in with Google Scholar, we found that it has been cited in more than 8000 books, reviews, and scholarly articles and studies. Interest in the essay and its ideas remains: About a quarter of those references have appeared since the article's 50th anniversary in 2017, when scientists and scholars revisited White's ideas about religiously informed views about the relationship between humans and the Earth. The question remains of interest to the media as well. In October 2020, Climate Nexus, in partnership with the Yale Program on Climate Change Communication and the George Mason University Center for Climate Change Communication, surveyed over 1800 registered voters in the U.S. (Interfaith Power and Light 2020) The survey asked questions about opinions on a range of pressing social issues and dug deeply with questions about climate change. Because survey respondents reported their religious affiliation, we can look at how views of humankind's relationship with the Earth and nature vary by religion. As you can see in Figure 13.1, the dominion view—that it is humankind's right to use the Earth and its natural resources for our own benefit—was rejected by a significant majority within *all* religious affiliations included! Instead, within each affiliation, between 64% and 90% of respondents said that humans have a responsibility to protect and care for the environment. There are variations among respondents from different religious traditions: At 36%, Other Christians are most likely to espouse a dominion view, while White establishment (mainline) Protestants (10%) and the unaffiliated (13%) were least likely. At 23%, White Evangelical Protestants fall roughly in the middle of the distribution of responses. The 2020 survey data, however, points to the ascendence of

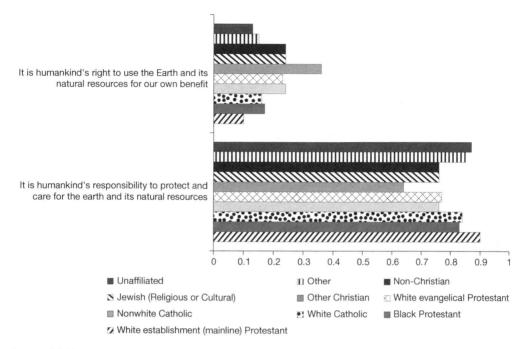

Figure 13.1 Views on the Relationship Between Humankind and the Earth, 2020

environment-friendly perspectives across religious traditions. We will return to the 2020 IPL survey data later in this chapter to explore current attitudes about climate change.

A researchable claim emerged from White's 1967 essay: that Christians—of varying sorts—are less concerned about the environment than people who are not Christian. In the 1980s and 90s, researchers explored the association among a range of indicators of religion and religiosity on one hand, and environmental beliefs and actions on the other. Researchers found, however, that people with strong personal religious beliefs in God or a higher power were *no more or less likely* to espouse environmentalism in attitude or action than people who did not have these beliefs. The same was true of frequency of church attendance, the importance that people said they placed on their religion, their religious affiliation, and their frequency of prayer: None of these religious variables consistently predicted environmental attitudes or actions (Boyd 1999; Eckberg and Blocker 1989, 1996; Guth et al. 1993, 1995; Hand and Van Liere 1984; Kanagy and Nelsen 1995).

In these studies, only religious fundamentalism (see Box 13.1) consistently predicted environmental attitudes and actions. In general, and all other variables being held equal, fundamentalist Christians were less likely to hold favorable views of environmentalists, less likely to support policies to protect the environment, and less likely to see the benefits of investing in environmental protection. In a sample drawn from Tulsa, Oklahoma, Eckberg and Blocker found that fundamentalists were less concerned than other people about the state of the environment. In national samples of clergy, religious activists, political activists, and the mass public, Guth et al. (1995) found that fundamentalists had more negative attitudes than others about environmental protections. Boyd (1999) found that fundamentalists were less likely to engage in environmentalist behaviors or to perceive danger in environmental risks.

Box 13.1 Fundamentalism: What's in a Name?

Researchers who study religion and environment have called **fundamentalism** by different names and operationalized it in a variety of ways. For example:

- Guth et al. (1993) refer to **conservative eschatology**, a combination of biblical literalism (self-reported belief that the words in the Bible are literally true) and "end times thinking" (self-reported belief in imminent catastrophe that will purify the world).
- Eckberg and Blocker (1989, 1996) refer to **sectarianism**, an index that combines measures including biblical literalism, a view of God as harsh and punishing, a belief in the value of obedience, affiliation with a conservative Protestant denomination, opposition to banning school prayer, rejection of Darwin's theory of evolution, belief in God's presence in everyday activities, and an appreciation for Gospel music.
- Boyd (1999) looked at **membership in a fundamentalist tradition**.
- Greeley (1993) focused on **biblical literalism**.

Each captures a similar aspect of religiosity: what is commonly called fundamentalist or evangelical belief, identity, and/or denominational affiliation.

However, other studies have found that, when other factors are accounted for, fundamentalist Christians were no more or less likely to espouse environmentalism than anyone else. What are those factors? When Greeley (1993) used data from the 1993 General Social Survey, a well-respected national survey, he found that the effects of fundamentalism dissipated once you accounted for political conservatism and a less gracious image of God (one that was more strongly associated with terms like "Father," "Master," "Judge," and "King" than with "Mother," "Spouse," "Lover," and "Friend"). Greeley concluded that it is not fundamentalism itself that drives anti-environmentalism among fundamentalist Christians. Instead, the predominantly conservative political leanings of such people and their predominant image of a judgmental God predict their opposition to environmentalism. Along similar lines, Kanagy and Nelsen (1995) found that when other factors—education, age, gender, and region—are controlled, religious variables, including fundamentalism, personal religion, and attendance at religious services, are not statistically significant predictors of environmentalism.

It is also important to note that, although statistically significant, the relationship between fundamentalist Christianity and environmentalism is not strong. For example, Eckberg and Blocker (1996) found that very little of the variation in environmental attitudes was predicted by religious variables—generally less than 3%, which means that more than 97% of the variation in environmental variables is due to other factors.

As sociologists, we are concerned not just with the attitudes and actions of individuals, even when they are shaped by social group membership. We are also concerned with social action by collectives and organized groups. For that reason, we now turn to religious *organizations*, and how they have responded to climate change and other environmental issues.

Religious Frameworks for Understanding the Human-Environment Relationship

Even before Lynn White's essay was published, Rachel Carson's *Silent Spring* (1962) sparked broad concern and reflection about environmental problems. As a foundation for calls to action, religious groups and leaders developed formal statements on where humans stand related to nature. Over time, the views of many religious groups have shifted, an evolution best illustrated by research on Religious Environmental Movement Organizations. Ellingson (2016) identified three distinct ethics or frameworks for understanding the relationship between humans and nature. "Steward-ship ethic" was the earliest framework, and typically identified individuals and their actions as the solution to environmental problems. Each of us is individually responsible to care for our part of the earth, but those responsibilities were not understood as linked to larger social forces that might be of interest to religious groups. The "Eco-Justice" framework emerged in the 1970s and 1980s and resulted in greater focus on how environmental degradation makes local, regional, and global inequalities worse. Environmental issues became tied to concern rooted in theology for the poor, weak, powerless, or vulnerable. The "Creation spirituality" framework expanded in the 2010s and centers on the sacredness of all of nature, and the interconnectedness of humans and nature in a world where people are neither more nor less important than any other living things.

Of course, some religious traditions, especially in non-Western and indigenous systems, have long been rooted in the "Creation Spirituality" that increasingly animates much Western religion. A literary example is found in the novel *Ceremony*, where Native American writer Silko (1977) describes a ritual that follows the killing of a hunted deer. As the deer lay in the throes of its death, Tayo—a Pueblo Indian of Laguna in New Mexico—covered the deer's head with his jacket (to the consternation of his cousin, who had rejected Native religious practices). After the deer died, Tayo's grandfather and uncle

> [W]ent to the deer and lifted the jacket. They knelt down and took pinches of cornmeal from Josiah's leather pouch. They sprinkled the cornmeal on the nose and fed the deer's spirit. They had to show their love and respect, their appreciation; otherwise, the deer would be offended, and they would not come to die for them the following year . . . Tayo wrapped the liver and heart in the clean cheesecloth [his grandfather] carried with him . . . Tayo held the bundle tighter. He felt humbled by the size of the full moon, by the chill wind that swept wide across the foothills of the mountain. They said the deer gave itself to them because it loved them, and he could feel the love as the fading heat of the deer's body warmed his hands.

Throughout *Ceremony*, Tayo seeks his proper place in nature, particularly in the landscape where he grew up in the southwest United States, after returning from serving as a soldier in World War II. Through the rituals and ceremonies of his people, he seeks balance and harmony as a small and mostly insignificant part of nature. This view of humans' relationships to nature might seem strange to you: the notion that we need to love and respect our food sources, the idea that the animal chooses to die to supply us with food, and Tayo's emotional connection to the source of his food. Even his sense of humility and gratitude might seem unfamiliar. But this passage embodies an alternative approach to relating to nature, one that emphasizes the inclusion of all living things in a single circle.

Szrot (2020) examined environment-related papal encyclicals of six Catholic popes over the last 60 years and found that these formal statements issued at the highest level of the Roman Catholic church went through a similar evolution in thinking to the one Ellingson identified. Early in the study period, the papal statements reflect an ethos of stewardship, where humans are viewed as having dominion over nature, and there was great confidence in human-generated science and technology to solve environmental problems. By the 1970s, however, the framework had shifted to one of concern about the impacts of environmental problems on human communities, social and economic inequality, and the prospects for world peace. Solutions came to be located increasingly in collective action on the part of governments, industry and other groups, a distinct move away from an individualistic stewardship ethic. Nonetheless, through the papacy of Benedict XVI, not

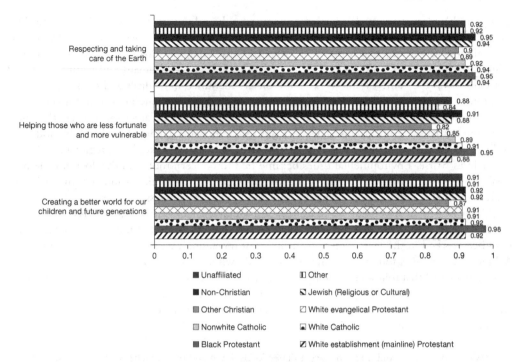

Figure 13.2 Reasons to Address Climate Change: Percent Responding Very Important or Somewhat Important Reason

nature, but humans and human communities, remained at the center of environmental concerns. In 2015, Pope Francis moved closer to an ethic of creation spirituality, asserting kinship rather than dominance over nature, when he wrote: "This sister [Mother Earth] now cries out to us because of the harm we have inflicted on her by our irresponsible use and abuse of the goods with which God has endowed her" (Pope Francis 2015).

We see these ethics or frameworks reflected in national polls as well. The 2020 Interfaith Power and Light survey on religion and climate change in the U.S. asked questions about *why* climate change needed to be addressed. In Figure 13.2, we share results for three reasons to address climate change, responses that most closely align to the frameworks identified by Ellingson (2016): (1) Respecting and taking care of the earth (roughly aligning with creation spirituality), (2) helping those who are less fortunate and more vulnerable (roughly aligning with eco-justice), and (3) creating a better world for our children and future generations (aligning with stewardship as generational justice directed at "our" descendants).

The results are broken down by broad groups of religious affiliation. While there are some small differences among groups, what is most striking is the high level of agreement with *each* of these reasons for addressing climate change across all groups. Across affiliations, we seem to be more similar than different in the lenses we bring to climate change action. Importantly, the results suggest that these ethics are not mutually exclusive but can be engaged simultaneously. Our frameworks for addressing climate change may be cumulative rather than one displacing another.

Religious Groups Speak About Climate Change

As the 2015 Paris Convention on Global Warming approached, more religious groups and leaders mobilized to issue formal statements on climate change (see Box 13.2 for excerpts of a sampling of statements from religious groups around the world). Most were in support of the voluntary targets for reduced carbon emissions by the middle of the 21st century. The statements reflected several common concerns that also align with the environmental ethics described by Ellingson (2016) and Szrot (2020):

- The inseparability of environment and human communities
- Inequitable impacts of climate change on developing countries, low-income communities, and communities of color
- Effects of climate change on other ecological crises including loss of biodiversity through an accelerating extinction of species
- Climate change's impacts on future generations
- Responsibility of wealthy nations for the impacts of climate change

Box 13.2 Excerpts of Formal Statements on Climate Change from Religious Organizations and Leaders

Group	Excerpt
AME Church Climate Change Resolution (2016)	We can move away from the dirty fuels that make us sick and shift toward safe, clean energy like wind and solar that help make every breath our neighbors and families take a healthy one, create new jobs that can't be outsourced, help protect the least among us and preserve what God bestowed.
The Time to Act is Now: Buddhist Declaration on Climate Change (2015)	We have a brief window of opportunity to take action, to preserve humanity from imminent disaster and to assist the survival of the many diverse and beautiful forms of life on Earth. Future generations, and the other species that share the biosphere with us, have no voice to ask for our compassion, wisdom, and leadership. We must listen to their silence. We must be their voice, too, and act on their behalf.
US Conference of Catholic Bishops *Global Climate Change* (2001)	Our obligations to the one human family stretch across space and time. They tie us to the poor in our midst and across the globe, as well as to future generations. The commandment to love our neighbor invites us to consider the poor and marginalized of other nations as true brothers and sisters who share with us the one table of life intended by God for the enjoyment of all … As people of religious faith, we bishops believe that the atmosphere that supports life on earth is a God-given gift, one we must respect and protect. It unites us as one human family. If we harm the atmosphere, we dishonor our Creator and the gift of creation. The values of our faith call us to humility, sacrifice, and a respect for life and the natural gifts God has provided.
Islamic Declaration on Global Climate Change (2015)	We call on all Muslims, wherever they may be, to tackle the root causes of climate change, environmental degradation, and the loss of biodiversity, following the example of The Prophet Muhammad (peace and blessings be upon him), who was, in the words of the Qur'an, 'a mercy to all beings.'

Group	Excerpt
The World Is Our Host: A Call to Urgent Action for Climate Justice (Anglican Bishops, 2015)	We accept the evidence of science concerning the contribution of human activity to the climate crisis and the disproportionate role played by fossil fuel-based economies. Although climate scientists have for many years warned of the consequences of inaction, there is an alarming lack of global agreement about the way forward. We believe that the problem is spiritual as well as economic, scientific and political, because the roadblock to effective action relates to basic existential issues of how human life is framed and valued: including the competing moral claims of present and future generations, human versus non-human interests, and how the lifestyle of wealthy countries is to be balanced against the basic needs of the developing world. For this reason the Church must urgently find its collective moral voice.
Holy and Great Council of the Orthodox Church Ecumenical Patriarchate (His All-Holiness Ecumenical Patriarch Bartholomew, 2015)	Climate change is much more than an issue of environmental preservation. Insofar as human-induced, it is a profoundly moral and spiritual problem. To persist in our current path of ecological destruction is not only folly. It is suicidal because it jeopardizes the diversity of our planet. Moreover, climate change constitutes a matter of social and economic justice. For those who will most directly and severely be affected by climate change will be the poorer and more vulnerable nations (what Christian Scriptures refer to as our "neighbor") as well as the younger and future generations (the world of our children, and of our children's children).
Bahai: Seizing the Opportunity: Redefining the challenge of climate change (2008)	Yet, in the face of the destructive impacts of climate change—exacerbated by the extremes of wealth and poverty—a need for new approaches centered on the principles of justice and equity is apparent ... To contribute to this important discourse, we assert that the principle of the oneness of humankind must become the ruling principle of international life.

Not all religious groups, however, agree that climate change is a pressing concern, or that coordinated governmental or international action is the way forward. For example, the most recent formal statement of the Southern Baptist Convention (Baptist Press 2008) expresses skepticism regarding human impacts on climate change and worries about the economic impacts of coordinated government action to curb it:

> proposals to regulate CO2 and other greenhouse gas emissions based on a maximum acceptable global temperature goal [are] very dangerous, since attempts to meet the goal could lead to a succession of mandates of deeper cuts in emissions, which may have no appreciable effect if humans are not the principal cause of global warming, and could lead to major economic hardships on a worldwide scale.

Although doctrinal statements may give the impression that agreement or unanimity within a given religious group, sometimes we see evidence of internal differences. For example, Evangelical

Christians, including some Southern Baptists, formed the Evangelical Climate Initiative (ECI) in the early 2000s. This group advocates for climate change action based on four core claims:

- Climate change is real and humans drive it
- Climate change will have significant impacts, especially on poorer communities
- Christians must respond to climate change
- Climate change is an urgent concern that needs immediate action from governments, businesses, churches, and individuals

The ECI statement was endorsed by over 300 Evangelical leaders. Their signatures were qualified, however, by a clear statement that each signed as an individual and not as a representative of their religious organization or ministry. The ECI statement has also been adopted by the Southern Baptist Environment & Climate Initiative. Here too signatories are careful to note that they speak as individuals and not as representatives of their larger faith tradition, hinting at the internal disagreements within the denomination.

As with many issues, viewpoints on climate change are often presented as polarized—if you are a part of this group, then you believe A. And if you are a part of that group, then you believe the opposite of A. Reality is more complicated, however. For example, the 2020 Interfaith Power and Light poll on climate change asked about if climate change is happening, if it is a crisis or major problem, and whether government action was needed. As Figure 13.3 illustrates, most respondents in *each* religious affiliation category believed that climate change really was happening.

More specifically, despite leader and institutional reservations about aggressive climate action, most White evangelical Protestants believe that climate change is happening, believe it is a crisis or a major problem, and strongly or somewhat strongly support government action to address it. Those in other religious affiliations are more likely to hold these ideas than are White evangelical

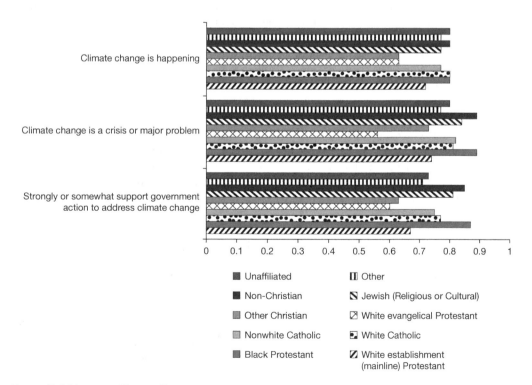

Figure 13.3 Views on Climate Change by Religious Affiliation

Protestants (and other Christians), but in all groups most respondents express concern about climate change. Religious affiliation may play a role, but religion is not definitive!

The 2020 IPL poll results align with other interesting things uncovered by research on religion and environmentalism. For example, researchers have found that believers do not always have the same views of environmental issues as "elites." Guth et al. (1995) found that religious variables explain between 22% and 44% of the variation in environmental attitudes and beliefs among a relatively small number of "elites," but less than 10% of the variation among the more numerous "masses" (ordinary, everyday believers). For the vast majority of believers, over 90% of the variation in environmentalism is explained by something other than the religion variables that Guth et al. tested. This matters because doctrinal statements are issued by elites, and we should not assume they uniformly represent all followers.

Other research suggests that looking at climate change's effects through the lens of religion does not convince people that action is needed. Severson and Coleman (2015) studied responses to a range of moral frames for climate change: Religion, secular morality, economic efficiency, economic equity, and science. Neither economic efficiency nor religion elicited support for climate change policies, not even among conservatives for whom those frames are generally thought to be most persuasive. Instead, a focus on science and economic equity was found to be effective at generating support for climate change action and lessening the political polarization around climate change.

Revisiting White: What Was His Point?

Research sparked by White's 1967 article in *Science* addressed important questions about what shapes environmental beliefs and actions. Along the way, however, we may have lost sight of the heart of White's argument. Remember, White never claimed that Christians in particular were less likely to be environmentalists. Nor did he contend that those who believe in the literal truth of the Genesis creation story are less likely to be active environmentalists. White's argument was more general. He argued that the Judeo—Christian worldview of human mastery over nature, a worldview that shaped centuries of technological and scientific development, so pervades modern Western culture that even those who do not claim a religious affiliation have adopted and enacted this belief. White (1967, 1205) points out that:

> It has become fashionable today to say that, for better or worse, we live in the "post-Christian age." Certainly the forms of our thinking and language have largely ceased to be Christian, but to my eye the substance often remains amazingly akin to that of the past. Our daily habits of action, for example, are dominated by an implicit faith in the perpetual progress which was unknown either to Greco-Roman antiquity or to the Orient. It is rooted in, and is indefensible apart from, Judeo-Christian teleology. . . . We continue today to live, as we have lived for about 1700 years, very largely in a context of Christian axioms.

White's point is deceptively simple: Scientists, engineers, entrepreneurs, and others—religiously motivated or not—adhere to the belief that humans can master the natural world. This belief has been infused with the Judeo-Christian worldview embodied in the Biblical creation story. This group includes, to at least some extent, you and almost everyone you know. Before you protest, consider these questions. Does your home have air conditioning? Does your water come from a reservoir formed by a human-made dam? Have you ever been cured by an antibiotic? Do you drive a car? Do you eat food other than wild berries gathered from the forest? If you answered "yes" to any of these questions, then you, like the rest of us in the United States and throughout much of the world, live a lifestyle that is made possible by our efforts to master nature. You have come to expect technology to tame the natural world and smooth it over for human habitation. You don't have to be religious to espouse this worldview. You just have to participate in a modern Western culture whose historic roots lie in a Judeo-Christian tradition, and whose impacts on the world's environment (and climate change) are increasingly felt everywhere. That is Lynn White's point, one that has been overlooked when researchers drew a specific hypothesis about fundamentalist Christians, or Christians in general, from his argument.

Ideas—even ones that have compelling historical evidence to support them—can be transformed in the process of creating testable hypotheses. White did not argue that fundamentalists are less likely to be environmentalists than non-fundamentalists. He argued that all of us live in a culture that is infused with the beliefs and practices of science and technology, and that science and technology themselves were driven in part by a worldview that posits humans' separation from and superiority over nature. As a result, whether or not we are Christian, we all struggle with how to live in environmentally friendly ways. Whether or not we are religious, almost all of us adhere to some elements of this separation of humans from nature and an ideology of mastery. White simply suggests its roots. In so doing, he argues for the power of religion to suffuse an entire culture: even when the religious belief itself dissipates, it remains deeply implicated in what we think and how we act.

14 Do We Need God to Do Good?

1 What is morality?
2 What are the roles of rules and community in morality and religion?
3 What is distinctive about religiously based moral systems?
4 Does religion ensure that we do good?
5 Are sociologists the spawn of Satan for acknowledging other moral systems?

In Fall 2021, Harvard's chaplains, representing diverse faith traditions from around the globe, elected Greg Epstein to be the president of their chaplains' group. This was noteworthy enough to be covered in the *New York Times*, *New York Post*, *New Yorker*, *Guardian*, National Public Radio (NPR), and a slew of other media outlets, albeit with a strong tilt toward the urban northeast of the US. What made Epstein's selection such an interesting choice? Well, Greg Epstein is an atheist perhaps best known for his 2010 book *Good Without God*. In that book, he focuses on shared values of secular humanists—tolerance, community, morality, values practiced wholeheartedly but without reference to religion. And he does this without denigrating those whose values arise from an explicitly religious framework.

Wall Street Journal columnist Daniel Henninger, on the other hand, has argued that we do need religion, above and beyond secular kinds of morality. He discussed the root causes of the financial crisis that came to a head in late 2008:

> What really went missing through the subprime mortgage years were the three Rs: responsibility, restraint and remorse. . . . Responsibility and restraint are moral sentiments. Remorse is a product of conscience. None of these grow on trees. Each must be learned, taught, passed down. And so we come back to the disappearance of "Merry Christmas." It has been my view that the steady secularizing and insistent effort at dereligioning America has been dangerous. . . . Northerners and atheists who vilify Southern evangelicals are throwing out nurturers of useful virtue with the bathwater of obnoxious political opinions. The point for a healthy society of commerce and politics is not that religion saves, but that it keeps most of the players inside the chalk lines. We are erasing the chalk lines.

He is not alone in thinking that religion is a necessary foundation for morality. But is he right? Or is the atheist, secular humanist who is president of Harvard's chaplains' group onto something?

Do We Need God to Do Good?

This question matters because, while religion remains a vibrant force worldwide, it also faces pockets of challenge. We discussed these challenges in Chapter 5. In most of Europe, for example, secularization has proceeded largely as predicted: State and religion are distinct spheres, identification

DOI: 10.4324/9781003182108-18

with religious groups has declined over time, and religion has been largely pushed out of the public sphere. In a number of societies, a national identity has developed independently of religion, and sometimes has explicitly pushed religion out of the way. The communist government in China and the mid-20th century secular government in Iran come to mind. And in the United States, religion remains a powerful force in politics and in the private lives of citizens but, as Henninger would most likely agree, it has been pushed out of public schools, and its role in government has become limited. We wonder what holds society together when religion is weakened or diminished, especially in the public sphere. Is morality integrally tied to religion? Can societies maintain a semblance of morality without religion?

Morality and Regulation

Though they are closely related, morality and religion are not the same thing. When we ask our students what "morality" is, they usually describe it as a way to regulate human behavior. To them, morality is about being able to tell right from wrong. It is about knowing how to behave. It is knowing rules, laws, folkways (patterns of conventional behavior in society), and all the stuff we take for granted. It is acting in predictable and acceptable ways. It is saying and doing the right thing and, just as important, not saying or doing things that are forbidden.

If you think about it, religion also acts as a regulatory system. It's the source of behavioral proscriptions and prescriptions: Do not, for example, kill, steal, lie, eat pork, dress immodestly, laugh at the misfortune of another, look an elder in the eye, or leave dog poop in a neighbor's yard. And do worship regularly, remember your ancestors, tithe, wash your hands carefully before a meal, remove your shoes to worship, and respect your parents. This is just the beginning—there are many more dos and don'ts that we won't list here. Of course, our list is drawn from several religions, and no single person is expected to adhere to all of them. The *what* of morality varies across societies. We tackle that later.

Sometimes the rules seem arbitrary. In the Bible, the book of Leviticus is full of rules that in a modern context seem picky and sometimes ridiculous. There are rules about clean and unclean animals, how to slaughter animals, how to shave, what you can and cannot eat and in what combinations, who can be a religious leader, and how religious celebrations should proceed. That's just the beginning! But seemingly arbitrary rules are not just limited to religion. Similarly odd rules, conventions, and patterns guide nonreligious life. Remind us again *why* we give the two-fingered wave to a passing car on a desolate rural road? (The two-fingered wave is *not* the same as flipping the bird! Instead, it is a simple acknowledgment of another driver—two fingers lifted off the steering wheel as you pass—that is the norm in rural areas.) Why does a man put the toilet seat down after, well, you know? Why do we address our elders more formally than we do our peers or juniors? This list, too, could be endless. Whether the rules are arbitrary or not, however, we generally adhere to most of them. The question is, why?

Morality and Community

Morality regulates our behavior. But sociologists understand that regulation is just a starting point for understanding morality. The rules are important. Equally important—maybe more important—is the community. By community, we mean the group from which morality emerges and to which moral behavior ties us. As we discussed in Chapter 4 on cohesion and conflict, engaging in collective religious rituals maintains and reinforces our religious communities by strengthening the ties among members and creating a sense of the larger group as an all-encompassing force. Similarly, adhering to moral rules integrally connects us to other people. Knowing and obeying these rules marks us as responsible members of society. Unfamiliarity with these rules—or worse, ignoring them—brands you as an outsider. Henninger (2008) gets this when he writes about "restraint" (i.e., adhering to rules, even when you would rather not) and "responsibility" to the larger group. We do not follow a vast array of rules just for ourselves. We do them for—and as members of—a community.

The sociological study of morality has its roots in the work of Durkheim (1858–1917). Durkheim firmly believed that morality and religion are more than just what an individual person does. They are social facts that emerge out of and operate in the context of human community. Both draw their strength from transcending the individual and infusing the community as a whole.

Moral rules are shared within the group and become *building blocks* of community. You may recall from Chapter 1 that Durkheim used the term "moral community" to describe the collective that is formed when a group of people adhere to shared beliefs and practices regarding the sacred. As Chapter 4 described, this is what religion *does*: It takes individuals and out of them builds a cohesive whole. This fact points us to an important quality of religion that is also shared by morality: Before either can regulate human behavior, each must first construct the group, by forming ties among people and creating boundaries between the group and outsiders. We must be able to tell who is *in* the group and who is *out*, who is a *member* and who is an *alien* or *outsider*. A rich sociological understanding of morality thus encompasses "the rules" and also sees how those rules are tied to the cohesiveness of the group and the boundaries around communities. We have to see both aspects of morality: its obvious regulation of the behavior of members *and* its role in building and maintaining the social group itself.

How effective morality is at regulating behavior depends on how attached people are to the community. Durkheim explained this nicely when he wrote about moral education. Society regulates our behavior through moral codes, he wrote. On the surface, that seems to suggest that these moral codes are oppressive, weighty constraints on individual behavior under which people chafe and suffer. But that is not, as it turns out, how we generally experience morality. Instead, as it regulates, morality simultaneously brings us into society and provides a sense of belonging to the larger group. Morality pushes us to think of others first—our family, community, or nation—and to understand selflessness as a virtue. Again, recall that religion does something similar, providing a mechanism by which individualism is transcended and society itself becomes central.

This does not mean that morality always works to keep people's behavior in line! We see plenty of instances where the rules get broken. For these instances we have Henninger's third "R"—remorse. But, at its most effective, morality works often enough to produce predictable behavior in an integrated, coherent society.

Membership and belonging provide powerful motives for people to follow society's moral rules. As Peter Berger so eloquently discussed in his classic *Invitation to Sociology* (1963), breaking the rules brings sanctions or punishments: disapproval, condemnation, gossip, the silent treatment, and sometimes even criminal proceedings. Rule-breaking also calls into question the strength of one's ties to the society and the sincerity of one's attachments and sentiments. "Who do you think you are?" you may wonder when someone cuts in line, speaks disrespectfully, absconds with your garbage bin, or otherwise acts in ways that suggest he or she is following a different set of rules. That is not a question that begs for a person's name! It's a question about the person's identity and social location, elicited by the perception that he or she is out of line. When rule-breakers make serious breaches or repeated offenses, they come to be seen as problematic or harmful to the community: uncaring about others, unreliable, or selfish. They are pushed to the edges of the community, if not evicted from it altogether. (Think ex-communication, ostracism, expulsion, and prison.) Exclusion from the group is the ultimate punishment. Morality draws boundaries around groups, and generally those within groups willingly go along with the dos and don'ts of that group in order to support the group and maintain membership in it. This is what Daniel Henninger refers to as keeping "most of the players inside the chalk lines."

What's Religion Got?

Although many communities are rooted in religious morality, religion is not the only possible basis for morality. Take, for example, a profession like medicine, where physicians adhere to ethical codes of conduct. Members follow principles for ethical decision-making (e.g., beneficence, autonomy), and the profession polices the boundaries around the community. At least in theory, miscreants who violate these principles are expelled from the community. Though it is not rooted in a religious tradition, the profession of medicine is nonetheless a moral community that regulates its members.

Another example is the military. Soldiers typically have a strong sense of community, bolstered by their mutual responsibilities to each other. The film *A Few Good Men*, which starred Tom Cruise and featured the now-famous line by Jack Nicholson's character ("You can't handle the truth!"), is a dramatic representation of the military as a moral community, with boundaries around the group and strict—if sometimes informal—codes of conduct. But though religious persons may serve in the military, and "God" is sometimes invoked in military settings, the military is essentially a secular institution. Nonetheless, it constitutes a powerful moral community, as anyone who has served in the military can tell you.

There are those who believe that a nonreligious morality is possible and desirable for their families. Critics of religion, including Sam Harris, who wrote *The End of Faith* (2004), would likely agree with them. Harris has himself proposed that religion be replaced by a rational approach to ethics akin to secular humanism. Is that really feasible? Can a morality that is not based in religion simply step in for religion, at no cost to the strength and effectiveness of the moral system?

Let's think about this. The rules that bind members of a secular moral community have significant force and legitimacy: It is widely accepted, for example, that doctors should "first, do no harm," and that members of the military should obey the legitimate commands of their superiors. But it is not hard to go back and find the human sources of these rules: the Hippocratic Oath and military doctrine. Religiously based moral systems are different because their human roots are obscured through beliefs and practices that, at least in our minds, link the moral system to a broader cosmic order.

In Chapter 1, we explored Peter Berger's claim that religion is our "audacious attempt to conceive of the entire universe as being humanly significant." By this, Berger means that religion is our way of making sense of our circumstances by linking them to a broader cosmic reality, a supposedly unchangeable and transcendent truth that exists outside us but to which we are connected. This cosmic order transcends human culture: It is understood to simply *exist* as part of the natural order, the way things are meant to be. By invoking religion as a basis of our moral system, we obscure the very human roots of our community. We assert that not humans, but God or some other higher power or order, made our community and established its rules. As Berger (1967, 26) puts it,

> The cosmos posited by religion . . . both includes and transcends man. The sacred cosmos [confronts] man as an immensely powerful reality other than himself. Yet this reality addresses itself to him and locates his life in an ultimately meaningful order.

Once they have been connected in this way to the transcendent, human communities take on an air of inevitability, as if the structure and rules of human society were set from outside that community and imposed on it by a higher power. This attitude, in turn, enhances the long-term stability of religiously based societies compared with secular ones.

It is not that such systems never change. Social change throughout recorded history argues against that conclusion. But social stability is strengthened when the moral system appears to participants as if it encompasses, but is also beyond, human experience. Let's return to the case of American civil religion. American government is clearly a human creation, one that students in the

United States learn about in grade-school history class. Human beings penned our founding documents: the Declaration of Independence, the U.S. Constitution, and the like. But as Bellah (1967, 5) noted in his analysis of key presidential inaugural addresses, one theme in particular

> lies very deep in the American tradition, namely the obligation, both collective and individual, to carry out God's will on earth. This was the motivating spirit of those who founded America, and it has been present in every generation since.

In specific historic eras, other themes emerge. The religious myth of exodus and escape from tyranny shapes our understanding of the Revolutionary War, with George Washington as the "messiah." The Civil War is often recounted using images of "death, sacrifice, and rebirth," with Abraham Lincoln serving as America's savior. The creation of Memorial Day, a commemoration of those who have died in war, "is a major event for the whole community involving a rededication to the martyred dead, the spirit of sacrifice, the American vision." (Bellah 1967, 11)

In the end, Bellah (1967, 12) concludes that American civil religion "is a genuine apprehension of universal and transcendent religious reality as seen in, or one could almost say, as revealed through, the experience of American people." But through that tradition, our understanding of our history, as well as our future, is infused with transcendent meaning. As a nation, we see ourselves as more than just a random collection of people thrown together willy-nilly. We see ourselves as having purpose and meaning, a collective self-conception that lends stability during treacherous historical times (e.g., revolution, civil war, other wars, presidential assassinations).

Although morality can and does exist in the absence of religion, religious foundations can significantly strengthen a moral system. Do we need God to do good? Probably not, but religion may help.

Does Religion Ensure that We Do Good?

In the 1980s and 1990s, scandals surrounding clergy became public. Televangelists came under fire for cheating on their spouses, religious leaders lived in high style off the contributions of their followers, and scores of Catholic priests were found culpable of child sexual abuse. As these scandals developed, our students expressed shock and disappointment. They were, of course, outraged by the offenses themselves: They disapproved strongly of marital infidelities, financial shenanigans, and abuse of children. But what troubled them even more was that *religious* persons, especially religious *leaders*, would engage in immoral or illegal behavior. They would exclaim, "How could they? They are supposed to be *religious!*" Implicit in this common first response is an assumption that people who are religious are, by the very fact of their religiosity, inherently moral and law-abiding. These events challenged this assumption. Of course, critics of religion regularly cite the evils perpetrated in the name of religion. As Hitchens (2007, 13) put so succinctly: "Religion poisons everything." While we do not agree with that blanket statement, we acknowledge that it reflects religion's mixed record when it comes to "doing good."

Our students were coming face to face with something that sociologists and criminologists had been exploring empirically for quite a while: the relationship between individual religiosity and deviant behavior. To be sure, criminologists have accumulated empirical support for the notion that religious people are more moral or law-abiding than are nonreligious people (Glueck and Glueck 1950; Nye 1958). As recently as 2008, psychologists who reviewed eight decades of research on individual religiosity and self-control concluded that more pious people exercise higher levels of self-control (Tierney 2008).

But, beginning in the late 1960s, the presumption that religious people are less likely to engage in immoral or illegal behavior was challenged by criminologist Travis Hirschi and sociologist of religion Rodney Stark. While they were analyzing data on adolescent religiosity and delinquency that were gathered in Richmond, California, Hirschi and Stark (1969) were taken aback to find that regular church attendance did not make a teenager less likely to engage in a range of delinquent behaviors. And conversely, being unreligious did not make teenagers more likely to engage in delinquent behavior. More than 20 years later, Stark (1996) revisited these findings. He noted that subsequent research had at least occasionally confirmed the lack of a relationship between religiosity and delinquency (e.g., see Burkett and White 1974), and he pithily summarized that, at least in some communities, "Kids on their way home from Sunday school were as likely to strip your car as were kids on their way home from the pool hall." As these examples illustrate, being religious does not always, or even consistently, ensure that you will engage in moral and legal behavior. Something beyond individual religiosity is at work. To solve this puzzle, Stark stepped back from the question of whether going to church prevents a kid from engaging in deviant behavior. Instead, he focused on the broader social context—he is, after all, a *sociologist*! And he noted something intriguing. Studies that found a relationship between religiosity and good behavior at the individual level usually focused on communities where a lot of people are religious and attend church regularly (e.g., the South, the Northeast). Religion is infused throughout such communities. On the other hand, studies that found religious kids to be no more or no less deviant than nonreligious kids typically drew their samples from communities where the overall levels of religiosity, throughout the community, were much lower (e.g., the West). This led Stark to posit a truly *sociological* explanation for the relationship between religion and deviance: In communities where overall levels of religiosity are high, being religious protects against or prevents deviance. But in communities where overall levels of religiosity are low, individual religiosity has no effect on deviance one way or the other. Stark (1996) argues that, even if you are religious, whether you draw on religion to guide your behavior in your day-to-day life depends largely on how religious your friends are:

> Teenagers form and sustain their interpretations of norms in day-to-day interaction with their friends. If most of a young person's friends are not actively religious, then religious considerations will rarely enter into the process by which norms are accepted or justified. Even if the religious teenager does bring up religious considerations, these will not strike a responsive chord in most of the others. This is not to suggest that nonreligious teenagers don't believe in norms or discuss right and wrong, but they will do so without recourse to religious justifications. In such a situation, the effect of religiousness of some individuals will be smothered by group interference to religion, and religion will tend to become a very compartmentalized component of the individual's life—something that surfaces only in specific situations such as Sunday school and church. In contrast, when the majority of a teenager's friends are religious, then religion enters freely into everyday interactions and becomes a valid part of the normative system.
> (164)

In sum, for religion to be *activated* as a protection from deviance at the individual level, it must be a strong presence in the community as a whole, especially among those with whom you regularly interact. Individual religiosity alone is not enough.

And so we come back to the value of sociology as a discipline. Sociology focuses our attention beyond the individual. It asks questions that are bigger than "Is a religious person less likely to be deviant than a nonreligious person?" It asks questions instead about the social context within which we are embedded, what that context looks like, and how it affects both individuals and groups. We concede that it is far easier to study individuals and to measure their qualities and characteristics. But it is vitally important that we also find ways to "see" the social world that exists all around us and to discern its powerful effects on us.

What about the bad behavior by ministers, described by sociologist Anson Shupe as "clergy malfeasance"? How can religious leaders so egregiously violate the teachings and rules of their own religious groups? Evidence of clergy malfeasance has shaken the faith of many believers and their trust in their leaders. And, of course, they are justified in their concerns and doubts. But focusing only on individual misbehaving clergy may lead us to overlook important dimensions of clergy deviance.

In his 1995 monograph, *In the Name of All That's Holy: A Theory of Clergy Malfeasance*, Anson Shupe raises the broader question of how religious organizations respond to clergy malfeasance. He astutely points out that when cases of clergy malfeasance come to light, they are usually not one-time occurrences. Instead, they are part of a larger pattern of deviance by the malfeasant, often extending over many years and sometimes across multiple congregations. Given this finding, Shupe argues that it is just as important to understand the organizational contexts within which clergy deviance occurs and where it is often absorbed and hidden for many years. In particular, he points to the authority structure of the group—is authority centralized outside the local congregation, or is it embedded within the local group?—as a key determinant of how religious organizations respond to the bad behavior of clergy. Do they put a stop to it? Do they neutralize it—that is, frame it as inconsequential or not so harmful? Do they normalize it—that is, frame it as typical and acceptable? The Catholic Church in the United States had a practice of removing from their churches clergy who had been accused of child sexual abuse. Sometimes priests were sent off for "treatment." Other times, they were immediately moved to other parishes. The new churches were not, as a general rule, informed about the priest's history. Such organizational practices provide a context that perpetuates bad behavior on the part of individuals. They also form the legal basis for large damage awards for victims.

The *response* is vitally important to long-term patterns of clergy deviance; it determines whether one bad act turns into a long string of such acts or whether malfeasant clergy are stopped in their tracks early on. As Shupe points out, the behavior that we find so objectionable on the part of clergy is a product of individual choices, but it happens within a larger social context that we would do well to understand.

Keep in mind too that social contexts are complicated. Thus far, our discussion of morality has suggested fairly Black-and-White rule systems. Do this! Don't do that! But when it is embedded in real social worlds, morality is often not so clear. Yes, child sexual abuse or stealing money from a church is bad behavior. But when an authority figure—one who is considered to reflect or be connected to the sacred—engages in the behavior, complications arise. Can a victim challenge a sacred authority? Will people believe a victim or a leader? Are colleagues of the leader prepared to respond definitively to malfeasance? When religious organizations encounter deviance by religious professionals, extensive chains of command and complex bureaucratic rules may protect victims by rooting out and punishing perpetrators . . . or, rules and hierarchy may actually buffer the mal-feasant clergy from the consequences of his or her actions. The religious *belief* system, the system of morality, is one part of this context. But the religious group and its structure and practices are also important parts of the equation. This is another instance where sociology—with its focus on structure, culture, and practice, along with the interactions among these things—enriches our understanding of perplexing situations.

A Note on Violence and Moral Communities

The role of community in forming and supporting moral codes helps explain another conundrum that often perplexes students and one that we explored in depth when we discussed religious violence in Chapter 6. That is, how can religions that espouse peace and love simultaneously elicit violence on the part of followers?

The boundaries around moral communities are key. Religious violence is almost always per-petrated against those who are viewed as existing *outside* the moral community—primitives, subhumans, nonbelievers, enemies, heretics, heathens, and infidels. Typically, outsiders are seen as untrustworthy with respect to the community's moral prescriptions and proscriptions: Because outsiders are not tied to the moral community in meaningful ways, members of the moral community are generally skeptical, at best, and downright disbelieving, at worst, that outsiders might be equally human or capable of living by the same rules that bind the community. It is not that outsiders are not expected to follow the rules—they are, because the moral community views the rules as applying to all. Instead, because they lack ties to the community, they are not trusted to follow the rules. More important, however, outsiders are not granted the same rights to be treated according to the code that applies to insiders. Different rules apply to outsiders to the community, rules that allow them to be targets for what we understand as religiously motivated violence, even when such acts would be impermissible against members of the community.

"Gook" is an ugly word. U.S. soldiers used it as derogatory slang for locals during the Vietnam War. A tragic low point of the war was the My Lai massacre, in which American soldiers killed 128 Vietnamese civilians—elderly people, women, and children. Psychologist Herbert Kelman and sociologist V. Lee Hamilton (1989) examined the massacre to identify its proximate and ultimate causes. They concluded that, among other factors, dehumanization was a significant contributor to the massacre. They wrote that

> the inhibitions against murdering one's fellow human beings are generally so strong that the victims must also be stripped of their human status if they are to be subjected to systematic killing. Insofar as they are dehumanized, the usual principles of morality no longer apply to them.
>
> (1989, 19)

As we noted earlier, morality is integrally tied to membership in a community; moral standards that apply to insiders do not apply to outsiders because they lack that membership. Kelman and Hamilton identified two interrelated components of dehumanization:

> Victims are deprived in the perpetrators' eyes of the two qualities essential to being perceived as fully human and included in the moral compact that governs human relationships: *identity*—standing as independent, distinctive individuals, capable of making choices and entitled to live their own lives—and *community*—fellow membership in an interconnected network of individuals who care for each other and respect each other's individuality and rights. Thus, when a group is defined entirely in terms of a category to which they belong, and when this category is excluded from the human family, moral restraints against killing them are more readily overcome.
>
> (19)

The process of dehumanization—which applies almost exclusively to *outsiders* to the group—goes far toward explaining why religious groups and their members may do to outsiders what they would never consider doing to their own members (e.g., murdering, torturing, kidnapping children).

Moral Relativism?!

Morality and religion are also complicated by their sheer variety, as we described in Chapter 2. Standards for behavior—prescriptions, proscriptions, laws, rules, taken-for-granted patterns—are not universal. Instead they vary, sometimes a lot, across settings. This is especially apparent when we step back and examine moral systems in societies other than our own. Some of what we see is familiar. But much of what we see seems strange: behavior that seems rude, odd ways of raising children, strange foods and eating rituals, unfamiliar notions about the roles of the elderly, teenagers, or women. The list seems endless.

We sometimes forget how strange our own moral system seems to outsiders. That is, we take for granted that our own moral system follows obvious, true rules. Of course it is wrong for men to marry men! Of course people should receive blood transfusions that are needed to save their lives! Of course an elderly parent must live with his children at the end of his life when he can no longer take care of himself! But in some other moral system, you will find the opposite statement to be the taken-for-granted truth: Men marrying men, fine with us! Accepting a blood transfusion leads to eternal damnation! My dad will be best off in a nursing home! How can that be if morality is *true*?

No matter how objectively true or universal a moral system may feel, moral systems do not precede human communities. Instead, they are products of human communities; they come from the community. As a result, what we think is "good" or "right" is largely determined by the community in which we are embedded. But it is hard for us to step back and critically examine our own moral system because it seems so true to us.

In a way, "Do you need God to do good?" is a trick question because it assumes that "good" is objectively knowable. You probably have some notion of what "good" *is*, but your notion is specific to your context. Someone else, in a different context, might well define "good" differently. For example, in the United States, many people believe that it is good and right to provide extraordinary life-preserving care to people who are gravely ill, whether the ill person is a child or a 95-year-old man. What is the good of medical technologies if you don't use them to preserve human life? There is always hope! In other cultures, however, what we do in hospitals to gravely ill people is viewed as cruel: sticking needles in people, shoving tubes down their throats, isolating them in sterile hospital rooms, interfering with the natural course of their illnesses, pounding on their chests to restart their hearts. What is obviously right to some is not right to others. Moral systems both define what is good and guide our behavior, with more or less success depending on the strength of the moral system. But we should not take the definition of what is right and good for granted, because someone from a different social context may dispute it!

Sociologists are no different from anyone else. We hold strong and particular moral commitments, although we may not all agree on what those commitments should be. We also know, at least intellectually, that "good" is defined and produced by the specific society of which we are a part. Thus, when we ask—"Do we need God to do good?"—we are not really asking whether we need religion to do the universally transcendent right thing. Instead, we are asking whether we need religion to steer people toward what a given society has defined as good.

At this point, you might be hearing a ringing in your ears. It might sound something like moral relativism . . . moral relativism . . . moral relativism: the idea that there are a variety of equally valid moral systems out there. Sometimes moral relativism is invoked analytically. In these cases, it reflects the empirical reality that moral systems vary across settings and presumes that morality is less a fixed truth and more a product of specific human societies. Taking a moral-relativist stance allows an observer to see multiple moral systems on their own terms. Often, however, moral relativism is invoked pejoratively, as a criticism of anyone who acknowledges the reality or validity of alternative systems. Those who use the term "moral relativism" pejoratively typically view morality—specifically, their own—to be an absolute, transcendent, universal truth. They see other moralities as inferior, less developed, or simply wrong.

However strongly we may believe in our own understandings of right and wrong, rejecting other systems out of hand is problematic. Why? Because it interferes with dispassionate observation of the unfamiliar: Feeling disgust or distaste for that which is unfamiliar makes it very hard to understand others on their own terms. Does that mean that sociologists are moral relativists who believe that "anything goes," as some claim? Of course not: Even as sociologists recognize the variety of moral systems and their functions in a range of societies, we retain personal moral convictions. For many of us, that includes a belief in an ultimate good or a single God. Just because we recognize a range of moral systems and take them seriously as objects of study does not mean that we deny the precepts of our own morality.

Concluding Thoughts

People do not need a "god" or a religion in order to do good. Nevertheless, religion most often strengthens human community, and does so because it lends stability by imbuing good behavior with transcendent meaning linked to a sacred cosmos. We don't just do something because a parent told us so, but because our religious community agrees and, ultimately, because the higher power in which we believe has ordained it as good and right. And, as we have discussed, neither individual religiosity nor religion collectively ensures that we do "good." Like other social institutions, religion is at least in part a human product. And like other institutions—politics, the military, education, family—it can work well or it can work poorly. It can do good or it can do harm.

The sociological lens provides tools to step back and examine religion's effects on our world today. And those effects are wide-ranging. There is a tremendous variety of religious belief and practice around the world. Religion forms our identity, not just our *religious* identity but how we understand race and ethnicity, nationality, social class, gender, and sexual identity. Religion molds our relations with other people—those in our religious group, those who believe something else, and those who reject religious belief altogether. It shapes how we view other nations and peoples and how we collectively interact with them. Religion is implicated in how we treat our natural world and whether we value scientific and technological advances. Some try to argue that religion is all good, and others that it is all bad. We merely argue that religion *is*.

Charles Darwin thought a lot about religion, especially as his developing theory of evolution began to challenge the religious beliefs with which he had been raised. He observed that "a belief in all-pervading spiritual agencies seems to be universal; and apparently follows from a considerable advance in man's reason, and from a still greater advance in his faculties of imagination, curiosity and wonder" (1871, 513). We concur. The varieties of religions, created by humans to connect themselves to a transcendent and sacred cosmos (which may or may not exist, but that is beyond the limits of science to know), are acts of creativity. Think about it. Rather than settling for what we can observe with our five senses, we seek the unseen. Rather than accepting life as mere random chance, we seek larger meaning. Rather than stumbling through each day, moment to moment, we search for order in what can appear a complex and chaotic world. And we do so through an endless variety of religions around the world. This variety and its impact on every corner of our lives is a testament to the richness of humanity.

Suggested Reading

Bellah, Robert. 1967. "Civil Religion in America." *Daedelus* 96(1): 1–21.
Berger, Peter. 1967. *The Sacred Canopy*. Garden City, NY: Doubleday.
Durkheim, Emile. 1973. *Moral Education: A Study in the Theory and Application of Sociology of Education*. New York: Free Press.

Bibliography

Abusharaf, Rogaia Mustafa. 1998. "Structural Adaptations in an Immigrant Muslim Congregation in New York." In *Gatherings in Diaspora Religious Communities and the New Immigration*, edited by R. Stephen Warner and Judith G. Wittner, 235–261. Philadelphia: Temple University Press.

African Methodist Episcopal (AME) Church. 2016. *AME Church Climate Change Resolution*. www.amechurch.com/wp-content/uploads/2016/07/AME-Climate-Change-Resolution.pdf Last accessed 1/9/22.

Aiken, William, Tatsushi Arai, Asoka Bandarage et al. 2015. *The Time to Act is Now: Buddhist Declaration on Climate Change*. https://fore.yale.edu/files/buddhist_climate_change_statement_5-14-15.pdf Last accessed 1/9/22.

Almond, Gabriel A., R. Scott Appleby, and Emmanuel Sivan. 2003. *Strong Religion: The Rise of Fundamentalisms Around the World*. Chicago: University of Chicago Press.

Almond, Gabriel A., R. Scott Appleby, and Emmanuel Sivan. 2006. *Evolution on the Frontline: An Abbreviated Guide for Teaching Evolution, from Project 2061 at AAAS*. Washington, DC: Author.

Almond, Gabriel A., R. Scott Appleby, and Emmanuel Sivan. 2008. *Questions and Answers on Evolution*. www.aaas.org/news/press_room/evolution/pdf/QA_Evolution.pdf

Ammerman, Nancy T. 1987. *Bible Believers: Fundamentalists in the Modern World*. New Brunswick, NJ: Rutgers University Press.

Anderson, Keith, and Elizabeth Drescher. 2018. *Click2Save Reboot: The Digital Ministry Bible*. New York: Church Publishing.

Anglican Consultative Council and the Anglican Communion Environmental Network. 2015. *The World is Our Host: A Call to Urgent Action for Climate Justice*. https://acen.anglicancommunion.org/media/148818/The-World-is-our-Host-FINAL-TEXT.pdf Last accessed 1/9/22.

Antoun, Richard T. 2001. *Understanding Fundamentalism: Christian, Islamic, and Jewish Movements*. Walnut Creek, CA: AltaMira.

Armstrong, Karen. 2005. *The Spiral Staircase: My Climb Out of Darkness*. New York: Anchor.

Association of Theological Schools. 2021. *Fact Book on Theological Education, 2020–2021*. Pittsburgh: The Association of Theological Schools.

Avishai, Orvit. 2008. "Doing Religion in a Secular World: Women in Conservative Religions and the Question of Agency." *Gender and Society* 22(4): 409–433.

Bader, Christopher D., Joseph O. Baker, and F. Carson Mencken. 2017. *Paranormal America: Ghost Encounters, UFO Sightings, Bigfoot Hunts, and Other Curiosities in Religion and Culture*. New York: New York University Press.

Bahai International Community. 2008. *Seizing the Opportunity: Redefining the Challenge of Climate Change*. www.bic.org/statements/seizing-opportunity-redefining-challenge-climate-change Last accessed 1/9/22.

Bailey, Amy K., and Karen A. Snedker. 2011. "Practicing What They Preach? Lynching and Religion in the American South, 1890–1929." *American Journal of Sociology* 117(3): 844–887.

Baker, Wayne E. 2005. *America's Crisis of Values: Reality and Perception*. Princeton, NJ: Princeton University Press.

Baltzell, E. Digby. 1964. *The Protestant Establishment: Aristocracy and Caste in America*. New York: Vintage Books.

Baptist Press. 2008. *2007 SBC resolution: 'On Global Warming.'* March 10. https://www.baptistpress.com/resource-library/news/2007-sbc-resolution-on-global-warming/

Barrett, David B. 2001. *World Christian Encyclopedia*. New York: Oxford University Press.

Basch, Linda, Nina Glick Schiller, and Christina Szanton Blanc. 1994. *Nations Unbound: Transnational Projects, Postcolonial Predicaments, and Deterritorialized Nation'states*. Basel, Switzerland: Gordon and Breach.

Basedau, Matthais., Georg Strüver, Johannes Vüllers, and Tim Wegenast. 2011. "Do Religious Factors Impact Armed Conflicts? Empirical Evidence from Sub-Saharan Africa." *Terrorism and Political Violence* 23(5): 752–779.

BBC. 2014a. "Buddhism: Theravada Buddhism." *BBC Religion and Ethics.* www.bbc.co.uk/religion/religions/buddhism/subdivisions/theravada_1.shtml

BBC. 2014b. "Hinduism: Texts." *BBC Religion and Ethics.* www.bbc.co.uk/religion/religions/hinduism/texts/texts.shtml

Beaman, Lori. 1999. *Shared Beliefs, Different Lives: Women's Identities in Evangelical Context.* St. Louis, MO: Chalice Press.

Beaman, Lori. 2003. "The Myth of Pluralism, Diversity and Vigor: The Constitutional Privileging of Protestantism in the United States and Canada." *Journal for the Scientific Study of Religion* 42(3): 311–325.

Beech, Hannah, and Hadi Azmi. 2021. "Transgender Woman Flees Malaysia After Prison Threat for Wearing Hijab." *New York Times*, October 21: A10.

Bellah, Robert. 1967. "Civil Religion in America." *Daedelus* 96(1): 1–21.

Bellah, Robert, Richard Madsen, William M. Sullivan, Ann Swidler, and Steven M. Tipton. 1985. *Habits of the Heart: Individualism and Commitment in American Life.* New York: Harper and Row, Publishers.

Berger, Peter. 1963. *Invitation to Sociology.* Garden City, NY: Doubleday.

Berger, Peter. 1967. *The Sacred Canopy: Elements of a Sociological Theory of Religion.* Garden City, NY: Doubleday.

Berger, Peter. 1992. *A Far Glory: The Quest for Faith in the Age of Credulity.* New York: Free Press.

Berger, Peter. 1999. "The Desecularization of the World: A Global Overview." In *The Desecularization of the World: Resurgent Religion and World Politics*, edited by Peter Berger, 1–18. Washington, DC: Ethics and Policy Center.

Beyer, Peter. 1997. "Religious Vitality in Canada: The Complementarity of Religious Market and Secularization Perspectives." *Journal for the Scientific Study of Religion* 36(2): 272–288.

Beyer, Peter. 2003. "Constitutional Privilege and Constituting Pluralism: Religious Freedom in National, Global and Legal Context." *Journal for the Scientific Study of Religion* 42(3): 333–339.

Bird, Warren, and Scott Thumma. 2020. *Megachurch 2020: The Changing Reality in America's Largest Churches-Report.* Hartford, CT: Hartford Institute for Religion Research.

Blau, Peter M., and Joseph E. Schwartz. 1984. *Crosscutting Social Circles: Testing a Macrostructural Theory of Intergroup Relations.* New York: Academic Press.

Blight, David W. 2018. *Frederick Douglass: Prophet of Freedom.* New York: Simon & Schuster.

Bloom, Paul. 2005. "Is God an Accident?" *Atlantic Monthly* 296(5): 105–112.

Blum, Edward J. 2016. "Slaves, Slavery and the Secular Age." In *Race and Secularism,* edited by Jonathan S. Khan and Vincent H. Lloyd, 77–98. New York: Columbia University Press.

Bock, Darrell, and Daniel B. Wallace. 2008. *Dethroning Jesus: Exposing Popular Culture's Quest to Unseat the Biblical Christ.* Nashville, TN: Thomas Nelson.

Boston, John. 2003. "At Long Last, Going to Church Finally Pays." *Online.* www.the=signal.com/News/ViewStory.asp?storyID=2906

Boswell, John. 1994. *Same-Sex Unions in Premodern Europe.* New York: Villard.

Bourdieu, Pierre. 1986. "The Forms of Capital." In *Handbook of Theory and Research for the Sociology of Education,* edited by John G. Richardson, 241–258. Westport, CT: Greenwood Press.

Boyd, H. H. 1999. "Religion and the Environment in the American Public." *Journal for the Scientific Study of Religion* 38(1): 36–44.

Bramson, Aaron, Patrick Grim, Daniel J. Singer et al. 2017. "Understanding Polarization: Meanings, Measures, and Model Evaluation." *Philosophy of Science* 84(1): 115–159.

Brasher, Brenda E. 2004. *Give Me that Online Religion.* New Brunswick, NJ: Rutgers University Press.

Brown, Davis. 2019. "Measuring Patterns of Political Secularization and Desecularization: Did They Happen or Not?" *Journal for the Scientific Study of Religion* 58(3): 570–590.

Brubaker, Pamela Jo, and Michel M. Haigh. 2017. "The Religious Facebook Experience: Uses and Gratifications of Faith-based Content." *Social Media and Society* (April–June): 1–11.

Bruce, Steve. 2000. *Fundamentalism.* Malden, MA: Blackwell.

Bruce, Steve. 2016. "The Sociology of Late Secularization: Social Divisions and Religiosity." *British Journal of Sociology* 67(4): 613–631.

Bunt, Gary R. 2000. "Surfing Islam: Ayatollahs, Shayks, and Hajjis on the Superhighway." In *Religion on the Internet: Research Prospects and Promises,* edited by Jeffrey K. Hadden and Douglas E. Cowan, 127–151. New York: JAI-Elsevier Science, Inc.

Burke, Kelsy C. 2012. "Women's Agency in Gender-Traditional Religions: A Review of Four Approaches." *Sociological Compass* 6(2): 122–133.

Burkett, Steven R., and Mervin White. 1974. "Hellfire and delinquency: Another look." *Journal for the Scientific Study of Religion* 13(4): 455–462.

Cadge, Wendy. 2005. "Lesbian, Gay and Bisexual Buddhist Practitioners." In *Gay Religion,* edited by

Scott Thumma and Edward R. Gray, 139–153. New York: Altamira Press.

Campbell, Heidi A. 2005. *Exploring Religious Community Online: We are One in the Network*. New York: Peter Lang Publishing, Inc.

Campbell, Heidi A. 2010. *When Religion Meets New Media*. London: Routledge.

Campbell, Heidi A. 2011. "Religion and the Internet in the Israeli Orthodox Context." *Israel Affairs* 17(3): 364–383.

Campbell, Heidi A. 2012. "How Religious Communities Negotiate New Media Religiously." In *Digital Religion, Social Media, and Culture*, edited by Pauline H. Cheong, Peter Fischer-Nielsen, Stefan Gelfgren, and Charles Ess, 81–96. New York: Peter Lang Publishing, Inc.

Campbell, Heidi A. (ed.). 2013. *Digital Religion: Understanding Religious Practice in New Media Worlds*. New York: Routledge.

Campbell-Reed, Eileen R. 2019. "No Joke! Resisting the Culture of Disbelief that keeps Clergy Women Pushing Uphill." *Crosscurrents* (March): 29–38.

Carlson, John. 2021. *Biden's Inaugural Speech Called for Americans to Embrace Civil Religion. What Does that Mean?* NBCnews.com. https://www.nbcnews.com/think/opinion/biden-s-inaugural-speech-called-americans-embrace-civil-religion-what-ncna1255084

Carson, Rachel. 1962. *Silent Spring*. New York: Houghton Mifflin.

Carter, Stephen. 1993. *The Culture of Disbelief: How American Law and Politics Trivializes Religious Devotion*. New York: Anchor.

Chai, Karen J. 1998. "Competing for the Second Generation: English-Language Ministry at a Korean Protestant Church." In *Gatherings in Diaspora Religious Communities and the New Immigration*, edited by R. Stephen Warner and Judith G. Wittner, 295–331. Philadelphia: Temple University Press.

Chai, Karen J. 2001a. "Beyond 'Strictness' to Distinctiveness: Generational Transition in Korean Protestant Churches." In *Korean Americans and Their Religions: Pilgrims and Missionaries from a Different Shore*, edited by Ho Youn Kwon, Kwang Chung Kim, and R. Stephen Warner, 157–180. University Park, PA: The Pennsylvania State University Press.

Chai, Karen J. 2001b. "Intra-Ethnic Religious Diversity: Korean Buddhists and Protestants in Greater Boston." In *Korean Americans and Their Religions: Pilgrims and Missionaries from a Different Shore*, edited by Ho Youn Kwon, Kwang Chung Kim, and R. Stephen Warner, 273–294. University Park, PA: The Pennsylvania State University Press.

Charles, Mark, and Soong Chan Rah. 2019. *Unsettling Truths: The Ongoing, Dehumanizing Legacy of the Doctrine of Discovery*. Downers Grove, IL: InterVarsity Press.

Chaves, Mark. 1994. "Secularization as Declining Religious Authority." *Social Forces* 72(3): 749–774.

Chaves, Mark. 1997. *Ordaining Women: Culture and Conflict in Religious Organizations*. Cambridge, MA: Harvard University Press.

Chaves, Mark, Peter J. Schraeder, and Mario Sprindys. 1994. "State Regulation of Religion and Muslim Religious Vitality in the Industrialized West." *The Journal of Politics* 56(4): 1087–1097.

Chen, Carolyn. 2008. *Getting Saved in America: Taiwanese Immigration and Religious Experience*. Princeton, NJ: Princeton University Press.

Cheong, Pauline Hope. 2013. "Authority." In *Digital Religion: Understanding Religious Practice in New Media Worlds*, edited by Heidi A. Campbell, 72–87. New York: Routledge.

Cheong, Pauline Hope, Peter Fischer-Nielsen, Stefan Gelfgren, and Charles Ess (eds.). 2012. *Digital Religion, Social Media, and Culture*. New York: Peter Lang Publishing, Inc.

Christ, Carol P. 2007. "Why Women Need the Goddess." In *Women's Studies in Religion: A Multicultural Reader*, edited by Kate Bagley and Kathleen McIntosh, 163–174. Upper Saddle River, NJ: Prentice Hall Publishers.

Christerson, Brad, Korie L. Edwards, and Michael O. Emerson. 2005. *Against All Odds: The Struggle for Racial Integration in Religious Organizations*. New York: New York University Press.

Christerson, Brad, and Michael O. Emerson. 2003. "The Costs of Diversity in Religious Organizations: An In-Depth Case Study." *Sociology of Religion* 64:163–182.

Christianity Today. 2001. "Eco-myths." *Christianity Today*, June. www.christianitytoday.com/ct/2001/juneweb-only/6-25-32.0.html?start = 1

Cloke, Paul, Callum Sutherland, and Andrew Williams. 2016. "Postsecularity, Political Resistance, and Protest in the Occupy Movement." *Antipode* 48(3): 497–523.

CNN. 2005. "School Board to Appeal Ruling to Remove Evolution Stickers." January 18. www.cnn.com/2005/LAW/01/18/evolution.stickers/

CNN. 2001. *Falwell Apologizes to Gays, Feminists, and Lesbians: September 14*. www.cnn.com/2001/US/09/14/Falwell.apology/

Cone, James H. 1969. *Black Theology and Black Power*. Maryknoll, NY: Orbis Books.

Cone, James H. 1986. *A Black Theology of Liberation*. Maryknoll, NY: Orbis Books.

Cone, James H. 2003. *The God of the Oppressed*. Maryknoll, NY: Orbis Books.

Congregation for the Doctrine of the Faith. 2003. *Considerations Regarding Proposals to Give Legal Recognition to Unions between Homosexual Persons.* www.vatican.va/roman_curia/congregations/cfaith/documents/rc_con_cfaith_doc_20030731_homosexual-unions_en.html

Cooper, Angela. 2021. "Using a Spiritual Director to Help Guide Your Way." *The New York Times*, January 13. www.nytimes.com/2021/01/13/style/self-care/spiritual-directors-faith-religion.html

Cooper, Anna J. [1892] 1988. *A Voice from the South.* New York: Oxford University Press.

Coreno, Thaddeus. 2002. "Fundamentalism as Class Culture." *Sociology of Religion* 63(3): 335–360.

Coser, Lewis A. 1956. *The Functions of Social Conflict.* Glencoe, IL: The Free Press.

Cousineau, Madeleine. 1998. "The Brazilian Catholic Church and Land Conflicts in the Amazon." In *Religion, Mobilization, and Social Action*, edited by Anson Shupe and Bronislaw Misztal, 85–99. Westport, CT: Praeger.

Cragun, Ryan T., J. E. Sumerau, and Emily Williams. 2015. "From Sodomy to Sympathy: LDS Elites' Discursive Construction of Homosexuality Overtime." *Journal of the Scientific Study of Religion* 54(2): 291–310.

Craig, Robert H. 1992. *Religion and Radical Politics: An Alternative Christian Tradition in the United States.* Philadelphia: Temple University Press.

Crawford, Sue E. S., and Laura R. Olson. 2003. "Clergy as Political Actors in Urban Contexts." In *Christian Clergy in American Politics*, edited by Sue E. S. Crawford and Laura R. Olson, 104–119. Baltimore: Johns Hopkins University Press.

Cronron, Kerith J., Shoshana K. Goldberg, and Kathyrn O'Neill. 2020. *Religiosity Among LGBT Adults in the U.S.* Los Angeles, CA: The Williams Institute.

Cunningham, Lawrence S. 2002. "Murder in Palermo: Who Killed Father Puglisi?" *Commonweal* CXXIX(17): (October 11).

Curtis, Susan. 1991. *A Consuming Faith: The Social Gospel and Modern American Culture.* Baltimore, MD: The Johns Hopkins University.

Dallas Morning News. 2005. *10 Ideas on the Way Out.* November 27: pp. 1P, 5P.

Darnell, Alfred, and Darren E. Sherkat. 1997. "The Impact of Protestant Fundamentalism on Educational Attainment." *American Sociological Review* 62(2): 306–315.

Darwin, Charles. 1871. *The Descent of Man.* New York: Penguin Classics.

Darwin, Helana. 2018. "Redoing Gender, Redoing Religion." *Gender and Society* 32(3): 348–370.

Darwin, Helana. 2020. "Navigating the Religious Gender Binary." *Sociology of Religion* 81(2): 185–205.

Davidson, James D., and Ralph E. Pyle. 2011. *Ranking Faiths: Religious Stratification in America.* New York: Rowman & Littlefield.

Davie, Grace. 1994. *Religion in Britain Since 1945: Believing Without Belonging.* Oxford: Blackwell Publishers.

Day, Katie. 2001. "Putting It Together in the African American Churches: Faith, Economic Development, and Civil Rights." In *Religion and Social Policy*, edited by Paula D. Nesbitt, 181–195. New York: Alta Mira Press.

Dearie, James. 2018. "Sourcing Enlightenment: Changing Media Breaks Open Spiritual Guidance for Younger Catholics." *National Catholic Reporter*, December 14–27: 1a.

Delahanty, Jack. 2018. "The Emotional Management of Progressive Religious Mobilization." *Sociology of Religion* 79(2): 248–272.

Demerath, N. J., and Rhys H. Williams. 1992. "Secularization Assessed: The Abridging of Faith in a New England City." *Journal for the Scientific Study of Religion* 31(2): 189–206.

Dias, Elizabeth. 2021. "Facebook's Next Target: The Religious Experience." *New York Times*, July 25. www.nytimes.com/2021/07/25/us/facebook-church.html

Dias, Elizabeth, and Ruth Graham. 2021. "A Movement Buttressed by Grievance and God." *New York Times*, January 11. www.nytimes.com/2021/01/11/us/how-white-evangelical-christians-fused-with-trump-extremism.html

Dilmaghani, Maryam. 2020. "Measuring Religious Polarization: Application with American and Canadian Data." *Studies in Religion* 49(4): 507–524.

Dobbelaere, Karel. 1999. "Toward an Integrated Perspective of the Processes Related to the Descriptive Concept of Secularization." *Sociology of Religion* 60(3): 229–247.

Dorrien, Gary J. 2015. *The New Abolition: W.E.B. Du Bois and the Black Social Gospel.* New Haven: Yale University Press.

Dorrien, Gary J. 2018. "True Religion, Mystical Unity, and the Disinherited: Howard Thurman and the Black Social Gospel." *American Journal of Theology and Philosophy* 39(1): 74–99.

Douglass, Frederick. [1845] 1995. *Narrative Life of Frederick Douglass.* Mineola, NY: Dover Publications.

Drescher, Elizabeth. 2011. *Tweet If You Heart Jesus: Practicing Church in the Digital Reformation.* New York: Morehouse Publishing.

Drumm, Rene. 2005. "No Longer an Oxymoron: Integrating Gay and Lesbian Seventh Day Adventist Identities." In *Gay Religion*, edited by

Scott Thumma and Edward R. Gray, 47–66. New York: Altamira Press.

Du Bois, W. E. B. [1935] 2007. *Black Reconstruction in America: An Essay Toward a History of the Part which Black Folk Played in the Attempt to Reconstruct Democracy in America, 1860–1880*. New York: Oxford University Press.

Durkheim, Emile. 1895 (1982 trans). *The Rules of Sociological Method*. New York: Free Press.

Durkheim, Emile. 1912 (1995 trans). *Elementary Forms of Religious Life*. Translated by J. W. Swain. New York: Free Press.

Durkheim, Emile. 1973. *Moral Education: A Study in the Theory and Application of Sociology of Education*. New York: Free Press.

Ebaugh, Helen Rose, and Janet Saltman Chafetz. 2000. *Religion and the New Immigrants: Continuities and Adaptations in Immigrant Congregations*. Walnut Creek, CA: AltaMira Press.

Echchaibi, Nabil. 2013. "Alt-Muslim: Muslims and Modernity's Discontents." In *Digital Religion: Understanding Religious Practice in New Media Worlds*, edited by Heidi A. Campbell, 190–198. New York: Routledge.

Eck, Diana. 2001. *A New Religious America*. San Francisco: Harper San Francisco.

Eckberg, D. L., and T. J. Blocker. 1989. "Varieties of Religious Involvement and Environmental Concern." *Journal for the Scientific Study of Religion* 13(4): 19–32.

Eckberg, D. L., and T. J. Blocker. 1996. "Christianity, Environmentalism, and the Theoretical Problem of Fundamentalism." *Journal for the Scientific Study of Religion* 35(4): 343–355.

Ecklund, Elaine Howard. 2005. "Different Identity Accounts for Catholic Women." *Review of Religious Research* 47(2): 135–149.

Ecklund, Elaine Howard. 2006. *Korean American Evangelicals: New Models for Civic Life*. New York: Oxford University Press.

Edgell, Penny. 1998. "Making Inclusive Communities: Congregations and the 'Problem' of Race." *Social Problems* 45(4): 451–472.

Edwards, Korie L. 2008. *The Elusive Dream: The Power of Race in Interracial Churches*. New York: Oxford University Press.

Ehrman, Bart. 2005. *Lost Christianities: The Battles for Scripture and the Faiths We Never Knew*. New York: Oxford University Press.

Ehrman, Bart. 2007. *Misquoting Jesus*. New York: HarperOne.

Ellingson, Stephen. 2007. *The Megachurch and the Mainline: Remaking Religious Tradition in the Twenty-First Century*. Chicago: University of Chicago Press.

Ellingson, Stephen. 2016. *To Care for Creation: The Emergence of the Religious Environmental Movement*. Chicago: University of Chicago Press.

Emerson, Michael O. 2006. *People of the Dream: Multiracial Congregations in the United States*. Princeton, NJ: Princeton University Press.

Emerson, Michael O., and Christian Smith. 2000. *Divided by Faith: Evangelical Religion and the Problem of Race in America*. New York: Oxford University Press.

Emerson, Michael O., Elizabeth Korver-Glenn, and Kiara W. Douds. 2015. "Studying Race and Religion: A Critical Assessment." *Sociology of Race and Ethnicity* 1(3): 349–359.

Episcopal Church. 2021. *LGBTQ in the Church*. www.episcopalchurch.org/who-we-are/lgbtq

Equal Justice Initiative. 2020. *Reconstruction in America: Racial Violence after the Civil War, 1865–1676--Report*. Montgomery, AL: Equal Justice Initiative, Inc.

Ethridge, Maurice F., and Joe R. Feagin. 1979. "Varieties of Fundamentalism." *Sociological Quarterly* 20: 37–48.

Evangelical Climate Initiative. 2006. *Climate Change: An Evangelical Call to Action*. www.christiansandclimate.org/statement/ Last accessed 1/9/22.

Evans, John H. 2002. "Polarization in Abortion Attitudes in U.S. Religious Traditions, 1972–1998." *Sociological Forum* 17(3): 397–422.

Fadiman, Anne. 1997. *The Spirit Catches You and You Fall Down*. New York: Noonday.

Feldman, Noah. 2008. "What Is It about Mormonism?" *New York Times Magazine*, January 6.

Fingerhut, Hannah. 2016. *Support Steady for Same-Sex Marriage and Acceptance of Homosexuality—Report*. Washington, DC: Pew Research Center.

Finke, Roger. 1992. "An Unsecular America." In *Religion and Modernization: Sociologists and Historians Debate the Secularization Thesis*, edited by Steve Bruce. New York: Oxford University Press.

Finke, Roger, and Rodney Stark. 2000. "The New Holy Clubs: Testing Church-to-Sect Propositions." *Sociology of Religion* 62(2): 175–190.

Foley, Michael W., and Dean R. Hoge. 2007. *Religion and the New Immigrants: How Faith Communities Form Our Newest Citizens*. New York: Oxford University Press.

Foner, Eric. 2014. *Reconstruction: America's Unfinished Revolution, 1863–1877*, Updated Edition. New York: HarperCollins Publishers.

Fredrickson, George M. 1981. *White Supremacy: A Comparative Study in American and South African History*. New York: Oxford University Press.

Freeman, Curtis W. 2007. '"Never Had I Been So Blind: W. A. Criswells Change on Racial Segregation."' *Journal of Southern Religion* 10: 1–12.

Fuist, Todd N. 2016. "'It Just Always Seemed Like It Wasn't a Big Deal, Yet I Knew for Some People, They Really Struggle with It.': LGBT Religious Identities in Context." *Journal for the Scientific Study of Religion* 55(4): 770–786.

Fussell, Paul. 1983. *Class: A Guide Through the American Status System.* New York: Touchstone Books.

Gallup Poll. 2001. "Americans Belief in Psychic and Paranormal Phenomena is Up Over Last Decade.'" *Online Report*, June 8, 2001. www.gallup.com/poll/4483/Americans-Belief-Psychic-Paranormal-Phenomena-Over-Last-Decade.aspx

Gallup Poll. 2005. "Paranormal Beliefs Come (Super) Naturally to Some." *Online Report*, November 1, 2005. https://news.gallup.com/poll/19558/Paranormal-Beliefs-Come-SuperNaturally-Some.aspx

Garces-Foley, Kathleen. 2007. *Crossing the Ethnic Divide: The Multiethnic Church on a Mission.* New York: Oxford University Press.

Gecewicz, Claire. 2018. *'New Age' Beliefs Common Among Both Religious and Nonreligious Americans.* Washington, DC: Pew Research Center.

Geertz, Clifford. 1966. "Religion as a Cultural System." In *Anthropological Approaches to the Study of Religion*, edited by M. Banton, 1–45. London: Tavistock.

Gerth, Hans H., and C. Wright Mills (eds.). 1964. *From Max Weber: Essays in Sociology.* New York: Oxford University Press.

Gervais, Christine L. M. 2012. "Canadian Women Religious' Negotiation of Feminism and Catholicism." *Sociology of Religion* 73(4): 384–410.

Glendinning, Tony, and Steve Bruce. 2006. "New Ways of Believing or Belonging: Is Religion Giving Way to Spirituality?" *The British Journal of Sociology* 57(3): 399–414.

Glueck, Sheldon, and Eleanor Glueck. 1950. *Unraveling Juvenile Delinquency.* Cambridge, MA: Harvard University Press.

Goode, Erich. 2011. *The Paranormal: Who Believes, Why They Believe, and Why It Matters.* New York: Prometheus Books.

Grant, August E., Amanda F. C. Sturgill, Chiung Hwang Chen, and Daniel A. Stout (eds.). 2019. *Religion Online: How Digital Technology is Changing the Way We Worship and Pray.* Santa Barbara, CA: Praeger.

Greeley, Andrew. 1993. "Religion and Attitudes toward the Environment." *Journal for the Scientific Study of Religion* 32(1): 19–28.

Greene, Anne-Marie, and Mandy Robbins. 2015. "The Cost of a Calling? Clergywomen and Work in the Church of England." *Gender, Work and Occupation* 22(4): 405–420.

Griffin, Wendy. 1995. "The Embodied Goddess: Feminist Witchcraft and Female Divinity." *Sociology of Religion* 56(1): 35–48.

Griffith, Derek M., and Emily K. Cornish. 2018. "What Defines a Man? Perspectives of African American Men on Components and Consequences of Manhood." *Psychology of Men & Masculinity* 19(1): 78–88.

Guth, James L., Linda Beail, Greg Crow, Beverly Gaddy, Steve Montreal, Brent Nelson, James Penning, and Jeff Walz. 2003. "The Political Activity of Evangelical Clergy in the Election of 2000." *Journal for the Scientific Study of Religion* 42(4): 501–514.

Guth, James L., J. C. Green, L. A. Kellstedt, and C. E. Smidt. 1995. "Faith and the Environment: Religious Beliefs and Attitudes on Environmental Policy." *American Journal of Political Science* 39(2): 364–382.

Guth, James L., L. A. Kellstedt, C. E. Smidt, and J. C. Green. 1993. "Theological Perspectives and Environmentalism among Religious Activists." *Journal for the Scientific Study of Religion* 32(4): 373–382.

Gutman, Herbert G. 1966. "Protestantism and the American Labor Movement: The Christian Spirit in the Gilded Age." *American Historical Review* 72(October): 74–101.

Gutterman, David S. 2005. *Prophetic Politics: Christian Social Movements and American Democracy.* Ithaca: Cornell University Press.

Hadden, Jeffrey K., and Douglas E. Cowan. 2000. "The Promised Land or Electronic Chaos? Toward Understanding Religion on the Internet." In *Religion on the Internet: Research Prospects and Promises*, edited by Jeffrey K. Hadden and Douglas E. Cowan, 3–21. New York: JAI-Elsevier Science, Inc.

Halker, Clark D. 1991. *For Democracy, Workers, and God: Labor Song Poems and Labor Protest, 1865–1895.* Urbana: University of Illinois Press.

Hamilton, David L., and Tina K. Trolier. 1986. "Stereotype and Stereotyping: An Overview of the Cognitive Approach." In *Prejudice, Discrimination, and Racism*, edited by John F. Davidio and Samuel L. Gaertner, 127–163. Orlando, FL: Academic Press.

Hammond, Philip E. 1974. "Religious Pluralism and Durkheims Integration Thesis.'" In *Changing Perspectives in the Scientific Study of Religion*, edited by A. Eister, 115–142. New York: Wiley.

Hancock, Rosemary. 2015. "Is there a Paradox of Liberation and Religion? Muslim Environmentalists, Activism, and Religious Practice." *Journal for the Academic Study of Religion* 28(1): 42–60.

Hand, C., and K. Van Liere. 1984. "Religion, Mastery-Over-Nature and Environmental Concern." *Social Forces* 63: 255–270.

Hane, Mikiso. 1991. *Premodern Japan: A Historical Survey*. Boulder, CO: Westview Press.

Hanf, Theodor. 1994. "The Sacred Marker: Religion, Communalism, and Nationalism." *Social Compass* 41: 9–20.

Harakas, Stanley. 2005. "The Stand of the Orthodox Church on Controversial Issues." *Greek Orthodox Archdiocese of America*. www.goarch.org/ourfaith/ourfaith7101

Harris, Sam. 2004. *The End of Faith: Religion, Terror and the Future of Reason*. New York: Norton.

Harris, Sam. 2006. *Letter to a Christian Nation*. New York: Knopf.

Hart, Stephen. 1992. *What Does the Lord Require: How American Christians Think about Economic Justice*. New Brunswick: Rutgers University Press.

Hartford Institute for Religion Research. 2020. *Megachurch Definition—Report*. Hartford, CT: Hartford Institute for Religion Research.

Hartman, Keith. 1996. *Congregations in Conflict: The Battle over Homosexuality*. New Brunswick, NJ: Rutgers University Press.

Harvey, Paul. 2016. "Civil Rights Movement and Religion in America." In *Oxford Research Encyclopedia of Religion*, 1–22. New York: Oxford University Press.

Harvey, Paul. 2020. *Howard Thurman and the Disinherited: A Religious Biography*. Grand Rapids, MI: William B. Eerdmans Publishing Company.

Hechter, Michael. 1987. *Principles of Social Solidarity*. Berkeley: University of California Press.

Heclo, Hug. 2007. *Christianity and American Democracy*. Cambridge, MA: Harvard University Press.

Heidari, Nahid, Mehrdad Abdullahzadeh, and Sayid Ali Naji. 2021. "Lived Religious and Spiritual Experiences of Transgender People: A Qualitative Research in Iran." *Sexuality & Culture* 25: 417–429.

Henninger, Daniel. 2008. "Mad Max and the Meltdown: How We Went from Christmas to Crisis." *The Wall Street Journal*, November 20: A19.

Herberg, Will. 1955. *Protestant, Catholic, Jew: An Essay in American Religious Sociology*. Garden City, NY: Doubleday.

Herron, Arika. 2019. "Woman Says Roncalli Fired Her for Supporting 2 Employees Fired Over Same-sex Marriages." *Indy Star*, October 24. www.indystar.com/story/news/education/2019/10/24/woman-says-roncalli-fired-her-supporting-employees-fired-over-same-sex-marriages/2387527001/

Hewstone, Miles, Jos Jaspers, and Mansur Lalljee. 1992. '"Social Representations, Social Attribution and Social Identity: The Intergroup Images of Public and Comprehensive."' *European Journal of Social Psychology* 12: 241–269.

Hidayatullah, Aysha A. 2014. "Feminist Interpretation of the Qur'an in a Comparative Feminist Setting." *Journal of Feminist Studies in Religion* 30(2): 115–129.

Hirschi, Travis, and Rodney Stark. 1969. "Hellfire and Delinquency." *Social Problems* 17(2): 202–213.

Hitchens, Christopher. 2007. *God Is Not Great: How Religion Poisons Everything*. New York: Twelve.

Hogg, Michael A., and Dominic Abrams. 1988. *Social Identifications: A Social Psychology of Intergroup Relations and Group Processes*. London: Routledge.

Hollinger, David. 1995. *Postethnic America: Beyond Multiculturalism*. New York: Basic Books.

Holy and Great Council of the Orthodox Church Ecumenical Patriarchate. 2015. *Environmental Justice and Peace*. www.orthodoxcouncil.org/-the-green-patriarch- Last accessed 1/9/22.

Hoover, Steward M. 2012. "Forward: Practice, Autonomy, and Authority in the Digitally Religious and Digitally Spiritual." In *Digital Religion, Social Media, and Culture: Perspectives, Practices, and Futures*, edited by Pauline Hope Cheong, Peter Fischer-Nielsen, Stefan Gelfgren, and Charles Ess, vii–xii. New York: Peter Lang Publishing, Inc.

Hout, Michael, and Claude S. Fischer. 2002. "Why More Americans Have No Religious Preference: Politics and Generations." *American Sociological Review* 67(2): 165–190.

Hout, Michael, and Claude S. Fischer. 2014. "Explaining Why More Americans Have No Religious Preference: Political Backlash and Generational Succession, 1987–2012." *Sociological Science* 1(October): 423–447.

Houtman, Dick, and Stef Aupers. 2007. "The Spiritual Turn and the Decline of Tradition: The Spread of Post-Christian Spirituality in 14 Western Countries, 1981–2000." *Journal for the Scientific Study of Religion* 46(3): 305–320.

Howard, John W., and Myron Rothbart. 1980. "Social Categorization and Memory for In-Group and Out-Group Behavior." *Journal of Personality and Social Psychology* 38: 301–310.

Hunter, James D. 1989. *Culture Wars: The Struggle to Define America*. New York: Basic Books.

Iannaccone, Larry R. 1997. '"Toward an Economic Theory of Fundamentalism."' *Journal of Institutional and Theoretical Economics* 153: 100–116.

Interfaith Power and Light. 2020. *Poll: Voters of Faith Supporting Climate Change*. https://climatenexus.org/media/2015/09/IPL-National-Climate-Change-Poll-Press-Release.pdf Last accessed 1/9/22.

Intergovernmental Panel on Climate Change. 2021. *Climate Change 2021: The Physical Science Basis*. www.ipcc.ch/report/ar6/wg1/downloads/report/IPCC_AR6_WGI_Full_Report.pdf Last accessed 1/9/22.

International Islamic Climate Change Symposium. 2015. *Islamic Declaration on Global Climate Change.* www.ifees.org.uk/wp-content/uploads/2020/01/islamic_declaration_v4.pdf Last accessed 1/9/22.

Itzhaky, Haya, and Karni Kissil. 2015. "'It's a Horrible Sin. If They Find Out, I Will Not Be Able to Stay': Orthodox Jewish Gay Men's Experiences Living in Secrecy." *Journal of Homosexuality* 62: 621–643.

Jackle, Sebastian, and Georg Wenzelburger. 2015. "Religion, Religiosity, and the Attitudes Toward Homosexuality—A Multilateral Analysis of 79 Countries." *Journal of Homosexuality* 62: 207–241.

Jacobsen, Douglas. 2011. *The World's Christians: Who They are, Where They are, and How They got There.* Malden, MA: Wiley-Blackwell.

Janssen, Dirk-Jan and Peer Scheepers. 2019. "How Religiosity Shapes Rejection of Homosexuality Across the Globe." *Journal of Homosexuality* 66(14): 1974–2001.

Jenkins, Philip. 2002. *The Next Christendom: The Coming of Global Christianity.* New York: Oxford University Press.

Jenkins, Philip. 2004. *Dream Catchers: How Mainstream America Discovered Native Spirituality.* New York: Oxford University Press.

Jenkins, Philip. 2006. *The New Faces of Christianity: Believing the Bible in the Global South.* New York: Oxford University Press.

Jennings, Willie J. 2010. *The Christian Imagination: Theology and the Origins of Race.* New Haven, CT: Yale University Press.

Jeung, Russell. 2005. *Faithful Generations: Race and New Asian American Churches.* New Brunswick, NJ: Rutgers University Press.

Johnson, Curtis. 1989. *Islands of Holiness: Rural Religion in Upstate New York, 1790–1860.* Ithaca: Cornell University Press.

Jones, Jeffrey M. 2021. "U.S. Church Membership Falls Below Majority for First Time-Report." *Gallup Poll,* March 29, 2021. https://news.gallup.com/poll/341963/church-membership-falls-below-majority-first-time.aspx

Jones, Steve. 1999. *Almost Like a Whale: The Origin of Species Updated.* New York: Doubleday.

Juergensmeyer, Mark. 2003. *Terror in the Mind of God: The Global Rise of Religious Violence,* 3rd Edition. Berkeley: University of California Press.

Kallinen, Timo. 2019. "Revealing the Secrets of Others (on YouTube): New and Old in the Public Representations of Ghanaian Traditional Religion." *Suomen Antropologi* 44(1): 30–50.

Kanagy, Conrad L., and Hart M. Nelsen. 1995. "Religion and Environmental Concern: Challenging the Dominant Assumptions." *Review of Religious Research* 37(1): 33–45.

Kane, Nazneen. 2018. "Priestesses unto the Most High God: Gender, Agency, and the Politics of LDS Women's Temple Rites." *Sociological Focus* 51(2): 97–110.

Kanter, Rosebeth M. 1977. "Some Effects of Proportions on Group Life: Skewed Sex Ratios and Responses to Token Women." *American Journal of Sociology* 82: 965–991.

Kasselstrand, Isabella. 2019. "Secularity and Irreligion in Cross-National Context: A Nonlinear Approach." *Journal for the Scientific Study of Religion* 58(3): 626–642.

Keister, Lisa A. 2011. *Faith and Money: How Religion Contributes to Wealth and Poverty.* New York: Cambridge University Press.

Kelley, Robin D. G. 2008. *Freedom Dreams: The Black Radical Imagination.* Boston, MA: Beacon Press.

Kelman, Herbert, and V. Lee Hamilton. 1989. "The My Lai Massacre: A Military Crime of Obedience." In *Crimes of Obedience,* 1–20. New Haven: Yale University Press.

Kgatle, Mookgo S. 2018. "Social Media and Religion: Missological Perspective on the Link Between Facebook and the Emergence of Prophetic Churches in Southern Africa." *Verbum et Ecclesia* 39(1): 1–6.

Kim, Andrew Eungi. 2018. "Minjung Theology in Contemporary Korea: Liberation Theology and a Reconsideration of Secularization Theory." *Religions* 9(12): 1–17.

King, Martin Luther, and James M. Washington. [1963] 1991. *A Testament of Hope: The Essential Writings of Martin Luther King, Jr.* San Francisco, CA: HarperOne.

Kniss, Fred. 2003. "Mapping the Moral Order: Depicting the Terrain of Religious Conflict and Change." In *Handbook of the Sociology of Religion,* edited by Michelle Dillon, 331–347. New York: Cambridge University Press.

Kniss, Fred, and Paul D. Numrich. 2007. *Sacred Assemblies and Civic Engagement: How Religion Matters for America's Newest Immigrants.* New Brunswick, NJ: Rutgers University Press.

Krakauer, Jon. 2003. *Under the Banner of Heaven: A Story of Violent Faith.* New York: Doubleday.

Krogh, Marilyn C., and Brooke A. Pillifant. 2004. "Kemetic Orthodoxy: Ancient Egyptian Religion on the Internet." *Sociology of Religion* 65(2): 167–175.

Krull, Laura M. 2020. "Liberal Churches and Social Justice Movements: Analyzing the Limits of Inclusivity." *Journal for the Scientific Study of Religion* 59(1): 84–100.

Kurien, Prema. 1998. "Becoming American by Becoming Hindu: Indian Americans Take Their Place at the Multicultural Table." In *Gatherings in Diaspora: Religious Communities and the New Immigration*, edited by R. Stephen Warner and Judith G. Warner, 37–70. Philadelphia: Temple University Press.

Kurtz, Leslie. 1995. *Gods in the Global Village: The World's Religions in Sociological Perspective*. Thousand Oaks, CA: Pine Forge Press.

Kwon, Ho-Youn, Kwang Chung Kim, and R. Stephen Warner. 2001. *Korean Americans and Their Religions: Pilgrims and Missionaries from a Different Shore*. University Park, PA: The Pennsylvania State University Press.

Lawrence, Bruce B. 1989. *Defenders of God: The Fundamentalist Revolt Against the Modern Age*. San Francisco: Harper & Row.

Lechner, Frank J. 1991. "The Case Against Secularization: A Rebuttal." *Social Forces* 69(4): 1103–1119.

Lee, Robert. 1964. "Introduction: Religion and Social Conflict." In *Religion and Social Conflict*, edited by Robert Lee and Martin E. Marty, 3–8. New York: Oxford University Press.

Leiken, Robert S. 2005. "Europe's Angry Muslims." *Foreign Affairs*, July/August.

Lernoux, Penny. 1982. *Cry of the People*. New York: Penguin Books.

Levitt, Peggy. 2007. *God Needs No Passport: Immigrants and the Changing American Religious Landscape*. New York: The New Press.

Linville, Patricia W., Peter Salovey, and Gregory W. Fischer. 1986. "Stereotyping and Perceived Distributions of Social Characteristics: An Application to Ingroup—Outgroup Perception." In *Prejudice, Discrimination, and Racism*, edited by John F. Davidio and Samuel L. Gaertner, 165–208. Orlando, FL: Academic Press.

Liu, Yingling, and Paul Froese. 2020. "Faith and Agency: The Relationships Between Sense of Control, Socioeconomic Status, and Beliefs About God." *Journal for the Scientific Study of Religion* 59(2): 311–326.

Lizardo, Omar A., and Albert J. Bergesen. 2003. "Types of Terrorism by World System Location." *Humboldt Journal of Social Relations* 27: 162–192.

Luckmann, Thomas. 1967. *The Invisible Religion*. New York: The MacMillan Company.

Luhman, Niklas. 1989. "Functional Differentiation." In *Social Theory: Roots and Branches*, 2d Edition, edited by Peter Kivisto, 194–199. Los Angeles: Roxbury Publishing Company.

Lund, Stefan (ed.). 2020. *Immigrant Incorporation, Education, and the Boundaries of Belonging*. Cham, Switzerland: Springer Nature Switzerland.

Lundby, Knut. 2012. "Dreams of Church in Cyberspace." In *Digital Religion, Social Media, and Culture: Perspectives, Practices, and Futures*, edited by Pauline Hope Cheong, Peter Fischer-Nielsen, Stefan Gelfgren, and Charles Ess, 25–42. New York: Peter Lang Publishing, Inc.

Lynd, Robert S., and Helen Merrell Lynd. 1929. *Middletown: A Study in American Culture*. New York: Harcourt-Brace.

Lyon, Carter D. 2017. *Sanctuaries of Segregation: The Story of the Jackson Church Visit Campaign*. Jackson, MS: The University Press of Mississippi.

Madan, T. N. 2006. "Thinking Globally about Hinduism." In *The Handbook of Global Religions*, edited by Mark Juergensmeyer, 15–24. New York: Oxford University Press.

Mahaffy, Kimberly A. 1996. "Cognitive Dissonance and its Resolution: A Study of Lesbian Christians." *Journal for the Scientific Study of Religion* 35: 392–402.

Marsden, George M. 1980. *Fundamentalism and American Culture: The Shaping of Twentieth-Century Evangelicalism 1870–1925*. New York: Oxford University Press.

Marti, Gerardo. 2005. *A Mosaic of Believers: Diversity and Innovation in a Multiethnic Church*. Bloomington: Indiana University Press.

Martin, Michel. 2018. "Slave Bible from the 1800s Omitted Key Passages that Could Incite Rebellion." *National Public Radio*. December 9. https://www.npr.org/2018/12/09/674995075/slave-bible-from-the-1800s-omitted-key-passages-that-could-incite-rebellion

Marty, Martin E. 1964. "Epilogue: The Nature and Consequences of Social Conflict for Religious Groups." In *Religion and Social Conflict*, edited by Robert Lee and Martin E. Marty, 173–193. New York: Oxford University Press.

Marx, Karl. 1843 (1970 trans). *Contribution to the Critique of Hegel's Philosophy of the Law*. Cambridge: Cambridge University Press.

Masci, David. 2016. *How Income Varies Among U.S. Religious Groups*. Washington, DC: Pew Research Center.

Maxwell, Bill. 2003. "A Capital Suggestion for Church Diversity." *St. Petersburg Times online*. www.sptimes.com/2003/08/03/Columns/A_capital_suggestion_.shtml

McAllister, Ronald J. 1998. "The Mobilization of Prophecy: A Challenge to the Churches of Northern Ireland." In *Religion, Mobilization, and Social Action*, edited by Anson Shupe and Bronislaw Misztal, 160–173. Westport, CT: Praeger.

McCloud, Sean, and William A. Mirola. 2008. *Religion and Class in America: Culture, History, and Politics*. Boston, MA: Brill Publishers.

McDaniel, Eric. 2003. "Black Clergy in the 2000 Election." *Journal for the Scientific Study of Religion* 42(4): 533–546.

McGreal, Chris. 2006. "McDonald's Changes its Brand to Suit Kosher Appetites." *Guardian International Pages*, March 13: 25.

McGuire, Meredith B. 1997. *Religion: The Social Context*, 4th Edition. Belmont, CA: Wadsworth Publishing Company.

McKinley, Jr., James C. 2001. "Church and State: Seeking Complicity in Genocide." *The New York Times*, June 10.

McRoberts, Omar M. 1999. "'Understanding the 'New' Black Pentecostal Activism: Lessons from Ecumenical Urban Ministries in Boston." *Sociology of Religion* 60(1): 47–70.

Mears, Daniel P., and Christopher G. Ellison. 2000. "Who Buys New Age Materials? Exploring Sociodemographic, Religious, Network, and Contextual Correlates of New Age Consumption." *Sociology of Religion* 61(3): 289–313.

Migheli, Matteo. 2019. "Religious Polarization, Religious Conflicts and Individual Financial Satisfaction: Evidence from India." *Review of Developmental Economics* 23: 803–829.

Miller, Brian J., Peter Mundey, and Jonathan P. Hill. 2013. "Faith in the Age of Facebook: Exploring the Links Between Religion and Social Network Site Membership and Use." *Sociology of Religion* 74(2): 227–253.

Mills, C. Wright. 1959. *The Sociological Imagination*. New York: Oxford University Press.

Min, Pyong Gap. 2010. *Preserving Ethnicity Through Religion in America*. New York: New York University Press.

Mirola, William A. 2003a. "Asking for Bread, Receiving a Stone: The Rise and Fall of Religious Ideologies in Chicago's Eight-Hour Movement." *Social Problems* 50(2): 273–293.

Mirola, William A. 2003b. "Religious Protest and Economic Conflict: Possibilities and Constraints on Religious Resource Mobilization and Coalitions in Detroit's Newspaper Strike." *Sociology of Religion* 64(4): 443–462.

Mirola, William A. 2009. "Class Differences in Attitudes about Business, Economics, and Social Welfare among Indianapolis Catholics and Protestants." In *Religion and Class in America: Culture, History, and Politics*, edited by Sean McClud and William A. Mirola, 133–158. Boston, MA: Brill Publishers.

Montalvo, Jose, and Marta Reynal-Querol. 2000. "The Effect of Ethnic and Religious Conflict on Growth." IVIE WP-EC 2000-04. An updated version can be found in http://www.wcfio.harvard.edu/programs/prpes

Moore, Laura M., and Reeve Vanneman. 2003. "Context Matters: Effects of the Proportion of Fundamentalists on Gender Attitudes." *Social Forces* 82: 115–139.

Murphy, Caryle. 2016. *The Most and Least Educated U.S. Religious Groups*. Washington, DC: Pew Research Center.

Musa, Bala A., and Ibrahim M. Ahmadu. 2012. "New Media, Wikifaith and Church Brandversation: A Media Ecology Perspective." In *Digital Religion, Social Media, and Culture: Perspectives, Practices, and Futures*, edited by Pauline Hope Cheong, Peter Fischer-Nielsen, Stefan Gelfgren, and Charles Ess, 63–80. New York: Peter Lang Publishing, Inc.

Need, Ariana, and Geoffrey Evans. 2001. "Analyzing Patterns of Religious Participation in Post-Communist Eastern Europe." *British Journal of Sociology* 52(2): 229–248.

Neitz, Mary Jo. 2005. "Queering the Dragonfest: Changing Sexualities in a Post-Patriarchal Religion." In *Gay Religion*, edited by Scott Thumma and Edward R. Gray, 259–280. New York: Altamira Press.

Nesbitt, Paula D. 1993. "Dual Ordination Tracks: Differential Benefits and Costs for Men and Women Clergy." *Sociology of Religion* 54(1): 13–30.

Nesbitt, Paula D. 2016. *Why Gender Still Matters: Continuing the Toolkit into the Future*. www.episcopalchurch.org/cast-wide-the-net/why-gender-still-matters/

Ng, Nancy, and Andreas Fulda. 2017. "The Religious Dimension of Hong Kong's Umbrella Movement." *Journal of Church and State* 60(3): 377–397.

Niebuhr, H. Reinhold. 1932. *Moral Man and Immoral Society: A Study in Ethics and Politics*. New York and London: C. Scribner's.

Niebuhr, H. Reinhold. 1987 [1929]. *The Social Sources of Denominationalism*. Gloucester, MA: Henry Holt & Co.

Nye, Ivan. 1958. *Family Relationships and Delinquent Behavior*. Westport, CT: Greenwood Publishing.

Obama, Barack. 2008. *Transcript of Barack Obama's Victory Speech*, November 5. Chicago, IL. https://www.npr.org/2008/11/05/96624326/transcript-of-barack-obamas-victory-speech/

Ogland, Curtis P., and Ana Paula Verona. 2014. "Religion and the Rainbow Struggle: Does Religion Factor into Attitudes toward Homosexuality and Same-sex Civil Unions in Brazil." *Journal of Homosexuality* 61: 13334–1349.

O'Leary, Stephen D. 1996. "Cyberspace as Sacred Space: Communicating Religion on Computer Networks." *Journal of the American Academy of Religion* 64: 781–808.

Olson, Daniel V. A. 1993. "Fellowship Ties and the Transformation of Religious Identity." In *Beyond Establishment: Protestant Identity in a Post-Protestant Age*, edited by Jackson Carroll and Wade Clark Roof, 32–53. Louisville: Westminster/John Knox Press.

Olson, Laura J. 2017. "Negotiating Meaning through Costume and Social Media in Bulgarian Muslims' Communities of Practice." *Nationalities Papers* 45(4): 560–580.

Olson, Laura R. 2000. *Filled With Spirit and Power: Protestant Clergy in Politics*. New York: SUNY Press.

Olson, Roger E., Frank S. Mead, Samuel S. Hill, and Craig D. Atwood. 2018. *Handbook of Denominations in the United States*, 14th Edition. Nashville, TN: Abingdon Press.

Owens, J. Garfield. 1971. *All God's Chillun: Meditations of Negro Spirituals*. Nashville, TN: Abingdon Press.

Page, Sarah-Jane. 2014. "The Scrutinized Priest: Women in the Church of England Negotiating Profession and Sacred Clothing Regimes." *Gender, Work and Occupation* 21(4): 295–307.

Park, Jerry Z., and Joseph Baker. 2007. "What Would Jesus Buy: American Consumption and Spiritual Material Goods." *Journal for the Scientific Study of Religion* 46(4): 501–517.

Patillo, Mary. 2008. "Race, Class, and Neighborhoods." In *Social Class: How Does It Work*, edited by Annette Lareau and Dalton Conley, 264–292. New York: Russell Sage Foundation.

Pavlik, Steve. 1992. "The U.S. Supreme Court Decision on Peyote in Employment Division vs. Smith: A Case Study in the Suppression of Native American Religious Freedom." *Wicazo Sa Review* 8(2): 30–39.

Pearce, Lisa D., and Melinda Lundquist Denton. 2011. *A Faith of their Own: Stability and Change in the Religiosity of America's Adolescents*. New York: Oxford University Press.

Peart, Norman A. 2000. *Separate No More: Understanding and Developing Racial Reconciliation in Your Church*. Grand Rapids, MI: Baker Books.

Perry, Samuel. 2022. "American Religion in the Era of Increasing Polarization." *Annual Review of Sociology* 48: 1.

Perry, Samuel L. 2015. "Bible Beliefs, Conservative Religious Identity, and Same-sex Marriage Support: Examining Main and Moderating Effect." *Journal for the Scientific Study of Religion* 54(4): 792–813.

Perry, Samuel L., and Andrew L. Whitehead. 2016. "Religion and Public Opinion toward Same-Sex Relations, Marriage, and Adoption: Does the Type of Practice Matter?" *Journal for the Scientific Study of Religion* 55(3): 637–651.

Peterson, Richard A., and N. J. Demerath, III. 1942. "Introduction." In *Millhands and Preachers*, by Liston Pope, xvii–xl. New Haven: Yale University Press.

Pettigrew, Thomas, and Joanne Martin. 1987. "Shaping the Organizational Context for Black American Inclusion." *Journal of Social Issues* 43: 41–78.

Pevey, Carolyn, Christine L. Williams, and Christopher G. Ellison. 1996. "Male God Imagery and Female Submission: Lessons from a Southern Baptist Ladies' Bible Class." *Qualitative Sociology* 19(2): 173–193.

Pew Forum on Religion and Public Life. 2008. *Trends in Candidate Preferences among Religious Groups*, November 3. http://pewforum.org/docs/?DocID=349

Pew Forum on Religion and Public Life. 2012. *Nones on the Rise: One-in-Five Adults Have No Religious Affiliation*. Washington, DC: Pew Research Center.

Pew Research Center. 2007. *Muslim Americans: Middle Class and Mostly Mainstream*. Washington, DC: Pew Research Center.

Pew Research Center. 2014. *The Changing U.S. Religious Landscape: Findings from the 2014 U.S. Religious Landscape Survey*. Washington, DC: Pew Research Center.

Pew Research Center. 2015a. *The Future of World Religions: Population Growth Projections, 2010–2050*. Washington, DC: Pew Research Center. www.pewforum.org/2015/04/02/religious-projections-2010-2050/

Pew Research Center. 2015b. *U.S. Catholics Open to Non-traditional Families*. Washington, DC: Pew Research Center.

Pew Research Center. 2015c. *America's Changing Religious Landscape: Christians Decline Sharply as Share of Population, Unaffiliated and Other Faiths Continue to Grow*. Washington, DC: Pew Research Center. www.pewforum.org/2015/05/12/chapter-2-religious-switching-and-intermarriage/

Pew Research Center. 2015d. *U.S. Public Becoming Less Religious*. Washington, DC: Pew Research Center. www.pewforum.org/2015/11/03/u-s-public-becoming-less-religious/

Pew Research Center. 2016. *The Gender Gap in Religion Around the World*. Washington, DC: Pew Research Center. www.pewforum.org/2016/03/22/the-gender-gap-in-religion-around-the-world/

Pew Research Center. 2017a. *The Changing Global Religious Landscape*. Washington, DC: Pew Research Center. www.pewforum.org/2017/04/05/the-changing-global-religious-landscape/pf-04-05-2017_-projectionsupdate-00-07/

Pew Research Center. 2017b. *More Americans Now Say They're Spiritual but Not Religious*. Washington, DC: Pew Research Center. www.pewresearch.

org/fact-tank/2017/09/06/more-americans-now-say-theyre-spiritual-but-not-religious/

Pew Research Center. 2019. *In a Politically-Polarized Era, Sharp Divides in Both Partisan Coalitions—Report*. Washington, DC: Pew Research Center. www.pewresearch.org/politics/2019/12/17/in-a-politically-polarized-era-sharp-divides-in-both-partisan-coalitions/

Phillips, Rick. 2004. "Can Rising Rates of Church Participation be a Consequence of Secularization?" *Sociology of Religion* 65(2): 139–153.

Pope Francis. 2015. *Encyclical Letter: Laudato si' of our Holy Father Francis on Care for Our Common Home*. Rome: Vatican. www.vatican.va/content/francesco/en/encyclicals/documents/papa-francesco_20150524_enciclica-laudato-si.html   Last accessed 1/9/22.

Pope, Liston. 1942. *Millhands and Preachers*. New Haven: Yale University Press.

Pouschter, Jacob, and Nicholas Kent. 2020. *The Global Divide on Homosexuality Persists—Report*. Washington, DC: Pew Research Center.

Povoledo, Elisabette, and Ruth Graham. 2021. "Vatican Prohibits Blessing of Same-sex Unions." *New York Times*, March 16: A13.

Presbyterian Church, USA. 2006. *Theological Task Force on Peace, Unity, and Purity of the Church, Final Report*. www.pcusa.org/peaceunitypurity/

Presbyterian Church, USA. 2008. *Book of Order*. Louisville, KY: General Assembly of the Presbyterian Church, USA.

Prickett, Pamela J. 2015. "Negotiating Gendered Religious Space: The Particularities of Patriarchy in an African American Mosque." *Gender and Society* 29(1): 51–72.

Promise Keepers. 2008. *History of Promise Keepers*. www.promisekeepers.org/about/pkhistory

Putnam, Robert D., and David E. Campbell. 2010. *American Grace: How Religion Divides and Unites Us*. New York: Simon & Schuster.

Quammen, David. 1997. *Song of the Dodo: Island Biogeography in an Age of Extinction*. New York: Scribner.

Raboteau, Albert J. 2004. *Slave Religion: The "Invisible Institution" in the Antebellum South*. New York: Oxford University Press.

Rashi, Tsuriel. 2013. "The Kosher Cell Phone in Ultra-Orthodox Society: A Technological Ghetto within the Global Village?" In *Digital Religion: Understanding Religious Practice in New Media Worlds*, edited by Heidi A. Campbell, 173–181. New York: Routledge.

Reimer, Sam. 2007. "Class and Congregations: Class and Religious Affiliation at the Congregational Level of Analysis." *Journal for the Scientific Study of Religion* 46(4): 583–594.

Rhoades, Todd. 2004. *Paying People to Attend Church Plan Fails*, September 23. www.mmiblog.com/monday_morning_insight_we/2004/09/index.html

Riesebrodt, Martin. 1990 (1993 trans). *Pious Passion: The Emergence of Modern Fundamentalism in the United States and Iran*. Translated by D. Reneau. Berkeley: University of California Press.

Riesebrodt, Martin. 2000. "Fundamentalism and the Resurgence of Religion." *Numen* 47: 266–287.

Rinaldo, Rachel. 2019. "Obedience and Authority among Muslim Couples: Negotiating Gendered Religious Scripts in Contemporary Indonesia." *Sociology of Religion* 80(3): 323–349.

Robbins, Mandy, and Anne-Marie Greene. 2018. "Clergywomen's Experience of Ministry in the Church of England." *Journal of Gender Studies* 27(8): 890–900.

Robinson, Leland W. 1987. "When Will Revolutionary Movements Use Religion?" In *Church—State Relations: Tensions and Transitions*, edited by Thomas Robbins and Roland Robertson, 53–63. New Brunswick, NJ: Transaction Books.

Rodriguez, Eric M., and Suzanne C. Ouellette. 2000. "Gay and Lesbian Christians: Homosexual and Religious Identity Integration in the Members of a Gay-Positive Church." *Journal for the Scientific Study of Religion* 39(3): 333–347.

Roof, Wade Clark. 1998. "Modernity, the Religious, and the Spiritual." *The Annals of the American Academy of Political and Social Science* 558(July): 211–224.

Roof, Wade Clark. 1999. *Spiritual Marketplace: Baby Boomers and the Remaking of American Religion*. Princeton: Princeton University Press.

Rose, Fred. 2000. *Coalitions Across the Class Divide: Lessons from the Labor, Peace, and Environmental Movements*. Ithaca, NY: Cornell University Press.

Rowell, Reverend Jeren. 2003. "The Law of Love." In *Sermon delivered at the Inaugural Chapel of the Wynkoop Center for Women in Ministry, Nazarene Theological Seminary*. www.wynkoopcenter.org/index.php?option=com_content&task=view&id=40&Itemid=69

Savastano, Peter. 2005. " 'Saint Gerard Teaches Him that Love Cancels that Out': Devotion to St. Gerard Maiella among Italian American Catholic Gay Men in Newark, New Jersey." In *Gay Religion*, edited by Scott Thumma and Edward R. Gray, 181–202. New York: Altamira Press.

Schieman, Scott. 2010. "Socioeconomic Status and Beliefs about God's Influence in Everyday Life." *Sociology of Religion* 7(1): 25–51.

Schieman, Scott, Christopher Ellison, and Alex Berman. 2010. "Religious Involvement, Beliefs about God, and the Sense of Mattering Among Older Adults." *Journal for the Scientific Study of Religion* 49(3): 317–335.

Schleifer, Cyrus, and Amy D. Miller. 2017. "Occupational Gender Inequality among American Clergy, 1976–2016: Revisiting the Stained-Glass Ceiling." *Sociology of Religion* 78(4): 387–410.

Schnabel, Landon. 2015. "How Religious are American Women and Men? Gender Differences and Similarities." *Journal for the Scientific Study of Religion* 54(3): 616–622.

Schnabel, Landon, Conrad Hackett, and David McClendon. 2018. "Where Men Appear More Religious Than Women: Turning a Gender Lens on Religion in Israel." *Journal for the Scientific Study of Religion* 57(1): 80–94.

Schnoor, Randal F. 2006. "Being Gay and Jewish: Negotiating Intersecting Identities." *Sociology of Religion* 67(1): 43–60.

Schroeder, Ralph, Noel Heather, and Raymond M. Lee. 1998. "The Sacred and the Virtual: Religion in the Multi-User Virtual Reality." *Journal of Computer-Mediated Communication* [Online] 4(2). www.jcmc.indian.edu/vol4/issue2/Schroeder.html

Schwadel, Philip. 2011. "The Effects of Education on Americans' Religious Practices, Beliefs, and Affiliations." *Review of Religious Research* 53(2): 161–182.

Schwadel, Philip. 2012. "Social Class and Finding a Congregation: How Attendees are Introduced to Their Congregations." *Review of Religious Research* 54(4): 543–554.

Schwadel, Philip. 2016. "Does Higher Education Cause Religious Decline? A Longitudinal Analysis of the Within- and Between-Person Effects of Higher Education on Religiosity." *The Sociological Quarterly* 57: 759–786.

Schwadel, Philip, and Aleksandra Sandstrom. 2019. *Lesbian, Gay, and Bisexual Americans are Less Religious than Straight Adults by Traditional Measures—Report.* Washington, DC: Pew Research Center.

Scully, Sean. 2005. "Breathtaking Inanity: How Intelligent Design Flunked its Test Case." *Time,* December 20.

Sered, Susan Starr. 1994. *Priestess, Mother, Sacred Sister. Religions Dominated by Women.* New York: Oxford University Press.

Severson, Alexander W., and Eric A. Coleman. 2015. "Moral Frames and Climate Change Policy Attitudes." *Social Science Quarterly* 96(5): 1277–1290.

Sherkat, Darren E. 2017. "Sexuality and Religious Commitment Revisited: Exploring the Religious Commitments of Sexual Minorities, 1991–2014." *Journal for the Scientific Study of Religion* 55(4): 770–786.

Shulman, Robin. 2008. "Humanist parents seek communion outside church." *The Washington Post,* December 21: A10.

Shupe, Anson. 1995. *In the Name of All That's Holy: A Theory of Clergy Malfeasance.* Westport, CT: Praeger Publishers.

Silko, Leslie Marmon. 1977. *Ceremony.* New York: Penguin.

Simmons, L. B. 1994. *Organizing in Hard Times: Labor and Neighborhoods in Hartford.* Philadelphia: Temple University Press.

Slama, Martin. 2018. "Practising Islam through Social Media in Indonesia." *Indonesia and the Malay World* 46(134): 1–4.

Smidt, Corwin, Sue Crawford, Melissa Deckman, Donald Gray. Dan Hofrenning, Laura Olson, Sherrie Steiner, and Beau Weston. 2003. "Political Attitudes and Activities of Mainline Protestant Clergy in the Election of 2000: A Study of Six Denominations." *Journal for the Scientific Study of Religion* 42(4): 515–532.

Smith, Adam. 1776 [1965]. *An Inquiry into the Nature and Causes of the Wealth of Nations.* New York: Modern Library.

Smith, Christian. 1996a. *Disruptive Religion: The Force of Faith in Social Movement Activism.* New Brunswick, NJ: Rutgers University Press.

Smith, Christian. 1996b. *Resisting Reagan: The U.S. Central American Peace Movement.* Chicago: University of Chicago Press.

Smith, Christian. 1998. *American Evangelicalism: Embattled and Thriving.* Chicago: University of Chicago Press.

Smith, Christian. 2003. *The Secular Revolution: Power, Interests, and Conflict in the Secularization of American Public Life.* Berkeley: University of California Press.

Smith, Christian, and Robert Faris. 2005. "Socioeconomic Inequality in the American Religious System." *Journal for the Scientific Study of Religion* 44: 95–104.

Smith, Christian, and Melinda Lundquist Denton. 2005. *Soul-Searching: The Religious and Spiritual Lives of American Teenagers.* New York: Oxford University Press.

Smith, Drew R. 2001. "Churches and the Urban Poor: Interaction and Social Distance." *Sociology of Religion* 62(3): 301–313.

Smith, J. Harold. 1950. *God's Plan for the Races.* University of Central Arkansas Archives and Special Collections. Fayetteville, AR: University of Arkansas Libraries.

Smith, Peter J., and Elizabeth Smythe. 2017. "Faith Groups and Justice: A Source of Solidarity or Division in the Global Justice Movement the

World Social Forum and Occupy Wall Street as Case Studies." *Globalizations* 14(7): 1140–1156.

Smith, Timothy L. 1978. "Religion and Ethnicity in America." *The American Historical Review* 83: 1155–1185.

Sointu, Eeva, and Linda Woodhead. 2008. "Spirituality, Gender, and Expressive Selfhood." *Journal for the Scientific Study of Religion* 47(2): 259–276.

Southern Baptist Climate Environment and Climate Initiative. 2008. *A Southern Baptist Declaration on the Environment and Climate Change.* www.baptist-creationcare.org/node/1/ Last accessed 1/9/22.

Spiro, Melford. 1966. "Religion: Problems of Definition and Explanation." In *Anthropological Approaches to the Study of Religion*, edited by M. Banton, 85–126. London: Tavistock.

Stacey, William, and Anson Shupe. 1982. "Correlates of Support for the Electronic Church." *Journal for the Scientific Study of Religion* 21(4): 291–303.

Stack, Liam. 2020. "On a Remote Rosh Hashana, Tradition and Technology Meet." *New York Times*, September 19: A5.

Stack, Liam. 2021. "Brooklyn Diocese Fires Gay Teacher Who Wed." *New York Times*, October 28: A21.

Stanton, Zack. 2021. "How the 'Culture War' Could Break Democracy," *Politico*. https://www.politico.com/news/magazine/2021/05/20/culture-war-politics-2021-democracy-analysis-489900 Last accessed 12/12/2021.

Stark, Rodney. 1996. "Religion as Context: Hellfire and Delinquency One More Time." *Sociology of Religion* 57(2): 163–173.

Stark, Rodney. 1999. "Secularization, R.I.P." *Sociology of Religion* 60(3): 249–274.

Stark, Rodney. 2015. *The Triumph of Faith*. Wilmington, DE: ISI Books.

Straarup, Jorgen. 2012. "When Pinocchio Goes to Church: Exploring an Avatar Religion." In *Digital Religion, Social Media, and Culture*, edited by Pauline Hope Cheong, Peter Fischer-Nielsen, Stefan Gelfgren, and Charles Ess, 97–111. New York: Peter Lang Publishing, Inc.

Sukhmani, Pal, and Chetan Sinha. 2016. "Religious Fundamentalism, Right-Wing Authoritarianism, and Homophobia Among Hindus." *Indian Journal of Health and Wellbeing* 7(7): 717–721.

Sullivan, Kathleen. 2000. "St. Catherine's Catholic Church: One Church, Parallel Congregations." In *Religion and the New Immigrants*, edited by Helen Rose Ebaugh and Janet Saltzman Chafetz, 210–233. Walnut Creek, CA: AltaMira Press.

Sullivan, Susan Crawford. 2011. *Living Faith: Everyday Religion and Mothers in Poverty*. Chicago: Chicago University Press.

Sumerau, J. E. 2012. "That's What a Man is Supposed to Do: Compensatory Manhood Acts in an LGBT Christian Congregation." *Gender and Society* 26(3): 461–487.

Sumerau, J. E., and Ryan T. Cragun. 2015a. "Contemporary Religion and the Cis-gendering of Reality." *Social Currents* 3(3): 293–311.

Sumerau, J. E., and Ryan T. Cragun. 2015b. "The Hallmarks of Righteous Women: Gendered Background Expectations in the Church of Jesus Christ of Latter-Day Saints." *Sociology of Religion* 76(1): 49–71.

Sumerau, J. E., Ryan T. Cragun, and Lain A. B. Mathers. 2016. "Contemporary Religion and the Cisgendering of Reality." *Social Currents* 3: 293–311.

Sumerau, J. E., Lain A. B. Mathers, and Ryan T. Cragun. 2018. "Incorporating Transgender Experience Toward a More Inclusive Gender Lens in the Sociology of Religion." *Sociology of Religion* 79(4): 425–448.

Swarts, Heidi J. 2008. *Organizing Urban America: Secular and Faith-based Progressive Movements*. Minneapolis: University of Minnesota Press.

Sweet, Julia. 2015. "The Russian Orthodox Church and Social Movement Protests: Is Unity Possible?" *The International Journal of Religion and Spirituality in Society* 5(4): 77–85.

Swenson, Donald. 2014. "The Subjective Secularization of Great Britain." *Implicit Religion* 17(2): 165–182.

Szrot, Lukas. 2020. "From Stewardship to Creation Spirituality: The Evolving Ecological Ethos of Catholic Doctrine." *Journal for the Study of Religion, Nature and Culture* 14(2): 226–249.

Tajfel, Henri. 1978. "Social Categorization, Social Identity and Social Comparison." In *Differentiation Between Social Groups: Studies in the Social Psychology of Intergroup Relations*, edited by Henri Tajfel, 61–76. London: Academic Press.

Taylor, S. E. 1981. "A Categorization Approach to Stereotyping." In *Cognitive Processes in Stereotyping and Intergroup Behavior*, edited by David L. Hamilton, 83–114. Hillsdale, NJ: Erlbaum.

Thomas, George M., and Douglas S. Jardine. 1994. "Jesus and Self in Everyday Life: Individual Spirituality through a Small Group in a Large Church." In *I Come Away Stronger: How Small Groups Are Shaping American Religion*, edited by Robert Wuthnow, 275–299. Grand Rapids, MI: William B. Eerdmans Publishing Co.

Thumma, Scott. 1991. "Negotiating a Religious Identity: The Case of the Gay Evangelical." *Sociological Analysis* 52: 333–347.

Thumma, Scott, and Dave Travis. 2007. *Beyond Megachurch Myths*. San Francisco: Josey-Bass Publishers.

Thumma, Scott, Dave Travis, and Warren Bird. 2005. *Megachurches Today 2005*. http://hirr.hartsem.cdu/org/faith_megachurches.html

Thurman, Howard. 1949. *Jesus and the Ddisinherited*. Boston, MA: Beacon Press.

Tierney, John. 2008. "For Good Self-Control, Try Getting Religious about It." *New York Times*, December 30.

Tisby, Jemar. 2019. *The Color of Compromise: The Truth about the American Church's Complicity in Racism*. Grand Rapids, MI: Zondervan.

Tschannen, Oliver. 1991. "The Secularization Paradigm: A Systematization." *Journal for the Scientific Study of Religion* 30(4): 395–415.

Turkle, Sherry. 1995. *Life on the Screen: Identity in the Age of the Internet*. New York: Simon and Schuster.

United Federation of Metropolitan Community Churches. 2005. www.mccchurch.org/AM/Template.cfm?Section=Home

United Methodist Church. 2004. *Book of Discipline*. Nashville, TN: United Methodist Publishing House.

U.S. Catholic Bishops. 2000. *Welcoming the Stranger Among Us: Unity in Diversity*. Washington, DC: United States Catholic Conference, Inc.

U.S. Catholic Bishops. 2001. *Global Climate Change*. www.usccb.org/resources/global-climate-change-plea-dialogue-prudence-and-common-good Last accessed 1/9/22.

Usman, Sushil K. 1998. "Islam and Social Movements in Asia: The Case of Malaysia." In *Religion, Mobilization, and Social Action*, edited by Anson Shupe and Bronislaw Misztal, 100–109. Westport, CT: Praeger.

Vaid, Urvashi. 1995. *Virtual Equality: The Mainstreaming of Gay and Lesbian Liberation*. New York: Anchor Books.

Van de Port, Mattijs. 2006. "Visualizing the Sacred: Video Technology, 'Televisual' Style, and the Religious Imagination in Bahian Candomble." *American Ethnologist* 33(3): 444–461.

Viana, Francisco. 1993. "O Fim do Romantismo [The End of Romanticism]." *Veja*, April 28: 74–75.

Vidich, Arthur, and Joseph Bensman. 1958. *Small Town in Mass Society: Class, Power, and Religion in a Rural Community*. Princeton, NJ: Princeton University Press.

Voas, David, and Mark Chaves. 2016. "Is the United States a Counterexample to the Secularization Thesis?" *American Journal of Sociology* 121(5): 1517–1556.

Voas, David, Daniel V. A. Olson, and Alasdair Crockett. 2002. "Religious Pluralism and Participation: Why Previous Research is Wrong." *American Sociological Review* 67(2): 212–230.

Voltaire. [1733] 1980. *Letters on England*. Translated by L. Tancock. Middlesex. England: Penguin.

Wagner, Rachel. 2013. "You are What You Install: Religious Authenticity and Identity in Mobile Apps." In *Digital Religion: Understanding Religious Practice in New Media Worlds*, edited by Heidi A. Campbell, 199–206. New York: Routledge.

Wallace, Ruth A. 1993. "The Social Construction of a New Leadership Role: Catholic Women Pastors." *Sociology of Religion* 54(1): 31–42.

Warner, R. Stephen. 1993. "Work in Progress Toward a New Paradigm for the Sociological Study of Religion in the United States." *American Journal of Sociology* 98: 1044–1093.

Warner, R. Stephen. 1998. "Immigration and Religious Communities in the United States." In *Gatherings in Diaspora: Religious Communities and the New Immigration*, edited by R. Stephen Warner and Judith G. Wittner, 3–34. Philadelphia: Temple University Press.

Warner, W. Lloyd, and Paul S. Lunt. 1941. *The Social System of a Modern Community*. New Haven, CT: Yale University Press.

Weber, Max. 1947. *The Theory of Social and Economic Organization*. New York: Free Press.

Weber, Max. 1967 [1922]. *The Sociology of Religion*. New York: Beacon Press.

Wedam, Elfriede. 2003. "The Religious 'District' of Elite Congregations: Reproducing Spatial Centrality and Redefining Mission." *Sociology of Religion* 60(1): 47–64.

Wedow, Robbee, Landon Schnabel, Lindsey K. D. Wedow, and Mary Ellen Konieczny. 2017. "'I'm Gay and I'm Catholic': Negotiating Two Complex Identities at a Catholic University." *Sociology of Religion* 78(3): 289–317.

Wells-Barnett, Ida B. 1895. *A Red Record: Tabulated Statistics and Alleged Causes of Lynchings in the United States, 1892-1893-1894*. Chicago, IL: Donohue & Henneberry.

White, Jr., Lynn. 1967. "The Historical Roots of our Ecologic Crisis." *Science* 155(3767): 1203–1207.

Whitehead, Andrew L. 2014. "Male and Female He Created Them: Gender Traditionalism, Masculine Images of God, and Attitudes toward Same-Sex Unions." *Journal for the Scientific Study of Religion* 53(3): 479–496.

Whitehead, Andrew L. 2017. "Institutional Norms, Practical Organizational Activity, and Loose Coupling: Inclusive Congregations' Responses to Homosexuality." *Journal for the Scientific Study of Religion* 56(4): 820–835.

Wikipedia. 2008. *Sicily*. http://en.wikipedia.org/wiki/Sicily

Wilcox, Melissa M. 2003. *Coming Out in Christianity: Religion, Identity, and Community*. Bloomington, IN: Indiana University Press.

Wilder, D. A. 1981. "Perceiving Persons as a Group: Categorization and In-group Relations." In *Cognitive Processes in Stereotyping and Intergroup Behavior*, edited by David L. Hamilton, 213–257. Hillsdale, NJ: Erlbaum.

Wilkins-Laflamme, Sarah. 2017. "Secularization and the Wider Gap in Values and Personal Religiosity Between the Religious and Nonreligious." *Journal for the Scientific Study of Religion* 55(4): 717–736.

Wilson, Bryan. 1982. *Religion in Sociological Perspective*. New York: Oxford University Press.

Wirtz, John G., Prisca S. Ngondo, and Philip Poe. 2013. "Talking with Us or at US: How U.S. Religious Denominations Use Organizational Web Sites to Communicate with their Constituents." *Journal of Media and Religion* 12: 165–180.

Wood, James R. 1970. "Authority and Controversy: The Churches and Civil Rights." *American Sociological Review* 35: 1057–1069.

Wood, Richard L. 2002. *Faith in Action: Religion, Race, and Democratic Organizing in America*. Chicago: University of Chicago Press.

Woodbury, Robert D., and Christian S. Smith. 1998. "Fundamentalism et al.: Conservative Protestants in America." *Annual Review of Sociology* 24: 25–56.

Woodhead, Linda. 2007. "Gender Differences in Religious Practice and Significance." In *The Sage Handbook of the Sociology of Religion*, edited by James Beckford and N. J. Demerath, III, 550–570. Los Angeles: Sage.

Woodhead, Linda. 2008. "Gendering Secularization Theory." *Social Compass* 55(2): 189–195.

Wuthnow, Robert. 1988. *The Restructuring of American Religion*. Princeton, NJ: Princeton University Press.

Wuthnow, Robert. 1994. *"I Come Away Stronger": How Small Groups are Shaping American Religion.*

Grand Rapids, MI: William B. Eerdmans Publishing Company.

Wuthnow, Robert. 1998. *After Heaven: Spirituality in America Since the 1950s*. Los Angeles: University of California Press.

Wuthnow, Robert. 2005. *America and the Challenges of Religious Diversity*. Princeton, NJ: Princeton University Press.

Yamane, David. 1997. "Secularization on Trial: In Defense of a Neosecularization Paradigm." *Journal for the Scientific Study of Religion* 36(1): 109–122.

Yancey, George. 2001. "Racial Attitudes: Differences in Racial Attitudes of People Attending Multiracial and Uni-racial Congregations." *Research in the Social Scientific Study of Religion* 12: 185–206.

Yang, Fenggang. 1999. *Chinese Christians in America: Conversion, Assimilation, and Adhesive Identities*. University Park, PA: The Pennsylvania State University Press.

Yang, Fenggang, and Helen Rose Ebaugh. 2001. "Transformation in New Immigrant Religions and Their Global Implications." *American Sociological Review* 2: 269–288.

Ying, Xie, and Minggang Peng. 2018. "Attitudes toward Homosexuality in China: Exploring the Effects of Religion, Modernizing Factors, and Tradition Culture." *Journal of Homosexuality* 65(13): 1758–1787.

Yip, Andrew K. T. 1997. "Dare to Differ: Gay and Lesbian Catholics' Assessment of Official Catholic Positions on Sexuality." *Sociology of Religion* 58: 165–180.

Yukich, Grace, and Ruth Braunstein. 2014. "Encounters at the Religious Edge: Variation in Religious Expression Across Interfaith Advocacy and Social Movement Settings." *Journal for the Scientific Study of Religion* 53(4): 791–807.

Index

Note: Page numbers in *italics* indicate figures and in **bold** indicate tables on the corresponding pages.

9781032021454